FERRYBOATS

LAN

TO

FERRYBOATS

A LEGEND ON PUGET SOUND

by

M.S. Kline and G.A. Bayless

Bayless Books

SEATTLE

Bayless Books, Seattle 98109
© 1983 by Bayless Books
All rights reserved. Published 1983
Printed in the United States of America
Library of Congress Cataloging in Publication Data
Kline, Mary Stiles, 1953-
    Ferryboats: legend on Puget Sound.

Bibliography: p.
Includes index.
1. Ferries—Washington (State)—Puget Sound—
    History.
I. Bayless, George A. (George Albert), 1925-
II. Title.
HE5783.W3K54 1983 386′.6′097977 83-19681
ISBN 0-914515-00-4

Dedicated to
Walter Green and William O. Thorniley

TABLE OF CONTENTS

Acknowledgements	ix
Introduction	1
Ferries Across the Bay	3
150 Years of the Black Ball Flag	15
The Steamer Fleets Join Forces	25
Three Sisters	45
Canadian Pacific Railway vs. Puget Sound Navigation Company	67
Clear the Decks for an Au-to-mo-bile	81
Steamboat Men Turned Ferryboat Operators	107
Competition Among Ferry Lines	123
Lake Washington's Floating Bridges	143
Competition Heats Up	159
Ferries and Freight: Transport and Commerce	181
Foshay Comes to Town	195
An Era of Labor Relations and Strife	203
A Streamlined Super Ferry	225
San Francisco Ferries Come North	249
Blackballed: The End of the Line	283
The Legacy: Washington State Ferries	305
Ferry Register	333
Development of P.S.N. Auto Ferry Fleet	347
P.S.N. Fleet List	348
K.C.T.C. Fleet List	352
Origin of Ferry Names	354
Excerpts from Federal Title 46—Shipping	358
Scrapbook	360
Bibliography	379
Index	383
Authors' Page	401

ACKNOWLEDGEMENTS

The real joy in writing a book like this one comes from the people you meet, the stories that are told and the reliving of incidents long forgotten. This is a book recounted by history's participants. The authors hope that it will generate even more story-telling, families sharing knowledge with younger generations and the provocation of even more scholarly research. It serves as a guide to important incidents, a reference authority. It is intended as incentive to preserve the region's past while seeking to understand the present. (It is not the last word; it is only the beginning.)

Three years of research, interviewing and writing created a book based on a collection that took over 50 years to gather. William O. Thorniley, writer, photographer, promoter, public relations representative for Puget Sound Navigation Company, Chinook jargon linguist, president of Olympic Peninsula Hotel & Resort Owners, was a collector of print type, Puget Sound ship photos, brochures, logs, letters, lists, memorabilia and whatever struck him as savable. Bill Thorniley had an archival instinct for ferryboating on Puget Sound. He was a writer for *The Marine Digest* from its first year of publication. There he published a popular series of steamboat histories and wrote a mariner's personal column called "The Beachcomber." When Jackson Corbet, Jr., founder, editor and publisher of *The Marine Digest* died in 1943, William O. Thorniley assumed the interim position of editor and production manager for Mrs. Corbet until the journal was sold. Many of Thorniley's files are the original photos and stories written for *The Digest*. No one else cared to save them.

Thorniley joined Puget Sound Navigation Company in 1928. He served a short time on its vessels before his promotion talents were recognized by the company. Captain Torger Birkeland (Caxton Printers, Caldwell, Idaho 1961) writes in his book *Echoes of Puget Sound*:

> Again my clothes were hung up in the familiar mate's room on the SOL DUC and I was happy for an opportunity to again sail with my old friends and shipmates who were still there to welcome me back. Captain Frese was now sailing deep waters as chief mate of the S.S. WESTISON. Cap would never fail to visit Colman Dock and his old friends when in port. On such a call one evening he came aboard and roused me out of bed to introduce his ship's carpenter, a tall, lanky lad who would like to ship on the SOL DUC as quartermaster. As it happened we did have an opening just then, and so the happy-go-lucky William O. Thorniley, bubbling over with pep and ambition, commenced his career with the Puget Sound Navigation Company, a relationship which was to continue for many years."

Soon Thorniley assumed management of all public relations, printing of schedules and brochures, advertising, radio programs and press releases. Thorniley set up his own telegram service with personal funds, calling it the "Thorniley Reminder Service." He circulated birthday and anniversary greetings to hundreds of Puget Sound residents, printed on his own press. He and his wife, Mary, published a popular newsletter called *The Christmas Chimes,* a mixture of anecdotes and favorite verses. They printed it with their antique type and for this Thorniley was dubbed the "Pastime Printer." The old presses and type collection now form a popular museum exhibit at Seattle's West Coast Paper Company.

Bill Thorniley was recognized on the Seattle waterfront at an early age. He collected and snapped photos of the steamboatmen of the day. He preferred personal, unposed shots and for those who were uncooperative about picture-taking, Thorniley hid his camera within a candy box. He disguised himself as a hawker when he boarded ships and at just the right moment, when the unsuspecting crew member was perfectly registered— "click"—Thorniley had his photo.

His collections grew as people recognized his interests. Many items were delivered to him for safekeeping. Other collectables were the honest result of requisitions from people's unvalued memorabilia and "old junk."

Experienced archivists marvel at Thorniley's cataloging procedures, too. Photos were identified and often dated; events were sited, and corresponding documentation could be found after researching boxes and boxes of file papers.

Thorniley was one of the early founders and contributors of the *Newsletter* for Puget Sound Maritime Historical Society. He interviewed individuals, wrote copy, assembled photos and printed the paper. It was the forerunner of the Society's quarterly journal known today as *The Sea Chest*. He was also a major contributor to McCurdy's *Marine History of the Pacific Northwest*, written by Gordon Newell, furnishing ferry and steamer information and photographs.

Correspondence files show that Thorniley communicated with researchers around the world. He was known as a leading authority on Puget Sound's maritime history.

Co-author George Bayless was a neighbor of Thorniley's as a youngster. He purchased Bill Thorniley's private maritime collection following Thorniley's death in 1979. The collection mounted as more and more boxes were uncovered. Thorniley had built shelves behind shelves. Dusty boxes were unearthed that had not been opened for years. Mr. Bayless assembled the materials according to their familiar order, catalogued photographs and safely stored and protected the items. His methodical organization eased research practices when Mary Kline began the initial review of materials for publication. Not surprisingly, there was enough for at least three books.

After lengthy consideration and assemblage of documents, it was evident that the photographs and documentation existed for the compilation of a thorough history of Puget Sound ferryboating. But the collection lacked the cohesive character that had once been generated by the vivacious personality of Bill Thorniley. The adhesive thread was lost with his passing. Here was a collection derived from the *people* who created Puget Sound's ferry fleet, their photos and their stories. The authors needed to know more about these people, who they were, and how they ticked.

At the instigation of Harold Graham, the authors were introduced to Walter Green, a contemporary and close friend of Bill Thorniley. His career with Puget Sound Navigation Company paralleled Thorniley's throughout the thirties and early forties. Mr. Green stayed with the Black Ball Line until its sale to the State of Washington in 1951. Then he joined with Bob and Lois Acheson in building Black Ball Transport, Inc., operators of the ferry COHO between Port Angeles and Victoria.

Mr. Green has a dynamic personality that commands the attention of all and the close friendship of many. Through him, the authors were introduced to many of his associates in Puget Sound Navigation Company, retirees of Washington State Ferries and people within the present ferry system. His accurate recollections guided the selection of pertinent data and embellished dry documentation. He contributed major insight and understanding of the operation of ferries on Puget Sound. Green helped the authors tell the story the way Thorniley and his friends felt is should be told.

Thomas William Thorniley and Jessie Thorniley Quick, children of William O., continued to uncover pertinent collection materials and recall stories that guided the use of Thorniley's files.

The Peabody family was generous and helpful in sorting fact from fiction in over 150 years of recorded family history, some of which has been pertinent to the ferryboat story, all of which was fascinating. Larry Peabody read most of the chapters dealing with Black Ball history. He and his brother Woody also added information and personal stories through interviews. Occasionally the authors received a phone call from Larry with yet another great memory recalled. Mrs. Marie Peabody provided pleasant recollections and news clippings of her late husband Captain Alexander Peabody. Margaret Peabody Smith collected family albums and reconstructed family geneology.

Manuscript readers were sought to guide the substance and accuracy of individual chapters and the overall message conveyed. Harold Graham (and Betty), Walter Green and the infallible Robert C. Leithead reviewed all of the material. Captain Robert Matson contributed valuable information and photos, particularly dealing with Kitsap County Transportation Company, the Lake Washington ferries and union organization. Captain Russel Taylor detailed his recollections of the early steamboat days through interviews. Philip Spaulding, a former apprentice of designer Carl Nordstrom and a nationally-known naval architect in his own right, granted interviews, gave technical documentation and provided designs for the ferry BEELINE, used as art work on endsheets of this book.

Tim Dwyer of *The Marine Digest* loaned 20 years of his magazine, dating from 1922-1943 for research. Captain Merle Adlum reviewed labor organization materials and provided personal information about Captain John Fox. J. Knox Woodruff, Puget Sound Freight Lines, reviewed the freight chapter. Mrs. Lois Acheson, President of Black Ball Transport, Inc. and Mrs. Mary Lieseke, President of Horluck Transportation Company graciously granted interviews to the authors. Richard E. Brown, acknowledged California ferry expert reviewed the California ferry chapter and corresponded with scholarly research from his own files. Joshua Green, Jr. recalled entertaining anecdotes from his father's repertoire of steamboating tales. Jack Embree and Mary Keenholtz gave the authors insight to Alex Peabody as an employer and business manager, also valuable recollections about the sale of Puget Sound Navigation Company to Washington State. Ralph White reviewed the closing chapter and offered his suggestions, loaning important photos as well.

The Northwest Ferry Retirees served as a resource group, providing contacts, identifying photos, telling stories, defining technicalities, and mainly giving everyone a good time.

Editorial and production staff for this book included Harriet DeLong as the astute editor and supporting friend, and Nelda R. Hair, a woman of numerous talents and skills, many of which were taxed herein to produce this book. Brad Evans reviewed the manuscript for clarity and composition. Oakley Lotz researched statistics for the register of ferries in the appendix. His good humor kept serious debates lighthearted.

Production was greatly assisted by the professional suggestions and cooperation of individuals within the printing industry: Howard Rosenthal of the University Printing Company, now Forward Press, Seattle; Sam Boren of West Coast Paper Company, Seattle (he bought more than his share of the coffee, too); Jim Wilson and Celeste Christensen of The Type Gallery, Seattle, and Harry Emerson of Lincoln & Allen, Portland. They have helped the publisher produce a book that may be considered a truly Northwest "product."

The dust jacket and layout designer, Herbert E. Carlson is the *best* to be found. His wisdom and patience kept the authors' cluttered minds free from worry in that department.

There are numerous contributors to whom the authors owe generous thanks. Some may be erroneously overlooked here but their efforts were equally appreciated. Thanks to: Clinton Betz, Elliott Burdett and the Colman Family, Sid Campbell, Alice Collingwood, Harry and Matilda Dring, John F. Henry, Jack Kutz, Greg Lange, Tom Macbride, Col. Dick McFarland, Tom McKey, Robert W. Parkinson, Barry Provorse, Jervis Russell, Karen Stern, Captain D. A. Webb.

A number of institutions were helpful for locating research materials and photographs. Thanks to: Allen Knight Maritime Museum at Monterey, Astoria Maritime Museum, Oregon; The Bancroft Library at University of California at Berkeley; Boeing Archives, Seattle; Coast Guard Museum, N.W., Seattle; Museum of History & Industry, Seattle; National Maritime Museum at San Francisco; Northwest Seaport, Seattle; Provincial Archives, Victoria, B.C.; Puget Sound Maritime Historical Society, Seattle; Transportation Institute, Seattle; University of Washington Archives and the Northwest Collection, Seattle and the Washington State Archives in Olympia.

We owe a very special and sincere thanks to our families, close friends and the crew of Bayless Bindery who guided and supported our efforts throughout the creation and production of this book. Thanks to them, our goals were achieved and we have endured.

Galena

Age 5 (1983)

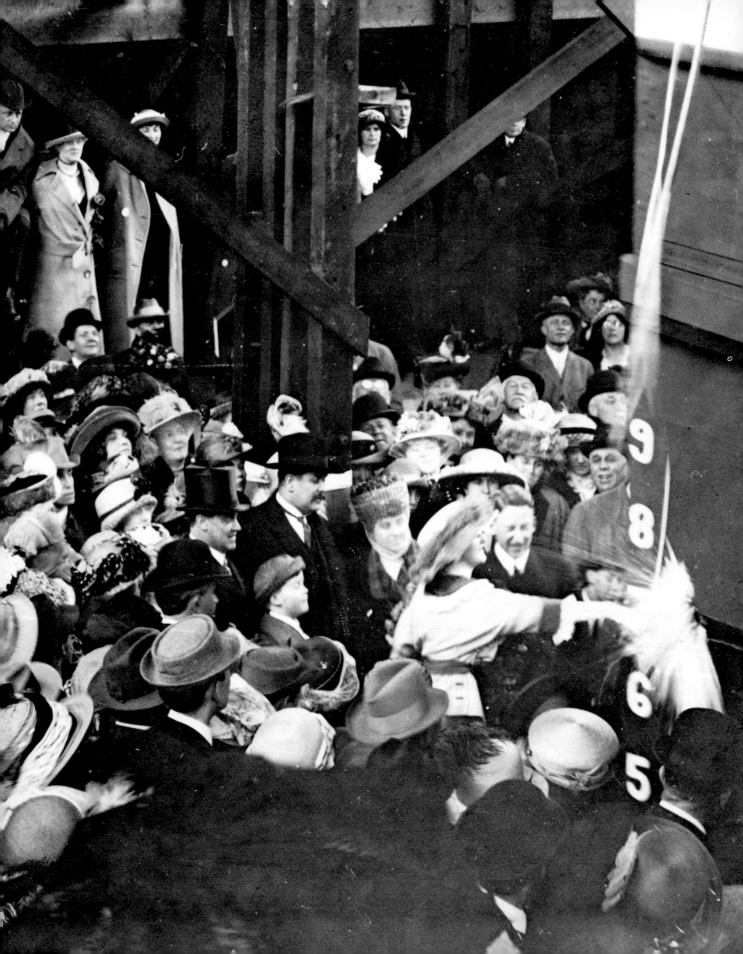

INTRODUCTION

" 'The Evergreen Playground' is the name given to that part of Western Washington and British Columbia that borders Puget Sound and the waters adjacent to it. It is a region of high mountains and beautiful valleys, of a marvelous inland sea with more than two thousand miles of shoreline, of crystal lakes and rushing rivers, of fertile fields and beautiful cities."

Black Ball Ferry Line's 1929 brochure describes the Puget Sound region of yesterday and today. Visitors from around the world journey to the region to enjoy its splendor, open spaces, and metropolitan cities. Joining island communities, major cities and peninsulas is the world's largest and most modern ferry fleet. Owned today by Washington State Ferries, it is comprised of routes and ferry designs pioneered by steamboatmen and business investors who were eager to develop this rich frontier.

Ferry and steamboat routes linked the Sound communities. These water highways may be traced to the Native Americans who navigated the inland waters with superbly built canoes. American, British and Canadian settlers appreciated the Indian's form of transportation and adopted it for their own use.

Compared to the other western territories, Washington was late in receiving railroads. Pacific Coast shipping was a more direct tie to the rest of the world. It was generally faster than overland wagon travel and cheaper for the transport of commodities. Port Townsend, located just inside of the Strait of Juan de Fuca, became the major American port for the Northwest in international shipping before 1900. Victoria, B.C., just across the Straits, was the metropolitan center at that time for the entire region.

As the population grew, attracting farmers and industrialists, major Washington cities evolved inland. Seattle, Tacoma, Everett and Bellingham were busy population centers. Farming communities developed on the Sound's islands and Kitsap Peninsula. Steamboats served as passenger and freight boats. They were Puget Sound's predominant form of transportation until the introduction of the automobile.

Automobiles rejuvenated the entire region. People were eager to take their cars to outlying communities. Trucks answered the demand to haul significant quantities of freight. But ferries, in the absence of bridges, would have to transport them cross-Sound.

In less than a decade the automobile ferry replaced every steamer on every major Puget Sound route. Independent small companies were forced out of business through consolidation or dominance of larger corporations which could finance construction of new auto-carriers. Only two independent companies survived.

During the 1920s and 1930s Puget Sound's population continued to increase. By the late 1930s war production at the Bremerton Navy Yard attracted even more people and tended to concentrate the population within the Seattle-Tacoma region. The ferry commuter, as well as the traveler, was a source of income to the primary ferry company at that time.

Puget Sound Navigation Company, the Black Ball Line, controlled all major ferry routes between 1935 and 1951. It managed its fleet as a regulated monopoly, subject to the laws and route certificates of Washington State, the growing demands of the labor movement, and the public's persistance for better service and newer ferries.

The public sector would have the last word. Total control of the Puget Sound ferry fleet was delivered into their hands. Washington State purchased Puget Sound Navigation Company and most of its vessels in 1951. The ferries were passed to government ownership, to serve the needs of Washington State residents. Today Washington State ferry routes are still the major highways crossing Puget Sound.

CHRISTENING THE SOL DUC

FERRIES ACROSS THE BAY

Whistles tooted and boats scurried in every direction. Competing steamers raced toward the Seattle waterfront to be first to collect waiting passengers and freight. The black and white swarms of the "Mosquito Fleet" dashed from their piers headed toward their next destination: Tacoma, Bremerton, Bellingham, Port Townsend and the numerous stops along the way. The little ships lent life and zest to the ports of Puget Sound.

Tall-masted sailing ships and black-hulled steam schooners dotted the harbors in lines or anchored singly in bays, waiting their turn to load fragrant lumber from the forests. Deep-waisted squareriggers carrying lime and coal discharged thousands of crewmen who would build new homes and new businesses on Puget Sound. The little steamers delivered them to nearby cities and towns, providing the only reliable means of transportation for nearly 60 years.

Such was the setting the day the first ferryboat entered service on the Sound. The year was 1888. Ten years before, the small steamboat NELLIE had been taken off the Seattle to Milton (West Seattle) run. For a time the only way to cross the bay was by two rowboats equipped with auxiliary sail power. Elliott Bay and its tidelands still flooded the land where highways, bridges and businesses lie today. Harbor Island, the manmade stepping stone to West Seattle, had not yet been imagined, much less built.

The vessels referred to as steamers on Puget Sound had sleek, even lines running bow to stern with a single pilothouse forward. The steamers carried freight and passengers with only an occasional vehicle. Often they did not run on a regular schedule but restricted their trade to an approximate daily sailing from a designated port. They stopped at tiny communities, farms and businesses on demand.

Ferryboats were generally bigger and more cumbersome in design. They were documented to carry vehicles as well as freight and passengers. They ran on a particular route with a specified schedule as an

CITY OF SEATTLE, PUGET SOUND'S FIRST FERRY BOAT

extension of a highway. A ferry, unlike the trim steamers, was often double-ended. They usually had two pilothouses and a propeller at each end.[1] Early ferryboats had steam engines and were technically classified with the steamers as steamboats. They served similar functions and emerged from the same heritage.

Seattle's first ferryboat, the steam-driven sidewheeler CITY OF SEATTLE, entered regularly scheduled service on New Year's Eve, 1888. She had been built in Portland, Oregon that same year by John Steffen, for the West Seattle Land and Improvement Company at a cost of $35,000.

NEWCOMERS TO PUGET SOUND

She was casually referred to as the jitney ferry, meaning that a five cent fare was collected. She had been introduced to the run by the Improvement Company at the outrageous fare of 15 cents. Her owners quickly reduced the fare to five cents when they realized that it was more profitable to sell their property in

[1]The definition of "ferryboat" may be challenged by the confusion of opinions. These opinions and rulings have been expressed and sometimes altered on the basis of governmental and legal regulations, design inspection, operation of the vessel, nomenclature and personal preference. The general qualifications include: 1) a vessel that operates on a regularly scheduled run over a body of water; 2) a vessel that functions as an extension of a highway; 3) a vessel that is documented to carry passengers, freight and vehicles and is often double-ended (propellers at each end and two pilothouses). See Appendix for U.S. Coast Guard Regulations.

MOSQUITO FLEET STEAMERS

SEATTLE, 1888

WEST SEATTLE FERRY TERMINAL AT FIRST AND MAR-
ION ST., SEATTLE

West Seattle than to sell ferry tickets. The five cent fare was a success from the start. A "big nickel" was painted on the side of her terminal.

The CITY OF SEATTLE served this run for the next 25 years, ushering in a legendary era of ferryboating in the Pacific Northwest.

THE FIRST ONE

By the summer of 1889, the CITY OF SEATTLE was making 10 round trips daily. The landing had become so popular that that year a narrow-gauge cable car line was built to carry people up the hill to where the West Seattle Land and Improvement Company had lots for sale. The crests of West Seattle—Sunset and Palm Avenues—soon became the dwellings of lawyers, bankers, shipbuilders and tradesmen who went to and from their daily routines over the water. Like today's ferryboat commuters, they met twice daily to discuss politics and newspaper accounts of the day's events.

Remnants of the popular ferry landing in West Seattle, connecting with the Seattle terminus at Marion Street, are difficult to locate today. Ferry Avenue Southwest slants northeasterly from Fire Station No.29, cuts across California Avenue Southwest and rambles down a steep ravine to a jumble of ancient piling standing in haphazard manner near the shore. It was here that one of the busiest ferry landings on Puget Sound operated; today Seattle is extending a waterfront park across this property.

As a ferryboat, the CITY OF SEATTLE was remarkably fast and often made her two-mile run in eight minutes. She was 121 feet long, 33 feet in width, and drew 5 feet of water. Her horizontal engines of 270 horsepower were equipped with a locomotive firebox boiler.

All passengers, horses and wagons, supplies and freight were carried on the main deck of the ferryboat. The upper deck consisted of a single square pilothouse built around the stack and facing in both directions.

As time went by, competition reared its ugly head. The little steamer GARDEN CITY, passenger carrier only, came onto the West Seattle run in 1904 with 17 round trips daily, but she lasted only a short time. There were scarcely enough people in West Seattle to support such frequent service.

As enterprise would have it, the LADY OF THE LAKE appeared with a fare of only four cents. The CITY OF SEATTLE countered with commuter fares, "40 rides for a dollar." Who could make money at

these prices? Who could pay a crew from the revenues? The LADY OF THE LAKE settled the issue one day when she burned on the ways in the repair yard.

LADY OF THE LAKE

The need for a bigger ferry (not more frequent service) grew apparent. Construction of a ferry was begun in Tacoma in 1906. June 27, 1907 was a banner day for West Siders. The WEST SEATTLE, hailed as the largest and finest ferry north of San Francisco, went onto the run. She was a sidewheeler, 145 feet long with a beam 48.7 feet and a draft of 7 feet.

The same day, the Luna Park Natatorium, a short walk north of the ferry landing, opened with a fun zone, the "longest bar in the world," and a big dome covering three swimming pools. A strip of stores had sprung up at the landing. The Seattle Yacht Club built its first headquarters there. The West Seattle Boathouse rented small craft for leisurely afternoon rowing; salmon fishing skiffs could be hired at 25 cents an hour. Several small shipyards enjoyed a brisk business.

The first street car operating around the Bay from Seattle to Luna Park made its debut that June, too. The beginning of the streetcar ultimately spelled the doom of the ferryboats to West Seattle, but their demise was not immediately apparent.

A CHANGE OF PACE

With the completion of the new ferryboat, the older CITY OF SEATTLE was free to operate directly to Luna Park at Duwamish Head. The summer of 1907 marked the peak of travel on these routes. During July

FERRY WEST SEATTLE   *MATSON COLL.*

of that year, 103,000 ferry passengers were carried. Competition from the streetcars proved disastrous, however, and the ferry line was soon in financial difficulties. Service was curtailed and the CITY OF SEATTLE was sold to San Francisco interests for the Martinez-Benecia Route. The WEST SEATTLE was purchased by the Port of Seattle in June, 1913, and continued to go into the red.

The CITY OF SEATTLE experienced a hazardous journey south as she left her namesake city in 1913. While under tow of a steam schooner,[2] she broke loose in a storm and was adrift several hours. She had been boarded up at both ends for the trip, but before she cleared Cape Flattery the boards were gone. She made the voyage with the waves sweeping her driveways.

The West Seattle landing began to lose its lustre. The Seattle Yacht Club moved to fresh water moorage at Montlake after the Lake Washington Ship Canal locks at Ballard opened in 1916. The small shipyards folded and their drydocks were towed to Lake Union. Prohibition forced the closure of the "world's longest bar" at Luna Park and salmon fishing dwindled in Elliott Bay; the old West Seattle Boathouse was out of business, too.

Seattle's infamous incendiary at last extinquished the park by torching it in the early 1930s. The City Park Department filled in the swimming pools to prevent accidents or lawsuits. The property was eventually rejuvenated into an attractive outlook plaza at Duwamish Head.

The Port of Seattle divested their interests in the ferry service by donating the WEST SEATTLE to King County, September 22, 1919. The county soon realized that this gift would not be a profitable one nor could it be financially self-sustaining. County commissioners tried operating the WEST SEATTLE to Tacoma without kindling any interest in this scheme. By 1920 they had abandoned all hope of successful operation and leased the ferry to the Kitsap County Transportation Company. This company layed up the vessel at Houghton on Lake Washington and operated her as a relief ferry for their Vashon Heights run.[3]

[2]Steam schooners were large steam freight carriers that evolved primarily on the West Coast just before the turn of the century. In most cases they did not carry sail. Their name was derived from their use as engine-powered replacements for the sailing schooners that once carried supplies between Western port cities. The steam schooner was specifically designed to carry lumber even though they carried other types of freight as well.

[3]Kitsap County Transportation Company in turn leased the ferry and operation to Pierce County for the Point Defiance-Gig Harbor run, May through September 1921. There was a nominal charge of 50 cents for automobiles.

Captain Russ Taylor, master of the WEST SEATTLE for a few short months late in her career with King County, recalled how the passengers of the West Seattle ferries were of tougher calibre than most of us are today.

The CITY OF SEATTLE did not have the luxury of a passenger or second deck that would segregate passengers from the freight deck. Ladies in long day dresses and gentlemen in business suits were expected to be seated on the main deck where the freight was loaded and stowed. The butcher and grocer hauled their wagons there pulled by teams of drays. Automobiles were driven aboard this main deck where crew members were instructed to watch their language when passengers were nearby.

Captain Taylor remembered the abruptness with which county officials appeared one day to inform the WEST SEATTLE crewmen that they no longer had jobs

CAPTAIN RUSSEL TAYLOR

LUNA PARK NATATORIUM

A WOMAN AT THE WHEEL

aboard the ferryboat. When the ferry was scratched from the county operating budget, so too were the men who operated her. The smaller steamer AQUILO was brought from Lake Washington for West Seattle service.

In 1922 the Kitsap County Transportation Company officially took over the route and began to operate the WASHINGTON on the Seattle-Vashon Heights run for the county. All officers' jobs were permanently terminated. Captain Taylor sought employment elsewhere. Eventually he became a highly respected master with the Puget Sound Navigation Company and later, with the Washington State Ferries.

Captain Taylor's first command, the old WEST SEATTLE, met with a far less distinguished fate. She became a barge for the stowage of fishing nets. On San Francisco Bay, the CITY OF SEATTLE was dealt a finer hand of cards for her future. She was operated between Martinez and Benecia by her purchasers, the Martinez & Benecia Ferry and Transportation Company. She also served on the Mare Island-Vallejo Route with a carrying capacity of 500 passengers and 19 vehicles. Her original machinery remained intact. Aside from placing a wheelhouse on each end, no extensive alterations were made to her upperworks. Her name was never changed while in operation.

On Puget Sound some of the masters of the CITY OF SEATTLE included Captain J.L. Oliver, Captain William I. Waitt, Captain Joseph A. Monroe, Captain Alex Wood, Captain Frank Price, Captain Ed Jensen, Captain Bert McMillan and Captain George Bullene. She carried no mates. James O'Neill, John A. Snyder, Manly Danforth, Charles Woods and Patrick Gard were her engineers.

Few of the more modern vessels have lasted as well as the CITY OF SEATTLE. Puget Sound's oldest ferryboat survives at this writing in Sausalito, California, moored at the Yellow Ferry Harbor. She has been remodeled into a home and office for the marina's proprietor. Because of the ravages of time she is supported on piling. She is still known as the CITY OF SEATTLE and yes, you've guessed it, she *is* painted yellow.

GROWTH AND ITS EFFECT ON STEAMERS

It is difficult to say if steamers and their many routes arose from the needs of the settlements or if

CITY OF SEATTLE AT THE YELLOW FERRY HARBOR, SAUSALITO, CALIF.

SOUND COMMUNITIES BUILT NEAR THE WATER

LURA MAUD, BORN OF SENSIBLE NEEDS AND PRACTICAL DESIGN.

they actually precipitated the development of communities. Early day settlers on Puget Sound built near the water. Lumber was their primary source of revenue. Water transportation afforded the cheapest and quickest means of export at a time when roads and wagons were not always readily available. It was easier to use man's environment than to reorder it with manmade roads.

Steamers were built in all shapes, sizes and colors. They were born of sensible needs, available materials and instinctive character of design. They were operated by small crews who, as often as not, built the vessel, shared its ownership, planned its route, contracted potential customers, collected tickets, and then ran the boat. The steamers affected the daily lives of every resident of Puget Sound. They provided the only contact with the outside world on weekly or semi-weekly runs. Life would have been intolerable without them.

Seattle was an exciting boom town, born of the

GOLD RUSH SUPPLIES WERE PROVIDED THROUGH SEATTLE

gold fields of Northern California, sustained by the lumber and mining industry of the region and rejuvenated by the gold fever of the Alaskan Yukon discovery. Puget Sound ports had supplied San Francisco's thirst for building supplies throughout the Gold Rush of the 1850s and later following the destructive earthquakes and fires. By the late 1890s Seattle had become

the jumping off point for fortune seekers of the Klondike.

Supplies and transportation were provided through Seattle. For many people headed north, this city was their last brush with civilization. As they boarded the steamship or another vessel that had been requisitioned in some dubious state of flotation, they bid farewell to the muddy streets of a Western waterfront town. They returned several years later to find the city remarkably transformed from the profits of the gold fields and the businesses that supplied the hopeful prospectors.

Most steamers on Puget Sound bays and inlets were designed for service that lent itself to single-ended (one pilothouse forward with a propeller at one end) operation, rather than the double-ended ferryboat with a pilothouse on each end and two propellers or sidewheels. The single-end had the advantage of speed underway. But the intricate operation of backing, or even turning the vessel from the pier for the return trip, was time consuming and occasionally hazardous if the captain failed to clear the dock.

The double-ended ferryboat afforded easier access and egress for vehicular traffic, but wagons were not particularly prevalent or necessary on cross-Sound freight haulage. Passengers walked to the town dock for boarding and walked again at their destination on the other side. Freight was loaded on handcarts from wagons at the piers until the early 1930s. The passengers carried baskets, crates and sacks of produce, eggs or other commodities in their arms. Generally there was plenty of stowage space within the cabin.

Elevators were installed aboard steamers to facilitate freight and motor car handling after 1910. As the automobile gained in popularity, turntables were placed on the vessels to turn cars around and allow them to exit the ship over the same end they had entered. Originally cars were treated as any other form of freight. They were elevated or lowered from the pier to the deck of the steamer, depending upon the tide level.

Piers were designed to accommodate the handling of freight and passengers for the single-ended steamer

PASSENGERS AND FREIGHT WERE BOARDED ON STEAMERS AT THE TOWN DOCK.

and not the blunt-nosed ferryboat. The only ferry dock in Seattle until about 1921 was the one at Madison Street for the West Seattle run.

The evolution of the ferryboat on Puget Sound must be attributed to both passenger steamers and the steam scows and barges that hauled freight. Many innovations, including the Barlow elevator, designed by Harry Barlow of Seattle, were considered for use aboard these little freight steamers. Steamships of the ocean trade were strong influences for passenger accommodations with luxurious decor and quality service. Many early ferryboats sported similar amenities. It was not until recent years and prohibitive costs, as well as stringent U.S. Coast Guard fire codes that mandated the exchange of charm and comfortable appointments for practicality aboard the ferries.

Ferries today still combine many of the traits of those early day workboats. Washington State ferries carry passengers and commuters to their numerous destinations around the Sound. They carry automobiles. They still carry commodities from the outlying communities into the city. Handcarts have been replaced with semi-trucks and trailers but the purpose is the same: to bring the residents and businesses of the state closer together over the water highways of Puget Sound.

THE S.S. BEAVER

Steamboats were already on Puget Sound when the majority of settlers began to arrive. A distinquishing maritime heritage was in progress and newcomers recognized the advantages.

As early as 1835 the British Hudson's Bay Company introduced the first steam vessel to the Pacific Ocean, destined for its new home on the Columbia River. Launched in the presence of the King of England and 150,000 spectators on the Thames River, the S.S. BEAVER sailed for the New World.[4] Dubious about steam navigation at the time, the BEAVER's owners rigged her as a brig with her machinery in place but without sidewheels attached. Under canvas, Captain D. Home made speedy time and reached the Columbia River ahead of his consort, the bark COLUMBIA, after a passage of 163 days.

The engines were found to "work extremely well"[5] and cutting cord wood for fuel became an immediate occupation for the crew. Indians were later recruited for this task.

The BEAVER entered service without delay, carry-

S.S. BEAVER, FIRST STEAMBOAT IN THE PACIFIC

S.S. BEAVER ENDED HER DAYS AT THE ENTRANCE TO VANCOUVER HARBOR.

ing goods and collecting furs for all the company's ports between Puget Sound and Alaska. She visited every bay, river and inlet on the Sound and made at least one trip a year to Alaska with cargoes of produce, goods and supplies for the Russians from whom Hudson's Bay Company leased property for their company posts. The steamer towed an occasional Russian vessel and served as an all-around workboat.

The BEAVER underwent extensive overhaul in 1860 and was fitted with staterooms to run with pas-

[4]S.S. BEAVER built in Blackwall, County of Middlesex, May 7, 1835, by Green, Wagran & Green. The owner's representative was William Armit, secretary of the Hudson's Bay Company. Dimensions: 101.4' length, 20' beam, 11' depth of hold and 109.12 gross tonnage. Engines and boilers were built by Bolton & Watt.

[5]The log of the BEAVER. Reproduced with omission of exact dates in *Lewis and Dryden's Marine History of the Pacific Northwest*, pp.15-17.

sengers between Victoria and New Westminster, B.C. She was chartered by the Imperial Hydrographers as a survey ship for several years; was refitted as a towboat in 1874; suffered extensive damage by fire to her upperworks in 1880. She struck a rock in Burrard's Inlet and sank in 1883. The BEAVER's timbers were still sound. The vessel was raised and returned to tugboating service until 1888. At that time she was once again licensed as a passenger carrier between logging camps on Burrard's Inlet until her fatal trip in July, 1888. She ended her days on the rocks at the entrance to Vancouver Harbor.

The BEAVER served as one of the forerunners of the Mosquito Fleet and met many of the conditions of the definition of a ferryboat. She was a tugboat and a passenger boat. She navigated most of the inland waters and tributaries of Puget Sound. She was an extension of the wagon roads. She was, in a sense, *the* existing highway.

By the early 1850s Puget Sound settlements had grown to the extent that inter-community trade was nearly as desirable as the trade with other Pacific Coast ports. It would be another 30 years before the railroads would be interested in this region. They were concentrating their efforts in California and introducing ferryboats on San Francisco Bay. Puget Sound communities depended on natural waterways to provide portal-to-portal access without significant financial investments. Steamboats proved to be the convenient answer.

Ingenuity, perserverance and a solid measure of common sense led the maritime business entrepreneurs to evolve a system of steamers and ferryboats that would one day become the largest inland water fleet in the United States. Elliott Bay was once black with busy little boats shuttling back and forth; swarming like mosquitos to the Seattle piers. Settlers from all parts of the world became accustomed to this dependence on the water but not without some hesitation which had its amusing moments.

One well-known story was told by former State Senator Robert T. M'Donald in the *Seattle Daily Times* September 17, 1944. Some members of the legislature visited Seattle in 1859, he recalled,

> "On the morning of their departure at 5:30, which was about the time they expected to be called, they heard a loud whistle. Supposing it came from the steamer, they lost no time in getting down to what seemed

in the darkness the dock. In their haste, they soon entered what they believed was the engine room of the steamer. After waiting there some time, one of the members asked the engineer how soon he would leave for Olympia. 'This sawmill doesn't run to Olympia, sir,' was the reply."

Steamers changed the lives of the Indians. They preferred to hire the steamboat to tow their canoes home if they could afford it. J. Willis Sayre, in his book, *The Early Waterfront of Seattle*, writes,

> "A never to be forgotten sight in the 1870s, '80s and '90s was the coming in each autumn of whole flotillas of Indian canoes from down-Sound. Hundreds of Indians would congregate on their way to and from their job picking hops in the Puyallup Valley.

> "They made their headquarters on Ballast Island[6] near the foot of Washington Street, and when they weren't singing they were gambling. Most of them spent all the money they had earned with Seattle merchants and went home broke and happy. They never cared about paddling their canoes if they could afford to hire a steamboat to tow them. On one occasion in 1885, the QUICKSTEP came into the harbor towing a string of Indian canoes a quarter mile long."

QUICKSTEP

S. W. JOSEPHINE ON AN EXCURSION

Steamers and ferries were a source of pleasure in those days, too. Spectators and passengers enjoyed the constant racing and competition among all the boats. The steamboat motto was, "Nothing sacred and all in fun."[7] Boats carried convention crowds from Seattle's waterfront to the picnic grounds in North Seattle. There was no other way to get there except by walking.

Canadian trade was forecast in the early years of the Sound's settlement, as witnessed by the influence of the Hudson's Bay Company on the Columbia River and in British Columbia. Victoria was already much larger than Seattle by the 1860s. San Francisco's steamship lines ran regularly to the Canadian port, although there was no regular service to Seattle. Steamer service to Canada from Sound ports was born of necessity and proved to be entertaining and popular for passengers. Washington State Ferries and Black Ball Transport, Inc. continue these runs successfully for the same reasons.

Seattle's waterfront celebrated the evening of July 21, 1869, when Secretary William H. Seward steamed into the harbor on the WILSON G. HUNT. He had just concluded the purchase of Alaska for the United States. His speech to Seattleites predicted a glorious future for Washington Territory. He was correct.

Alaska's rich ore and mineral deposits, including the glittering gold of the Klondike, was soon to be a major source of revenue to northwestern businesses. Maritime commerce and waterborne traffic is as significant now between these two states as it was at the turn of the century. Petroleum and natural gas reserves of Alaska have simply replaced the demand for gold.

The story at hand is significantly tied to the success of one Seattle steamship line. The Alaska Steamship Company was the parent company of one important Puget Sound ferry fleet and through their original design and scope of purpose, the progenitor of the Alaska State Ferry System.

Hundreds of steamers and ferryboats have traveled over 40 different routes on Puget Sound. Bridges and vehicles have never replaced them. Most of these routes were incorporated into the modern ferry system.

Residents of the Sound often rely on this system to carry them to and from work, to football games, to medical assistance, to universities, to dinner on-the-town, to a weekend camping trip or to a Sunday picnic. Visitors enjoy the ferries for recreational purposes. Produce and dairy products cross from island to mainland on the ferries. Freight and commercial haulage continue as major factors in the present day success of the fleet.

Lifestyles have changed; the ferries are fast and the finest in the world. Dependence on this reliable waterway and the vessels that navigate it, remains constant.

[6]Ballast Island no longer exists. Once located near the foot of Washington Street in Seattle, it was where sailing vessels offloaded their ballast of cobblestone and rock onto this island pile. Ballast islands may be found in most ports of the world that were once patronized by sailing ships.

[7]Wilbur Thompson, "When It Was Fly on the Flyer," *The Sea Chest,* December 1981.

150 YEARS OF THE BLACK BALL FLAG

While the church clock chimed ten, Captain James Watkinson signaled his mate to trim sails and cast off lines. A blizzard was raging in New York's harbor near the East River Pier that blustery cold fifth day of January 1818. But the captain's orders were explicit; the packet ship JAMES MONROE would keep the word of her owners and sail for Liverpool "on time."

The snow storm raised havoc with the new packet's speed. It was not until four o'clock in the afternoon that she cleared Sandy Hook Bar, only 17 miles from her departure point. Making up time on the Atlantic crossing, the JAMES MONROE landed her passengers January 28, just three weeks later.

This trim ship carried a curious black ball insignia on her main royal mastheads and another on the foretopsail. It was from this peculiar symbol, of which no substantiated information was found, that the Black Ball Line drew its name. The flag was soon identified as an emblem of prompt, reliable service. That flag would one day be carried to the Pacific Northwest to be flown for nearly another sixty years on ferries of Puget Sound. It endured nearly a century and a half on the North American continent.

Cornelia and Enoch W. Peabody raised eight children in their New England home. Several sons followed the sea, but Charles, their third eldest, chose not to follow his father as shipmaster of Black Ball packets. He selected the business prowess of his uncle and namesake, Charles H. Marshall. Marshall was at the helm of the Atlantic Black Ball Line until his death in 1865.

Charles Marshall and Cornelia Peabody's father, Benjamin Marshall, had been one of the five original textile importers who conceived the idea of sailing their trading vessels on schedule with or without a full cargo. Such an idea was unheard of at the time and seemed unprofitable. But businessmen and travelers were tired of lengthy delays, persisting sometimes as long as a month. They welcomed the scheduled sailing wholeheartedly.

Benjamin Marshall had two other sons, Alexander

BLACK BALL PACKET SHIP

C. and Edward C. who joined him and Charles H. in the packet business. These two became shipmasters and good friends of another Black Ball comrade, Captain Enoch W. Peabody. Captain Peabody married their sister, Cornelia, in 1855 and sailed with her across the Atlantic on his packet ship for a honeymoon trip.[1] Peabody was master of the MANHATTEN until 1855, the NEPTUNE until after the Civil War, and the CHARLES H. MARSHALL, the last ship constructed for their packet service, circa 1869.

Charles E. Peabody was born to Cornelia and

Enoch in Brooklyn, New York in 1857. He received a thorough education, first at the Polytechnic Institute in Brooklyn and then at Heidelberg University in Germany. After spending three or four years in Europe, young Charles returned to New York's Wall Street as a broker in stocks and bonds. It was here that Peabody became closely acquainted with his father's cousin, Charles H. Folger, Secretary of the U.S. Treasury in President Chester A. Arthur's cabinet. Folger was heir to the Folger coffee empire.

Folger's son and Charles Peabody attempted a

[1]Cornelia Marshall Peabody kept a diary of this honeymoon voyage. It has been preserved in the Peabody family as an historical keepsake. The diary reveals intimacies, tragedies and human relations reflective of the period and crossing the Atlantic on a sailing ship.

farming venture in Minnesota but soon recognized their ineptitude for agriculture. Secretary Folger respected the aggressive young man. Due to political persuasiveness, Charles Peabody was appointed special agent for the U.S. Treasury Department for the West Coast. Here he would deal with such issues as the management of the U.S. Revenue Cutter Service then under the Department of the Treasury; care and treatment of Eskimos residing in Alaskan Territory; and the annoying persistence of shipmasters smuggling illegal Chinese aliens across the Canadian border into Puget Sound and the Washington Territory.

THE GREAT WILD WEST

So it was that at the tender age of 25, Charles Peabody headed west to stake his fortune and establish his good name. On that train trip across the country, Charles met Miss Lilly Macaulay, his future bride.

Peabody was stationed in Port Townsend, Washington Territory, at the entrance to Puget Sound. It was 1882 and Tacoma, Olympia, Seattle and Port Townsend were all vying to become the center of Washington civilization. Each city sought to be the territorial capital, which would shortly achieve statehood, and the terminus for the long overdue railroad. Port Townsend was a logical center for maritime transport and the transfer of goods from ship to rail. The federal government already utilized the city for a number of their head offices, including U.S. Customs, Revenue Cutter Service,[2] and the Treasury Department. There were several army and navy forts within close proximity. Nestled just across the Strait of Juan de Fuca was Victoria, British Columbia, one of the most cosmopolitan cities on the West Coast at that time.

The Northwest was a region burgeoning with business deals and a good home for an ambitious man seeking prosperity. An early day lumber king on Vancouver Island, William J. Macaulay, appreciated Peabody's motivation and talents. He joined the young entrepreneur in the late 1880's in negotiating a deal with Robert Dunsmuir for some of his Vancouver Island timber holdings.

James Macaulay had begun his lumber business in Manitoba at what was then called Rat Portage, an illustrative name that later changed to Canora. After

[2]The U.S. Revenue Cutter Service considered locating their academy at Port Townsend instead of their final choice at New London, Connecticut, home of the present day U.S. Coast Guard Academy.

CHARLES E. PEABODY WHEN HE MOVED WEST

PORT TOWNSEND, WASHINGTON TERRITORY

TALBOT COAL YARD, PORT TOWNSEND

milling all of the available timber at that site, Macaulay moved his family and business to Victoria where he became a very wealthy man.

Macaulay, Peabody and Dunsmuir formed the Victoria Lumber & Manufacturing Company at Chemainus, B.C. Today the operation continues with considerable modernization as the McMillan, Bloedel & Powell River Company. Peabody became temporary business manager of the new lumber company and married his partner's daughter.

The Victoria Colonist carried the following announcement, May 27, 1891:

"Cupid's Work

"Mr. Charles Peabody of Port Townsend was married to Miss Lily Macaulay [sic]. The wedding took place at the residence of the lady's parents, Rev. Father Nicholaye officiating. The happy couple left for Harrison Hot Springs after the ceremony."[3]

Mr. and Mrs. Charles Peabody made their home in Port Townsend. Peabody was already a prominent businessman involved with the local coal industry, lumber operations, and management of the Merchant's Bank, owned by Ladd & Tilton. Charles Peabody, Walter Oakes and George Roberts became aligned in a business venture known as the Pacific Wharf Company, August 8, 1891, involving extensive dock property holdings in Port Townsend. Stockholders included D.B. Jackson, 118 shares; Charles Peabody, 200; H. Elling, 36; W. Oakes, 118; Melville Nichols, 14, and George Roberts, 14. The Articles of Incorporation stated a capital investment of $59,000. The purpose was the "acquiring, purchasing, holding by contract as lease, and the chartering of steamships, vessels, watercraft, and the maintenance and operation of same in all lawful business, trade, commerce, and the navigation upon oceans, sounds, bays, straits, tide waters, lakes, rivers, canals." Walter Oakes was chairman of the board and Peabody was president.

The first three of eight sons were born to Charles and Lilly in Port Townsend. Family names had become a tradition: Charles Macaulay, Folger (for the U.S. Secretary) and Alexander Marshall.

Seattle, like the rest of the country, was beginning to recover from the economic panic of 1893 when barter and trade had replaced the specie of the realm. Lumber mills on Puget Sound were humming again and 50,000 residents of Seattle were beginning to see light at the end of the once dark tunnel. There were no

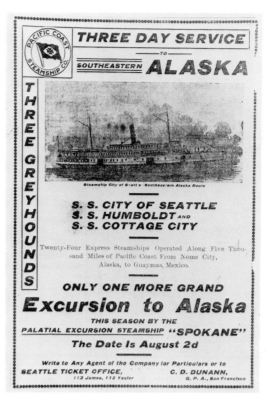

indications to forecast a gold rush in the North at this time, but there were placer mines in various districts of Canada and Alaska that were producing valuable ores. Southeastern Alaska had a number of small centers of prospective importance. Gold discoveries had been attracting increasing numbers of people to Alaska via the Northwest. The existing Pacific Coast Steamship Company and a few other packets were apparently meeting all the transportation demands.

Three gentlemen were closely watching Alaskan discoveries and transportation opportunities. They were willing to gamble on the future. They had fresh ideas for the steamship service and believed the public was ready to accept some improvements. Charles Peabody, George Roberts and George Lent brainstormed ideas for the Alaskan trade and sought other interested investors. They were joined by Melville Nichols and Walter Oakes.

It was not until January 21, 1895, that they publicly announced the organization of the Alaska Steamship Company, incorporated under the laws of the State of Oregon. This insignificant group debated at first about

[3] The Macaulay mansion was known as Pinehurst. Its architecture included a romantic tower overlooking the sea. It is presently undergoing restoration in Victoria. Macaulay later built a more imposing mansion near Government House. It was called the Highlands, because of the Scotsman's heritage. This mansion today is recognized as one of the most beautiful homes in Victoria.

CREW'S PORTRAIT FOR CITY OF KINGSTON

CAPTAIN GEORGE F. ROBERTS AND CAPTAIN DUNCAN

J.G. NORD AND MELVILLE NICHOLS

CHARLES PEABODY IN 1888

18

calling it the Merchant's Steamship Company[4] but somehow "Alaska" had a more adventuresome appeal.

The founders of Alaska Steam were typically men of the maritime trades, experienced in business and company management. Each investor played a supporting role in the success of the company: Charles Peabody, the well-educated and connected banker with numerous lumber and industrial ties; Captain George Roberts, shipmaster of the CITY OF KINGSTON, who later served as master of Alaska Steam's vessels; George Lent, chief engineer of the CITY OF KINGSTON with unlimited engineering experience and a knack for negotiating sales; Captain Melville Nichols, a Puget Sound pilot; Walter Oakes, son of the president of the Northern Pacific Railway Company and transportation entrepreneur in his own right.

The new company bought the 140 foot steamer WILLAPA and placed her on the routes between Puget Sound and Southeastern Alaska. Some Alaska sourdoughs credited the WILLAPA for bringing on the discovery of the Alaskan-Yukon gold vein that led to the great Klondike Strike in 1898. Gold had been mined as early as 1892 in the Yukon, but the WILLAPA's fare was much less expensive than the rates of the Pacific Steamship Company. Many more prospectors could afford exploration. A ruthless rate war ensued between the two companies with Pacific Coast cutting their fares to less than half the normal fee in an attempt to drive Alaska Steam out of business.

The public was apparently resentful of Pacific Coast's unsportsmanlike attitude toward the fledgling company. The monopoly had been run with a tight rein which the travelers resented. The people began to patronize the WILLAPA and "loaded to utmost capacity"[5] she sailed from Schwabacher's Wharf on her first voyage, March 3, 1895. A profitable load was aboard: 79 passengers, 22 horses, sleds for a mining party, and several hundred tons of miscellaneous cargo.[6]

Captain Roberts was at the helm of the WILLAPA, steering her for ports-of-call such as Ketchikan, Juneau, Dyea and Sitka. The WILLAPA returned to Seattle on St. Patrick's Day and the townspeople considered her success a milestone in fulfilling the prophecy of Secretary Seward that that city would one day be the trade center for supply of the north.

THE WILLAPA

The WILLAPA had a lengthy history of service in the Northwest prior to her employment with Alaska Steamship Company. Launched as the bar tug GENERAL MILES at Astoria, Oregon on June 15, 1882 by the Illwaco Navigation Company, she was one of the largest and finest boats in this service. She had a length of 100 feet, 22 foot beam and a 10 foot depth of hold. As a steamer she was designed for service on and crossing the bar. Her history began even earlier than 1882. She was originally built in 1879 as a sailing schooner.

The GENERAL MILES was practically a sister ship of the GENERAL CANBY which was later one of the pioneer steamers of the Sound's Port Orchard run. Captain John Henry D. Gray, grandson of Captain Robert Gray who discovered the Columbia River and Grays Harbor, had an interest in the GENERAL MILES and at times served as her master. He was in command when the GENERAL MILES went to the rescue of the QUEEN OF THE PACIFIC, aground at the mouth of the Columbia River. Captain W.P. Whitcomb was master almost continuously until 1889 with chief engineers William Clough, succeeded by Edward Taylor and Charles Smith.

The MILES did a general freight, passenger and towing business to and from Portland, having no set

[4]This name was suggested due to their service for the merchants of Alaska. *The Marine Digest*, September 1944.

[5]*Alaska Sportsman Magazine*, December 1960.

[6]Ibid. Officers on the first voyage were: Captain George Roberts, master; Captain J.G. Nord, mate; Captain George Francis, pilot; William Van Tassel, chief engineer; Oswin Spieseke, first assistant; and Courtland Taylor, purser. On the second trip, C.V. LaFarge succeeded Taylor as purser and Captain Francis was succeeded by Captain Leonard. One year later Captain Harry Gillespie and Captain "Chilkat" Jensen took command.

19

THE WILLAPA RAN BETWEEN PUGET SOUND AND SOUTHEASTERN ALASKA.

schedule and going wherever trade warranted. She was one of the first boats on the Grays Harbor route and did much to build up that part of the country. Her freight accommodations were limited and her passenger provisions only fair, but pioneers of that day were a hardy lot and put up with conditions that today would bring no end of complaints.

Early in 1889 the MILES was sold to Fred Strong of Portland and the Coast Steamship Company which had been organized by Strong, Charles F. Beebe, and F.K. Arnold to secure a larger portion of trade for Portland from the small towns along the coast. Soon after this, Captain Herbert F. Beecher leased the GENERAL MILES and brought her to Puget Sound for service between Port Townsend and the San Juan Islands. Here she carried freight in connection with passenger steamers J.B. LIBBY and POINT ARENA. When, on November 10, 1889 the LIBBY burned, the GENERAL MILES ran for a while in her place. In this service she carried passengers and freight between Port Townsend and the Islands, making one trip a week to Seattle. After operating on the island run for less than one year, she returned to Portland.

In 1890 she ran between Portland and Willapa Harbor, from which she afterwards drew her name. She was hauled out at Portland in 1891 and cut in two, then lengthened 36 feet. She was relaunched as the passenger steamer WILLAPA. Her new dimensions were 136 feet by 20 feet by 10 feet, depth of hold. She had a fore-and-aft compound engine[7] and a Scotch

marine boiler. She was extensively refitted and upon her reappearance, was considered a very fine vessel indeed.

The WILLAPA usually operated in Grays Harbor trade but when business was offered she would make trips to Coos Bay, Willapa Harbor and other Coast ports. By 1894 she was again on Puget Sound. She was chartered by the Hastings Steamboat Company of Port Townsend and it was perhaps at that time that Charles Peabody and his associates became aware of her.

Alaska Steamship Company purchased the steamer February 26, 1895. The WILLAPA became the first ship of the new steamship company. The historic Black Ball flag, a black ball on a red field, the banner that had graced the mastheads of fast sailing packets since 1818 on the Atlantic, was unfurled on the WILLAPA. The flag was considered the family crest.

The Black Ball flag was flown aboard ships of the Alaska Steamship Company until sale of that company to Guggenheim interests in 1909. Peabody retained his right to the flag and in 1928, his son, Captain Alexander Marshall Peabody, flew the flag once again on Puget Sound.

Upon delivery of the WILLAPA to Alaska Steam, work was immediately started to put the vessel in first class condition. She was overhauled and refitted under the direction of George Lent. She was not a fancy vessel by any means, but she filled a need, and from the

[7]The compound engine had cylinders with 15″ and 32″ diameters and a 28″ stroke. The boiler had a working pressure of 110 pounds.

start received the wholehearted support of the territory she served. The WILLAPA always carried a good load and being inexpensive to operate, she proved a moneymaker for the company.

Bound for Mary Island, Alaska, 2:30 A.M., Friday, March 19, 1897, the WILLAPA stranded on Regatta Reef, Seaforth Channel. She had been in a heavy snow storm for several hours and visibility was nearly impossible. The schooner GABRIOLA and canoes from the Indian village nearby assisted in removing passengers and freight. Several head of horses could not be removed and were shot. The passengers were taken to Bella Bella, B.C., to await the arrival of the steamer EDITH which, as soon as word was sent to Seattle, was furnished by the company to finish the trip.

The WILLAPA was first considered a total loss but was later purchased from the underwriters by British Columbia interests. After salvaging, she was repaired and refitted and placed in operation by Canadian Pacific Railway Company. Under the British flag she was used as a relief boat. At one time she even returned to the Alaska run.

The WILLAPA was again purchased by American interests in November 1902 and once more flew the American flag. A few days later she was resold to the Bellingham Bay Transportation Company and renamed the BELLINGHAM. In connection with the steamer DODE she operated between Seattle and Bellingham with through-service maintained to Blaine and Point Roberts. On this run she met opposition from the UTOPIA and the famous GEORGE E. STARR.

In December, 1903 the BELLINGHAM was towing the steamer DODE to Bellingham when a collision occurred with the well-known steamer FLYER. The DODE was somewhat battered but the BELLINGHAM escaped with minor injuries. Within a few weeks the BELLINGHAM came under management of the Inland Navigation Company also owned by Charles E. Peabody and associates. She was operated on the Port Townsend Mill run for a short time[8]. Later she was laid up and underwent overhaul under the direction of a Peabody cousin, Captain Howard Penfield.

Looking like a brand new boat, the BELLINGHAM entered the Strait run, Port Angeles to Clallam, later to Neah Bay. After one summer on the Strait she replaced the LYDIA THOMPSON on the San Juan Island run, (Seattle-San Juan Island-Whatcom). Her commander, Captain Penfield, was succeeded by Captain Sam Barlow.

The BELLINGHAM's crew recalled that the vessel was possessed by a ''ghost whistle,'' a low moaning sound that could plainly be heard in certain parts of her cabin when she was laboring in a heavy sea.

January 11, 1907 the BELLINGHAM was called upon to replace the ALICE GERTRUDE, a steamer that had been lost at Slip Point, Clallam Bay. Captain Barlow left her command here for the ROSALIE and was followed by Captain Charles E. Kalstrom. Kalstrom continued aboard the BELLINGHAM until his death in 1917.[9] The BELLINGHAM was on the Strait run most of the time.

CAPTAIN HERBERT F. BEECHER, SON OF A PREACHER

The BELLINGHAM's boilers were considered to be in too poor a condition for operation by 1918. She passed out of commission as a passenger vessel and her fittings and machinery were salvaged by Neider & Marcus. Parts of her machinery were said to be cut into shrapnel and used in France during World War I.

For several months the old BELLINGHAM lay forsaken and bare. Many supposed that the first vessel to fly the Black Ball flag had passed into history. She was a proven heroine of many battles against the elements in her career. Her rival carriers had not yet seen the last of her.

[8]Captain William Doney was her master on the Seattle-Port Madison, Kingston, Port Ludlow, Port Townsend and way ports run.
[9]Captain Kalstrom's death occurred aboard the WAIALEALE. D.J. McDonald was with Kalstrom as chief engineer for several years on the BELLINGHAM.

UTOPIA—THE OPPOSITION

LYDIA THOMPSON HEADED FOR THE LANDING

S.S. DODE IN 1898

In March 1919, the BELLINGHAM's hull was sold to H.C. Strong of the Sunny Point Packing Company. After some alterations at King & Winge Ship Repair yard, she reappeared as the barge BELLINGHAM. She was equipped with two cargo winches, driven by a vertical donkey boiler. She had two masts and carried sail! They were not much used.

In the fall of 1922 her owners decided that she was just too good a boat to be used as a sail barge. She was hauled out at Taylor's Mill and a few planks were replaced. A 200-horsepower Fairbanks-Morse semi-diesel engine was installed at Lake Union Drydock & Machine Works in Seattle, as well as extensive alterations made to her upperworks.

THE BELLINGHAM REPLACED THE ALICE GERTRUDE.

Once again the vessel was fitted out for operation between Seattle and Ketchikan and other Southeastern Alaska ports. She was operated by the Northland Transportation Company as the NORCO. In the late 1920's she was sold into brief ownership by the Citizen's Light and Power Co. of Ketchikan[1] then J.E. Berg of the same city. From 1941 to 1946 she was owned by Ketchikan Cold Storage and offered for sale by Puget Sound Marina, Lake Union, Seattle. Otis Shively of Seattle purchased her.

The brave little steamer Ex-WILLAPA faced a repugnant death for one that so diligently served the Black Ball flag. The vessel that had incessantly endured hardships, ended her career in a blaze of glory. During the summer of 1950 she participated in the ritual of the annual Seattle celebration known as Seafair. The NORCO (Ex-WILLAPA, Ex-GENERAL MILES, Ex-BELLINGHAM)was presented to the Puget Sound Maritime Historical Society for the sacrificial burning of "Neptune's barge."

The vessel was stuffed with fireworks and other combustibles and towed into Elliott Bay by the tug GOLIAH. She was torched and blazed in a spectacular fire for hours, refusing to sink. During her final moments, Captain Alexander Peabody sent the Puget Sound Navigation Company's ferry KALAKALA to signal the final salute of whistles and air horns. All the ships in the bay joined the final farewell to this pioneer of the Black Ball flag. Fireboat DUWAMISH and harbor patrol boats extinguished her fires and pumped gallons of water into this trusty ship that refused to die. At last her beaten and charred hull had no recourse but to sink into the deep waters of Seattle's harbor.

Within one year, the Black Ball flag was lowered on the Peabody fleet of Puget Sound. Like the proud WILLAPA, the company passed into legends of history.

THE BELLINGHAM OF THE INLAND NAVIGATION CO.

[1]This company was controlled by W.B. Foshay who forfeited these investments during the stock market crash of 1929.

THE STEAMER FLEETS JOIN FORCES

The Klondike Gold Rush was gaining momentum and the steamship companies forgot their rate wars while business and Seattle boomed. By the end of 1897 Charles E. Peabody had reorganized the Alaska Steamship Company with Frank E. Burns and Carl H.E. Stoltenberg. They joined as stockholders and upped the capital from $30,000 to $40,000.[1]

Turning to their associate, D.B. Jackson, they chartered the steamer ROSALIE with an option to buy. It was time to replace the WILLAPA. The ROSALIE was approximately the same size with an equal carrying capacity.

The ROSALIE was booked within 24 hours of announcement of her new service. She headed north for Alaska Steamship Company, July 31, 1897. The official passenger list records 93 people, but there were probably closer to 150 aboard. These trips proved so successful that the company exercised its option that fall and bought the ROSALIE.

The ship's first master under Alaska Steam was Captain George Roberts. He ran her from Seattle to Skagway with wayports. When Roberts left to take command of the company's S.S. CITY OF SEATTLE, he was succeeded by Captain John A. "Dynamite" O'Brien. He continued with the steamer until fall of 1900.

As the gold stampede mounted, so grew the fleet of Alaska Steam. They added the DIRIGO, FARRALON, and the DOLPHIN. Later they built the steamship JEFFERSON at Heath Shipyard in Tacoma[2] and named it in honor of the county in which the company had formally organized. These gentlemen had an eye for opportunity. They were youthful and willing to take risks.

The Seattle Post-Intelligencer, September 9, 1901, announced that the Puget Sound Navigation Company, owner and operator of the ROSALIE, was now providing service on the Seattle-Victoria run. The company had secured four mail routes on the Sound, including Neah Bay, Port Angeles, Port Townsend and the San Juan Islands. This would be the company's bread and

ROSALIE, FIRST OF THE P.S.N. FLEET

butter.

Puget Sound Navigation Company was organized by Peabody and his stockholders about 1898. It was considered an inland water subsidiary of Alaska Steamship Company. The Articles of Incorporation show that it was registered in the State of Nevada. That was certainly inland. It also provided for lenient corporate laws and taxes concerning steamboat operation.

Alaska Steam executives soon recognized the

Str. Rosalie,
P. Angeles, Wn.

increasing demand for service on Puget Sound. Here was an opportunity to recycle some of their smaller vessels as they became obsolete for the strenuous Alaska employment. The size of crowds traveling to Southeastern Alaska where prospectors and suppliers could connect with the Chilkoot Trail and Skagway were multiplying. The first vessels of the Alaska Steam fleet could no longer accommodate even a third of the passengers and freight dealers who sought passage and cargo space.

[1]Financial figures were taken directly from corporate papers and official audits unless otherwise stated.

[2]C. Calkins, *High Tide*

STEAMERS OF THE GOLD STAMPEDE:

DOLPHIN

ALASKA STEAMSHIP COMPANY'S
S.S. CITY OF SEATTLE

JEFFERSON

DIRIGO

A letter written by the late Captain H.T. Shaver[3] recalls the conditions aboard Alaska steamers at that time:

"A year later, in 1899, as I have said before, my mother and I went from Seattle to Skagway on the old ROSALIE, and it was one of the most interesting trips in my life.

"The vessel was crowded as usual, and while there were not too many people going to seek their fortunes in the mines, there were a lot of people aboard such as newspaper men, merchants, bankers, and others who were going to establish a business.

"I remember quite well that there were a lot of gamblers in the passenger crowd, and they used to draw a white chalk line on the upper deck and throw silver dollars to the chalk line, and the one that got the nearest, picked up all the dollars. I hung around on the other side of the chalk line, and if the dollars started to roll overboards toward the edge, I would chase them and give them back to the owners. Every once in a while, one of them would give me a dollar for the service, and by the time I arrived in Skagway, I had fifty dollars stashed away, or rather my mother did.

"I remember that we landed at Morre's Dock, and I have a picture of the ROSALIE, taken in 1899 at the dock. The night before, the tide was in and we were laying very nicely alongside the dock, and of course we stayed aboard the night. The next morning as I went out on deck, I couldn't find the dock, but just a bunch of piling, and then I happened to look topside and found that the dock was about 20 feet above us, and we were practically laying on the mudflats at the head of Lynn Canal."

The steamer ROSALIE was built in Alameda, California for C.L. Dimond of San Francisco in 1893. She was intended as an excursion vessel but this idea was abandoned. She operated as a ferry between San Francisco and Vallejo for a short while before heading north.

After one or two trips between Southeastern Alaska, commanded by Captain Patterson, she was sold by Dimond for $50,000 to D.B. Jackson, considered one of the great transportation organizers on Puget Sound.[4] Four months later, on October 5, 1894, Jackson and his associates incorporated as the Northwestern Steamship Company.

Their company placed the ROSALIE in the command of Captain Charles Ames, better known to most as "Big Ames" due to his extraordinary stature. He and Captain William Williamson, pilot, ran the

[3] *The Sea Chest,* Vol. 13, page 130.

[4] D.B. Jackson was one of the major stockholders and associates of Charles Peabody in the Pacific Wharf Company in Port Townsend. He was the grandfather of the former Washington State Governor, Daniel Jackson Evans. Evans is president of The Evergreen State College in Olympia, Washington.

CREW OF THE ROSALIE—1903

steamer between Tacoma, Seattle, and Victoria until autumn of 1897.

When the PORTLAND steamed into Seattle with a ''ton of gold'' the Alaska Steamship Company chartered the ROSALIE from Jackson to step up their Alaska runs and replace the WILLAPA. Soon she proved too small for even this popular run and the company executives placed her under the management of their new company, Puget Sound Navigation Company. She ran in opposition to two Sound steamers, the UTOPIA and the SEHOME.

The fare to Victoria was dropped to 25 cents by the navigation company and competition waxed hot and heavy until the UTOPIA, too, was purchased by Puget Sound Navigation. She was commanded by Captain Henry Carter and later by Captain A.N. McAlpine. With the exception of short periods when the ROSALIE ran to Bellingham and Strait ports, she continued on the Victoria route until 1904. She was then

transferred to the San Juan Island route and remained there for the rest of her career.

In 1907, Captain Samuel Barlow left the command of the BELLINGHAM to become master of the ROSALIE. He served aboard her continuously from the time she entered the Island run with Captain A. Hansen as his mate. John D. Goff was engineer throughout the latter years of her service.

The ROSALIE was always a popular boat. She entertained a special place in the heart of Charles Peabody according to his sons. Her cabin was furnished with Pullman car seats, and fittings throughout were equally luxurious.[5] With a rated speed of 12 knots, it no doubt pleased Mr. Peabody to ride his vessel on inland waters in comfort.

[5]The ROSALIE measured 136'6'' x 27'.

TRANSPORTATION ORGANIZER D.B. JACKSON

C.H.J. STOLTENBERG (Far Right) ABOARD ROSALIE

ONE OF THE FIRST STEAMERS TO ALASKAN GOLD

ROSALIE'S DINING SALON

A TOUCH OF ELEGANCE

PORTLAND CARRIED A "TON OF GOLD" TO SEATTLE.

UTOPIA, BUILT IN SEATTLE, 1893

Throughout her varied career, the ROSALIE seemed equally well-suited to inside and outside routes. To quote Captain Harry Barlow, Sam Barlow's brother, "When she was on the Alaska run they used to slow her down off Four Mile and bring her in with a tug. When Sam had her on the Island run they used to ring a slow bell 200 yards off the docks."[6]

TICKEE-ONE, TICKEE-TWO, TICKEE-THREE

A letter written on the stationery of Puget Sound Navigation Company, dated and marked, "S.S. ROSALIE, January 3, 1911"[7] reads:

"Mr. F.E. Burns
General Manager P.S.N. Co.
Seattle, Washington

"Dear Sir:

I beg to advise you that the present whistle on the ROSALIE does not give satisfaction as an echo whistle and it is necessary for us to have a good echo whistle for the Island rout.

Yours Respectfully,
Samuel Barlow
Master, S.S. ROSALIE"

We can only wonder today if Captain Barlow received his new whistle. On the morning of December 11, 1912, the ROSALIE piled up on Smith Island in a heavy morning fog. She was later pulled off by the MORNING STAR, suffering no serious damage.[8]

The echo system of navigation is one which is practiced even today on Washington's ferries. Ferry captains thread fog-bound Puget Sound by ear as well as radar. Some of the mates and skippers become experts at this method while the old masters in the day of the ROSALIE depended on it totally. Ferries and steamers had the same route, the same course, and mostly the same speed in a fog as they had in fair weather.

The oldtime pilot logged his course devotedly, jotting down running time on each compass bearing, charting an invisible track in the water. This was particularly important, as Captain Barlow mentions on the San Juan island runs. In some cases the passes are so narrow that an Olympic broad jumper could make it ashore at low tide. Even amateurs could swim it and if the water was not quite so deep, one could wade. Should the fog roll in as it is prone to do, particularly in fall and winter months, sometimes for a week at a time, the master resorted to his log.

SAN JUAN ISLAND'S SKIPPER, CAPTAIN SAMUEL BARLOW

Finding a fair day several weeks before in his log, when the tides were similar to these fog-ridden ones, the captain begins to follow the invisible groove he mapped that previous time. He is "running out his time" with watch, tachometer and compass. The variants of tidal currents and the velocity of the winds are the unpredictable factors altering his chart through pea soup.

The captain blows his high-pitched whistle to determine his relative position to the land. Counting the seconds after he has blown his horn, "tickee-one, tickee-two, tickee-three" he hears a low sizzling sound of echo, ahead. A long, solid running echo indicates the shoreline. A solid echo fairly long, indicates land nearby. The captain proceeds along his course, identifying his position by blasting his whistle and listening for its response.

Trained ears catch a double echo or the harsh or smooth tones of the sound. Each tone is interpreted from long habit and experience on the route. In a very dense fog, within very tight quarters, a lookout is sta-

[6]*The Marine Digest,* February 24, 1923.

[7]This letter was loaned to the authors by Walter Green, via Black Ball Transport, Inc. It was originally in the possession of Captain Louis Van Bogaert who was first mate and pilot of the ROSALIE at the time of its writing.

[8]The ROSALIE did not meet her doom until early morning, June 22, 1918, when a fire was discovered that spread rapidly. She was a total loss at her moorings in the West Waterway of Seattle.

GARLAND

ALICE GERTRUDE

CHARLES PEABODY (center) AND ROBERT MORAN (left) IN SEATTLE'S PIONEER SQUARE

Beautiful San Juan Islands

PUGET SOUND NAVIGATION CO.
COLMAN DOCK, SEATTLE.

tioned to assist the captain in watching for land or other floating objects such as nearby ships. Echo voices warn the pilot if he is too close. He glides on past the land whether he sees it or not.

Once clear, the master may take an echo off the last headland to insure correct departure from the pass he has just navigated. He runs out his time on the logged course, until close quarters again call for more whistling.

Echo pilotage is a tradition on Puget Sound. It is a science which cannot be rigidly taught. It is an instinctive response developed by the pilot who in good weather has memorized his route and the ragged shorelines that respond to his whistle in a fog.

Fundamental is the fact that sound will travel through fog at approximately 1080 feet per second, depending upon the temperature. Using this scale and rounding it off to 1000 feet for a safety margin, the captain counts a round trip for outbound whistle and returning echo by the second. A single second puts 500 feet between the boat and the shore. A ten-count echo means nearly one mile or over 5000 feet, so most pilots do not listen for echoes longer than that.

Ferryboat passengers today may observe this procedure if caught in a fog. Should you notice a crew member standing on the bow and the whistle blowing at various intervals while crossing, count the seconds and you will know just how close the ferry is to land.

Some ferry captains took their echo training with them elsewhere. Captain Russ Taylor recalls how he was one of the few American pilots who could navigate the Chinese Yangtse River during the 1930s.

"It was easy," he said, "I did it with echoes."

GREEN'S MOSQUITO FLEET

Seeking to enlarge their service of Puget Sound routes, the owners of Puget Sound Navigation Company absorbed the entire fleet of the Thompson Steamboat Company for about $300,000 in January 1902. There were six vessels included in the sale: the ALICE GERTRUDE, LYDIA THOMPSON, MAJESTIC, GARLAND, PROSPER and EVANGEL.

Charles Peabody became president and general manager of the navigation company and continued as manager of Alaska Steamship Company. Walter Oakes was president and treasurer of Alaska Steam. The services of both companies were closely controlled by a few people.

Meanwhile, an exceptional young man made

34

YOUNG JOSHUA GREEN

try. Seattle's potentially inexpensive power resources would provide the greatest manufacturing opportunities. The senior Green was a dreamer whose thinking proved far ahead of his time.

Joshua Green received a good education. He attended a private academy in Jackson, Mississippi, followed by two years at Maupin's University School in Ellicott, Maryland. Upon his arrival in Seattle, he immediately sought employment.

His father became acquainted with Mr. Bailey Gatzert,[9] head of Schwabacher Brothers and Company, the leading grocery and hardware firm in town. Through Gatzert, Green secured a job as chainman on a crew surveying the Seattle, Lake Shore and Eastern Railroad. But he loved the water so much that Gatzert helped him get a job as purser on the shallow-draft freight and passenger boat, HENRY BAILEY. It belonged to the Skagit Railway and Navigation Company.

SEATTLE MAYOR BAILEY GATZERT

strides toward his personal goal as a leader of shipping on the Sound. Joshua Green was born in Jackson, Mississippi and arrived in the Puget Sound region with his parents in 1886.

Green lived to the age of 105 years. He made significant contributions to the development of reputable steamboat and ferry service before his early retirement from marine enterprise in 1926.

Washington was a Pandora's Box of riches when Green recognized his prospects on arrival at age 16. His family had taken the typical route at that time, crossing the country by rail to Tacoma and taking the steamboat to Seattle.

Mr. and Mrs. W.H.H. Green had left their war-torn and bankrupt homeland in the South to seek a region of better opportunities for their sons, Joshua and Hal. Their grandfather's cotton mill had been burned by the Yankees, punishment for manufacturing cloth for Confederate uniforms. His bank, too, was stripped of every coin.

Though the Civil War had ended by the time Joshua Green was born in 1869, the ravages of war and Reconstruction were too much for the Greens to bear. Their father carefully reasoned that Seattle, Washington Territory had the greatest prospects in the nation due to the rains running down the Cascade Mountains. The precipitation could be harnessed to furnish more water power than anywhere in the coun-

[9]Schwabacher Bros. and Co. was established in Seattle in 1869 with Gatzert as the resident partner. Gatzert was a leader of commerce in the city. He became president of Seattle Drydock & Shipbuilding Company in 1888, an investor in the Metropolitan Electric Railway Company, Great Western Iron and Steel Works, president of People's Savings Bank in 1890, president of the Seattle Chamber of Commerce until the spring of 1890, and president of the Puget Sound National Bank in 1891. Frederick James Grant's *History of Seattle* writes of him in 1891:

"... Mr. Gatzert has a remarkable liberality of views and generosity in act, he has assisted almost every worthy enterprise, and was particularly forward in assisting the coal industry in its struggling days."

Green's shipmates on the HENRY BAILEY were Captain Sam Denny, master; Peter Falk, mate; Henry Denny, first engineer; and Frank Zickmund, second engineer. The Dennys were related to Seattle's founding family who landed at Alki Point in 1851.

Green claimed to have been lucky in his companions aboard the freight boat. Seattle's waterfront was "full of drunks" at that time and notoriously bad.[1] Green attributed his lifelong frugality to the lessons learned at the hand of mate Peter Falk. Falk always encouraged him to save a nickel and "walk home rather than taking the cable car, regardless of the distance."[2]

Green convinced Sam Denny, Falk and Zickmund to collaborate with him and buy the sternwheel steamboat FANNY LAKE and a scow for $5000. This, no doubt, required persuasiveness on Green's part. His life's savings amounted to about $250 while the others had very little money saved for investment.

Bravely the four men went to see banker Jacob Furth. He loaned them $1250 apiece from Puget Sound National Bank. It is said that he required no collateral, although the bank would have owned a sternwheeler and a scow if the borrowers had not paid their debt.

The four partners left the HENRY BAILEY to operate the FANNY LAKE. The latter was a freighter so no effort was made to carry passengers in competition with the former on the same route. Green found that he could buy oats and hay directly from the farmers on the Skagit River; haul it to loggers and sawmillers to trade for cut lumber. The lumber was then taken back to the farmers and sold at a profit.

In his trading company venture, Green ran into competition with George T. Willey, hay and grain merchant. The ANNIE M. PENCE was purchased to assist the FANNY LAKE. This flourish of business induced Willey to join Green and his associates in a corporation. It seemed wiser than expending energy in a ruthless battle.

The new enterprise was known as the LaConner Trading & Transportation Company. Willey remained on shore while Green worked on the boats with the other stockholders. By this time, Green, too, held a master's and pilot's license.

Several tragedies struck the little company in the early 1890s. Green claimed, though, that hard work and ingenuity saved the company.

[1] Lucile McDonald interview with Joshua Green, January 17, 1965.
[2] Ibid.

HENRY BAILEY'S CREW: (l to r) CAPTAIN SAM DENNY, MATE PETER FALK, FRANK ZICKMUND AND JOSHUA GREEN

LACONNER, 1895

COMPETITOR AND PARTNER, GEORGE T. WILLEY

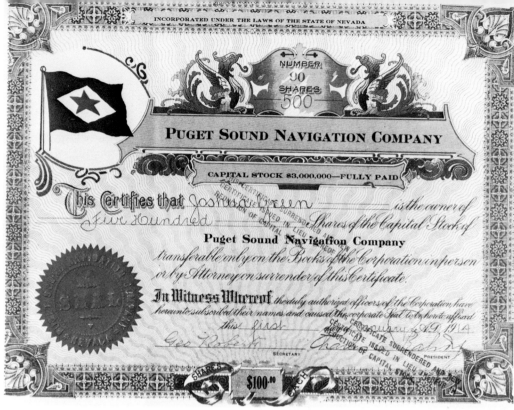

C.E. PEABODY (c.front) WITH CREW ABOARD THE
ROSALIE

FAIRHAVEN WAS ADDED TO LACONNER TRADING &
TRANSPORTATION COMPANY

FAIRHAVEN WAS BUILT IN 1889

T.W. LAKE BORE HER BUILDER'S NAME

In 1893 the wooden steamer FANNY LAKE met her fate in a boiler fire. Captain Alexander Wood, George Benson, mate, and the engineer Alex Riddel, had loaded 25 tons of hay at Dr. Calhoun's farm near LaConner, then they tied up at the pier to await the tide. The crew barely had time to escape with their lives and the vessel was a total loss. The FANNY LAKE, built in 1875, was valued at $5000 and was insured for $4000.[3]

There was more trouble the following year. The financial panic of 1894 did not aid the company in its struggles to grow. The second of several mishaps hit them when the other now uninsurable hay carrier ANNIE M. PENCE was destroyed by fire.

The partners learned that they had undertaken a volatile business that literally could send their profits up in smoke. The company's financial resources were strapped. The loss was a sobering jolt to this honest crew of hardworking fellows. The outlook was glum.

THE T.W. LAKE

In desperate need of another boat, the partners decided that they would rebuild the ANNIE M. PENCE. Green discovered that by naming the rebuilt vessel for the shipbuilder, the cost of reconstruction would be reduced by as much as two thousand dollars. The work performed was excellent. The vessel emerged from the yard as the T.W. LAKE, advertising the builder's name for years to come.

Launched at Ballard in the fall of 1895, the T.W. LAKE was the last vessel built by the pioneer shipbuilder whose name she bore. T.J. King, one of the eventual founders of the well-known King and Winge Shipbuilding Company, was the superintendent of the

Lake yard, in charge of the ship's construction. R.F. Westover, ship carpenter, built her superstructure.

The T.W. LAKE was 95 feet in length with a beam of 20 feet and depth of hold of 6 feet, 6 inches. All the timber used in the vessel had been hand-selected. LaConner Trading Company sought a vessel they could use for years to come and the builder was creating a monument to his skill. Consequently, there were few carriers on the Sound that were built as conscientiously.

The T.W. LAKE was built for the specific needs of the local freight business. She was one of the first boats on Puget Sound to be equipped with a winch for hauling freight up the slip at low tide. She had twin screws and steam engines of 40 horsepower each.[4]

In early days the T.W. LAKE carried large quantities of iron ore from Bellingham to Tacoma. She spent a number of seasons bringing grain from the LaConner district under the command of the company captains Sam Denny, Peter Falk, and Joshua Green. Frank Zickmund was her first engineer.

T.W. LAKE's first owners sold the vessel in the spring of 1905 but she continued to operate the local freight trade. A Barlow marine elevator became standard equipment for her in 1916 and two years later, she was rebuilt. The hull was reconstructed from the boiler room forward and the rest of her wood hull was replaced wherever the need was apparent. Her open bow was closed in, increasing her freight capacity. Her steam engines and boilers were replaced with two 45-horsepower Fairbanks-Morse C.O. engines. At one time the T.W. LAKE was commanded by Captain Harry Barlow, designer of her elevator.[5]

Only two minor collisions in which the T.W. LAKE sustained no appreciable damage, marred the freight boat's career until fatal disaster in 1923. At 7:15 on the evening of December 5 while bound for Roche Harbor with 500 barrels of lime, this little freighter of Green's original fleet was wrecked. Conjectures abound about how and where the disaster occurred but none of the

[3]Ibid.

[4]Her fore-and-aft compound engines with cylinders 7 and 12 by 10 inches were built by A.L. Kelsall of the Northwestern Ironworks.

[5]NRUnder the ownership of Merchants Transportation Company, the T.W. LAKE was commanded by Captain Harry Barlow, Captain C.C. Blythe, Captain Jack Smith, Captain A.B. Burnham, Captain George Browner, Captain Charles Schuman, Captain Frank Winchester, Captain Al McDougall and Captain E.S. Mason. Engineers included Felix Kayo, Henry Grounds, Harry Whitworth, Miles Coffman, E.E. Emmons, Walter Brit, Al Solibakke and Joseph Larsen.

crew of 15 men lived to tell the tale. A terrible storm blew up that night but the details will never be known.

Search teams spent days near the scene of the wreck looking for bodies and pieces of wreckage that might give a clue to the dreadful event. The only conclusion they reached was that the T.W. LAKE was swept off her course while crossing the western end of Guemes channel. Struggling against the fury of wild wind and a strong ebb tide, she was dashed to pieces on Belle Rock.[6]

AN OPPORTUNE MERGER

LaConner Trading & Transportation Company's business prospered and more vessels were acquired by them. They were able to increase the size of their fleet and the number of routes served while minimizing competition on the runs through consolidations. The company bought the E.D. SMITH and equipped her with a scow-type bow. They purchased the UTOPIA and the GEORGE E. STARR for the Seattle-Anacortes run. In his later years, Joshua Green remembered the STARR:[7]

> "This was a faithful little boat. If you put a load on her the side paddlewheels went so far down into the water she would hardly go ahead! She ran from Bellingham to Seattle. We had a full load of canned salmon on her and she was so slow that it cost us more to feed the passengers than the passage money amounted to. We had a peck of troubles in those days, too. It wasn't all easy sailing."

The company continued to expand its fleet. They bought the STATE OF WASHINGTON, FAIRHAVEN and the sternwheeler LACONNER. They built the CITY OF DENVER for some people from Colorado who wanted to take her to the Klondike but forgot to pay the bill. She remained in the LaConner fleet. All told, the company that had started out with one old boat and a scow was operating about 12 boats by 1900, carrying passengers as well as freight. Joshua Green was beginning to do well.

At this time the company was also operating the INLAND FLYER[8] to Bremerton in competition with steamboatman H.B. Kennedy. The latter had a bigger and better steamer, the ATHLON, built in Portland. He purchased her for the Port Orchard route in April 1901. On July 27, 1901, H.B. Kennedy and LaConner Trading Transportation Company combined to end competition on the run, but the INLAND FLYER and the ATHLON continued to be separately owned.

They called the run the Port Orchard Route. Meanwhile, Joshua Green had purchased Sam Denny's interest in LaConner Trade but the other partners remained stockholders for a time. Zickmund and George Willey later became involved in outside interests and they, too, decided to sell. Green had earlier acquired some of Willey's stock but *The Seattle Post Intelligencer,* May 2, 1903, carried a story stating that Alaska Steamship Company, owners of Puget Sound Navigation Company, had purchased the controlling stock of LaConner Trading & Transportation Company. The recorded value of Willey's stock was $100,000.[9] After the sale, Green was left with about

INLAND FLYER (l) AND SEATTLE SPIRIT (r)

[6]Captain E.S. Mason was in command and Joseph Larsen was chief engineer at the time of the disaster. Captain Mason's body was not recovered.

[7]*The Sea Chest,* Volume 8, page 87.

[8]Ibid. The INLAND FLYER was the first vessel to use oil fuel on the Sound. "Standard Oil Company just remunerated us in the handsomest way you ever saw!" [Joshua Green].

[9]*Seattle Post-Intelligencer,* May 2, 1903. Willey was a hay and grain merchant with a business on the Seattle waterfront. Green singled him out as a man who knew his business and would be a hard worker and good investor.

ATHLON, BUILT IN PORTLAND

CITY OF DENVER, BUILT FOR THE KLONDIKE BUT NEVER MADE IT

PARTNERS OF JOSHUA GREEN IN LaCONNER TRADING TRANSPORTATION COMPANY:

FRANK ZICKMUND

CAPTAIN SAMUEL DENNY

40 percent interest, Peter Falk had two or three percent[1] and Charles E. Peabody controlled the majority.

The company formed as a result of this merger was the reorganized Puget Sound Navigation Company. La-Conner Trading & Transportation Company was not to lose its prosperous identity, though, or its ingenuous leader. Peabody served as president of the enlarged corporation throughout the transitional period[2] and then assumed chairmanship of the board. As president, he was succeeded by Joshua Green. Captain Peter Falk became vice president and Walter Oakes was secretary-treasurer.

The combined fleet of the navigation company totaled sixteen vessels plus one operated, the ATHLON. Vessels owned by the Puget Sound Navigation Company would now fly a houseflag designed with the advice of Mrs. Green. It consisted of a red star on a white diamond on a blue field. Only Alaska Steamship Company continued to fly the Peabody Black Ball flag.[3]

So began the company that would one day build a fleet of ferryboats that would surpass all American ferry fleets in size, quantity and routes served.

MR. AND MRS. PETER FALK

[1]Captain Peter Falk remained a major stockholder in Puget Sound Navigation Company until his death May 17, 1924. Falk was born in Borgholm Bada, Sweden, but came to the United States early in his life. He entered Puget Sound steamboating as a young man and became chief officer of the steamboat CITY OF QUINCY in 1888. He left that vessel to become mate on the HENRY BAILEY where he met his future partners in the LaConner Trading & Transportation Company. Falk retired 15 years before his death.

He had commanded a number of famous Puget Sound ships including the GEORGE E. STARR, UTOPIA and the INLAND FLYER, the latter being his last ship. *The Marine Digest*, p.8., May 24, 1924 editorial remarks that reading a sketch of Falk's career, ''one closes with the thought: Here was a man and a career that were really worthwhile.''

[2]It was temporarily known as the Inland Navigation Co., organized by Alaska Steam stockholders to acquire corporate properties.

[3]Green later recalled the story of the flag's selection in *The Sea Chest*, Volume 8, page 83: ''I remember very well when my wife and I were in New York City years ago and went into one of their leading ship chandlery establishments and gathered a lot of talent around us and agreed unanimously on the design and creation of the house flag.'' Puget Sound Maritime Historical Society has adopted this flag as its official banner.

[4]Meeker, the author and pioneer, and Green were historically linked. As purser of the FANNY LAKE, Green made frequent trips to Meeker's hop ranch for cargoes and deliveries in the late 1800's.

"Ezra Meeker, just before he died
  Said there's another steamboat that
  I'd like to ride;
Joshua Green said what will it be ...?
The GEORGE E. STARR or the ROSALIE."[4]

    William J. Fitzgerald, age 8
    Former Seattle Fire Chief

SIDE PADDLE GEORGE E. STARR, BUILT IN SEATTLE, 1879

ROSALIE

THREE SISTERS

The development of a ferryboat fleet on Puget Sound would be incomplete without the story of three steamships that came to the Northwest at the hands of Puget Sound Navigation Company. Their introduction served as an illustration of this company's sensitivity to public demands and intuition for business success.

Each of these vessels was eventually converted into a ferryboat but their popularity must be attributed to their early days as luxurious "liners" on the Sound. At the time of their introduction they were a welcome reminder to Sound residents of the sophisticated culture of the Eastern seaboard many had left behind. They would bridge the eras by recalling for passengers the pleasures of steamboating and the practicality of ferryboats.

Charles Peabody and Joshua Green made a powerful team when it came to business acumen and ingenuity. Backed by a staunch group of financial and highly-motivated supporters, the leaders of this company were to build a foundation that would withstand the rigors of time in the face of catastrophes and severe depression. They seemed always to adapt to public needs ahead of their contemporaries, giving their company the edge needed to survive adversity.

Two subsidiaries of Alaska Steam, the Straits Steamship Company of Oregon formed in 1905 and the International Steamship Company in 1906 were each organized with a capital stock of $250,000.[1] No record survives to demonstrate the service they performed. Papers show that George Lent sold the INDIANAPOLIS to International Steamship Company for $1 in February 1906.[2] It is assumed that they were used to charter vessels and acquire certificates for the routes between Seattle and Victoria and intermediate points. In July 1903, Puget Sound Navigation Company had begun operating on this route with the CLALLAM.

The CLALLAM met with a disaster that set the new company on its heels and forced it to begin looking for a more reliable steamship to operate. The company formed another subsidiary in 1906, known as the Puget

MAKE NO MISTAKE ABOUT THE IDENTITY OF THE HONORED GUEST ABOARD THE INDIANAPOLIS

Sound Day Line, to bring steamships from the Great Lakes to Puget Sound. These three vessels that traveled around the Horn, the INDIANAPOLIS, CHIPPEWA and IROQUOIS,[3] would leave an indelible mark on the lives and hearts of many who were associated with them.

Puget Sound Day Line was incorporated under the laws of the State of Maine to accommodate banking and insurance procedures for the operation of one of the vessels from Chicago, Illinois, and to purchase two ships from Detroit, Michigan. The corporate investors in the Day Line looked like a roll call of Alaska Steamship Company stockholders: Charles Peabody, George Lent, George Roberts, and Frank Burns. Edward Beach of New York (brother-in-law of Charles Peabody) was the only newcomer.

Puget Sound Day Line was incorporated October 29, 1906,[4] but it was not until 1909, after the three vessels were safely delivered to the Northwest, that Joshua Green[5] became a stockholder and was elected

[1]*Report of the Investigation of the Earnings, Property, Operations, Rates, Services and Facilities of the Puget Sound Navigation Company, May, 1947,* Department of Transportation, State of Washington, page 11. This document states that the Straits Steamship Company was organized in 1903 but record books indicate 1905.

[2]Leithead, Robert C. Shown in records in his possession.

[3]Much of the history of these three vessels was drawn from unpublished accounts found in William O. Thorniley's files. An article dealing with the IROQUOIS is dated January 1, 1970, with signatures of Captain Louis Van Bogaert and Captain Frank E. Hamilton at the bottom of the last page of the typewritten account. However, copies of this history were not found in the Louis Van Bogaert Collection, Puget Sound Maritime Historical Society.

[4]The Puget Sound Day Line was incorporated after the INDIANAPOLIS was brought to the Northwest. The corporation was involved with its ownership and especially its operation. The corporation may have been formed as a result of P.S.N.'s experiences in purchasing the INDIANAPOLIS from Eastern owners.
The Puget Sound Day Line's incorporation papers were found in the A.M. Peabody Collection, Museum of History & Industry, Seattle.

[5]In the biography of Joshua Green, *The Green Years,* Green claims that he was responsible for hearing first of the possible sale of these steamships. Records show that Joshua Green was not a Puget Sound Day Line stockholder nor did he negotiate for the purchase of these vessels. George Lent acted on the company's behalf in all three cases.

president of the company. Charles Peabody was vice president, C.H.J. Stoltenberg was secretary-treasurer. George Lent and Frank Burns were on the board of directors. It is possible that the company remained separate from the Puget Sound Navigation Company for some time, chartering the steamships to the parent company for operation. In order to reduce liabilities of ownership, this procedure was commonly practiced.[6]

LAUNCHING OF THE INDIANAPOLIS

At a time when women in America were speaking out for the right to vote, the steamer INDIANAPOLIS did her part in introducing new roles for her "sisters." The launching of this good ship, May 5, 1904, was not only an important social affair, but a "first." W.K. Greenbaum, general manager of the Indiana Transportation Company, owners of the newly built vessel, is credited with the idea of a "Ladie's Launching." Not only would a woman traditionally christen the vessel with champagne, but women would pull the trigger that would release the ship on the launching ways! It was simply unthinkable.

A statewide contest was held to select the sponsor and several maids of honor. Miss Eula Clay performed her duties with vigor and delight as sponsor, swinging the bottle at the steamer's bow just after the maidens had pulled the trigger. Dignitaries such as Governor W.K. Durban and his staff, prominent businessmen, and residents of the large nearby cities in Indiana, turned out in force to witness this colossal event.

The INDIANAPOLIS proved worthy of the occasion and was known as a very fine ship. [Who would admit otherwise?] This popular run was between Michigan City and Chicago, making two round trips a day. Built as a day boat, the INDIANAPOLIS had three decks. The social hall was on the main deck aft with the purser's and steward's offices and baggage check room. The cabin on the promenade deck was finished in mahogany, decorated in white and gold gild, carpeted

red throughout. The cabin aft had eight staterooms and the lunchroom was located in the forward hold or orlop deck.[7] The captain's and officers' quarters were on the hurricane deck aft of the pilot house. Interior fittings were estimated to have cost over $10,000.[8]

The INDIANAPOLIS stayed on her route only two seasons, proving inadequate for capacity crowds. She was sold to George Lent for operation by Puget Sound Navigation Company, October 15, 1905.

The INDIANAPOLIS was drydocked five days after this sale in Toledo, Ohio, at Craig's Shipyard, the original builder. She was outfitted for her long voyage around South America via the Straits of Magellan. Salt water condensors, evaporators, and fittings were installed; she was strengthened on the main deck; side ports and gangways were sealed.

Embarking on one of the lengthiest voyages undertaken in years, the INDIANAPOLIS left Toledo October 31, 1905, in the care of Captain John J. Johnson, master, and Chief Engineer C.F. Bishop.[9] She took on supplies, coal and fresh water in New York where spars and sails were stepped to conserve fuel. Leaving New York December 12, she arrived in Port Townsend, February 10, 1906. She had traveled a total of 18,000 miles in one of the best records for time of any vessel of her class. Her engines were never stopped with mechanical difficulties. The longest part of her journey—Coronel, Chile to San Francisco—was taken under sail without stops. She arrived in the Northwest just fifty-one days after her departure.

The steamer was overhauled in Seattle and refitted in drydock. New boilers were fitted; coal-fired furnaces were exchanged for oil-fired furnaces. The dining room was relocated on her main deck.

The INDIANAPOLIS entered her new run April 1, 1906 on the Seattle-Port Townsend-Victoria run, making the trip in five hours. The Canadian Pacific steamship PRINCESS BEATRICE was quickly withdrawn since she was no match for the Great Lakes speeder.

[6]Most corporations were not the sole owners of their vessels because of tax liabilities and legal opinions. The practice of individual ownership or small subsidiaries within major shipping companies was common to the sailing ship era and continues in modern use.

[7]Deck below the lower deck.

[8]From William O. Thorniley's unpublished article.

[9]Captain John Johnson was a veteran master from Alaska Steam and Chief Engineer Charles F. Bishop, former Port Engineer for La-Conner Trading & Transportation Company was considered one of the finest steamboat engineers on the West Coast.

CHIEF ENGINEER CHARLES F. BISHOP

CAPTAIN HOWARD PENFIELD

But the popular "INDIAN's" stardom was ruthlessly challenged that summer. The PRINCESS VICTORIA came charging in to skim the profits of the tourist trade, then neatly withdrew at the close of the season. The INDIANAPOLIS was left to wrestle with the less profitable off-season business. Competing with the Canadian Pacific was not to be a piece of cake.

FLYING FISTICUFFS ON THE FLYER

Captain John Johnson continued as master of the Lakes steamer for the 1906 season and then returned to Alaska Steam. He was relieved by veteran skipper Howard Penfield,[1] a former mate of the BAILEY GATZERT, in March 1907.

When the CHIPPEWA and the IROQUOIS arrived on the Sound in 1907, Captain Penfield was eager to challenge the fabulous FLYER for dominion of the Seattle-Tacoma trade. The FLYER's owner, Captain U.B. Scott had suspected a fight was brewing and had already converted the FLYER's boilers to fuel oil. This added a bit to the legendary speed of the steamboat.

Scott was a fighter of endurance and had already met loggerheads with the Northern Pacific Railroad

who inaugurated fast local train service between the two cities about the same time the FLYER seriously entered the run. But the railway's "Business Man's Express" was only mildly successful while the water route was still the favorite mode of transportation for travelers.

Much of the FLYER's success was attributed to her beautifully tuned triple expansion engine of 2000 horsepower capacity. So smooth was its operation that it seldom ran at full power nor could riders detect vibrations. The engine was an exact duplicate of the one designed by Neifie and Levy of Philadelphia for J.P. Morgan's yacht CORSAIR. So well built was this engine that it was estimated to have revolved more than two billion times during the FLYER's 30 year career. It was still found in perfect order when the vessel was scrapped.[2]

[1] Captain Howard Penfield was a cousin of Charles Peabody whose son, Norman Penfield Peabody, was named for him. A conflicting source states that Penfield took command of the CHIPPEWA when she arrived and did not transfer to the INDIANAPOLIS until January 13, 1908. At that time he was relieved by Captain John J. Livingston who served until May 14, 1908, when Captain A.N. McAlpine took command of the CHIPPEWA.

Prior to the INDIANAPOLIS's arrival on the Seattle-Tacoma route, the FLYER reached a settlement with the Northern Pacific Railroad to honor railroad tickets aboard the FLYER. Burning 24 cords of wood a day the FLYER kept a strict schedule of one hour and forty minutes running time between the two cities. The FLYER's crew enjoyed heckling the INDIANAPOLIS by honoring the tickets of the INDIAN just as the steamer was loading passengers.

Captain Penfield was a master who earned his papers on the quarterdeck of a sailing ship and prided himself on a well-kept, spit and polish ship. The INDIAN's brasswork sparkled, while the crew members were expected to adhere to a rigid code of discipline. The watches were changed *exactly* on time and crew members left by the lee door from the wheelhouse.

Racing of Puget Sound Navigation boats was strictly forbidden by the management and insurance underwriters. Captain Everett B. Coffin of the FLYER tended to take advantage of the situation and razz Captain Penfield incessantly. Fearing that the trusted Captain Penfield might succumb to the mortal throes of apoplexy, the company officials (who no doubt received significant chiding themselves) agreed at last to a "trial of speed" between the two ships. The epic race that ensued from Seattle to Tacoma resulted in a draw, sparking a lively debate to the point of fisticuffs. The issue of designating a champion for this race was never resolved.

The INDIANAPOLIS was generally a slower vessel than the FLYER, although her plush interiors and elegant style continued to generate rivalry for the FLYER at least another five years.

Competition ended in June of 1911 when the Columbia River & Puget Sound Navigation Company sold the FLYER to the Seattle-Tacoma & Everett Route, Inc. In 1913 that company sold her to the Inland Navigation Company (Puget Sound Navigation Company).

The INDIANAPOLIS went to court, so to speak, when she collided in a dense fog, December 14, 1910, with the wooden steamer KITSAP. The accident occurred only 400 yards from the Seattle shoreline. There the KITSAP sank. The vessel was later raised, despite the extreme depth of water, repaired and reinstated into service for her owners, Kitsap County Transportation Company. The already touchy relationship between the KITSAP's owners and the navigation company was not improved by the mishap or the

SEATTLE-TACOMA ROUTE
The Scenic Route
STEAMSHIPS
"TACOMA" and "INDIANAPOLIS"

LEAVE SEATTLE FOR TACOMA	LEAVE TACOMA FOR SEATTLE
7:00 A. M.	7:15 A. M.
9:00 A. M.	9:00 A. M.
11:00 A. M.	11:00 A. M.
1:00 P. M.	1:00 P. M.
3:00 P. M.	3:00 P. M.
5:00 P. M.	5:00 P. M.
7:00 P. M.	7:00 P. M.
9:00 P. M.	9:00 P. M.

LEAVES SEATTLE FROM COLMAN DOCK, FOOT OF MARION STREET. (TAKE OVERHEAD WALK AT CORNER OF FIRST AVENUE AND MARION STREET.)

LEAVES TACOMA FROM MUNICIPAL DOCK (11TH STREET BRIDGE.)

60c — SINGLE TRIP — 60c
$1.00 — ROUND TRIP — $1.00

Puget Sound Navigation Co.
Colman Dock (Foot of Marion St.)
MAin 2222   Seattle, Wash.

[2]Thompson, W. and A. Beach, *Steamer to Tacoma*, Bainbridge, Wa., 1963. The FLYER was rebuilt in 1918 by Puget Sound Navigation Company as the WASHINGTON, serving another decade as spare boat and excursion vessel.

ensuing court dispute.

The INDIAN is believed to have introduced yet another first for women. When a wireless was installed aboard the vessel, Mrs. R.H. Tucker was employed as a wireless operator. She is believed to have been the first female wireless operator in the world.[3]

In early 1933, after nearly 27 years of steamer service on Puget Sound, the INDIANAPOLIS was dry-docked at Lake Washington Shipyards where she was converted to an autoferry. Her main deck forward was cut away; her bow was rounded off for loading and unloading in ferry slips. A turntable was installed aft to turn the cars around so that they could exit over the entry portal. A lunch counter and galley for passengers and crew was relocated aft on the passenger deck. The officers' quarters, smoking lounge and dining salon were cleared away. The INDIANAPOLIS emerged with a car-carrying capacity of 33 and space for 750 passengers. The luxury liner was no more.

CAPTAIN EVERETT B. COFFIN OF THE FLYER

For the seasons of 1934 through 1937, the INDIAN was placed on the Edmonds-Port Townsend run. She was sold to Seattle Iron and Metals Corporation on the Duwamish River in December 1938. Her final document was surrendered August 23, 1939 at Seattle and endorsed, "dismantled, and abandoned as unfit for future use." The INDIANAPOLIS had been scrapped.

CHAMPAGNE AGAIN

Mrs. George T. Arnold broke a bottle of bubbly over the bow, christening the new vessel CHIPPEWA. It was a side launching, Saturday, June 23, 1900, at Craig's Shipyard[4] in Toledo.

CHIPPEWA was built as a day boat with three decks. The social hall was aft on the main deck with the dining salon aft of it; the galley was below decks. The social and dining salons were furnished in mahogany and trimmed in white; the main cabin was finished in the same manner but carpeted throughout.

The vessel went into operation on the Great Lakes for the Arnold Transportation Company on Mackinac Island. She created quite a sensation upon her arrival at Mackinac July 9, 1900. The steamer ALGOMAH blew a cordial welcome on her whistle but many mistook it for a fire alarm. Pandemonium broke loose and a real crowd was on the pier to meet the CHIPPEWA that day.

CHIPPEWA was joined by the steamer IROQUOIS, August 30, 1901, and both vessels operated on the same route for the Arnold Transit Company until their ultimate sale to Puget Sound Navigation Company October 3, 1906. The CHIPPEWA carried a price tag of $125,000.

After outfitting the CHIPPEWA for the same voyage already successfully completed by the INDIANAPOLIS, Captain Charles C. McClure and Chief Engineer C.F. Bishop were underway for Puget Sound. Not many lake boats making the trip around South

[3]The INDIANAPOLIS, CHIPPEWA and IROQUOIS are reputed to have been the first ships on the Pacific Coast to be equipped for wireless communication. Jay Wells, *The Seattle Times*, July 19, 1970, page A21.

[4]George L. Craig, owner of Craig's Shipyard, was born May 11, 1864 in New York City. He learned shipbuilding from his father, John Craig, and studied drafting under Frank E. Kirby. He was general manager of the Craig Shipbuilding Company from 1895 to 1907. He died at LaJolla, California on March 7, 1941.

George T. Arnold, born in Michigan in 1845, was a successful vessel operator around Mackinac Island from 1878 to 1921. He died at the island September 16, 1922.

Arnold and Craig were closely associated from 1900 to 1910 in building the CHIPPEWA, IROQUOIS, CHIPPEWA II, and the MACKINAC.

America to the West Coast had as many problems as the CHIPPEWA.

Leaving Hoboken, New Jersey, February 18, 1907, it was not until March 24 that she limped into the Straits of Magellan with three boilers, bad weather, head winds, engine trouble and relieved of one anchor. CHIPPEWA was averaging 23 tons of coal per day. Eighty-three days and fourteen hours after the date of departure, or 1920.5 tons of coal later, the CHIPPEWA tied up at the Port Townsend dock. Company officials were taken aback. The INDIANAPOLIS had made the same journey in a remarkable 51 days. The engineer, C.F. Bishop, who made both trips, was just as badly shaken.

CHIPPEWA was placed on a number of the Puget Sound routes, including the Seattle-Port Townsend-Victoria run. She was busy the spring of 1908 when Teddy Roosevelt's "Great White Fleet" anchored in Elliott Bay from March 23 through 26. Hundreds of

vessels were enlisted to serve as excursion boats while Americans and Canadians shared their enthusiasm for this spectacular show.

The CHIPPEWA underwent a major rebuild in 1915 when wooden deckhouses were replaced with shiny new steel ones. Forty-eight staterooms provided berths for 160 passengers. Puget Sound Navigation thought they were preparing their vessel for an excursion route to British Columbia, but World War I intervened.

The U.S. Shipping Board requisitioned the vessel from lay-up status for use as a recruit training ship in Seattle. Alterations soon transformed the passenger steamer into a training ship. After several training cruises around the Sound and one to Astoria, Oregon, the war was won. Captain J. Howard Payne, a future competitor of the Black Ball flag, commanded the training ship. The CHIPPEWA was returned to the navigation company and the steamship remained idle until 1926.

By the mid-twenties, Puget Sound was in need of as many autocarriers as could be built or converted. CHIPPEWA was selected by the navigation company for this purpose and rebuilt to carry 90 cars, 2000 passengers, manned by a crew of 30. She operated steadily until 1932 when she was again rebuilt. Her steam boilers and immense engines were just too slow. This time her cabins were finished in mahogany with new interior fittings and furnishings. A 2130 horsepower, eight cylinder Busch Sulzer diesel engine replaced her steam, increasing her speed to 15.5 knots.

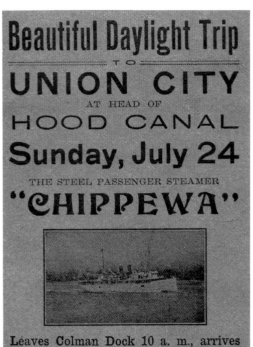

Beautiful Daylight Trip
TO
UNION CITY
AT HEAD OF
HOOD CANAL
Sunday, July 24
THE STEEL PASSENGER STEAMER
"CHIPPEWA"

Leaves Colman Dock 10 a. m., arrives Union City 3 p. m.; leave Union City 5 p. m., arrive back 9:30 p. m.

This Excursion is being given by "The Greeters" an organization of Seattle Hotel Clerks

A TRIP TO HOOD CANAL

The steamer ride along Hood Canal is, we might say, an abbreviated trip to Alaska. The Olympic Mountains, lying to the westward along the Canal, are almost equal to the mountains along both sides of the "inside passage" to Skagway. There is very little margin of low or level land between the waters of Hood Canal and the Mountains, which rise almost from the water's edge. In some places the rocky walls rise perpendicularly from the water, which is so deep, and in which the rock wall goes down so straight, that deep draught vessels can tie up alongside. The coloring of the mountain sides is splendid. First, there is a ribbon of white or bright yellow sand, then the bright green of the willows or small brush, and then the different shades of fir and cedar intermixed with patches of bare, rocky cliffs and burned and dead timber, and at the top, the everlasting snow. In the afternoon, along towards sunset, the light and shadow effects are indescribably beautiful. The trip is almost a steamboat ride amongst mountains. It certainly is one along the side of mountains.

If you want a one day's outing in the way of a steamboat ride combined with a mountain trip, just try the cruise up Hood Canal. You cannot be disappointed, and you surely never will regret it.

Take a little lunch with you or get something to eat aboard the steamer.

ROUND—$1.00—TRIP

Tickets on sale at all Hotels and at 612 First Avenue and Colman Dock

PUGET SOUND NAVIGATION COMPANY
COLMAN DOCK
SEATTLE, WASHINGTON

BLACK BALL LINE

April 4, 1932

Mr. Wm. O. Thorniley,
Santa Lucia Inn,
Salinas, California.

Dear Bill: -

We were so glad to get your letter and you can't imagine how Mr. Klaboe laughed when I showed it to him.

We have in our possession a very excellent story penned by Harriet Geithmann on her typewriter. It is certainly a very hot effort and should make Mr. Kiloline happy when he sees it, and we want him to be happy. Also, we will send him a dozen or so photographs, which he can go through and pick to suit his caprice. Copy for a new ad will probably leave this office on Thursday or Friday; the story and photos I will airmail to him tomorrow.

On Friday I left the Colman Dock office, of this Company, and collected up town a very distinguished and jovial company, Capt. Ames, Capt. Fisher, Mr. Short and Mr. Ote—. We then drove out to the Chippewa arriving about 11:00 o—. At 1:00 o'clock she put forth. As soon as we were out i— channel the diesel engines in the Chippewa were hooked o— and away she went. We had a very pleasant trip around t— lake and the engine behaved beautifully. She was turned a 175 r.p.m. and developed a speed of about 14.15 nautic— miles. With the additional revolutions to bring her up 210 she should show the required speed.

The representatives of the Busch-Sulzer Company were her— and everybody seems very well pleased with the ship. Sh— is the most beautiful thing on Puget Sound, and, to the be— of my knowledge, there is nothing on either coast to com— with her. The ferries that I have seen in New York, New Orleans, etc., can't hold a candle to her.

It is twenty minutes after five now and if this letter i— any longer Mrs. Tallman will not be able to finish it by 5:30. She sends you her very best and says she can hard— wait until you get back, don't you Mrs. Tallman.

After 1947 the Black Ball Line used the CHIPPEWA mostly as a relief and standby ferry. She operated on the Anacortes-San Juan Islands-Sidney route and the Seattle-Manchester route. In 1949 she operated on the Seattle-Winslow route, except summers, when she ran between Anacortes and Sidney, B.C.

The CHIPPEWA faithfully served the Peabodys until the majority of the fleet was transferred to Washington State in 1951. She operated on the Anacortes-San Juan Island-Sidney run until finally sold out of service June 25, 1965, to Foss Launch and Tug Company, Seattle. They, in turn, sold her November 2, 1966, to the Isthmian Line, Inc., Seattle, who sold her to the Columbia Steamship Company, Seattle, July 24, 1967.

On December 5, 1967, the CHIPPEWA was traded to the United States Maritime Administration in exchange for the PIERRE VICTORY. At the time, the old ferryboat was lying idle on Lake Union. On January 13, 1968, the Maritime Administration sold the CHIPPEWA to Donald V. Clair of Oakland, California. She was drydocked at Todd Shipyard prior to departure, boarded up and housed-in for protection against the weather for the tow down the merciless coastline to Oakland.

The tug ONEYANA was on her way home to Honolulu at the time. Clair contacted a broker, Robert E. Landweer, to have the tug tow the CHIPPEWA. Leaving Seattle on May 21, 1968, in charge of Captain Don Hallanger, they encountered heavy weather in a 70 mile gale of Cape Blanco. ONEYANA took the ferry into Drakes Bay where they discovered the damage was fairly light. She had lost a mast and there was some water in the shaft alley of the hull. They arrived in San Francisco Bay six days after departure.

Following the vessel's arrival at Clay Street Pier, the CHIPPEWA was to be converted into a maritime museum. Before such efforts were underway, fire caught the caretakers by surprise, June 23, 1968, causing damages of $30,000 and provoking the end to Clair's dreams for a museum.

CHIPPEWA was sold to Donald Craven on August 30, 1968, and was towed to Stockton. There she was moored at Paradise Point fishing resort located on Disappointment Slough near King Island. The owners planned to use the hull for a replica of the old CHRYSOPOLIS, a famous luxury ferryboat of the Bay Area. In October, 1970, the vessel was cut down and stripped to the hull, still in Disappointment Slough. As of 1983, the CHIPPEWA's sad hull remains barely afloat at Collinsville, California.

U.S.S. CONSTITUTION IN ELLIOTT BAY

PEABODY FAMILY

BLACK BALL FERRY
M. S. Chippewa
Seattle - Bremerton ● Navy Yard Route

THE REMARKABLE TRIO

The third vessel of this Great Lakes threesome was the cumbersome IROQUOIS. This steamer generates the fondest recollections of all. She was known to many thousands on Puget Sound throughout her existence there until 1970. The IROQUOIS is in Alaska now. Like the CHIPPEWA she was built at Craig's Shipyard for T.T. Arnold Transit Company. She was launched July 16, 1901, and commenced daily service, running with the CHIPPEWA between Petoskey, Harbor Springs, Mackinac Island and the Soo.

During hay fever season thousands of people sought relief by crowding the hotels in that part of the country. Several Pullman passenger trains would pull into Petoskey and Harbor Springs daily. However, after the hay fever had bloomed itself out, these two vessels were not financially successful. Their route was much too long for a day boat, covering nearly 145 miles each way. By October the IROQUOIS and CHIPPEWA tied up.

The following three seasons the IROQUOIS was chartered by George Singler's White Star Line for a run known as the Isle Royale Route. Finding this charter unprofitable because of a short tourist season, the IROQUOIS was chartered in 1905 to the Chicago and South Haven Line.

On June 12, 1906, the IROQUOIS was chartered to the Niagara and St. Lawrence Navigation Company for operation of a 75-day season on Lake Ontario and the upper St. Lawrence River. A news item in the *Thousand Island Sun,* Sunday, August 19, 1906, stated that she carried the largest excursion load of 1300 passengers from Ogdensburg to St. Alexandria. But alas, the crowds were not big enough to prevent her lay-up September 15 at Mackinac Island.

By October 3, 1906, negotiations for the sale of the IROQUOIS to Puget Sound Navigation Company were completed. Known as the Puget Sound Day Line, the company paid $127,000 for this staunch 223.6' steamship.

On the way to the shipyard for voyage outfitting, the IROQUOIS towed her running mate CHIPPEWA to New York where they arrived in tandem December 8, 1906. Heavy spars were stepped and the IROQUOIS was rigged with main and foresails as well as studsails on both masts. These would steady her in heavy seas and reduce coal consumption. Some accounts also state that in those early years following the disasters entailing loss of human life on steamers, any vessel traveling west of Port Townsend was required by law to carry sails.[5]

[5]Thorniley materials state that this law was in effect from 1904 to 1918, but no evidence of federal regulation could be traced.

Under the able command of Alaska Steam's Captain John J. Johnson[6] the IROQUOIS left Hoboken at 8:00 A.M., January 23, 1907. She stopped at St. Lucia, British West Indies and Montevideo, Uruguay, for coal, fresh water and supplies before proceeding without delay through a calm Straits of Magellan. She reached Coronel, Chile, for refueling and supplies without harm.

The IROQUOIS made the long stretch to San Diego, California, under sail to help conserve coal reserves. She was fortunate to have fair winds all the way. The weather was smooth and the equipment ran perfectly. She arrived at Seattle for drydocking and general overhaul 66 days out of New York.

THE STATEMENT OF GENERAL AVERAGE AND COLLISION CLAIM CASE OF THE STEAMER IROQUOIS NEW YORK TO SEATTLE

This statement prepared by Johnson & Higgins, Average Adjustors, on September 7, 1907, at Seattle, revealed some fascinating details about the IROQUOIS's first trip west. The statement gives the following introduction:

"1907

"*January 22* This vessel left New York bound for Seattle

"*January 30* While attempting to make a landing at the dock at Port Castries, St. Lucia, she came into collision with and damaged the S.S. TROLD which was lying alongside the dock.

"Claim was made upon the IROQUOIS for the damage which the TROLD sustained. A Board of Arbitration was appointed which assessed the damage at $1,000-. and the claim was settled for this amount.

"She proceeded upon her voyage and nothing worthy of note occurred until she arrived at Coronel, Chile.

"*March 7th,* While lying at anchor in this port, the propeller became fouled in her mooring lines. It was necessary to obtain assistance of a diver and to cut them away. After this had been done, she proceeded and in due course arrived at Seattle."

The sworn affadavit of the master claims it was the "negligence of the engineer" which caused both incidents. The captain paid the surveyors to inspect the damage to the TROLD but these two could not agree on the cost of repairs. Captain Johnson must have then negotiated with the TROLD's master to reach an agreement to pay $1,000. This reasonable settlement was due to the fact that damage was incurred above the waterline; the TROLD would not be delayed for repairs, and the vessel's damaged hull plates could be restored at the owner's convenience. Captain Johnson executed his duties with international diplomacy.

All told, even with collision claim, Puget Sound Navigation Company spent only $2,770.62 for the IROQUOIS's 18,000 mile trip, exclusive of crews' wages which would not have amounted to more than $400. Coal amounted to $1,300, purchased after departure from New York. Other supplies purchased at Port Castries enroute were 100 oranges, one bunch of bananas, 100 pounds white lead, 50 pounds vine lead, two cans varnish, two dozen sandpapers, ten pounds of putty, one pound of lard candles and three panes of glass.[7] They took on three thousand gallons of water and paid for "police supervision."

Waterfront Scene,
Pt. Townsend, Wash.

[6]Master of the INDIANAPOLIS for the same voyage.

[7]*Statement of General Average and Collision Claim Case of the Steamer IROQUOIS New York to Seattle.*

In Seattle oil burners were placed under the IRO-QUOIS's four Roberts water tube boilers.[8] Two lifeboats and more staterooms were added, bringing the total to 53 with a new cabin placed aft on the hurricane deck. She was fitted with wireless and her new capacity with these changes accommodated 800 overnight passengers and 1000 day passengers.

Under the charge of Captain Charles Byrdsen, the Sound's IROQUOIS made a trial run June 15, 1907, and was placed on the Seattle-Bellingham-Vancouver regular run July 1. She was a welcome addition to the Puget Sound fleet.

CAPTAIN CHARLES BYRDSEN

The Seattle Star, dated May 17, 1912, shows that the IROQUOIS tried a new route as well as the traditional ones:

"With Mayor Seymour of Tacoma, Mayor Beckwith of Victoria, representatives from the Commercial Club of Tacoma, the Chamber of Commerce from Seattle and the Victoria Board of Trade, and steamship officials and newspaper men from Seattle, Victoria and Tacoma, the new steel steamer IRO-QUOIS completed her maiden voyage yesterday. She sailed from Tacoma Wednesday night, coming to Seattle and from there to Victoria, where the guests were taken for an automobile tour of the city.

"The IROQUOIS will begin a new fast freight and passenger service between Tacoma, Seattle and Victoria."

IROQUOIS plied the Sound routes until the United States Shipping Board requisitioned her in June 1918 for recruiting. Alterations similar to those undergone by the CHIPPEWA transformed the IROQUOIS into a training ship. Short cruises were made on inland waters until the end of World War I; she returned to her owners in 1919.

BACK TO THE EAST

Green and Peabody made the decision to sell the IROQUOIS to her former charterers, the Chicago and South Haven Steamship Company, just one year after her return to them by the U.S. Government. The new owners, represented by Captain Frank Dority, came to Seattle to prepare the vessel for her return voyage to the Great Lakes. This time the voyage would be shorter, through the Panama Canal.

Captain John Johnson was called out of retirement to act as ocean master. Upon her arrival in Montreal July 30, 1920, Captain Dority assumed command. The IROQUOIS resumed the old "fruit" run between Chicago and South Haven, Michigan, August 19, bringing freshly picked fruits to market.

Once again the IROQUOIS faced financially troubled waters. Several bad fruit seasons on Michigan's west shore and a very light passenger business contributed to her downfall. After seven years her new "old"

[8]Boilers built by Marine Boiler Works, Toledo. Each boiler measured nine and one-half feet by nine feet. The triple expansion steam engine with cylinders measuring 21-34-58 inches with a 30 inch stroke was left intact.

UPPER DECK OF THE IROQUOIS

*S.S. IROQUOIS (fnt row) DON CARROLL, PURSER; CAP-
TAIN HARRY I. ANDERSON, (bck row) GEORGE GREGG,
FREIGHT CLERK; WALTER GREEN, TRAFFIC REPRESEN-
TATIVE; VIC AMBROSE, STEWARD.*

*IROQUOIS PLIED THE SOUND ROUTES FOR MANY
YEARS*

CAPTAIN HARRY ANDERSON

owners were again in dire straits. Detroit Trust Company held a $166,500 mortgage on the IROQUOIS. They foreclosed. The vessel was sold at sheriff's auction June 6, 1927 to another company in the throes of economic worry. By September 1927, she was on the marshall's block. This time, the successful bidder was Puget Sound Navigation Company. After seven years the IROQUOIS was returning home.

Captain Harry Anderson and Chief Engineer W.A. Teederman were sent out by the company to guide the vessel to Seattle. They would follow the same route in reverse as when she had returned to the Great Lakes via the Panama Canal. She arrived at Seattle November 22, just 44 days out of Montreal. She spent the remainder of that season at Lake Washington Shipyard undergoing a rebuild. She became a night steamer for the Seattle-Port Townsend-Port Angeles-Victoria run[0]. She was widened to provide more deck room. Her cabin was panelled and loading doors were installed on the bow and the sides. She retained her original water tube boilers but her main deck now accommodated 40 to 50 automobiles. She was fitted with 45 two-passenger staterooms, six double suites, two bridal suites[1] and accommodations for 400 day passengers and 160 night passengers.

Speakers provided radio music and programs in a number of public rooms and a dance floor graced the front salon. The IROQUOIS sailed nightly from Seattle to Victoria at midnight in an agreement with Canadian Pacific who ran a day boat from Seattle to Victoria.

Captain Carl Stevens[2] was in command. Parties and entertainment took place aboard the IROQUOIS that are still remembered. The nightly run operated until 1947 when the IROQUOIS was replaced with the newly built CHINOOK. The IROQUOIS faithfully served the run for twenty years with only a few skippers, Captain Stevens, Captain Harry Anderson, Captain Louis Van Bogaert and Captain Lyle Fowler. Captain Van Bogaert and Chief Engineer John Gustafson were in charge most of that time.

After 1947 the IROQUOIS was essentially idle, relieving the CHINOOK intermittantly until 1952. Unlike many of the Black Ball ferries, this vessel was not sold to Washington State but to a new company called Black Ball Transport, Inc. She would operate strictly as a freight boat for her new owners, carrying highway trailers in a nightly Seattle-Port Townsend-Port Angeles-Victoria route, known as the "paper run." Crown Zellerbach shipped paper, mainly newsprint, from their Port Angeles mill to Seattle.

Black Ball Transport, owned by Bob and Lois Acheson and stockholders like Walter Green, sent the IROQUOIS to drydock for major renovations before the start of her new freight service. Afterwards, she was barely recognizable as the passenger liner she had once been. Reconstruction work was carried out at Tacoma Boat Building Company under the watchful eye of Captain Henry C. Grandy, owner's representative, and Harold Graham, chief engineer. Her steam engines were replaced with a 1600 horsepower Fairbanks-Morse diesel engine.

[0]IROQUOIS relieved the steamer SOL DUC on this run the summer of 1928. The SOL DUC then replaced the KULSHAN I on the night run Seattle-Anacortes-Bellingham, primarily for freight.

[1]The IROQUOIS was noted as the only passenger ship in America with twin beds in her bridal suites. One old timer said that that decor ruined more honeymoons than any other single thing he could think of in his time!

[2]Captain Stevens entered Puget Sound seafaring in 1908 with Everett Tug & Barge Company. He joined P.S.N. in 1914 and proceeded to command almost every ship in the fleet, including the SOL DUC and the KALAKALA. In 1942 he became a Puget Sound pilot and served as president of the Pilot's Association for six terms. He commanded deep sea ships of the Tacoma Oriental Lines and American Mail Line. He retired in 1960 from the Pilot's Association. He passed away at his home in Seattle in September, 1962.

THE IROQUOIS HAD STYLE

THE STEAMER WAS A POPULAR EXCURSION VESSEL

Black Ball Line

Toast and Coffee	20c
Hot Cakes and Coffee	25c
Side Order Ham or Bacon	25c
Eggs, Toast and Coffee	40c
Ham and Eggs, and Coffee	55c
Bacon and Eggs, and Coffee	55c
Omelet, Plain	40c
Cereals with Cream	15c
Toast, Marmalade and Coffee	25c
Sliced Orange	25c
Grape Fruit (Chilled)	20c
Doughnuts and Coffee	15c
Butterhorn and Coffee	15c
Pie and Coffee	15c
Coffee or Milk	10c
Chocolate	10c
Tea	10c
Soup	10c

STEAKS

T-Bone Steak with Potatoes and Toast	85c
Sirloin Steak with Potatoes and Toast	75c
Club Steak with Potatoes and Toast	60c
Pounded Steak with Potatoes and Toast	50c
Hamburger Steak with Potatoes and Toast	40c

SALADS

Lettuce, with Choice of Dressing	25c
Sliced Tomatoes	20c
Lettuce and Tomato Salad	30c
Combination Salad	35c

GOOD MORNING INVADERS!

OLYMPIC

HERE'S YOUR BREAKFAST

☆ ☆ ☆

TOMATO JUICE	STEWED FIGS
STEWED PRUNES	ORANGE JUICE
STEWED APRICOTS	HALF GRAPEFRUIT
DEL MONTE PEACHES	PRESERVED GRAPEFRUIT

☆ ☆ ☆

GRAPE NUTS	BRAN FLAKES
ROLLED OATS	CORN FLAKES
CREAM OF WHEAT	SHREDDED WHEAT

☆ ☆ ☆

BUCKWHEAT OR WHEAT CAKES

DRY OR BUTTERED TOAST, ORANGE MARMALADE

WHEAT CAKES WITH LITTLE PIG SAUSAGES, HAM OR BACON

LITTLE PIG SAUSAGES	TWO EGGS, ANY STYLE
HAM OR BACON AND EGGS	FRENCH TOAST AND JELLY

☆ ☆ ☆

TEA	COFFEE	SWEET MILK	HOT COCOA

S. S. IROQUOIS - - BLACK BALL LINE

CAPT. LOUIS VAN BOGAERT, MASTER   E. J. O'CONNELL, CHIEF STEWARD

CAPTAIN LOUIS VAN BOGAERT

Lois Acheson, president of Black Ball Transport, Inc., and Harold Graham, former chief engineer of the IROQUOIS who served with Captain Louis Van Bogaert for Puget Sound Navigation Company, reminisced one afternoon[3] about their fondest memories of the old vessel.

"Well, I'll tell you one thing," Lois Acheson remarked, "you never should have ridden from Port Angeles to Victoria aboard the IROQUOIS if you had a tendency to get seasick."

"She could roll like the dickens," agreed Harold Graham.

"She certainly could."

Graham further recalled, "Especially after her bow and bow doors were rebuilt. They were perfectly flat, like the sideport doors, and closed at a "V" angle. Two or three times we were caught in the Straits when we really shouldn't have been out. One time in particular, we left Victoria and she was sticking her nose way into those big flat doors forward. As a matter of fact we were down there trying to brace her up and she was rolling a good 25 to 35 degrees."

"Yes, we used to have trouble explaining to our customers how we happened to be dumping so much paper," said Mrs. Acheson. "Every time you guys would do that we had to pay a claim to Crown."

Mr. Graham happened to think, "Remember the time we had that barge with those darn little cabbages, uh, brussel sprouts? We had a truck load of crates of brussel sprouts and the darn truck turned over and broke open many of those crates. We had brussel sprouts everywhere you tried to walk. They rolled into drain pipes and scuppers and what a mess. We had just all the water we wanted to contend with, I'll tell you, with those darned cabbages stopping up the drains. I never have liked brussel sprouts since then! ... but safety wise, the IROQUOIS was a good ship."

"Good old girl, I miss her," replied Mrs. Acheson.

Mr. Graham concluded, "Everyone had a fond spot in their heart for her. Every single person that worked on her, I believe."

The IROQUOIS made her last trip on the Victoria run August 30, 1969. A new labor contract that year ran the cost of operating a self-propelled freight vessel so high that the IROQUOIS was offered for sale from her lay-up berth in Seattle's Lake Union, January 1, 1970. The freight she once carried was transferred to trucks. After a year or two, a buyer for the vessel was finally found. She was taken to Alaska where she rests

CHIEF ENGINEER HAROLD GRAHAM

today as a fish processing plant.

The era of the three "grand old sisters" on Puget Sound had come to a close. All three vessels built on and for the Great Lakes were much more content and suited to the waters and the people of Puget Sound. The people, too, have changed, but many fond memories remain in their hearts for the era of style and refined taste that once graced their waters. These steamships catered to a lifestyle that has vanished in the Pacific Northwest.

[3]Authors' interview, October 29, 1981.

VICTORIA, THE "OLD WORLD CITY" OF THE NORTH-
WEST, WAS THE DESTINATION OF MANY PUGET SOUND
STEAMERS AND FERRYBOATS

CANADIAN PACIFIC RAILWAY VS. PUGET SOUND NAVIGATION COMPANY

The Seattle-Victoria steamboat and ferry route has enjoyed a long and traditional popularity among residents and visitors in the Pacific Northwest. The route's notoriety deserves a closer look as a distinctive contributor to the need and acceptance of automobile ferryboats on the Sound.

Victoria, once the larger of the two cities, was a more formal and metropolitan city with international shipping and communication. Located on the Pacific coastline and not inland as Seattle is on Puget Sound, the British influence and broad European interests influenced the growth and charm of Victoria. Puget Sound residents found that this Canadian city revitalized their somewhat less urbane and isolated perspectives of the world beyond their inland sea. There is little doubt that Victoria invigorated their desires to build a comparable American city within Washington. Seattleites broadened their plan to encompass the robustness and success of San Francisco. Fortunately for consistency, the early architecture of all of these cities was similar.

Port Townsend, the settlement federally selected to be the focal center and port for Washington Territory, was located across the Straits from Vancouver Island. This city established long lasting business and governmental ties with Victoria, B.C., the Provincial capital. It was natural that Tacoma and Seattle, in competition with Port Townsend for territorial and railroad recognition, would early on establish transportation ties with the Queen's city in British Columbia.

James R. Hunt and John Hart Scranton began a Seattle-Victoria run with their steamer CONSTITUTION as early as 1857. This route would be served by numerous vessels in the years to come. Most of these vessels were under American registration. The original round trip of the CONSTITUTION required one week!

Alaska Steamship Company and its subsidiary, Puget Sound Navigation Company, initiated the Port Townsend-Port Angeles-Victoria schedule in 1902.

CLALLAM CREATED A DEMAND FOR THE PRINCESS BEATRICE

The ROSALIE and the MAJESTIC made two round trips daily in the summer. The 97 foot GARLAND substituted for the MAJESTIC during the winter months when business was slack.

The Board of Trade of Victoria, B.C. and local business representatives called on the Canadian Pacific Railway and the Pacific Coast Steamship Company, the competitors of Alaska Steamship Company, in an attempt to interest either company in challenging the Puget Sound Navigation Company's dominance of the Victoria run. They wanted a spacious, modern and fast ship.

At that time Pacific Coast Steam had all their vessels committed to other runs due to the Klondike gold rush. For the same reason Canadian Pacific Railway showed no interest in their proposal.

VANCOUVER HOTEL, VANCOUVER, B.C.

[1]Leithead, ''Canadian Pacific Triangle Route,'' *The Sea Chest*, September, 1967.

The rush for gold occurred at points within both American-owned Alaskan Territory and Canadian-owned Yukon Territory. The C.P.R. operated some of the sleekest and speediest steamships, known as the EMPRESS ships, in ocean service from the Pacific Northwest. Canadian Pacific built a railroad through the Canadian Rocky Mountains to Victoria, B.C. A series of attractive hotels were built by the Railway to accommodate passengers. The Empress Hotel in Victoria, circa 1908, and the Vancouver Hotel in Vancouver, B.C. are two famous ones.

After the completion of the rail line, the company began a vigorous campaign to promote tourism. They needed trade for the new line. Other luxury resorts were built along the way at such places as Lake Louise, Glacier and Banff. It was no coincidence that prompted Canada's first national parks to be located along this system through the Rockies. Washington Territory and Alaska ultimately benefited from the serious promotional efforts of the C.P.R.

The Canadian Pacific Railway's extensive holdings in Canada and the Yukon Territory, including this elaborate network of well-serviced trains, made them a potent transportation power on the North American continent. Their sternwheelers on the Yukon River, based at Whitehorse, Y.T., connected with rails from British Columbia. The C.P.R. was both a competitor and informal business associate in the transport of prospectors, tourists and entrepreneurs to the Klondike and Alaskan ports. They competed with American shipping firms in the transport of people and supplies north. They carried passengers by steamship from British Columbia or overland by rail to Alaska. Their railway also connected with Skagway, Alaska, the jumping-off point for Alaska Steam's passenger vessels from Puget Sound.

Pacific Coast Steam and Canadian Pacific Railway operated fine, well-appointed steamships, offering a touch of refinement and luxury. Canadians were sorely disappointed when both companies refused to meet Puget Sound Navigation Company in contest for the Victoria-Seattle route. The P.S.N. boats were slightly understated in their decor. They did not meet the Canadians' preferences.

The northern neighbor's clamor was momentarily stilled in July 1903, when Puget Sound Navigation Company introduced their new wooden 155 foot CLALLAM to the Seattle-Victoria run. Built at Heath Yards in Tacoma, the CLALLAM was designed to operate with the steamer MAJESTIC between Tacoma,

The BEAUTIES and WONDERS of PUGET SOUND

TACOMA · SEATTLE · EVERETT ROUTE

INTERNATIONAL STEAMSHIP COMPANY

THE INLAND NAVIGATION COMPANY

General Offices
COLMAN DOCK — SEATTLE, WASH.

Seattle, Port Townsend and Victoria. The vessel was equipped with 44 staterooms and a fore-and-aft compound engine of 800 horsepower. She had a cruising speed of 13 knots.

Introduction of the CLALLAM was of the first order of business for Puget Sound Navigation Company in 1903. The company's separation from Alaska Steamship Company gave them autonomy to work out the individual services of inter-Sound routes and the maintenance needed for a fleet of passenger boats on these routes. The offshoot company that began operation with the outgrown vessels of the Alaska service had graduated to an operation of substantial size and demand. This company's growth, like its parent, would experience major setbacks.

Six months after introduction, January 9, 1904, the CLALLAM encountered a stormy sea and foundered on her crossing to Victoria. The ill-fated steamer had left her Tacoma landing on schedule the day before. She picked up passengers and freight at the foot of Washington Street in Seattle. There, a peculiar incident is said to have transpired.

Sheep destined for Victoria slaughter houses were customarily led aboard ship by a bellwether sheep who boarded his charges and returned to Seattle after escorting the flock to Victoria.[2] That day this stubborn sheep emphatically refused to step aboard the CLALLAM. He was left behind when the ship departed.

As the steamer left Port Townsend to cross the Straits, a gale was rising. From the Canadian side she was spied one-half hour out of Victoria. The ship was rolling heavily and appeared to be proceeding off course. A Canadian steamer and Puget Sound Tug Boat Company's SEA LION and RICHARD HOLYOKE were dispatched for rescue, but despite an all night search the CLALLAM could not be found.

Aboard ship, Captain George M. Roberts,[3] 55 years old and a veteran of 29 years on Puget Sound ships, realized that his vessel was taking water at a dangerous rate in the heart of a tremendous storm. The captain had retired to his bunk after leaving Port Townsend for his customary mid-afternoon nap. Sensing that the CLALLAM was pitching over badly he went to the pilothouse to check. First Officer G.W. Doheny had the wheel. Chief Engineer Scott A. Delauney signaled from the engine room and called up that a port was stove-in. Captain Robert's sent Doheny to investigate.

A previously broken and repaired deadlight,[4] located about 18 inches above the waterline on the port side was sprung. The power of the storm's crash-

CAPTAIN GEORGE ROBERTS COMMANDED THE TRAGIC CLALLAM

[2]The majority of mutton sold on Vancouver Island and within the City of Vancouver was shipped via Seattle on the Sound steamers. Due to a lack of refrigeration, as many as 500 or 600 head of sheep would be shipped on the hoof aboard night steamers like the CLALLAM. Steamers had probably carried livestock from the time of their introduction to the Sound.

Cattle herds were often a problem, demanding that ships' crews pinch-hit as part-time cowboys, keeping animals out of the produce and freight while trying to prevent them from falling overboard. Occasionally they did that anyway, following one another into the bay in herd-like fashion. The steamer's lifeboats were lowered for the round-up. Just imagine—"stampede on the steamer."

[3]Captain George Roberts was one of the founders of Alaska Steamship Company and a shareholder in the CLALLAM.

[4]A fixed porthole with an iron cover that screws down over the glass.

THE SEATTLE POST-INTELLIGENCER.

VOL. XLV., NO. 57.   SEATTLE, WASHINGTON, SUNDAY, JANUARY 10, 1904.—FORTY-FOUR PAGES.   PRICE FIVE CENTS.

FIFTY-FOUR DROWN IN WRECK OF THE CLALLAM

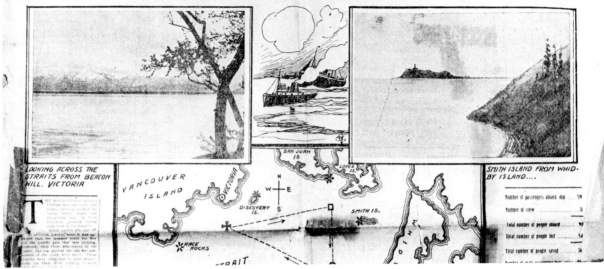

LOOKING ACROSS THE STRAITS FROM BEACON HILL, VICTORIA

SMITH ISLAND FROM WHIDBY ISLAND....

Number of passengers aboard ship	59
Number of crew	31
Total number of people aboard	90
Total number of people lost	54
Total number of people saved	36

ing waves had stove-in the deadlight. The engine room crew had stuffed blankets into the opening, nailing boards over the top of these.

In the meantime the bilge section of the line pump and the syphon were choked with coal and debris. Reserve pumps were started but they, too, were quickly clogged.

Water was rising rapidly in the bilge. About this time the deadlight's repair with blankets and boards gave way. The ship's porthole once again exposed the vessel to surging waters.

Mate Doheny did not return to the pilothouse. The engineer reported in person to the captain the alarming situation and his suggestions for saving the ship. The captain was appalled when personal inspection revealed that the engine room crew was wading waist-deep in water. The plunger pumps were defective and the engineer had started the main circulating pumps improperly, pumping seawater into the vessel. Rising water soon extinquished the boiler fires. The CLALLAM was at a standstill.

Confusion and panic could be felt throughout the ship. The captain had little choice but to order three lifeboats over the side for women and children. The front page story of the *Seattle Post-Intelligencer*, January 10, 1904, tells the grisly details:

"The Seattle-Victoria steamer CLALLAM was lost early yesterday morning midway between Smith Island and Dungeness Spit, at least fifty-four persons losing their lives in this disaster.

"Every person who put off in the lifeboats, lowered when it was apparent that the steamer could not live out the terrific gale that was blowing, drowned. Only those who stayed on the vessel, fighting against the sea for possession of the craft, were saved. These persons were compelled to fight desperately for their lives, rushing forward when the vessel turned on her beam ends, clinging frantically to the rails and finally slipping off the sides of the vessel into the water or to a life raft that had been lowered . . . "

The CLALLAM managed to stay afloat until mid-morning when the tugs SEA LION and RICHARD HOLYOKE located and rescued the survivors. Those husbands and fathers who stayed aboard witnessed the drowning of their wives and children. Many of the men were saved.

The newspaper account continues:

"The number of lives lost on the steamer may exceed 54. This is the total as given by the passenger list and reports received to date, but the passenger list takes no account of children under the half-fare age. That there were several of these aboard is likely. It is known already that Mrs. LaPlant died with a child that had not been entered on the passenger list, and three children of the Sullins family are also lost. It is possible that several small children drowned whose names are not known at present, owing to the fact that they were under age and did not pay the fare.

"The tug RICHARD HOLYOKE found the CLALLAM January 9 between San Juan and Smith Islands. Crew members secured a towline aboard the steamer and trying to take advantage of the winds and tides, headed for the American side, even though Victoria was closer than Port Townsend. The helpless CLALLAM suddenly rolled over and sank.

"It is a singular occurrence that the number of survivors from this city [Seattle] is light. There is a very heavy travel between Seattle and Victoria, but for some unexplained reason the percentage of Seattle passengers on the last trip of the CLALLAM was far below the average . . .

"Had all the passengers and crew remained aboard it is undoubtedly true that most of them would have been lost when the CLALLAM turned over and gave up the struggle. Others stronger and better able to care for themselves drowned with the relief tugs standing by, waiting to take them aboard."[5]

When the distress of the CLALLAM had first been noticed on shore, Puget Sound Navigation Company begged steamer and tugboat owners of Victoria to put out to relieve the distressed vessel. Victoria owners reportedly refused to risk their craft in the gale. One steamer, the MAUD, started out of Victoria Harbor but after striking the storm was compelled to run to the safety of homeport. They hurried an American fleet of six tugs to the rescue of the CLALLAM but they were several hours from the scene.

There were 36 survivors of the CLALLAM taken aboard the tugs, including Captain Roberts and Chief Engineer DeLaunay. Twenty-two of the thirty-one crewmen were saved, including three Chinese cooks, Toy Look, Ting Hung and Chin Ling. Of the rescued passengers, one was a prominent canneryman, one was a traveling man from Michigan, a railroad contractor from Montana, several mining men, and a number of men from Vancouver Island. One gentleman on his wedding trip lost his bride in the gale.

Those who perished included a surveyor and retired British officer; Captain Tom Lawrence, master of the steamer SCOTIA; a stock dealer and mining man, two members of the Vaudeville team Prince and Daniels, a timber cruiser, a Tacoma organist, a hardwood finisher, president of Seattle Iron & Steel Company, Homer M. Swaney; a streetcar conductor; and a customs inspector. The women who lost their lives included the wives and daughters of a restaurant owner, the manager of the Bank of Montreal, and a nurse at the Fanny Paddock Hospital in Tacoma. Exactly half the number of people aboard the CLALLAM that day lost their lives.

Superstitious seafarers believed that their original misgivings about the CLALLAM had been sadly justified. When the new steamer was launched the previous summer of 1903, two omens were noted.

The daughter of the Tatoosh Island weather observer had been selected by the residents of Clallam County to act as sponsor for their namesake vessel. The young woman missed the bow with the champagne bottle as the vessel slid down the ways with an unexpected speed. The CLALLAM's ensign was unfurled as she hit the water. A gasp rose from the crowd. The ensign was flying upside down, the universal distress sign for a ship at sea.

As a result of the CLALLAM's tragedy the U.S. Steamboat Inspection Service tightened their regulations. The CLALLAM's engineer was one of the first to lose his license. Captain Robert's certificate was suspended, as well. Passenger counts and safety precautions were initiated. On the whole, the vessels of Puget Sound became a safer fleet.

[5] *The Seattle Post-Intelligencer,* Sunday, January 10, 1904.

C.P.R. BECOMES INTERESTED

Victoria's Board of Trade renewed their overtures to the Canadian Pacific Railway for immediate introduction of a Canadian vessel on the Strait's run. In their determiniation, this company would provide more reliable service between Vancouver Island and the United States. The Canadian Pacific Railway was sympathetic and agreed to place their newly completed PRINCESS BEATRICE in operation. The company moved quickly. On January 20, 1904, the new ship was introduced to the run. The PRINCESS BEATRICE initiated the run that would eventually be known as the "Triangle-Route," serving Seattle, Vancouver and Victoria.

The PRINCESS BEATRICE was a fine steamer built at British Columbia Marine Railway at Esquimalt, B.C. A wooden vessel of 1,290 tons, measuring 193.4 feet in length, she was equipped with a triple expansion steam engine. She was capable of a speed of 13 knots. Licensed to carry 350 day passengers, the PRINCESS BEATRICE had berths for an additional 86 people in forty luxuriously appointed staterooms. Most PRINCESS steamers of the Canadian fleet were decorated with a richness and elegance that rivaled private yachts and Mississippi riverboats.[6]

The C.P.R. was eager to establish Puget Sound service but it was also hard-pressed by a severe shortage of vessels. The PRINCESS VICTORIA arrived from the Newcastle yard of Swan & Hunter, England, introducing yet another new standard for speed and elegance on inland waters. Her triple expansion 5,800 horsepower engines carried the new steamer at 20 knots. Intended for the Victoria-Vancouver, B.C. run, she had accommodations for 1000 day passengers and 76 staterooms and 152 berths. The PRINCESS VICTORIA relieved the PRINCESS BEATRICE on the Triangle Route in April 1904. She broke all speed records held on the Sound. She showed her American competitors that the C.P.R. intended to be a harbinger for a new type of service on Puget Sound.

THE FIGHT IS ON

Joshua Green and Charles Peabody decided to temporarily place Alaska Steam's DOLPHIN on the Victoria-Seattle run until a permanent replacement for the CLALLAM could be found. The MAJESTIC, which had been acquired through consolidation with LaConner Trading & Transportation Company, was rushed through a previously scheduled expansion of passenger accommodations. She emerged after remodeling February 4, 1904, renamed the WHATCOM.[7] She carried 80 overnight passengers in 38 staterooms with a capacity for 240 day travelers. The WHATCOM's triple expansion steam engine carried the vessel at a speed of 15 knots.

Puget Sound Navigation Company anticipated increasing popularity of the Seattle-Victoria run and keenly felt the competition of the PRINCESS VICTORIA. The CLALLAM disaster had shaken the young company's confidence, but due to the success of Alaska Steamship Company in the gold rush, these partners were not financially strapped.[8]

In April of 1906, they introduced the Great Lakes steamship INDIANAPOLIS to challenge the Canadian Pacific's vessel. The INDIANAPOLIS's course included a stopover in Port Townsend for passengers and freight

THE REMODELED MAJESTIC BECAME THE WHATCOM

---

[6]Robert Turner's *The Pacific Princesses,* Sono Nis Press, 1977, quotes the Victoria *Daily Colonist* paper, "Everyone was delighted with the BEATRICE's speed and luxury. She was a gentlemen's club afloat with a special lounge for ladies so they could get away from the male stares and smoke."

[7]It was Charles Peabody's idea to name the vessels that they built for the Washington State counties. The WHATCOM was the third of those named, preceded by the JEFFERSON and the CLALLAM. "Whatcom" names a county, lake, creek and former city all in northwestern Washington. Whatcom was a Nooksack Indian chief whose name was said to have meant "noisy water." Meany, *Origin of Washington Geographic Names,* University of Washington Press, 1923.

[8]The CLALLAM was considered to be so safely built that Puget Sound Navigation Company insured her for collision and fire only. The vessel had cost $100,000 to build. McDonald, "The Worst Disaster in the Strait," *The Seattle Times,* January 6, 1963, page 12.

with the overall trip from Seattle to Victoria requiring less than five hours.[9] A similar trip today on more modern passenger vessels like the PRINCESS MARGUERITE or a Washington State ferry requires a comparable amount of time.

Rivalry between P.S.N. and C.P.R. was growing steadily. The INDIANAPOLIS, advertised as the "WHITE FLYER," was no match for the PRINCESS VICTORIA's speed. The real contest came one day in July 1906. The INDIANAPOLIS was just leaving Victoria with an excursion party in the early evening. They planned to leave just 45 minutes ahead of the PRIN-

CESS's regularly scheduled departure at 6:45 P.M. So anxious was the captain of the WHITE FLYER to get a headstart on the race, that he sailed early, leaving a few very unhappy excursionists behind. They joined the PRINCESS VICTORIA leaving at her usual time.

Three hours and 20 minutes later, at 10:20 P.M., the VICTORIA docked in Seattle. She had passed her rival at 9:44 P.M. near Jefferson Head. The INDIANAPOLIS made her way to the Seattle pier in the wake of the PRINCESS. Those passengers whom the captain of the INDIANAPOLIS had left behind were gloating. They found appropriate terminology and expression of feeling to greet the crew of the Puget Sound steamer. Crew members were said to have accepted "endearments of defeat" in a sporting manner.

The competition was fanned again in 1907 when Puget Sound Navigation Company introduced the CHIPPEWA and the IROQUOIS. A heavy summer tourist trade forced both companies to refrain from too much rivalry and concentrate on service. There was plenty of business for everyone.

The CHIPPEWA soon became a popular excursion boat on the Seattle-Victoria run. As the fall and winter months approached, though, the company's profits steadily diminished. Competitive pressure was intensified between the American and Canadian companies.

The PRINCESS ROYAL, newest of the Canadian Pacific's fleet, had been operating on the Alaska route but was switched to the Seattle-Victoria run to challenge CHIPPEWA. As the inclement weather of off-season approached, CHIPPEWA had fewer and fewer excursions. The loss of fares for both companies was significant with two vessels operating on the same run during the winter months. Clearly the companies needed to compromise. Neither wanted to risk the first move. They feared the loss of the chance to be sole operator on the route, if the other could be forced out of business. It was rumored that a rate war was imminent.

For economic reasons, P.S.N. decided to withdraw the CHIPPEWA from the run. They would operate Peabody's smaller favorite instead, the ROSALIE. Fare aboard the ROSALIE was cut to 50 cents per person while the C.P.R.'s fare remained the same $2. P.S.N. claimed not to be cutting rates to eliminate competition, but to successfully attract business from areas not formerly patronizing either system. [Few believed them.] The ROSALIE's rate was inspired to attract those who had less to spend on their travels as well. The Canadians maintained that people who traveled during the off-season were wealthy enough to pay more for the elegance and speed of the Canadian vessels.

All the bantering between the two companies erupted in a dramatic rate war,[1] reducing fares to the ridiculous price of 25 cents. Puget Sound Navigation Company established a new company route from Seattle to Vancouver, B.C., with the IROQUOIS in an attempt to further undercut Canadian service. They even investigated the possibility of returning their steamer BELLINGHAM (Ex-WILLAPA of the Canadian Pacific Navigation Company) to Canadian registry to compete on the Victoria-Vancouver run, but revised Canadian laws made these costs prohibitive.

[9]By virtue of the U.S. Government's Jones Act, foreign built vessels cannot transport and disembark passengers and freight between two United States ports. Because of this law, the C.P.R.'s vessels were limited to runs between Canada and one American port only, excluding them from competitive service of other ports along the Seattle-Victoria route. The Jones Act was designed to protect American shipbuilders and operators from foreign competition.

[1]An excellent account of the rate war is depicted in Turner, "The Great Rate War," *The Pacific Princesses,* Chapter III.

PRINCESS ELAINE

PRINCESS VICTORIA

C.P.R. maintained predominance throughout this lively battle with P.S.N. between 1907 through the spring of 1909. For the most part, passengers preferred the richness of decor aboard PRINCESS liners. The Navigation Company's Great Lakes steamers were a noticeable improvement, however, over former vessels of the line. The mighty Canadian Pacific Railway found it annoying that this new and comparatively small company was willing to antagonize their wrath and challenge their financial endeavors.

In a sense, both companies were ultimately rewarded for their perseverance. Their corporate strength improved while they established important footholds on Puget Sound and in British Columbia. The C.P.R. handily identified itself as a prominent passenger carrier between the U.S. and Canada. Their campaigns attracted thousands of tourists to the Northwest who contributed to the region's growth and commerce. In turn, P.S.N. recognized that it was not a match for the Canadian Pacific's passenger trade, but by raising standards on their ships, the company was able to develop freight routes on the Sound while underway for Canadian waters. The freight routes eventually would prove to be the reliable mainstay for the company.

Both companies were rewarded with heavy patronage in late May 1908, when the American Great White Fleet visited the Sound. The CHIPPEWA was humming with special excursions. The ROSALIE and the PRINCESS VICTORIA covered the regular runs with capacity crowds nearly every trip. The Fleet's arrival coincided with Victoria Day holiday, celebrating the King's birthday. Rates were slashed even lower to attract bigger crowds.

The summer of 1909 approached with anticipated heavy traffic to Seattle for the Alaska-Yukon Pacific Exposition. Joshua Green recognized that continuing the rate war was foolishness. The two companies had slashed their Seattle-Vancouver fares to rock-bottom prices. Now the railroads were beginning to grow uncomfortable. Neither company was anxious to tangle with the Northern Pacific or the Great Northern Railroads. Both operated rail service between Seattle and Vancouver.

Joshua Green approached his personal friend, Captain James Troup, head of the PRINCESS ships for the Canadian Pacific Railway. He suggested that they negotiate an armistice. Troup had every advantage at the time. It was not until May 1909 that a cautious set-

tlement was reached. At the invitation of the Northern Pacific Railway Company, Green and Troup traveled to St. Paul, Minnesota to meet with Northern Pacific's president, J.M. Hannaford. The railroad had suggested that they meet in a congenial atmosphere of neutrality to resolve the rate war.

Joshua Green retells the amusing story in his memoirs about the extremes he was willing to take in order to resolve their differences. He puffed away at the large cigar offered as a peace pipe to company officials in attendance. Green was a non-smoker, never having touched a cigar in his life. Midway through the meeting, Green begged to be excused. He hurried. A sudden and critical green nausea gripped in near collapse. He was able to return shortly, bravely explaining to the gentlemen present about his predicament. This set the conferees at ease. The outcome of their meeting was a verbal agreement suspending the great rate war. It was ended quietly, without public fanfare.

FERRIES OR OCEAN STEAMERS

A seemingly minor event occurred in 1909 which later had a tremendous influence on ferryboats. Early that year Puget Sound Navigation Company responded to a charge by a "contrived law" on behalf of the CHIPPEWA. It was believed that this obscure Canadian law was written to aid in the supremacy of the Canadian Pacific Railway.

American standards for steamboats allowed comparatively smaller vessels to legally carry more passengers per ship than the Canadian steamboat laws allowed. The CHIPPEWA, 100 feet shorter overall than the PRINCESS VICTORIA was licensed to carry 1250 passengers, while the PRINCESS VICTORIA carried only 1000. The new Canadian law stated that ocean steamers would be limited to carrying one passenger per two gross tons.[2] The gross tonnage of the CHIPPEWA was registered at 996, allowing only 498 passengers. The PRINCESS VICTORIA's registerage was 1943, allowing 971 passengers.

A very angry Charles Peabody, Chairman of Puget Sound Navigation Company, responded with a public statement. The CHIPPEWA and other navigation company vessels crossing Canadian waters were not ocean steamers,[3] but "ferries." Until that time, the only other vessels to have been referred to as ferries on the Sound were the CITY OF SEATTLE and the WEST SEATTLE. There were also ferryboats on Lake Washington at that time. All others were consistently referred to as steamers.

Peabody's response was uncontested by the Canadian government. He did volunteer to limit the number of passengers aboard the CHIPPEWA to 1000 to prevent overcrowding. Peabody set a precedent that day with the use of the word "ferry." Ferries would replace all steamers on cross-Sound service. It was a prophetic remark, too, since his son Alex would one day control the major ferry fleets of Puget Sound *and* British Columbia.

The C.P.R. continued to be a major but amiable competitor of P.S.N. even after the introduction of automobiles and double-ended ferries. The Canadian Pacific was popular with those who had money and influence as well as those seeking a brush with fame. Tourists from around the continent were attracted by the Canadian Railway's persuasive advertising.

In the early 1920s *The Marine Digest* told this anecdote:[4]

"When Captain J. C. Brownfield, manager of Washington Tug & Barge Company, and A.L. McNealy, manager of the Pacific Towboat Company, journeyed to Victoria, B.C. on the Canadian Pacific Steamship PRINCESS VICTORIA, they found that their fellow passengers included Doug Fairbanks and the divine Mary. Both men fled the place where Doug and Mary were supposed to be observing the scenery.

" 'It's the limit the way they fuss over these movie stars,' remarked Mr. McNealy, as they reached a lonely corner on the ship.

" 'Aye, aye to that,' returned Captain Brownfield.

" 'Also, amen, brother, amen,' put in a husky looking individual who sought refuge in the lonely corner of the vessel. He was smoking a black cigar.

" 'Well, well,' said Mr. McNealy, 'Here's Doug himself.'

[2]Leithead, "The Canadian Pacific Triangle Route," *The Sea Chest*, September, 1967.

[3]It is generally accepted among scholars and those who remember them so vividly, that the term "steamers," used particularly in reference to members of the Mosquito Fleet, carried passengers and freight, *not vehicles*. Unlike ferryboats, steamers were not designed or built to carry wagons or automobiles.

[4]*The Marine Digest*, September 30, 1922, page 6. This is an article written by William O. Thorniley.

PRINCESS MARGUERITE STILL SAILS BETWEEN VIC-TORIA AND SEATTLE

" 'Be merciful,' said Mr. Fairbanks, 'I crawled off here to have a quiet smoke. Sit down and join me.'

"That was the beginning of a long session. Reaching Victoria the towboat magnates and Doug headed for a Chinese junk that recently arrived there from the Orient. They inspected the strange looking craft from stem to stern.

"Mr. McNealy and Captain Brownfield found the irrepressible Doug a fine companion. He impressed them as a two-handed person who plays the man's part at any time."

Puget Sound Navigation Company was beginning to gain strength on the Sound in consequence of its revolutionary ideas, challenging all steamboat companies on inland waters. The Canadian Pacific Railway taught P.S.N. a number of valuable lessons. Foremost among these was how to dominate competitors. Puget Sound Navigation Company proved to be a fast learner with a very good memory.

CLEAR THE DECKS FOR AN AU-TO-MO-BILE

Many ferry riders are familiar with the frustrating experience of sitting in long ferry lines, idly waiting an hour or two for the chance to catch a ferry. When at last you are underway, you can breathe a sigh of relief and snooze in your car or wander to the passenger deck for a sandwich and a cup of coffee. Little thought is given to the people who make the ferry operate or navigate the correct course. You are there to rest and relax, as you anticipate a weekend away from home. Least of all do you think about your car, awaiting your return on the auto deck.

Woody and Larry Peabody, sons of the founder of Puget Sound Navigation Company, recall the days when loading your automobile aboard the cross-Sound boats was a different experience for everyone concerned. This was especially true from a crew member's viewpoint, the capacity served by most of the Peabody sons in their younger days.

The Peabody family owned a touring car. Occasionally they liked to take the family for a ride, or at least, part of the family. After all, there were eight sons. Sometimes they wanted to visit friends on the Peninsula or take a brief trip to Victoria. They enjoyed using their "machine."

But how was one to take this contraption on the steamer? Most vessels were not equipped to carry cars or wagons. But Peabody owned the company. The captain thought it was a good idea to help him.

An elevator was installed on the bow of several steamers to assist in the loading and off-loading of cargo at varying tide levels. Ramps or planks were placed leading onto the elevator, and the automobile was driven aboard ship.

The crew next faced the problem of the lack of overhead space in the vessel's superstructure on the cargo deck. The height of a touring car was tall. Consequently there were few choices if the vehicle was to be transported safely. The crew let the air out of the tires, removed the top (an early day convertible convenience), and removed the windshield. Can you imag-

ine watching the crew do this to your $4000 automobile in 1910?

Once the steamer reached its port of embarkation, the crew stood ready to reassemble the car. Praise be! It would be impossible to do this yourself.

Just imagine this process and then ponder the problem of approaching a dock with a long line of cars waiting to board. Think of the grumbling. But no, this threat to ultimate patience you were spared. You had to have an appointment for loading several hours in advance of scheduled departure time.

These methods continued to provoke concern that the crew would be able to put the car together again ... and that there would be a road when you reached the opposite shore. Automobiles were new to this part of the West and adjustments were required.

A newspaper clipping found in Captain Louis Van Bogaert's scrapbooks must have reminded him of days forgotten. Van Bogaert was a veteran of early steamers and automobiles. Entitled, "Takes Off Tires to Drive Machine Ashore from Ship," that article says that it had been many years since bystanders had seen an automobile with tires removed being driven off a vessel at the dock. When the SOL DUC was on the Victoria-Seattle route, this was a common sight. The driver could be seen removing tires so his machine would clear the low freight deck door.

The reporter noted that the previous afternoon the identical sight had brought back memories. A large travel-stained automobile was seen emerging from a vessel in the harbor with wheels denuded of tires. They were lashed in a lump to the rear of the luggage carrier.

Apparently this motorist had been forced to buy four tires in the United States but the only way he could gain duty free entry into Canada was to take them in as baggage and drive the automobile on the rims.

Perhaps the residents of Puget Sound were only slightly aware of the subtle changes occurring within the region. Distances were growing shorter, communities were expanding and people seemed to be everywhere in an area that was once wilderness. They also wanted to go places and see more of their new homeland.

AUTOFERRY CITY OF ANGELES

81

TOURIST CARRIED AUTOMOBILES FIRST

TYPICAL FERRY LINE

SOL DUC ON VICTORIA ROUTE

STEAMER ROUTES AND AUTOMOBILES

Captain William P. Thornton began his steamboating career at the age of 12 after moving to Friday Harbor from the nation's midwest. He was a deckhand on the LYDIA THOMPSON when she went aground in the San Juans in 1898. For a time, Thornton served on the U.S. Revenue cutters SCOUT, GUARD, and BEAR. He rejoined the Thompson Steamboat Company and was serving on the company's steamer GARLAND as mate when it was purchased by Puget Sound Navigation Company in 1902. Thornton obtained his master's papers and the new company transferred him to the crack ROSALIE as mate and pilot, and to the WHATCOM. For awhile in 1906 he served on the STATE OF WASHINGTON. It was here that our story will proclaim his fame.

Captain Thornton and his crew took a Stanley Steamer automobile from Hoodsport to Seattle on the STATE OF WASHINGTON. That Stanley Steamer is said to be the first automobile to be ferried across Puget Sound!

One ferry route in particular had the most immediate impact on the popularization of automobile ferryboats on the Sound. Early in December 1890, the U.S. Navy announced their decision to build a shipyard at Point Turner near Port Orchard. The general loca-

tion of the Navy drydock was to be named Bremerton in honor of James Bremer, who owned the original land track and plotted the townsite in 1891. Only eight years before this development, the first residence, a crude log cabin, was built on the site.

The Navy's announcement provoked a tremendous real estate boom at Port Orchard. Trade and reliable transportation between Seattle and Port Orchard was suddenly a priority for the steamer fleets.

Regularly scheduled service first appeared on the Seattle-Port Orchard run with the "steady, comfortable, smart little boat,"[2] [36 feet] called the HELEN. She was owned and operated by Captain W.H. Ellis. Three round trips a week were commenced in September 1885.

The HELEN was joined the following year by the 33 foot steamboat SEATTLE, owned and skippered by

[1] Newell, *Marine History of the Pacific Northwest,* Superior, 1966, p.681. Corroborated by tape recorded interviews.

Captain Thornton was later captain of the SIOUX, CHIPPEWA and the IROQUOIS. April 1914, he was appointed Port Captain for P.S.N. He served that office until 1920, retiring at that time to a mercantile business at Charleston, Washington. He later organized and ran the Elliott Bay Towing Company. He purchased and operated the Seabeck-Brinnon ferry route.

[2] Leithead and Van Bogaert, "The Navy Yard Route", *The Sea Chest,* Vol.2, pp.96-117.

Captain John H. Nibbe. He had formerly operated the sailing sloop SEA BIRD between Port Orchard and Seattle. These two vessels were barely the size of comfortable yachts today.

The HELEN and the SEATTLE remained on the run until mid-1888. The HELEN was replaced by the MOUNTAINEER, a 69′ x 16′ x 6′ propeller-driven vessel built on the Columbia River at Chinook, Washington. She had two whistles of startling volume. One was mounted vertically in the conventional manner; the other was mounted horizontally and equipped with a piston connected to a rod that extended into the pilot house for operation. This produced the effect of a calliope. It was guaranteed just as loud. The MOUNTAINEER retained her characteristic whistle when she was sold in 1891. She became a tugboat for the Stimson Mill Company, Seattle.

The freight and passenger sternwheeler SKAGIT CHIEF was introduced to the Navy Yard run in 1893 by drydock contractors, Barlow Brothers. This 137 foot vessel was to carry passengers and construction materials from Tacoma and Seattle to Port Orchard.

The first SKAGIT CHIEF was owned and operated on the East Pass Mail Route between Seattle, Tacoma and Bremerton. Captain George W. Barlow was the skipper who hauled most of the construction materials for the Bremerton Navy Yard. Captain Barlow was also the master of several other famous Sound vessels such as the STATE OF WASHINGTON, GREYHOUND and the MULTNOMAH.

Joshua Green's LaConner Trading & Transportation Company entered a joint agreement with H.B. Kennedy to operate LaConner Trading's INLAND FLYER and Kennedy's fast ATHLON on what was to become known as the "Port Orchard Route." By mid-May 1901, these two steamers were the regulars on the run; all others were considered opposition. This proved profitable and popular with sightseers, too. The battleships IOWA, OREGON, and WISCONSIN, plus two cruisers, were in drydock and on public display at the Bremerton Navy Yard.

It was not until 1908 that Puget Sound Navigation Company and H.B. Kennedy entered equal partnership with their two boats in a separate company called "The Navy Yard Route, Incorporated."[3] The company continued using this name until H.B. Kennedy's death in 1920. The title stuck as the name of the run for many years. The navigation company retained it in their advertising throughout the 1920's.

The regular Port Orchard boats were shifted from Pier 2 in Seattle to Puget Sound Navigation's terminal at Colman Dock when the partnership was formalized. This is where the Bremerton boats are found today.

The Navy Yard Route was to initiate some of the most significant changes in ferryboating in the region. The autocarrier came into its own as a result of this run. Bremerton was not only the site of one of the largest Navy Yards in the United States, it was also the transportation gateway to Washington's Olympic Peninsula.

[3]In February 1908, P.S.N. reorganized by increasing its capital stock from $500,000 to $1,500,000. They retired obligations which apparently had been outstanding on previously purchased vessels. These may have been the INDIANAPOLIS, CHIPPEWA and the IROQUOIS. The Navy Yard Route was then incorporated with 2,000 shares of stock, par value of $100 each, fully subscribed by H.B. Kennedy and Joshua Green in exchange for the steamers H.B. KENNEDY and TOURIST, together with an interest in the Port Orchard Route and a dock at Charleston. *Report of Investigation of Earnings of the Puget Sound Navigation Company,* May 1947.

CAPTAIN WILLIAM P. THORNTON

STATE OF WASHINGTON WAS FIRST STEAMER TO
CARRY AN AUTOMOBILE

HARRY BARLOW DESIGNED BARLOW ELEVATOR

SKAGIT CHIEF

OH! OLYMPIC
HIGHWAY TO THE OLYMPICS

(Oh! Olympia Gateway to the Olympics)

Words and Music by Rudo L. Fromme,
Supervisor Olympic National Forest

Piano Arrangement by Bernie F. Hume,
Secretary Olympia Chamber of Commerce

Published by -A. T. RABECK- Olympia, Wash.

P.S.N. PROMOTED THE OLYMPIC PENINSULA

CAPTAIN SAMUEL BARLOW

By the middle of 1915, the Bremerton steamer TOURIST under the command of Captain Samuel Barlow was to begin carrying cars twice daily. Because of the width and location of the TOURIST's boilers, only six cars could be carried each trip.

An ever-so-slight philosophical change had occurred with the announcement of autocarrier service aboard the TOURIST. The Navy Yard Route was the first to recognize the importance of accommodations for the auto, as well as for the passenger. Steamers serviced passengers and hand-trucked or carry-on freight. Existing ferryboats, like the CITY OF SEATTLE and the WEST SEATTLE, carried delivery wagons and buggies as well as passengers. But the TOURIST, a steamer, carried passengers, hand freight, vehicles, and *solicited* automobiles. It was a minor point but a signal that Puget Sound Navigation Company was using good sense. The company was willing to serve the present and anxious to prepare for the future in an effort to capture trade that was forthcoming.

The Navy Yard Route reviewed their vessel for other possible conversions. The H.B. KENNEDY like most steamers of her day had no space for autos. The KITSAP II was limited to a capacity for three cars. When the KITSAP II was acquired by the Navy Yard Route in 1917, thought was given to widening her main deck to carry cars. Shipyards were too busy at the time with war production so the alterations never occurred.

Small steamers were so overcrowded with walk-on passengers that the TOURIST's 5:00 PM trip out of Bremerton was switched to a dock within the naval station. There, yard employees boarded before townspeople were collected at the Bremerton wharf. It was

KITSAP II

soon apparent that a much larger vessel was needed for the route.

THE BAILEY GATZERT WALTZES AWAY WITH GLORY

Puget Sound Navigation Company looked around the Northwest for an appropriate vessel. They spotted the sternwheeler BAILEY GATZERT at Portland. Joshua Green was, perhaps, attracted to the vessel by her name. It was a poignant memory of the man who had opened employers' doors to him as a youth.

Purchase of the BAILEY GATZERT was quickly arranged with her owners, The Dalles, Portland & Astoria Navigation Company. She was towed to Seattle by the tug WALLOWA where she reentered Puget Sound service April 18, 1918.

The BAILEY GATZERT, one of the Sound's best-loved ferryboats was a sternwheeler launched at Ballard Marine Railway in the fall of 1890. She was built by John J. Holland for the Seattle Steam Navigation and Transportation Company, John Leary, president. Launched broadside, the new vessel moved away from the ways under her own steam. The launching party had made the hazardous journey to Ballard by train; was then carried by the new vessel on an excursion to Tacoma and returned safely to Seattle.

Without question, the BAILEY GATZERT was the finest vessel that had yet been launched on Puget Sound. She was named in honor of one of the region's outstanding pioneers who was a former mayor of Seattle.

The sternwheeler's interior decoration reflected the pride of the owners. Interior design was supervised by the British artist Harnett and the panels in the cabin were the work of his own hand. The panels of the engine room were the work of the versatile Captain

H.B. KENNEDY IN DRYDOCK

Howard Penfield, the first to hold the position of mate on the BAILEY GATZERT. Money was lavishly spent to make the BAILEY GATZERT a floating palace.

The new sternwheeler was taken to the Columbia River in 1892 where she was used for excursions until 1895. The *Bailey Gatzert Waltz* was written for the Lewis and Clark Centennial Celebration of 1905. The vessel was used as the Royal Barge for the Portland Rose Festival for several years. Eventually she was relegated to the upper river routes. By 1907 a new hull had to be constructed for her continued use. The house, built with such care, was found to be in excellent condition and was transferred to the new bottom. The Dalles, Portland & Astoria Navigation Company continued to operate the vessel on the Columbia River.

The BAILEY GATZERT's new hull was fully 17 feet longer than the original. She was immediately placed on the Bremerton run to help the TOURIST with auto-carrying duties[4] when Puget Sound Navigation Company purchased her. Everyone became aware of the new carrier because of her mellow chime whistle. It was designed by Captain U.B. Scott for the fast stern-wheeler TELEPHONE and shifted later from the BAILEY GATZERT to the CITY OF BREMERTON.

Captain R.B. Holbrook and Chief Engineer C.R.

Breyman were transferred from the TOURIST to take charge of the BAILEY GATZERT. The newly-arrived sternwheeler surpassed the TOURIST[5] as an autocarrier. She was assigned this exclusive duty with three daily round trips and four on weekends. The H.B. KENNEDY continued as a walk-on passenger carrier; the TOURIST began to haul freight only. The KITSAP II served as a standby boat.

Operating autocarriers became a challenge to some Puget Sound Navigation skippers and a dilemma to others. The change might be compared in the present to the operation of computerized ferries over the previous classes. The company moved their employees frequently to familiarize them with the routes, ports and vessels within their system.

Captain Holbrook was succeeded on the BAILEY GATZERT by Captain Wallace Mangan from the H.B. KENNEDY. Mangan was reassigned to the KENNEDY and Captain Harry Anderson took the BAILEY GATZERT's wheel. Anderson became the youngest

[4]In 1919 the Bremerton Car Ferry was organized and placed in operation to the Navy Yard. All of this stock was acquired by P.S.N. Ibid.

[5]The TOURIST's auto capacity was decreased from six to four due to the increasing size of automobiles at the time.

ELEGANT BAILEY GATZERT

WALLOWA TODAY IS HISTORIC ARTHUR FOSS

master in the Navy Yard's fleet.

Most steamers and ferryboats were not stopped by Seattle's widely acclaimed General Strike, the first in the nation, in February 1919. The company did take added precaution against strikers, though. All spare vessels were towed by the freighter COMANCHE from the tie-up yard in West Seattle to an anchorage near Port Orchard for the duration of the strike. This included the INDIANAPOLIS, CHIPPEWA, IROQUOIS and the POTLATCH.

Needing greater auto capacity, the BAILEY GATZERT entered Todd Shipyards in 1920. Her hull was sponsored out to accommodate 30 automobiles of the day. A 10-ton steam elevator, custom built by Washington Iron Works, Seattle, was installed to assist the loading and off-loading of vehicles. The BAILEY GATZERT became the first steamer on the Sound to be altered for the explicit responsibility of carrying automobiles.[6] She became the first true automobile ferry on the Navy Yard Route. The BAILEY GATZERT's reconstruction was remarkable in that it sparked a revolution of steamer conversions. Rebuilding, redesigning, new construction and new businesses sprang up that would exist until the last mosquito steamer had lost its regular run on Puget Sound. Within ten years, the automobile displaced nearly a century of passenger steaming on the West's largest inland bay. Overnight the old steamboats took the backseat to autoferries on all major Sound routes.

VETERAN CAPTAIN WALLACE MANGAN

CITY OF BREMERTON

One of Puget Sound Navigation Company's first vessels, the WHATCOM, was converted into the auto-ferry CITY OF BREMERTON in 1921, creating much fanfare. This procedure would be followed aboard numerous vessels of the navigation company's fleet and the boats belonging to other steamboat companies. The shipyard would begin by stripping off much of the superstructure above the main deck. The hull of the vessel was sponsored out, giving the boat increased breadth on the auto (main) deck; widening and rounding the bow, and sometimes the stern to fit landing slips. The WHATCOM's power plant was left intact along with the original engine room. Boiler uptakes were narrowed to assure height and width for automobiles. The passenger cabin was built above this deck; its overhead was topped by the boatdeck. The

[6]The FORTUNA on Lake Washington was altered for this purpose in 1919 but she was considered a lake ferry.

wheelhouse and the Texas deck[7] were here.

The result of reconstruction work was a single-ended, "drive-around" ferryboat. The CITY OF BREMERTON landed bow-in at the Seattle terminal. With the aid of a turntable in the stern, cars were looped around to the other side of the vessel and exited over the same bow that they had boarded. In this manner cars no longer were forced to back on or off the ferry in reverse gear as they previously had done.

Charleston was included as a stop on the Bremerton route at that time, but this landing had no ferry slip. Captain Russ Taylor describes the advantages of the CITY OF BREMERTON's turntable:[8]

"On a spring line, starboard side to, cars for exit on the turntable turned to the right, up the elevator to the dock level, two heavy gang planks pulled aboard, and the cars on their way. Cars for Seattle were taken on, thence to Port Orchard and Bremerton direct for a return voyage.

"Charleston was later eliminated [as a stop] and the elevator dismantled [an elevator was on the pier]. Seattle, Bremerton and Port Orchard had ferry slips, the bridge and apron resting on pontoons.

"The Bremerton arrivals backed into the slip, and the Mate gave signals to the pilothouse via electric bell [push button battery-operated doorbell] for maneuvering. In position, the engines were in reverse until signaled—one bell stop. Then closing in, one bell to forward, to slow. The back wash would roll the pontoons downward, and the Mate had to be on the ball, or he had a punctured apron.

"It was dicey at times, but the understanding between Mate and Captain was the main effort for a perfect landing. Under the apron, three bells, slow stern, to keep the ferry under the apron."

Todd Shipyard completed the CITY OF BREMERTON's conversion in 40 days for $100,000. The length of the vessel was not altered [167'4"]. Her beam was widened from 12 feet to 48 feet for six lanes of cars on the main deck. The vertical clearance was 11'6", ample height for trucks in 1921.

[7]Texas deck on a steamboat is the shortened upper deck where officers' cabins are housed.
[8]Letter from Captain Russel Taylor to Walter Green, April 22, 1982.

Captain Harry Anderson was transferred to the CITY OF BREMERTON from the BAILEY GATZERT. The vessel entered the Navy Yard Route November 19, 1921.

WHATCOM BECAME CITY OF BREMERTON

CITY OF BREMERTON

(opposite page) THE BARLOW ELEVATOR REVOLUTIONIZED AUTO AND FREIGHT CARRIERS

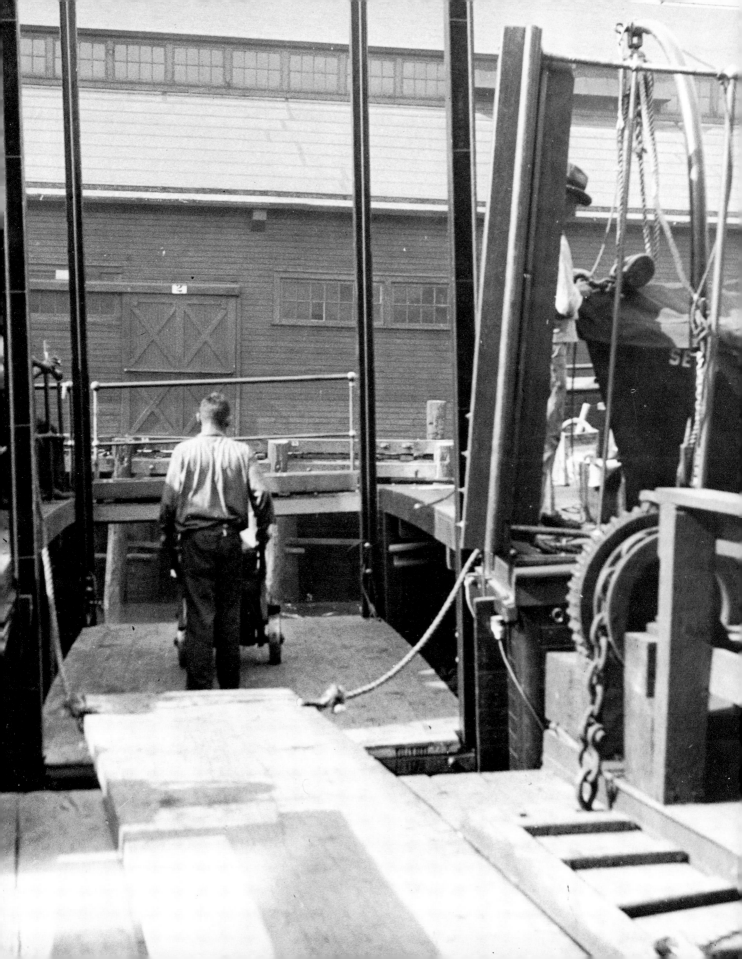

Captain Taylor recalls when he first shipped aboard the CITY OF BREMERTON:[9]

"I had earned my master's license in January 1920, and went captain on the ferryboat WEST SEATTLE shortly thereafter. We worked for King County and that same year they quit the ferry across from Seattle to West Seattle, replacing her with the little AQUILO from Lake Washington.

"When we all got 'fired,' I went with the Dodwell Line & Co. on the old FULTON, carrying paper from Seattle. I wanted to get my pilotage for complete Puget Sound and then that's when P.S.N. called me. They called one Sunday morning and said, 'Can you get down here with an application?'

"I went down and Larry Crowley, he was mate, was moving the CITY OF BREMERTON that morning into the slip. He had docked her, walked off and wouldn't come back. That's when they called me. I went there and with Harry Anderson's help, got the job."

A number of vessels followed the way of the CITY OF BREMERTON. In 1919 there had been only nine fer-ryboats in operation on Puget Sound.[1] By 1923 Puget Sound Navigation Company reported that they had handled 28,000 "machines" to and from Bremerton aboard the "fast and modern ferryboat" CITY OF BRE-MERTON. By August of that same year there were 23 fer-ries in operation on routes extending from Port Town-send to Tacoma and all major points between them.

The Kitsap County Transportation Company,[2] a long time competitor of Puget Sound Navigation Com-pany on several routes, introduced their first com-pany-owned ferry LIBERTY in 1923. Launched from the Lake Union Drydock Yard on Lake Washington and designed by Seattle naval architect, L.H. Coolidge, the LIBERTY entered the Seattle-Port Blakely run. She carried passengers only while awaiting completion of

[9]Authors' interview, January 28, 1981.

[1]These vessels were the WEST SEATTLE, Seattle-West Seattle run; WASHINGTON, Seattle-Vashon-Harper; VASHON ISLAND, Portage-Des Moines; PIONEER, Bremerton-Manette; CENTRAL, Everett-Clinton; gas WHIDBY, Mukilteo-Clinton; sidewheeler CITY OF TACOMA, Tacoma to Gig Harbor; TRANSIT, Titlow Beach-Berg's Landing-Fox Island; and the GUEMES, Anacortes-Guemes.

On Lake Washington three more ferries were in operation: LINCOLN, LESCHI and FORTUNA.

[2]Lyman Hinckley was president and Philip D. Macbride was secre-tary-treasurer of Kitsap County Transportation Company in 1923.

the Port Blakely ferry slip. One week later, she began carrying automobiles. She opened Bainbridge Island to further motorized traffic. The LIBERTY ran three round trips daily from Seattle. Within nine months she is said to have held a place of importance in the life of Bainbridge communities.

By April 1923, four more ferries were under construction for use on Sound routes. The steamboats CITY OF ANGELES and the PUGET of Puget Sound Navigation Company were rebuilt at the Johnson Yard at Port Blakely for $30,000 each. The steam ferry WHIDBY of the Whidby Island Transportation Company[3] was launched at the plant of John Martinolich in Dockton, Washington on March 16. The ferries CITY OF EDMONDS and MOUNT VERNON (Ex-ROBERT BRIDGES) made their appearances. The diesel ferry MOTOR PRINCESS, built at Esquimalt, B.C. by Yarrows, Ltd. made her first round trip for the Canadian Pacific Railway. She ran between Bellingham and Sidney, B.C. MOTOR PRINCESS was the first drive-on, drive-off ferry.[4]

The Marine Digest observed the relationship and progress of automobiles and the marine industry. Editorial comment, January 5, 1924:

> "Conversion of the Sound steamerships into ferryboats, with large space for automobiles, is one of the distinct developments of the new era of growth of the inland sea. The automobile for years hurt Puget Sound water traffic, but with the opening of the great Olympic Peninsula now rapidly becoming one of the national playgrounds for tourists, the increase in automobiling is beginning to help water traffic."

Due to the lack of a route, the CHIPPEWA joined the Navy Yard Route in 1926. She had been idle for years following a stint as a training ship for the U.S. Shipping Board in 1918. Her steel hull remained in excellent condition. Puget Sound Navigation converted her to an autocarrier at Lake Washington Shipyards, Houghton and the CHIPPEWA ferryboat reentered service May 23, 1926. She was licensed to carry 2000 passengers and 90 1926-style cars.

PORT CAPTAIN HARRY ANDERSON

[3]The name "Whidbey Island" was often spelled without the "e" in the early 1900s. Meany, *Origin of Washington's Geographic Names* states that it was erroneously spelled. Discoverer Captain George Vancouver named the island for his sailing master, Joseph Whidbey (spelled *with* the "e.") Charles Wilkes, who commanded the U.S. Exploring Expedition in 1841 and used Vancouver's reports, published the Wilkes' Survey in 1845 and his Puget Sound charts in 1848. Wilkes spelled "Whidby" *without* the "e." J.G. Kohl's "Geographical Memoir," published in *Reports of Explorations and Surveys,* Vol.12, Book 1, Wash. D.C., 1860, also used the "Whidby" spelling. Wilkes's and Kohl's reports were reprinted many times until 1900 when more detailed charts began to appear. The ferry and company name, as well as printed schedules, maps and brochures of the 1920s continued to spell "Whidby" without the "e."

[4]Joshua Green's friend and foe Captain J.W. Troup, manager of the C.P.R.'s B.C. Steamship Service, initiated the building of the MOTOR PRINCESS and her route. The vessel measured 170' x 42.8' x 11.5' of 1243 gross tons. She was built of fir and spruce deck sheathing. She was completed in 97 working days. The ferry carried 45 cars and diesel engines carried her at a speed of 14.5 knots. Clapp, "A Princess that Became A Queen," *Steamboat Bill,* Spring 1982.

CITY OF ANGELES

PUGET

MOUNT VERNON

STEAM FERRY WHIDBY

CITY OF EDMONDS

(opposite page) SEATTLE SCENES

E.W. PEABODY

THE EFFECTS OF AUTOMOBILES
ON THE NORTHWEST

It is interesting to observe the relatively quick rise to popularity and easy acceptance of the automobile, particularly in the West. Beginning as a novelty, they were soon elevated to a medium of pleasure and ''touring.'' Roads improved rapidly and Westerners could travel freely among the coastal states and British Columbia at minor expense. Autos and trucks were just as quickly utilized for practical and commercial purposes. As early as 1923, though, there were grumblings about traffic and the automobile's threatening presence. The mariner's source of news, *The Marine Digest,* April 7, 1923, editorializes this issue:

'Auto vs. Boat'

''A Saturday or Sunday afternoon on any of the Western Washington highways will quickly convince one that the auto has about reached its zenith as a medium of pleasure. If the weather is fair, the roads are crowded and there is not much fun in either driving or in riding. The element of risk is becoming worse all the time. Testimony to that effect can be found in the Monday newspapers.[5]

''The broad reaches of the Sound and the waters of Lake Washington, now invite the pleasure-seeker, offering him freedom from the reckless driver and surcease from the absent-minded pedestrian or the contrary cow. The cruiser, launch and the sailboat give safe access to the beauty spots that cannot be reached by automobile.

''Twenty odd years ago, the Sound used to be dotted with white-winged catboats of a Sunday afternoon, and Lake Washington had a great fleet of private launches. Then came the auto, increasing numbers until it eclipsed boating and yachting as a pleasure.

''But there are signs now that the eclipse is passing. The auto as a medium of pleasure, has about run its course, due to congested highways. But there is no congestion on the Sound or the lake.''

Naturally, ferryboat workers became amateur authorities on the style, size and varieties of automobiles. No doubt, this was a common topic of discus-

[5]In 1922 an average of 22 people were killed daily in automobile accidents in the U.S.A.

sion among them. As a matter of fact, ferry workers today are remarkable consultants if you are in the market for a new or used car. Those workers loading the ferries are adept at guessing the length and breadth of your car. They know which cars notoriously have trouble starting when it is time to disembark. They must be aware of erratic and irresponsible drivers. They probably know who reads the "Stop Your Motor"[6] and "No Smoking" signs on the car deck. As a matter of fact, the car deck of a Washington State ferry is an ideal center for the study of human behavior.

All in all, ferry workers are keen observers, but they do not always share the same opinion. This true story, written in 1927, illustrates the point:[7] [These two gentlemen were shipmates on Lake Washington many years ago.]

"A few Sundays ago, Captain Harry J. Wilson and Captain Russel Taylor got into an argument over the respective looks of the new automobile models. To settle the argument, they bought two copies of the Sunday edition of one of the big Seattle newspapers. From these papers each took an automotive section. The Beach Comber who happened to be present, looked over Captain Taylor's shoulder and glanced at the first picture. Now the auto in that picture may have looked all right, but perched on the radiator was a beautiful young woman in a bathing suit. The next picture showed a nifty sports model and in front of it stood the owner, a radiant creature who had forgotten to bring her skirt along. And so on. Every auto picture included a lovely display of leg.

"At the end of half an hour, Captain Taylor laid down his paper and turned to Captain Wilson.

" 'Well,' demanded Taylor, 'Are you ready to admit now that the Garter sports model has the Silken Eight beaten? Now frankly, which is the niftier automobile?'

" 'Automobile?' repeated Wilson in amazement. 'What are you talking about?'

" 'Why,' returned Taylor, 'you have just studied all of the new autos shown in the paper and now what's your judgement?'

" 'New autos in the paper!' again repeated Wilson, 'I don't think there were

any cars shown in that section of the paper. I didn't notice any cars.' "

THE CHANGING OF THE GUARD

The Navy Yard Route was definitely a money maker compared to many of the numerous ferry routes on the Sound. One reason is attributed to the initiative and promotion activities of the Puget Sound Navigation Company. This company should be credited with popularizing travel to the Olympic Peninsula and opening it to visitors.

The Navigation Company was the State's greatest travel bureau in those days. They no doubt took their cues from their competitors, Canadian Pacific Railway. The C.P.R. set an example of promotion technique, attracting tourists from around the world. The American Express Company sponsored similar tours to Alaska via Seattle. The federally-owned Alaska Railroad sponsored an active campaign to support the building of the railroad and attract travelers and industrialists to the United States' largest underdeveloped territory. Puget Sound Navigation Company was in a position to capitalize on the tourist campaigns of others.

The opening of the Pacific Northwest had a stimulating effect upon the region. Other steamboat and ferry operators, too, put tourism to good works. In June 1922, Captain J.L. Anderson began a water sightseeing trip that proved immensely popular with travelers. Over 3000 more passengers were handled that season than in any previous season. Throughout the summer the steamer ATLANTA made a two-hour tour each day of Elliott Bay, Lake Washington Ship Canal and the Locks, Lake Union and Lake Washington.

The Victoria-Anacortes Company, operating the MOUNT VERNON and the CITY OF ANGELES between Anacortes and Sidney, B.C., enjoyed a major portion of this trade. During the 1923 season they carried 19,800 passengers and 5200 automobiles. It was this company and this route that finally pushed the Canadian Pacific Railway into the decision to build and operate the MOTOR PRINCESS. They responded to a request from the Bellingham Chamber of Commerce to

[6]*The Marine Digest,* April 29, 1925. Collector of Customs, Millard T. Harston, announced the receipt of a letter from D.B. Carson, Commissioner of Navigation, attached to the Department of Commerce, Wash. D.C., warning against failure to stop motors of automobiles aboard ferryboats.

[7]*The Marine Digest,* September 3, 1927. William O. Thorniley was the Beach Comber.

run a Canadian ferry between Bellingham and Sidney.[8]

The Puget Sound Navigation Company took over the Anacortes-Sidney run from its founder, Captain H.W. Crosby, in 1924. They launched such a tremendous publicity campaign that the C.P.R. was forced to retreat. The MOTOR PRINCESS was placed on the Vancouver-Nanaimo run.

The Marine Digest kept a very close eye on the progress of the ferry companies. On January 12, 1928, they offered more insight to their rapid development:

'A GREAT FEAT'

"It is doubtful whether the general public has grasped as yet the full extent of what the Puget Sound Navigation Company and the Navy Yard Route have set out to do in making our section of the country a great goal for tourists. These two companies for years have been developing a plan whose fruition we are to see next summer. It is something far-sighted, something big.

"The plan will reach a climax next summer when the companies will have a new and modern ferryboat on the Port Angeles-Victoria route. They will then be able to offer automobile tourists an outing that probably cannot be duplicated anywhere. The pleasure-seekers will be able to take their autos from Seattle to Bremerton by ferry-boat. From Bremerton they will drive to Hood Canal. They will cross the beautiful canal by ferryboat. Then the great world of the Olympic Peninsula will lie before them, with all the lure and fascination of forests, mountains, and wilderness. After touring the wilderness, the autoists will drive to Port Angeles and thence across the Strait of Juan de Fuca to Vancouver Island on the new ferryboat. They will follow drives through the scenic wonders of the great island. After touring the island, autoists will drive to Sidney where they will board a ferryboat for Anacortes, passing through the San Juan Islands, famous as one of the world's beauty spots. From Anacortes the pleasure-seekers will drive back to Seattle, their starting point.

"That tour will soon become famous all over the United States and Canada. It will rank as a super attraction. It will give us a new status in the world of lovers of the outdoors beautiful."[9]

Relations between P.S.N. and C.P.R. began to improve as the Olympic Peninsula opened up. Both companies recognized the value of a circle of highways connecting British Columbia and Washington with speedy ferries. Competitiveness became overshadowed with cooperation. P.S.N. rebuilt the SIOUX in 1924 as the ferry OLYMPIC and introduced her to a new direct run between Port Angeles and Victoria. Travelers could also take the C.P.R.'s MOTOR PRINCESS to Bellingham that year, drive to Seattle, ferry to Bremerton, drive up the Olympic Peninsula, ferry from Port Angeles to Victoria and ferry to Vancouver. Any number of variations and sidetrips were possible. P.S.N. and C.P.R. boats were the common denominators to all routes.

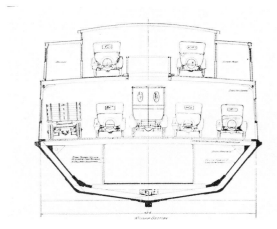

BROCHURE FOR C.P.R.'s MOTOR PRINCESS

[8]Clapp, "A Princess that Became A Queen," *Steamboat Bill.*

[9]One of the tasks of William O. Thorniley who was public relations director for P.S.N. for 20 years was to promote the Olympic Peninsula. He was also president of the Olympic Peninsula Hotel and Restaurant owners, a division of A.A.A.

By 1921 Joshua Green had acquired 48 per cent of the Navy Yard Route. The balance of the company stock was acquired by Puget Sound Navigation Company with the exception of six shares.[1] Captain William E. Mitchell was the manager of the Navy Yard Route at the time, having filled that office since 1917. F.E. Burns had retired from the general managership of P.S.N. by 1921 and Mitchell was promoted. He served in the combined office of general manager for both companies.

Mitchell was an example of the type of men who managed the steamers and ferries for the company. Born at Coupeville, Whidbey Island, in 1879, he was the son of Western pioneers. His father, Emerson Mitchell, was a native of Maine and spent early years of his life in the shipbuilding industry at Bath. He joined the gold rush to California in 1849. He headed further north in 1855. After his marriage to a New England sweetheart, Emerson Mitchell returned to Puget Sound in 1866. He was employed at Coupeville by Pope & Talbot's Puget Sound Mill Company until his death in 1907.

Captain William Mitchell lived at Coupeville until he was 17. It was the story of the boy and the farm. He spent his vacations driving a team of horses hitched to an old fashioned hay-hauling machine, giving him plenty of time to think about his future. The horses were changed each day at noon but Mitchell had to work from morning until night. Concluding that he was as good as a horse, the boy decided to enter steamboating. There he assumed he would receive treatment equal to the horse. The year was 1896.

Mitchell shipped as cabinboy on the LYDIA THOMPSON, operating between Seattle and Bremerton. The series of vessels he worked aboard included the WASCO, CITY OF DENVER, ALBION in the Seattle-Everett-Whidbey Island Route; the GREYHOUND, Olympia to Everett; the PERDITA on the Seattle-Hood Canal Route; and the INLAND FLYER, CAPITAL CITY, PORT ORCHARD and the STATE OF WASHINGTON on the Seattle-Navy Yard Route.

Mitchell worked his way up on the vessels from cabinboy, deckhand, and nightwatchman to mate and finally, master. He was skipper of the INLAND FLYER, CITY OF DENVER, PORT ORCHARD, ALBION, CAPITAL CITY, PERDITA and the STATE OF WASHINGTON.

Receiving his master's license in 1901, Mitchell commanded vessels of the Navy Yard Route from that time on. He was the first master of the new H.B. KEN-

[1]*Report of the Investigation of Earnings of the Puget Sound Navigation Company,* May 1947.

FERRY OLYMPIC

THE SLEEK AND FAST GREYHOUND

STEAMER PORT ORCHARD

NEDY in 1909, covering over 408,000 miles in that steamer during his eight years as commander.[2]

When Captain Mitchell joined the ATHLON in February 1901, that vessel constituted the entire fleet of the Navy Yard Route owned by H.B. Kennedy. Bremerton was a village of a few scattered houses and the Navy Yard was in its infancy. By 1925 Mitchell was directing the operation of the largest inland fleet in the nation. He continued as manager until 1929 and, having acquired stock in the Whidby Island Transportation Company and the Washington Route, Inc., he became president of those two corporations. In 1933, Mitchell was appointed general manager of Kitsap County Transportation Company, the major competitor of Puget Sound Navigation Company.

A number of changes were yet to occur within the Puget Sound Navigation Company. In retrospect, it is somewhat ironic that new people appeared within the company almost all at once. Following chapters will tell their stories.

Enoch W. Peabody, grandson of the late Captain E.W. Peabody of the Atlantic Black Ball ships, was at sea aboard the five-masted barkentine FOREST PRIDE on the night of August 12, 1926. They had sailed from Seattle July 2, two days before the holiday on the Fourth, so that the crew would not have to be paid for a day they did not work. That evening in August, "Woody" Peabody had a dream that his father, Charles E. Peabody, was dead. The next morning he reported the dream to his captain. He was smartly reprimanded for superstition and "making trouble for himself." The skipper reluctantly recorded Woody's remarks in the ship's log that day. A telegram was waiting at their next port. "Charles E. Peabody has passed away," it read.[3]

In July the following year, Joshua Green resigned as president of Puget Sound Navigation Company to resume his interest in banking. Gradually he had purchased controlling stock in the People's Saving & Trust Company. He was ready to assume its presidency. Joshua Green, master mariner, ship owner, and ferry fleet designer, retired from the sea.

P.S.N. CONVERTED A NUMBER OF THE STEAM PASSENGER CARRIERS TO FERRYBOATS, INCLUDING THE SPACIOUS IROQUOIS

[2] *The Marine Digest,* March 21, 1925, page 5.

[3] Authors' interview with E.W. Peabody, 1982.

STEAMBOAT MEN TURNED FERRYBOAT OPERATORS

A young man known as Henry A. Hansen, born at Cannon Falls, Minnesota moved west with his family to Tacoma in 1888. His father, Captain J.J. Hansen[1] bought the steamer and harbor tug QUICKSTEP. It was on this vessel that the founder of the second largest ferryboat company on Puget Sound gained his sea legs.

The Hansen family moved to Poulsbo nine years later, and played an active part in the affairs of the community. The family placed the QUICKSTEP on the mail run between Port Madison and Poulsbo. To improve their service they built another vessel, the steamer HATTIE HANSEN. The HATTIE HANSEN carried the mail for another ten years. The QUICKSTEP was traded to Captain Kraft on Lake Washington for machinery for yet another new vessel.

The family enterprise was so successful that the Hansens formed the Hansen Transportation Company. Through its operation they were among the first to run vessels between Seattle and Liberty Bay. Formally organizing in 1898, the company sponsors included Captain J.J. and H.A. Hansen, O.L. Hansen and Captain A. Hostmark.[2] Captain Henry Hansen was master of their boats, the HATTIE HANSEN and the SENTINEL, a steamer operated by the company for two years.

As steamboat operators the Hansens always insisted on strict observance of time schedules. One of the sons, O.L. Hansen had had an experience as a lad that forcibly impressed this need for rules on him. When visiting one of the small Sound communities that was served by a tiny steamboat, he boarded the vessel, homeward bound. A half-hour passed, then an hour. Hansen and the other passengers grew impatient. There was nothing they could do to improve the situation. Finally, after an hour and a half past the scheduled departure time, the truant skipper appeared. Indignant protest was voiced on all sides.

''Now look here,'' objected the master, ''I couldn't help it! My wife wanted to come to town to buy a new hat and I had to arguefy her out of it. She don't need a new hat. She got one three years ago.'' He stepped into the pilothouse growling that the passengers were ''derned unreasonable.'' O.L. Hansen never forgot the incident.[3]

Captains Hansen and Hostmark made a success of the original company after several years of diligent work. It was soon necessary to expand their enterprise. A bitter rate war ensued between Captain Hansen on the SENTINEL and Captain Moe of the Moe Brothers on the RELIANCE. Both skippers ran vessels across Dog Fish Bay.[4] These rate wars were notoriously ruthless. Steamboatmen would go to almost any lengths to attract passengers. They even resorted to baby-snatching on the assumption that the child's mother would follow. She was a paying-fare customer.[5] Races and the inevitable collisions were common. The vessels would try to beat their competition to the docks to be the first to load freight and passengers.

CAPTAIN A. HOSTMARK

[1] J.J. Hansen was engaged in the machinery business in Minnesota, selling harvesters and other farm equipment. He took the same business to Boxton, North Dakota, before moving to Tacoma and abandoning it for good. *The Marine Digest,* April 10, 1926, p. 7.

[2] Captain H.A. Hansen and O.L. Hansen were the sons of J.J. Hansen while Captain A. Hostmark was a son-in-law.

[3] Ibid.

[4] Later renamed as it is presently known as Liberty Bay. This was named for the two farms located there: Liberty Place and Liberty Bunch.

[5] Newell, *Marine History,* p. 111.

Fearing that land sales would drop because of the rate wars and to reassure the frightened passengers who had to tolerate poor conduct, Warren L. Gazzam, a land speculator, purchased the RELIANCE. He entered into an agreement with the Hansens to leave the RELIANCE on the Dog Fish Bay run and place the SENTINEL on the longer Harper-Colby-West Bainbridge Island-Brownsville run.

Gazzam was an insurance man too, and his associates acquired a substantial interest in the Hansen corporation. Officially the name was changed to Kitsap County Transportation Company, March 1905. The company's new smokestack emblem, the white collar, was a white metal band encircling the stack with a red or black "K" painted on each side of the collar. This emblem was soon recognized for its reputation of speed and service during nearly forty years on Puget Sound.

W.L.Gazzam became president and general manager of the Kitsap County company. He continued in that capacity until major changes occurred during 1917. The fast steamboats,the KITSAP[6] and the HYAK, were added in 1905 and 1908. Other vessels included the BURTON (1907-1910, 1911-1923), the FALCON (1913-1919), the VASHON II and the TOLO.The company later built the KITSAP II which made 21 knots on her trial trip.

The HYAK was chartered to Western Steel Corporation of Irondale, Washington, to operate from Seattle to Irondale and Port Townsend. The HYAK made two round trips per day. A bitter rate war raged between Puget Sound Navigation Company's president, Joshua Green, and W.L.Gazzam. That was the beginning of a

persistant competition that lasted until one of the companies could no longer withstand the battle.

In 1917 the Kitsap County Transportation Company's controlling interest changed hands again; this time it went to a man who was considered a youth in the tough steamboat business. Lyman D. Hinckley was 38 years old when he and his financial partner, attorney Philip D. Macbride, teamed up to purchase the company. Though younger than most, Hinckley was not a newcomer to steamboating. He could truthfully state his business introduction occurred when Benjamin Harrison was President of the United States. Hinckley landed a job on a Lake Union steamboat when he was only 13 years old.

Hinckley was born in a house on the west shore of Lake Union. His father, T.D. Hinckley was an early pioneer in Seattle. He had traveled west over the new road built in 1853 through Natchess Pass. T.D. Hinckley settled on the lake and worked as an engineer on the inland waters. He became known as one of the earliest steamboatmen on Puget Sound. Later he built the Hinckley Block on the southwest corner of Second Avenue and Columbia.[7]

Lyman Hinckley attended the old Denny School and Mercer School. At 13, with no further schooling available to him in Seattle, he held jobs as deckhand, fireman and engineer on the boats MAUD FOSTER[8]

[6]Built by Joseph Supple, Portland, Oregon.

[7]Circa 1890. *The Marine Digest*, May 5, 1923.

[8]Captain Harry Marsh, a resident of Seattle from 1889 until his death in 1936, was an engineer aboard the MAUD FOSTER which was the first steamboat on Lake Union in the early 1890s.

KITSAP II

KITSAP

VASHON II

STEAMER HYAK

and the D.T.DENNY. These vessels were engaged with log towing from the Western Mill on the lake[9] plus passenger and freight carrying across the lake to Edgewater and Brooklyn (University District).

In 1897 Hinckley left a job with the Great Northern Express to help build the Moran Brother's steamboats at Dutch Harbor, Alaska. They would navigate the Yukon River for the Klondike gold rush. Hinckley worked on the sternwheelers KLONDYKE, JOHN CUDAHY, and the T.C. POWER in the time-honored position of "rivet-holder."

The boilers for these riverboats were designed and manufactured in Seattle and one was placed in the hold of each ship. At Dutch Harbor the design was radically altered and the boilers were placed on the sternwheelers' decks. As a slender youth, Hinckley's job was to crawl inside each boiler to hold the rivets for fastening the boiler plates. His job was based on size not experience; he was the only man at Dutch Harbor small enough to get inside the boilers.

By the age of 18, Hinckley had already made three trips up the Yukon River and back. He was first on the T.C. POWER as oiler, then twice on the KLONDYKE as an unlicensed engineer. Returning to Seattle in 1898, he rejoined the Great Northern Express Company and became a messenger between Seattle and Kalispell, Montana.

After such a varied career, Hinckley decided that

he should reenter the water transportation field. His friendship with the young waterfront attorney, Philip D. Macbride, led to a business venture that included another mutual friend, George Russell[1]. The three partners organized the Kingston Transportation Company in 1913. They offered service between Ballard and Kingston, via way points in the passenger and freight operations.

Their first vessel was the gas boat MAY B.2, on which, for the first four months, Lyman Hinckley acted as master. George Russell took command for the next year and a half. The company bought the steamboat KINGSTON for the freight and passenger route between Seattle, Kingston and Port Ludlow. Russell shifted over to the berth of purser on the KINGSTON (Ex-DEFIANCE of 1901).In the years that followed the company extended their operations in the routes to

[9]Site of the present day U.S. Naval Reserve Station, Lake Union.

[1]George Russell once thought he would get away from the sea and its affairs, but the lure of salt water proved too much. He was born in Nova Scotia in 1879, coming west with his family at the age of 10. On completion of schooling at New Westminster, B.C., he entered the salmon cannery trade, working in the fishing and net departments. He moved to Seattle in 1902, returned to the salmon trade on the Fraser River, B.C., in 1903 and 1904 before returning permanently to Seattle. In 1904 he began working for T.D. Hinckley in property management. He stayed in association with that company and the T.D. Hinckley estate until 1913 when the Kingston Transportation Company was formed.

Port Townsend, San Juan Islands and Bremerton. On the latter run they operated the BREMERTON (Ex-KITSAP). Russell served as purser on these routes also.

Hinckley managed the office affairs for the company and forged steadily ahead as a prominent Puget Sound steamboat operator. Partner Macbride prospered as one of the city's foremost attorneys. Later, he became president of the Board of Regents of the University of Washington.[2] In 1917 this team purchased the well-established Kitsap County Transportation Company from W.L. Gazzam. Hinckley became president, Macbride was secretary-treasurer and Captains A. Hostmark and H.A. Hansen and O.L. Hansen[3] continued as stockholders and members of the board of directors. George Russell became purser of the fast steamboat HYAK in the Seattle-Poulsbo route. He later became superintendent of the Kitsap company. He had obtained a mate's license by that time and could serve

as pilot in Puget Sound waters.

Kitsap County Transportation Company was one of the first to invest in the construction and ownership of autoferries. In the winter of 1922-23 they rebuilt the steamer LIBERTY into the autoferry LIBERTY.[4] The company would prove that they could build a profitable business in ferryboating. The conditions under which the LIBERTY's trial run was staged attracted attention to the company. They were not soon forgotten.

Lyman Hinckley had invited a large number of prominent individuals to accompany the LIBERTY on the trial trip from Seattle to Bainbridge Island and return. As the guests assembled on the old ferry dock at the foot of Marion Street, they found a 35-mile an hour gale whipping up heavy, frothing Puget Sound seas. The foam-crested swells tempted the guests to turn tail and retreat to warm comfortable homes and offices. There was indecision and irate discussion on all sides. One kindly gentleman saved the event. Captain J.S. Gibson[5] came along ready to go aboard. With a stern and determined stance, he glared at the hesitant throng.

"All right gentlemen," he said. "Come on, it's time to go aboard." He headed for the ferry slip.

"But what about the storm?" someone called out.

"Just a little blow," returned the captain. "Why the Sound's as smooth as a millpond." He strode aboard. Everybody followed. The affair was considered a pleasant outing for most guests that day. Some did suffer from *mal de mer* and the wind blew one distinquished guest's hat overboard. Refreshments were served in the cabin aft of the pilothouse on the upper deck, where the effect of plunging waves was felt the most.

The Hinckley regime of Kitsap County Transportation Company improved service with their own ferry KITSAP in 1925 to Vashon Island. They continued to serve Bainbridge Island, Poulsbo (passenger only) and the mainland points on the other side of the Sound. By 1923, the company owned and operated seven fast carriers and leased two of the King County ferryboats. Of its own fleet, the HYAK ran between Seattle and Poulsbo, the BREMERTON was on the Seattle-Port Madison-Manzanita-Brownsville route; the VASHON II covered the Seattle-Rolling Bay run; the SUQUAMISH[6] was on the Seattle-Fletcher Bay run; the ferryboat LIBERTY[7] carried vehicles on the Seattle-Port Blakely route, and the VERONA served as a relief and freight carrier. The company leased the county ferryboats WASHINGTON

[2]Philip D. Macbride, born in Iowa City, Iowa, March 21, 1887, was the son of Dr. Thomas Macbride, widely known as the president of the University of Iowa. (*The Marine Digest*, January 30, 1926, p. 5). Philip Macbride became the president of the Shipowner's Association, vice president of the Kitsap County Transportation Company and a large property owner of the Seattle business section. He was the financial influence that eventually intertwined a number of Puget Sound transportation companies, as well as serving as their legal counsel.

[3]O.L. Hansen sold his interest in the company September 15, 1925 when he retired to devote his time to a mercantile business in Poulsbo. He and his partner, Captain Hostmark, handled automobiles, hardware and groceries.

[4]The LIBERTY replaced the steamer MONTICELLO on the Seattle-Port Blakely run. She was commissioned at the end of February 1923.

[5]Founder of the International Stevedoring Company, Captain Gibson devoted the last 15 years of life to the advancement of Elliott Bay, giving Seattle vigorous leadership, helping to stabilize the city as the premier port of the Pacific Northwest. (This story was retold in *The Marine Digest,* July 24, 1943, p. 1).

[6]Leithead, "The White Collar Line," *The Sea Chest,* Volume 5, p. 8. The SUQUAMISH was the first diesel-powered passenger carrier in the United States; she was also known as the "HYAK'S PUP."

[7]LIBERTY ferryboat: Ex-CITY OF EVERETT, Ex-steamer LIBERTY, LIBERTY ferryboat, then BALLARD ferryboat.

SUQUAMISH UNDER CONSTRUCTION

STEAMER BREMERTON WAS ON THE SEATTLE-PORT
MADISON-MANZANITA-BROWNSVILLE ROUTE

(opposite page) LIBERTY FERRYBOAT BUILT FOR KITSAP
COUNTY TRANSPORTATION COMPANY

and WEST SEATTLE for service on the Seattle-Vashon Heights-Harper route.

CAPTAIN CHANCE WIMAN

With the company's lease for the King County vessels and the acquisition of the steamer VERONA,[8] Kitsap County Transportation Company hired one of the most fascinating characters of the Puget Sound passenger fleet. Captain Chance Wiman had navigated the inland waters for 40 continuous years. He played a distinctive role as a participant and an observer of one of the most gripping labor events on the Sound.

Chauncey E. Wiman was a resident of Washington from 1874 until 1935. He was born in Belleville, Ontario, Canada, in May 1863, to Mr. and Mrs. S.P. Wiman. In 1874, his father moved the family to Olympia to engage in the logging industry. Chance Wiman followed suit, occupied in the same business until May 1, 1884.

It was that spring day that Wiman sauntered aboard the Sound freighter LOTTIE at her dock in Olympia and changed the course of his life. He asked Captain Patrick Doyle, the master, for a job. He was hired as deckhand and the LOTTIE, a propeller vessel, got underway. She carried lime from Roche Harbor to the up-Sound ports. Seattle and Tacoma were then small but bustling communities. Port Townsend was still the shipping center of Puget Sound. It was there that the Customs House seemed established for all time; it was there that ships from around the world entered and cleared.

Wiman changed over to the sternwheeler MESSENGER at the end of the first summer, 1884, working in the freight and passenger business in the Shelton-Olympia-Tacoma route.[9] Passenger fares charged were $1 for the trip from Tacoma to Olympia. The Seattle-Olympia fare was $1.50.

One year as deckhand aboard the MESSENGER was enough for Wiman. He transferred to the sternwheeler CLARA BROWN. The CLARA BROWN was carrying freight and passengers in the Shelton-Olympia-Tacoma-Seattle run, too. Once each week the vessel made a side trip, going either to Roche Harbor for lime or to the LaConner flats for oats and potatoes.

Most of the Sound carriers burned cord wood for fuel. Steaming coal at that time was not widely used due to its outrageous price, $2.50 to $3.00 a ton.[1]

Wiman stayed three years on the CLARA BROWN as a deckhand, fireman, then mate. When he obtained

CAPTAIN CHAUNCEY E. WIMAN

[8]The steamer VERONA was sold to Kitsap County Transportation Company by the Union Navigation Company of Poulsbo in 1923.

[9]Later a route of the Puget Sound Freight Lines and their carriers.

[1]*The Marine Digest*, May 10, 1924, p. 7. The *Digest* compared these prices with their current prices at $5 a cord of wood and $6 to $6.50 per ton of coal. They blamed these increases on "higher costs of production."

SUQUAMISH

his master's license, he was appointed to the command of the ESTELLA. This vessel had been chartered for one year to the Tacoma Chamber of Commerce. In an effort to build up trade, the Chamber of Commerce operated the vessel between Tacoma and Sydney (Port Orchard), near Bremerton. At the end of the year, Wiman was appointed master of the DES MOINES, operating between Tacoma and Gig Harbor. He held that command slightly more than three years. About 1894 he decided to get into business for himself.

Wiman bought half-interest in the passenger and freight service organized by F.B. Bibbins on the Tacoma-Quartermaster Harbor run. Their company was called Bibbins & Wiman. They owned and operated the steamer SOPHIA and built the NORWOOD in 1899 at the Haskell & Crawford yard in Old Town, Tacoma. Their partnership dissolved in 1904 when Bibbins retired. The NORWOOD was sold to F.G. Reeve, the Washington Route president, in 1905.

Wiman believed in family involvement in business. U.S. Marine Inspection records show that Gertrude Wiman, his wife, was granted a second class pilot's license in 1907 at Seattle. She is believed to be the second woman in the Pacific Northwest to pilot steamboats.[2]

Wiman and John Manson[3] joined efforts to form the Vashon Navigation Company. They built the

steamer VASHON at the Martinolich Yard at Dockton, Vashon Island. Manson was the former engineer of the Puget Sound Dry Dock Company, owned by St. Paul & Tacoma Mill Company. Its Dockton drydock was the only one on Puget Sound for large vessels. The partners built the VERONA in 1910 at Martinolich's Yard and seven years later built the VASHON II at the yard of Charles E. Taylor[4] at Burton, Vashon Island.

The VERONA afforded Captain Wiman, her master, a permanent docket in Northwest history. It was also an incident that changed the course of his life.

[2]Captain Minnie Hill, Portland, Oregon, was licensed to pilot the sternwheeler GOV. NEWELL. She was reputedly the *first* woman to hold a steamboat license in this region. Newell, *Marine History*, p. 132.

[3]Peter Manson, Captain John Manson's brother, formed the marine construction company of P. Manson & Son with his son, Harry E. Manson (born 1891 in Tacoma). Nephew Harry worked on the vessels of the Vashon Navigation Company and learned some of his earliest lessons from Captain Wiman. After graduation from the University of Washington in 1914, Harry joined his father's firm. He was also one of the owners of the Tacoma Machine Works and the Vashon Navigation Co. Manson Construction Company built a number of the docks, piers and shoreside facilities for the ferry fleets of Puget Sound.

[4]Taylor later became manager of the Lake Washington Shipyards in the 1920s.

On Sunday morning, November 5, 1916,[5] Captain Wiman landed the VERONA at a Seattle pier for her regular run to Everett. Laughing and singing labor songs, over 200 men purchased tickets for passage aboard the VERONA. An equal number awaited the arrival of the steamer CALISTA.[6] The majority of Wiman's passengers that day were a high-spirited lot from the membership of the Industrial Workers of the World, casually referred to as the "Wobblies." They were headed for a march on the City of Everett to demonstate to the "sheriff and vigilantes . . . the boss-ruled gang of Everett,"[7] that the mill owners would not be allowed to crush union organization.

Everett citizens had been tipped off to the impending invasion of the VERONA's passengers. The sheriff and his deputies were planted on the Everett pier fully armed. They were prepared for any battle that might ensue. Hundreds of spectators lined the hillside above the waterfront, displaying human curiosity, anquish and fear.

Wiman approached the pier in Port Gardner Bay with some trepidation. As the engines slowed, cheers rang from the supportive spectators and were returned by the VERONA's union crowd. The sheriff and his deputies moved toward the landing as a deckhand tossed the mooring line to the wharfinger who secured it to a piling. The gangplank was quickly in place. The Wobblies pushed en masse to disembark; the Everett sheriff stepped forward, his gun raised. He shouted at them to halt.

A gunshot rang through the air. Pandemonium ignited on the pier. Shots were fired from land and ship. Gunfire raked the VERONA's deck as deputies fired from concealed portholes on tugboats surrounding the steamer. Wobblies and VERONA's crew were caught in their crossfire. After what must have seemed an eternity, but actually lasting only two or three minutes, the VERONA's engines were engaged at full speed; and bursting the ship's lines, Captain Wiman speedily steered the VERONA into the safety of the bay.

Wobblies aboard ship silently anticipated more violence as they neared Seattle. Officials waited there with warrants for their arrest. Having had enough for

[5]VERONA had replaced CITY OF EVERETT on December 18, 1915.

[6]CALISTA was launched at Quartermaster Harbor August 12, 1911, for the Island Transportation Company and named for the mother of Captain H.B. Lovejoy, manager of the firm. (*The Sea Chest*, Vol. 4.) CALISTA received the engine and boiler from the company's steamer WHIDBY, consumed by fire May 9, 1911.

[7]Clarke, Norman H., *Mill Town*, p. 200.

this round, the labor group realized that theirs was a battle fraught with tears and strife, not just their laughter and songs. Five men were known to be dead or dying, 27 lay wounded on the deck. No one had counted the number of men who had fallen over the side in the fight.[8] History has not recorded the name of the delinquent VERONA's purser if, indeed, there was one that day. A count of the number of paid fares did not exist; no one guessed when the passengers boarded that such a record would be so important.

Captain Wiman sold out his interests in the VERONA and the Vashon Navigation Company in 1919. He joined King County's ferryboat fleet as master of the double-ended ferryboat VASHON ISLAND. Later he commanded the ferry WASHINGTON, operating in the Seattle-Vashon Heights-Harper route. At the end of 1921 Kitsap County Transportation Company assumed control of the county ferry fleet on the Sound, retaining Captain Wiman aboard the WASHINGTON. He served on that vessel until the company built the diesel-powered autoferry KITSAP, the first of the company's ultra-modern motor fleet. Wiman was promoted to command the new vessel and stayed on her bridge until his retirement to a Vashon farm in 1928.

In retirement, Wiman is said to have found that raising a flock of geese was as difficult as managing a steamboat.[9]

VERONA

STEAMER CALISTA LOADED UNION MEN FOR EVERETT

[8]It is estimated that between 6 and 12 perished this way. An equal number of Everett deputies were wounded and/or killed on the pier. Ibid, p. 207.

[9]Captain Wiman passed away September 12, 1935, aged 72, after 44 years of service on the Sound.

FAST FERRY SERVICE FOR A CHANGE

Kitsap County Transportation Company was prepared to establish the initial *fast* ferry service between downtown Seattle and Port Blakely in 1923. Under the terms of the contract with Port Blakely Mill Company, one of the Kitsap Company's passenger carriers was to be converted to a ferryboat for the new service. The mill company[1] owned 1600 acres of undeveloped land on Bainbridge Island, including 1000 acres at Port Blakely. This land was to be developed and opened up to buyers. Direct ferry service for commuters was essential. The company expected the newly converted carrier to provide 35-minute service on the Seattle-Port Blakely run.

The Kitsap Company assumed operation of the Port Blakely Mill Company's steamer MONTICELLO until the launching of the LIBERTY in 1923. The LIBERTY carried 35 automobiles. When conditions warranted, the mill company was to join the Kitsap stockholders in building a larger, faster vessel, carrying 65 to 75 automobiles and costing approximately $200,000.

In April 1923, the Kitsap County Transportation Company purchased the Poulsbo Transportation Company and all interests. The sale included the Union Navigation Company of Poulsbo, owners of the VERONA which was operated by the Poulsbo Transportation Company. The deal also included machinery from the wrecked ATHLON and an uncompleted wooden hull on the ways at Lemolo.

It was a very busy spring for a growing ferry company. Philip Macbride sold his stock in the company to Lyman Hinckley. In March 1924, the company launched the ferry HIYU for the Fletcher Bay-Brownsville route. The HIYU's Chinook Indian jargon name translated, meant "plenty, much"[2] but the little HIYU measured only 65 feet long with a 28 foot beam.

The Marine Digest gave the following account of the launching in the March 15, 1924 issue, accompanied by a photo of Miss Alice Moran:

"The Lake Washington Shipyards, a corporation headed by Charles A. Burkhardt, of Seattle, staged its first launching last Saturday afternoon when it sent the hull of the new automobile ferryboat HIYU into the water for the Kitsap County Transportation Company. The yard is located at Houghton, near Kirkland on the east shore of Lake Washington. Charles E. Taylor, veteran Northwest shipbuilder, who is manager of the plant, was warmly congratulated on the success of the initial launching.

"Miss Alice Moran, daughter of Sherman Moran who was associated with his famous brother, Robert Moran, in founding the Seattle steel shipbuilding industry, christened the new ferryboat. With the sponsor on the christening platform were her parents; Mr. and Mrs. Taylor; Miss Hazel L. Hopkins; Lyman Hinckley, president of the Kitsap County Transportation Company; and James King, manager of the King and Winge Shipbuilding Company.

"The Houghton yard originally was established in the war period [WWI] by Captain John L. Anderson and changed hands several times in the period following the war. Last year it was bought by Lake Washington Shipyards. All through the winter, manager Taylor kept a force of more than 200 men steadily employed. As shown in the photograph in this department, the plant is now engaged in repair, overhaul and installation work on a large fleet of commercial vessels, including nearly 30 cannery tenders. The yard this week completed the last of eight scows built for Alaska Consolidated Canneries.

"Manager Taylor reports that the outlook for the coming season is bright."

MISS ALICE MORAN

[1]Partners D.E. Skinner and John W. Eddy owned Port Blakely Mill Company.
[2]William O. Thorniley's papers, "Origin of Indian Names of Puget Sound Vessels, Past and Present."

The photograph accompanying the article on Lake Washington Shipyards identifies the vessels as follows:

"In the ways near the center is seen the new cannery tender under construction and between this hull and the water is the hull of the new ferryboat HIYU, ready for the launching. To the right appears the Alaska cannery motorship VIRGINIA IV and beyond her, at the end of the dock, is the codfisher ALICE, getting ready for the coming season. On the ways to the right of the VIRGINIA IV is the cannery tender ALF of Alaska Consolidated Canneries. The white sailing vessel on the right is the schooner BIANCA and moored on her right side appears the motorship MURIEL. All told there were 25 cannery tenders at the plant in addition to the vessels named. The white steamship on the extreme right is the PRINCETON, now owned by Captain A.R. Bissett of Vancouver, B.C."

Lyman Hinckley was stricken with a fatal heart attack in December 1924. The future of the Kitsap County Transportation Company seemed unpredictable as the new year approached in the face of the young president's death. Hinckley had been one of the few leading men of the Seattle waterfront to be licensed both as master and marine engineer for waters of Puget Sound. The company recovered from the shock of Hinckley's death by retiring part-owner George Russell from the company vessels and bringing him ashore as superintendent of the company. He continued in that capacity for several years.

Sherman Moran, formerly the vice president, succeeded to the company's presidency. Bert S. Murley was appointed general manager.

Murley, who had been associated with Kitsap County Transportation Company for eight years at the time, was 39 years old. Born in Plattsville, Illinois in 1885, he was, like a number of other Seattle shipping men, raised on a farm in the corn belt. It was there that he learned to work hard and use his own initiative.

At the age of 21, Murley reasoned that a seaport city had every opportunity to be found in an inland city with the additional opportunities provided by the sea and ships. Murley packed his bags and arrived in Seattle about 1906.

He logged for a time, patiently scouting out his future. In 1907 he moved to Poulsbo, where he opened a hardware business and no doubt became acquainted with the Hansen family, by then already associated with the Kitsap County Transportation Company, as well as the mercantile trade. Murley observed that Poulsbo depended upon shipping for its intercourse with the world, especially as a homeport of the great Puget Sound halibut fleet. Its atmosphere was, and is today, maritime.

Murley switched from hardware to shipping in October 1916 when he became the assistant of W.L. Gazzam, controlling stockholder of the Kitsap company. The following spring, when Hinckley and associates bought out Gazzam's interest, Murley was immediately promoted to general agent. His remarkable record in this capacity later secured him the job of general manager. In this position, Murley was executive head of the ferry fleet. He continued in that position throughout the later sales of the company to John Anderson, to the Puget Sound Navigation Company and the Black Ball Line until the Kitsap County Transportation's "White Collar Line" was totally dissolved. Thus, Murley served the same company under four regimes: Gazzam, Hinckley, Anderson and Peabody.

March 28, 1925, a brief notice appeared in *The Marine Digest*:

"Captain John L. Anderson, who with associates recently purchased the Hinckley interests in the Kitsap County Transportation Company, on Wednesday afternoon was elected president and manager of the company. The election was held at a meeting of the trustees of the corporation in its offices at Pier 3.

"Other officials elected are Philip Macbride, vice president; Alpheus Byers, general counsel; Bert S. Murley, secretary and treasurer. Mr. Macbride and Mr. Byers were associated with Anderson when they acquired controlling interest in the Kitsap County Transportation Company. Papers for the transfer of interest of the late Lyman Hinckley in the company to Captain John Anderson and associates were signed last week."

The Puget Sound Navigation Company's dominance of the passenger routes would be newly challenged with Anderson's ownership of Kitsap County Transportation Company. The Kitsap County company would be responsible for some of the finest ferries ever built on the inland sea.

FERRIES AND STEAMERS REQUIRED MAINTENANCE, HERE K.C.T.C. BOATS ARE FOUND AT KING & WINGE SHIPYARD

COMPETITION AMONG FERRY LINES

The automobile changed steamboating in the Pacific Northwest; autoferries changed marine enterprise on Puget Sound. Steamboat operations represented, for the most part, family or individually owned vessels and controlling companies. The dog-eared phrase "everybody and his brother" was literally true within the mosquito fleet. As the cities grew, the steamers began to identify major routes while eliminating those which were less popular or profitable. Competition rates influenced mergers and improved service. Shipbuilding, crafts and tradesmen, and materials and equipment became readily available on the Sound's shores when communities began to recognize their dependency on water routes for their livelihoods and transportation. The automobile forced the construction of roads and highways, influenced the growth of businesses dealing in fuel and engines, and signalled the introduction of automobile ferries for Puget Sound. But autoferries represented a significant investment, whether steamboats were to be converted or if new construction was awarded. The State was already licensing operators for specific routes by the early 1920's. Those companies who had controlled the routes the longest were generally awarded the licenses. The one-man steamboat operation was already a scarcity on the inland waters by the early twenties.

There were several major companies competing for supremacy of the routes. It was difficult to guess in those early days of ferryboating which ones would achieve their goals. Accommodating automobiles aboard boats proved to be a major investment, but a popular one. Not only were vessels designed and altered to accommodate automobiles but the engines of those vessels had to have adequate propulsion. Gasoline and diesel engines of this size and capacity were in a relatively developmental stage in the twenties. On the Sound, a number of those engines were placed in ferryboats as respectable "experiments."

For the most part, alterations and new construction of ferryboats for operation on the Sound were per-

formed by architects and shipyards within the region. Few, if any, ferries were purchased outside of the area in the 1920s, although a few Sound ferries were purchased by California buyers.

A number of smaller ferryboat proprietors achieved a degree of success in their businesses which should not be overlooked. Eventually, most of these companies and their vessels were absorbed by the Puget Sound Navigation Company or the Kitsap County Transportation Company, if their routes survived at all. But their contributions to the evolution of a modern ferry fleet were significant.

THE ACTIVE WASHINGTON NAVIGATION COMPANY

Mitchell Skansie, president of the Washington Navigation Company, operators of the ferry system between Tacoma and the islands and peninsula across the Sound from Tacoma, remarked about some of the technical problems and financial encumberances of running ferryboats:[1]

"... in 1922 we purchased our first ferry, the CITY OF TACOMA (II).It was powered at that time with twin steam engines and for a time we continued to operate her that way. She cost us from $1500 to $1600 a month for fuel, and we had a hard time getting by. So we later replaced the steam engine with a pair of 180 hp Fairbanks-Morse diesels which cost us only $300 a month for fuel and we applied the rest of the previous expense on the purchase of the new motors, and before we knew it, we had them paid for. We could say the same thing about the other diesel engines of the same type that we have bought. They have practically paid for themselves in their saving over steam in a comparatively short time."

Mitchell Skansie and his brother, Joe, also a principal company factor, were born to a family of fishermen and shipbuilders. The Skansies were among the earliest

[1]Pratt, "The Active Washington Navigation Company," *Pacific Motorboat*, Jan., 1938, pp. 26-7.

LAUNCHING THE CROSLINE

CITY OF TACOMA   *CAPT. R. MATSON*

purse seiners of Puget Sound. Two of their brothers continued in that profession. In 1912, Mitchell and Joe founded the Skansie Shipbuilding Company at Gig Harbor. During the period of 1912 to 1929, they built over 180 purse seiners and cannery tenders in addition to a number of commercial craft and some of the Sound's finest yachts.[2] The Skansie name became a hallmark for quality boatbuilding. They are said to have built the first gasoline launch for seine fishing on the Sound while most fishermen were still using muscle and oars to power their skiffs.

The Skansies started ferryboating in 1922 when they secured a contract from Pierce County to operate a ferry on the run between Steilacoom-Anderson Island-McNeil Island-Long Branch. They operated the small ferry TRANSIT, owned by Captain E.B. Elwell. The ferry was 65 feet long and carried 13 cars on two decks. It was formerly operated as a freighter on the Navy Yard Route. The Skansies associated with A.M. Hunt, a member of a Tacoma family with a permanent place in the history of Puget Sound shipbuilding and shipping.

Five of the seven Hunt children, Emmet E., A.M., A.R., L.B., and F.M. Hunt were successful as masters, engineers and owners of Sound steamboats. A.M. Hunt, coming from Michigan in 1876, settled with his parents near Wollochet Bay[3]. He never lived more than 20 miles from the old family home.

The post office was established at Artondale on Wollochet Bay in 1878. The eldest brother Emmett established the mail route between Steilacoom and the new post office. He began a 20-mile run with a 13 foot rowboat, making the trip once a week. By 1882, he had built the tiny steamboat, BABY MINE, 26 feet by 8 feet, powered with a four-by-four oscillating engine. Brother A.M. Hunt joined Emmett as chief engineer of the tiny craft.

Four years later, the BABY MINE was replaced with the GYPSEY QUEEN. When she was sold to Seattle interests, A.M. Hunt became purser on the MESSENGER and then the JOSEPHINE. From 1889 until 1892, the Hunt brothers operated the steamboat SUSIE of the Fox Island Clay Works and then built the steamboat VICTOR, placing her in the Tacoma-Quartermaster and Gig Harbor service in 1892.

In 1898, the brothers were joined by the younger A.R. Hunt, and celebrated his introduction to their business with the construction of the famous SENTINEL for the Tacoma-Seattle route. The CREST was built to replace the VICTOR for the Gig Harbor route in 1900. By 1902 the SENTINEL had ceased to operate at a profit. The Hunt brothers dissolved their partnership. Emmett took the CREST and the Gig Harbor route, while A.M. took the SENTINEL and another steamer, the CLARA BROWN, which had been purchased on speculation. A.M. sold these boats a short time later.

SHIP DESIGNER A.M. HUNT

[2]Ibid.

[3]*The Marine Digest,* 12/5/1925, p. 5. Wollochet was also known as "Cut Throat Bay."

124

BURTON

SENTINEL

SUSIE

ATALANTA

A.M. Hunt joined with Frank Bibbins to form the Tacoma & Burton Navigation Company in 1905. Hunt designed the BURTON, built that year, and the MAGNOLIA, built in 1908. A.R. and L.B. Hunt eventually purchased Bibbins's interests in the company and a shipyard was established on the Puyallup River where A.M. Hunt superintended the building of steamboats. These included the ARIEL, built in 1912, and the ATALANTA, built in 1913 for the Gig Harbor route. In 1918, the ATALANTA was traded to the Washington Route for the FLORENCE K. A.M. Hunt retired from the steamboat business to establish Hunt Bros. Boat Repair Yard at Tacoma.

In 1921, A.M. Hunt designed and built the ferryboats CITY OF TACOMA and GIG HARBOR at the Hunt Bros. yard. He continued as secretary of the new corporation, and later ferries of the Skansie fleet were all constructed in the Skansie Bros. yard.

The Skansies served the original Hunt Bros. route with fast, modern ferryboats and expanded their runs to include Steilacoom, Anderson Island, McNeil Island and Long Branch. The county granted them another contract in 1925 for the run between the foot of Sixth Avenue, Tacoma, and Fox Island and East Cromwell. Then in 1927 the county extended contracts for the balance of their runs, including service between Point Defiance and Gig Harbor and between Point Defiance and Vashon Island.

With the exception of the CITY OF TACOMA, the Skansies built all of their ferries in their own yard and used oil-fueled Fairbanks-Morse engines in each of them. The company owned five other boats: 1) ferry DEFIANCE, built in 1927, 165 feet in length, 48 foot beam, two F.M. engines of 360 and 240 hp, operated between Point Defiance, Gig Harbor and Vashon Island; 2) ferry SKANSONIA, built in 1929, 165 feet in length, 48 foot beam, powered with two F.M. engines, 210 hp each, operated on the Gig Harbor-Point Defiance and Vashon Island run; 3) ferry CITY OF STEILACOOM, built in 1924, 110 feet in length, powered with 200 hp F.M. engine, operated between Steilacoom, Anderson Island, McNeil Island-Long Branch; 4) ferry FOX ISLAND, (Ex-WOLLOCHET) built in 1925, 100 feet in length, 32.5 foot beam, 150 hp F.M engine, built for service to Day and Fox Islands, later a standby ferry; 5) ferry VASHONIA, originally the RELIEF of the Washington Company, stripped to the deck and enclosed in a new hull of greater length, beam and depth. The gasoline engine in the VASHONIA was replaced with a 150 hp F.M. diesel, which was installed in the original engine room. These conversions were completed in 1932.

The Skansies also built the ferryboat ELK which was later sold to Crosby Lines and renamed the AIRLINE. Ownership of the AIRLINE was eventually transferred to Puget Sound Navigation Company and operated by Peabody in the 1930s.

The CITY OF TACOMA, originally built with steam engines and intended to carry only 30 cars, was hauled out at Western Boat Building Company in 1924, cut in two and lengthened to 170 feet. She was repowered with two 180 F.M. engines. Her car carrying capacity was increased to 50 autos. The CITY OF TACOMA operated from Point Fosdick to Sixth Avenue, Tacoma. A.M. Hunt directed the redesign and reconstruction of the CITY OF TACOMA.

Hunt also directed the construction of the double-ended ferryboat GIG HARBOR, built in 1925. It was similar to the rebuilt CITY OF TACOMA but the GIG HARBOR was shorter lived. The ferry burned June 10, 1929.

Pacific Motorboat, June 1925, told about the progress of the diesel engine within the ferryboat industry in this region:

"One of the most interesting and rapidly developing work boat services to which the heavy oil engine has proved itself adapted is that of the automobile ferry. In no locality has this application grown to greater proportions than on Puget Sound. Up to the past several years the number of these craft was relatively small. Such ferries as were in service were mainly propelled by steam and functioned more as incidental connections between 'out-of-the-way points than as main units in a well-knit transportation system.

"... When the demand for these ferry routes first began to make itself felt, an attempt was made to meet it with the conventional steam-powered ferry boat. It was not long, however, before enterprising transportation companies who had already seen the performances of the heavy oil engine in other lines of service, introduced it to the ferry system with the result that it will now be only a short time until the demonstrated economy and efficiency of the oil engine will have entirely supplanted the more expensive methods of propulsion."

Mitchell Skansie was sold not only on diesel engines but on the use of Fairbanks-Morse engines. He replaced the DEFIANCE 240 hp engine with a Fairbanks-Morse 375 hp in the late thirties.

"We have the utmost satisfaction with them, not only in economy but also in their reliability and long life. When one stops to consider that these boats run twelve hours a day, every day of the week, that some of them cover about 45,000 miles a year in distance, it is readily seen that not only is steady performance necessary but that the wear and tear is greater than in almost any marine service I know of. We have very few layups, and none of them through any faults in the power plants." [4]

People who rode the ferries of the Washington Navigation Company are said to have believed in the success and growth of the company, based on a business-like operation, good service and enterprise in building up business on the various runs that they served. One Vashon Island commuter stated, "The Skansies have been instrumental in developing the summer home and permanent population of the entire south end of Vashon Island. They have done this by rendering good boat service. They have not hesitated to make the service as frequent and adequate as the requirements for the run necessitated, and whenever an extra boat is needed to take care of peak travel, they make it a point to see that one is available. In this way they have not only benefited their patrons but have also been able to expand their own business by making it attractive and convenient for people to live in the districts they serve." [5]

[4] Pratt, "The Active Washington Navigation Company," *Pacific Motorboat*, Jan. 1938, pp. 26-7.
[5] Ibid. p. 26.

Pierce County built a new Gig Harbor terminal in 1928 for the ferryboats of the Washington Navigation Company. The construction was handled by P. Manson & Son with a contract for $39,400. *The Marine Digest,* February 18, 1928, makes special note of the construction materials and costs executed for the terminal:

"A bridge 280 feet long is being built which will lead to a steel span 96 feet long. The pontoon which supports the outer end of the span is now being built at the plant of Tacoma Machine Works at a cost of $4,000. It is 26 by 30 feet with a depth of eight feet. It is a composite construction, including 40,000 feet of lumber and eight tons of steel. The planking used is four inches in thickness and is sheathed with one-inch creosoted fir. Over 220 creosoted piles will be used for the construction of the terminal. Included in the contract is the building of the 60 foot roadway a quarter of a mile long to connect with the present county highway. The new terminal which is at the entrance to Gig Harbor will supersede the present slip inside the harbor."

Pierce County, unlike other counties of the state, controlled *all* the routes and operation of ferries within the county. Generally speaking, Pierce County's control encompassed more routes and greater distances than any other single county. By the early thirties, one company, the Washington Navigation Company, operated ferries exclusively on these routes. Bureaucratic control had its pluses and minuses when severe depression gripped the Pacific Northwest.

CITY OF STEILACOOM

RALPH WHITE

DEFIANCE

RALPH WHITE

FOX ISLAND

CAPT. R. MATSON

(opposite page) CREDITS:
RELIEF

GIG HARBOR

WILLIAMSON COLL. P.S.M.H.S.

ELK

VASHONIA

CAPT. R. MATSON

FERRY WOLLOCHET

CAPT. R. MATSON

In mid-1935, the Washington Navigation Company petitioned the United States District Court for the right to reorganize its financial structure under the federal bankruptcy laws, Judge E.E. Cushman, presiding. The state supreme court had recently ordered the company to refund to Pierce County $126,000 of subsidies paid in the previous three years, on the grounds that the county commissioners had no legal right to pay the subsidies. County Attorney Harry H. Johnston and his assistants opposed reorganization of the company as endangering the $126,000 claim of the county. The Washington Navigation Company was granted the right to reorganize, but they lost the greater battle for existence within a short time. Progress in the county took its toll.

The Narrows Bridge, third longest suspension bridge in the world, collapsed like a house of cards less than one year after this wonder of the world opened for automobile traffic. Washington Navigation Company folded in a similar manner. The Tacoma Narrows Bridge was opened July 1, 1940, putting out of business the hard-pressed ferries of the Skansie Bros. on the Gig Harbor run. From the day it was opened, the bridge was viewed with some apprehension by the public.[6] No sooner had it opened than it began to stage hair-raising antics. Not only did it sway from side to side, but it developed an undulating, galloping movement, lengthwise at times, so that an automobile traveling over it seemed to be riding waves. Officials and engineering experts proclaimed the bridge essentially safe and yet, in winds of less than 45 miles an hour, this symbol of progress crumbled. Skansies' ferryboats had never encountered such problems. The Narrows Bridge disaster was a timely argument for the disadvantages of change and modern convenience.

Washington State purchased the SKANSONIA and the DEFIANCE to operate between Titlow Beach (Tacoma) and Point Fosdick (Olympic Peninsula) following "Galloping Gertie's" collapse. William Skansie of Gig Harbor was awarded the contract to operate these two ferries for the state over the protest and lower bid of Captain John Anderson, Lake Washington ferryboat operator. Anderson had bid the price of $12,905 a month for the operation of the two ferries, while Skansie bid $14,000 per month for operation. The Department of Highways' acting director, James A. Davis, stated that Anderson's bid did not meet contract specifications. The call for bids was let December

[6]*The Marine Digest*, 11/16/1940, p. 2.

130

SKANSONIA

TACOMA NARROWS BRIDGE

ANOTHER ENERGETIC FERRYBOAT OPERATOR OF PUGET SOUND—CAPTAIN HARRY CROSBY

24, 1940, with a required submission date of December 28, 1940. The short time allowed for completion of the bids and the fact that Skansie was well acquainted with the vessels he had formerly owned, gave him a definite advantage over Anderson.

This contract with a private operator expired 18 months later. The second call for bids introduced the Black Ball Line to the run. Puget Sound Navigation Company operated the SKANSONIA and the DEFIANCE for Washington State. The company never owned the vessels, although they did purchase the former Skansie ferry, VASHONIA, in 1943, selling her for scrap in 1950.

Skansie brothers continued to operate the smaller ferry runs such as McNeil and Fox Island for a number of years. The McNeil Island boats were privately operated on county lease until the penitentiary that was located there was closed in 1980. The Skansies lost their most profitable run, Tacoma to Gig Harbor, in the early forties because of the bridge. They were virtually eliminated from the ferryboat business at that time.

In 1921, ferryboats were providing auto service on many runs but there was not *convenient* transportation for cars to Victoria and Vancouver Island. The traveler's choice consisted of the aging steamer SOL DUC of the Puget Sound Navigation Company, crossing the Strait of Juan de Fuca, or the Canadian Pacific Railway's boats from Seattle or Nanaimo, B.C. Only a few cars could be accommodated on any of these vessels. The cars had to be taken apart in order to load them through narrow sideports on the boats. A talented man who recognized the exploding potential of the ferryboat business and whose restless spirit was eager for challenges where a profit might be turned, moved quickly.

Captain Harry Crosby, tugboat operator, steamboatman, salvage expert, Alaska cannery owner, property investor, and bonafide capitalist, had a different idea when it came to ferry routes. He dreamed of a ferry terminal at Anacortes. Boats could carry cars and passengers through the beautiful San Juan Islands and disembark at Sidney, B.C., 18 miles north of Victoria on Vancouver Island. Anacortes and Victoria business people publicly lent their support.

Crosby purchased the four year old kelp harvester, HARVESTER KING, for use as his ferry, paying only $12,000[7] for a power scow already equipped with a square bow and stern. Slight alterations kept the Fairbanks-Morse "CO" engine placed well aft to provide three lanes for eight to ten cars on the main deck. A passenger deck was located on the second deck with a raised pilot house forward of the passenger cabin. The bold lettering across three-quarters of the length of the vessel identified this peculiar craft as the "VICTORIA-ANACORTES FERRY."

The sternwheeler GLEANER was chartered to assist the new service and was altered to carry 25 cars. On both vessels, automobiles were driven over the bow and backed off the ship over the bow at the end of the run. The GLEANER also landed at steamboat docks where cars were loaded at her sideports with a freight elevator.

Inaugurated April 26, 1922, the new run for autos was an immediate success for Crosby. Fares were $4 one-way and $6 round-trip for autos under 3,000 pounds ($5 and $8, respectively, for larger machines). Passengers paid $1. Six hundred cars and 3,000 passengers were carried that first June. Originally advertised as a "three hour crossing," that slogan was later modified to read, "less than five hours." It was the HARVESTER KING that couldn't keep up.

Recognizing the inadequacies of the HARVESTER KING, Captain Crosby considered building a new ferryboat. In October 1922, the Anacortes-Sidney Ferry Lines requested bids for a ferryboat 146 feet by 34 feet by 9 feet for their American-Canadian route. Built with a 500 horsepower diesel engine, it was to maintain a speed of 12 knots. Accommodations aboard the ferry would include space for 35 autos, a lunch room, smoking room, rest room for women, and a gas station for automobiles.

"The vessel will be open at both ends for a distance of thirty feet so that motorists may sit in their cars and view the scenery while the ferry is plying from shore to shore," stated *The Marine Digest*, October 28, 1922.

Summer traffic warranted a better ferryboat. Crosby turned to the Puget Sound Navigation Company. They chartered the recently converted CITY OF ANGELES to him, and her skipper, Captain Louis Van Bogaert, delivered her to Crosby. Crosby was to com-

HARVESTER KING

CITY OF ANGELES

CITY OF ANGELES

mand the vessel the first month. The CITY OF ANGELES loaded 40 cars onto two decks, using an elevator to raise and lower autos to the second deck. She was initiated into service May 10, 1923, providing additional waystops at Orcas and Roche Harbor.

Captain Crosby turned to an associate of his with the same surname but no relation, Roy W. Crosby, when the need for yet another ferry was evident. Roy Crosby had a maritime background and experience with automobiles—a rare breed in 1923.

[7]Leithead, "Captain Harry Crosby—Puget Sound's Energetic Ferry Operator," *The Sea Chest*, Vol. 12, pp. 27-34.

Roy Crosby, orphaned at the age of 12, made his way to Tacoma from Minnesota at the age of 16 after completing high school.[8] Crosby worked on the steamships OHIO, plying the Nome trade, and the ROBERT DOLLAR, sailing to San Francisco. He worked one season in a Nome mining camp and returned to Tacoma with $1000 savings in his pocket.

In 1905, Crosby joined the automobile business with the Mitchell, Lewis Motors Company of Racine, Wisconsin, manufacturers of the Mitchell car. He worked through the company factory at Racine and joined the sales force shortly thereafter. He was transferred to San Francisco and in 1910 he was sent to Seattle to establish the Elliott Bay branch of the company. When the Seattle branch closed, so successful was his work with the company, that he was offered a position as manager of the Kansas City branch. But he had cast his lot with Seattle for all time. He joined the Hudson's car force and later became manager of the Locomobile Company of Seattle.

Crosby returned to maritime affairs in 1915 in association with Captain Harry W. Crosby making a number of important shipping deals. So pleased was he with his success that he formed the Crosby Marine Corporation in 1921 owning and operating steamships on the West Coast.

In 1923, the Crosbys joined forces again to purchase for a song the Port of Seattle's unreliably powered diesel passenger ferry, ROBERT BRIDGES. For $38,000 they rebuilt the vessel at Ballard Marine Railway, altering the vessel to carry 28 cars and 400 passengers. They converted her from a double-ender to a single-ender with a propeller at one end only driven by a new Fairbanks-Morse diesel engine.[9] Australian hardwood formed the auto deck, making it one of the "finest dance floors on the Pacific Coast."[1]

The ROBERT BRIDGES was rechristened the MOUNT VERNON to the delight of Mount Vernon, Washington's chamber of commerce. Her run was initiated July 30, 1923. The summer season for the Crosbys was an overwhelming success. Predictions for the fall were not slighted "owing to the abundance of Chinese pheasants in the islands, much travel is expected during the hunting season."[2] Patronage of the MOUNT VERNON was not given a rest until December that year when a storm and high tides washed out the ferryslip at Sidney.

The following summer introduced some new problems for this rewarding venture. Another common rate war was evident when the Island business of three little steamers was threatened by the CITY OF ANGELES and the MOUNT VERNON. The ALVERENE of the Kasch Transportation Company,[3] the SAN JUAN II of the San Juan Transportation Company,[4] and the SPEEDER, owned by Captain Norman L. Driggs were all on similar runs in the San Juan Islands. They were forced to match rates with the more affluent and aggressive Crosbys. Most of these little companies had had vessels on the Island runs since the early 1900s, and were no doubt taken aback when ferryboats threatened their trades. Puget Sound Navigation Company recognized the potential of the route and the ultimate threat to their crossing between Port Angeles and Victoria. They resolved the rate issue by purchasing the run from Crosby. The little vessels could not compete with the powerful presence of Puget Sound Navigation Company and stopped trying after a time.

[8]*The Marine Digest,* 11/3/1923, p. 5.

[9]Leithead, "Captain Harry Crosby ...," *The Sea Chest.*

[1]*The Marine Digest,* 7/21/1923, p. 10.

[2]*The Marine Digest,* 9/15/1923, p. 4.

[3]William H. Kasch, owner of Kasch Transportation Company, was born in Iowa in 1872 and moved with his family to Anacortes in 1890. His father established one of the first grocery stores there. Kasch acquired the MOLLIE K. about 1901 and began operating her for "towing and general jobbing" (*The Sea Chest,* Vol. 16, No. 1, p. 12). Named for his mother, the MOLLIE K. was the first gas boat to operate out of Anacortes. Kasch entered the passenger business between Anacortes, Friday Harbor and Bellingham with the YANKEE DOODLE in 1909. His later vessels of the fleet included the CITY OF ANACORTES, BAINBRIDGE, and the ALVARENE. Kasch died January, 1926, and company operations passed to his brother, Frank Kasch.

[4]The San Juan Transportation Company was started in 1909 by John S. McMillan of the Roche Harbor lime interests, placing the steamer SAN JUAN II on the run Seattle-Roche Harbor, connecting with the BURTON for Bellingham. Company interests were later sold to Captain Charles K. Maxwell. Maxwell operated the SAN JUAN II until it was lost off Blakely Island, Christmas Day, 1929. (Ibid.).

Crosby, however, was not satisfied with retirement from ferryboating. The Skansies sold him their 66 foot ELK, built at their yard in Gig Harbor, to create a new run between Old Town, Tacoma, and the head of the bay at Gig Harbor in May 1924. The ELK was single-ended, propelled at one end only, but sporting two wheelhouses, one at each end, to aid in backing into slips. The Skansies had operated the ELK on the Steilacoom-Anderson Island-Long Branch run. The ferry carried only 10 or 12 cars. Crosby ran the ELK in competition with Pierce County ferries and faced tremendous difficulties.

Since his Tacoma run was failing miserably, Crosby switched the ELK to another run. It operated cross-Sound between the Ballard Dock[5] and Kingston in Kitsap County. This run, too, had its disadvantages since the ferry had to pass through the Lake Washington Ship Canal each time on its four round-trip daily schedule.

A newspaper clipping in the Thornley files, dated July 4, 1924, sheds some light on this operation:

"Ballard Ferry Starts Operating
"Commercial Club Builds Dock for Vessel—Busy Meeting of Organization Plans Many Activities

" ... The ferry committee reported that the Ballard-Kingston ferry started operating Sunday and barring some trouble at Kingston was on the way to being a successful venture. When Capt. Harold Crosby reached Kingston on the Sunday afternoon trip, he found the dock barred from him by the Edmonds ferry, which laid there thirty-five minutes after it was scheduled to leave, in an effort to keep the Ballard ferry from landing its passengers. Mr. Crosby finally nosed in and got his passengers off, leaving word that he intended to get into the dock according to the terms of his lease, or sue the port officials. The troubles will be ironed out, as the people of Kingston are aroused over the unfair tactics used by the other ferry.

"Secretary [Dwight] Hawley reported that he had ordered the construction of the dock at the Ballard end, as the council had shown no inclination to provide any funds, as they once tacitly agreed to do. The work cost about $350 and this will be made up by subscriptions later on.

"The people at Suquamish are very anxious to have the Ballard ferry land there and as soon as they provide a dock it will be taken from Kingston and operated to Suquamish, with two trips during the day to Seabold. That will give a more direct route, saving about twenty minutes on the run. This will give a short route to Bremerton, also."

The route lasted from June until fall, since the one and one-quarter hour crossing could not compete with the 30 minute crossing from Edmonds to Kingston. Sound Ferry Lines, owned by the Joyce brothers, operated the Edmonds run.

Captain Crosby was not yet beaten. The ELK did not return to the Ballard run the following summer. Crosby devised a plan for a short crossing from Alki Point to Manchester on the Olympic Peninsula. He lengthened the ELK 38 feet, gave her a new engine and a new name, the AIRLINE. Roy Crosby and several other investors joined the captain again to form the Crosby Direct Ferry Lines. Ferry slips were built at Alki and Manchester. The new company and route was inaugurated April 12, 1925.

"With elaborate ceremonies, ferry service from Alki Point, Seattle, to Manchester was dedicated last Sunday afternoon. Miss Esther Oland, native daughter of Manchester, christened the ferry landing at Alki Point and Miss Mary Schutt, native daughter of West Seattle, christened the landing at Manchester. Mayor C.A. Hanks of Port Orchard and Miss Olund arrived from across the Sound in an airplane piloted by aviator Edward Hubbard. Miss Schutt and Mrs. M.A. Wilkens of the Seattle Park Board made the journey from Alki Point to Manchester in the airplane. Following the ceremonies at Alki Point the guests made the trip to Manchester in the ferryboat AIRLINE. Commercial Clubs of Manchester and Port Orchard were hosts for the delegation on an automobile tour of Kitsap County."[6]

The Crosbys ordered a new ferry to be built at the Marine Construction Company on the Duwamish River. The 142 foot, 65-car ferry CROSLINE was expected to cost $250,000. It was designed by Seattle architect L.H. Coolidge. The 600 horsepower heavy

[5]Ballard Dock at the foot of 24th Avenue N.W., Seattle.
[6]*The Marine Digest*, 4/18/1925, p. 15.

134

AIRLINE   *CAPT. R. MATSON*

oil engine was designed by Harry W. Sumner and built by the H.W. Sumner Co.

But the AIRLINE proved so popular that Crosby purchased the 18-car ferry GLORIA from A.R. Hunt in Tacoma to relieve his ferry on weekends until the new vessel was ready. Still a steam-powered ferry, he renamed it the BEELINE.[7]

Crosby's rates and shorter distance to the peninsula won him favor and passengers from the usual riders of the Puget Sound Navigation Company and the Kitsap County Transportation Company. Puget Sound Navigation Company charged $2 one-way and $2.50 round trip for the run on the Navy Yard Route to Bremerton. Kitsap County Transportation Company shortened their Vashon Heights and Harper route (five miles south of Manchester) to terminate at Fauntleroy rather than Seattle. With this route they slashed their fares to $1.00 each way, car and driver. Crosby wanted fresh business for the AIRLINE. He met his competitors' rates with a fare of 50 cents, car and driver. Protests raised before the State Department of Public Works forced Crosby to raise his fares to 85 cents, one way, and $1.50 round trip. The other companies were only slightly appeased.

The CROSLINE entered the Alki run that summer. The Navy Yard Route immediately lowered its fare to $1 one-way and $1.75, round trip. This was a real bargain for motorists since the Navy Yard run was twice the distance. Crosby continued to carry cars, trucks and passengers in such quantity, though, that a merger of the Puget Sound Navigation Company with the Crosby Direct Ferry Lines occurred in the early part of 1926. Three ferries, two docks and the certificate for the route, was included in this deal. Puget Sound Navigation Company ran the route until the Alki ferry slip washed out in 1936 and the terminal was shifted to Colman Dock.

Crosby was considered an inventive promoter with sound ideas for ferryboating. His career in this field lasted only four years, but his attention to the promise and future of the Sound's ferries was a hallmark of their popularity. Two of his major routes survive today. The Anacortes-Sidney run remains a monument to his imagination. The Vashon-Fauntleroy route was started by Kitsap County Transportation Company when Crosby's rate war provoked them into strong competition for a shorter and less expensive Seattle-Vashon route.

"His turbulence and inventiveness definitely helped shape Puget Sound ferryboating."[8]

[7]Drawings for the BEELINE were furnished by Philip Spaulding, Seattle naval architect, who drew them during his apprenticeship to Carl Nordstrom. A sketch of the BEELINE appears on the endsheets of this book.

[8]Leithead, "Captain Harry Crosby..." *The Sea Chest.*

CROSLINE AT ALKI POINT

FERRY CROSLINE

FERRY BEELINE

A FERRY OWNER AND SKIPPER WHO WORE SKIRTS

Puget Sound is notorious for its colorful maritime operations, but one of the ferry lines has a story with an unusual twist. Berte H. Olson became the first female automobile ferryboat operator on Puget Sound. She was one of a family of 14 children raised on Whidbey Island. Her father was a ship's carpenter and most of her brothers became commercial fishermen. She, too, fished on a troller off Cape Flattery and married a fisherman, Agaton Olson. With him, she entered the ferryboat business in 1921. They had twin three year old sons at the time.

Mrs. Olson was awarded a state contract for ferry service between Camano and Whidbey Islands, otherwise known as the Utsalady [Camano]-Oak Harbor [Whidbey] route. Her husband's fish boat, the RAINBOW, was mustered to tow a scow that carried cars between the islands.

Business proved profitable so Berte Olson had two ferries built in 1924. The first, named DECEPTION PASS, was launched by Ballard Marine Railway in their Salmon Bay Yard in June of that year. She was designed 68.8' long by 24' beam and was equipped with a 40 horsepower gasoline engine. The DECEPTION PASS would run across Deception Pass between Whidbey and the mainland at Anacortes. The second ferry, the ACORN, created slightly more attention when she was launched the following September.

Designed by L.H. Coolidge, Seattle naval architect, and built by Ballard Marine Railway Company, the new ferry ACORN maintained an average speed of nine knots on her trial trip on Lake Washington. Because of the design of her forward body, the new vessel attracted keen attention from Puget Sound transportation circles and *Pacific Motorboat Magazine*.[9] The forward body was worked into a model form by Coolidge that was unlike anything previously seen on the Sound.

"A cross-section of the bow is slightly concave. The new vessel has an overhanging clipper stem and although her beam is 25 feet, the surface disturbance is very slight when she moves through the water. The bow is especially adapted for use in comparatively lumpy water!

"While the forward body is of the unusual design indicated, the after body is the conventional V bottom type. The vessel was

BERTE H. OLSON

built for the Olson Bros. [Berte's company name] of Oak Harbor. She has space for 16 automobiles. With her beam of 25 feet, she is 65 feet long and is equipped with a 75-horsepower diesel engine."

The ACORN was launched Thursday, September 25, 1924, without ceremony or sponsor when the new ferry took her first trip. She was scheduled for service at the end of the following week.

When Berte and her husband divided their business ventures in the early thirties, Mrs. Olson con-

[9]Quoted in *The Marine Digest*, 11/1/1924, p. 10.

† "Lumpy water" in Olson's proposed route between Whidbey Island and Camano Island, is common.

tinued to run the ferry operations they had initiated on Whidbey Island.[2] Captain Alexander Peabody, then new to the operation of Puget Sound Navigation Company, took a guardian interest in Berte's operation and assisted her throughout the years. He transferred ownership of the CENTRAL II, a 65 foot ferry built by Captain Willis Nearhoff at Clinton, Whidbey Island, to Mrs. Olson when Puget Sound Navigation Company bought Nearhoff's Mukilteo-Clinton route and the CENTRAL II.

Puget Sound Freight Lines chartered the CENTRAL II from Mrs. Olson in 1931 to run with their vessel, the PIONEER, on the Gooseberry Point-Orcas Island crossing. The CENTRAL II was destroyed by fire that summer. Puget Sound Freight Lines sold their route to Puget Sound Navigation Company and the PIONEER was given to Mrs. Olson.

Mrs. Olson's livelihood was severely threatened with the opening of the Deception Pass Bridge, built by the W.P.A. in 1935. It ended her profitable Deception Pass crossing and she disposed of her ferryboat of the same name.

Recognizing Mrs. Olson's predicament, Captain Peabody turned over the Port Gamble-Shine route to her. She started that service with the ACORN and Puget Sound Navigation's CLATAWA.[3]

OLSON'S DECEPTION PASS

[2]Agaton Olson and his brother moved their ferry operation to Long Branch, Washington, and in 1939 they built the motor ferry TAHOMA at Tacoma. This boat had a service speed of 12 miles an hour, measuring 65' x 26.9'. The TAHOMA, powered with a 135 hp Atlas diesel, was operated between Steilacoom and McNeil and Anderson Islands. It carried 10 cars. The firm later acquired the ferry PIONEER from Berte Olson to operate between Puget and Taylor Bar, providing service for the upper Sound peninsula district and Olympia.

[3]The CLATAWA, a former Sound steamboat, was converted to a ferry early in 1924 at the King and Winge Shipyard, Seattle, for the Whidby Island Transportation Company in the Everett-Whidbey routes. She was acquired by P.S.N. during their takeover of the Whidby Company in the late twenties.

PIONEER

CLATAWA

NEARHOFF'S CENTRAL II

(top, opposite) ACORN

Romantic WHIDBY ISLAND!

BLACK BALL FERRY LINES
PUGET SOUND NAVIGATION COMPANY
Colman Dock,, Seattle
Uptown Office 1306 Fourth Avenue
MAIN 2222

The Marine Digest, March 21, 1936, tells about the transaction:

> "The Puget Sound Navigation Company has announced the sale of the Port Gamble-Port Ludlow ferry route to the Olympic Navigation Company of Port Gamble, which is now operating the service from Port Gamble to Shine. The transaction included the sale of the motor ferry CLATAWA and transfer of the certificate to Mrs. Agaton Olson, who formerly operated across Agate Pass."

The Port Gamble-Shine run saved motorists 120 miles by crossing Hood Canal directly rather than driving around the south end of Hood Canal.

Berte Olson expanded her operation to include the Seabeck-Brinnon [near Dabob Bay and Duckabush] crossing in 1939. The CLATAWA and the ACORN were shifted to this run. She purchased the LAKE CONSTANCE (Ex-CITY OF KINGSTON, Ex-RUBAIYAT) as a spare boat for the run.

Mrs. Olson actively managed the operation, maintenance, ship repairs and slip construction for her ferry company. She might have been known as a Tugboat Annie had it not been for her dizzy pace which included all purchasing and taking the wheel of the ACORN or the LAKE CONSTANCE across the canal. She had polished seamanship.

The CLATAWA was a larger ferry than the formerly mentioned ones. It required more than Berte's "dog ticket" on the water. Even though she was probably qualified to sit for her full master's license, she never found the time. "Sometimes as a woman, I think I have too much to do," remarked Captain Olson one day.[4]

In anticipation of increased traffic across Hood Canal with the completion of the Agate Pass Bridge in 1950, Berte Olson's colorful ferry operation between Port Gamble and Shine saw its last days. Captain Alexander Peabody, stalwart friend and confidant, approached Mrs. Olson with an offer to buy the route franchise. Berte's little ferries would not handle the increased number of motorists crossing the bridge. Captain Peabody, though in the midst of battle with the State of Washington for the survival of private ownership of his company, purchased the run.

[4]Wright, "Floating Bridges," *The Saturday Evening Post,* April 5, 1941, p. 40.

Ceremonies dedicated Puget Sound Navigation Company's Lofall-Southpoint crossing June 10, 1950. The ACORN and the LAKE CONSTANCE were sold. Mrs. Olson retired from the inland sea.

This charming, enterprising female entrepreneur, nicknamed "Little-but-Oh-My!", a licensed ferryboat master and operator, passed away in June 1959, aged 77. Ferryboating was never again quite the same.

CAPTAIN ALEXANDER PEABODY AND BERTE OLSON

LAKE WASHINGTON'S FLOATING BRIDGES

Flag's flew at half-mast on ferries and steamers, silken folds drooping in the morning light. Thousands of residents on Lake Washington, glancing out over the quiet waters Sunday morning, May 18, 1941, saw the flags and knew that they had lost a pioneer. It was fitting that the flag John L. Anderson venerated should be the means of breaking the sad news to the lake communities he had faithfully served for half a century.

Captain Anderson was the eldest of four children, born in Gottenberg, Sweden in 1868. After attending public school until the age of 14, he exchanged his textbooks for the sea. He sailed with an uncle who owned a fleet of sailers carrying lumber and ore. On young John's second trip across the Atlantic, he was taken ill and left to recover in a hospital in Quebec; the vessel returned to Sweden without him. After his recovery he went to Shreiber, Ontario, where he worked in a hotel and then entered the employ of the Canadian Pacific Railway. He was superintendent of a road gang, engaged in painting cars and stations.

Anderson made his way to Seattle in 1888 when he shipped as deckhand on the freighter POINT ARENA for one year and then transferred as deckboy to the steamship GEORGE W. ELDER. His duty was to polish brass work; he was a diligent deckboy. Under the command of Captain J.C. Hunter, the GEORGE W. ELDER made voyages to Sitka, Juneau, San Francisco and Portland.

After a year, Anderson came ashore to work for the Stetson-Post Mill in Seattle for the winter. This included duty aboard the mill's tugboat RAINIER. He left the mill a short time later to work on the steamboats of Lake Washington.

In 1871 there was a horsedrawn passenger carriage service from Yesler Wharf to the foot of Yesler Way on Lake Washington.[1] By 1888 the Lake Washington Cable Railway had formed and the first cable car ran up Yesler Avenue from Seattle's waterfront and out to Leschi Park where the coal-fired steam plant supplied power to the cable.[2]

An amiable but persistent fellow by the name of Charles C. Calkins arrived on this scene from the midwest. He quickly made a small fortune as a land spec-ulator of the latter 1800s. Calkins was quite a salesman with the gift of persuasion. He had visions of building a hotel, gardens, home sites and a vessel for transportation, all without industrial smog [it was a concern then, too] on the lovely wooded shores of the lake. He selected his site on Mercer Island and purchased it from Mr. Gardner Proctor. His company was called the Lake Washington Land and Improvement Company. The site was to be called "East Seattle."

Calkins built the hotel for $30,000 and invested another $70,000 in residences at Leschi Park. The C.C. CALKINS was launched March 21, 1890 and enrolled May 2, 1890. It was built by W.C. Peterson with a length of 74.8 feet, 16.3 foot beam, and depth of 5.5 feet. A crew was recruited. Among them was the deckhand John Anderson.

CAPTAIN JOHN ANDERSON   CAPT. R. MATSON

[1]Yesler Way no longer extends to the lake.

[2]Anderson built his first home near this site in 1895, overlooking the lake at the end of the Yesler cable line.

When the first boat service to Mercer Island began, Calkins wanted at least one man with deep sea experience in the crew. Anderson served that role. The rest of the crew included Captain H.M. Race, master; a chief engineer, a purser and a fireman. Anderson spent a good deal of time going through the various departments of the deck and engine room.[3] He fired the boilers under superintending engineer, E.W. Dieckhoff[4] and shortly sat for his master's license.

On November 15, 1890 there was a change of ownership of the C.C. CALKINS and Captain L.B. Hastings became master. John Anderson stayed on.

During President Harrison's trip to Seattle in 1891, his itinerary included a trip to Calkin's East Seattle Hotel. The President boarded the KIRKLAND at Leschi Park to cross the lake. In concert, all the whistles of the escort fleet opened up and the C.C. CALKIN's steam calliope on the upper deck played *Home Sweet Home* as the boats proceeded to East Seattle.

On December 12, 1891, ownership changed again and Captain George H. Rodgers took command of the steamer. When Rodgers left in 1892, young Anderson was asked to take command. But the panic of 1892 jeopardized the plans of the C.C. CALKIN's owners and soon after, the steamer was laid up. She later suffered a fire at Houghton and was rebuilt as the steamer BLANCHE in 1898.

Anderson was able to buy an interest in the propeller-driven steamboat WINNIFRED. This transaction was carried out in conjunction with a partner, Jimmy M. Coleman. Coleman owned the steamer VIXEN in operation on Lake Sammamish at the time. The WINNIFRED, 52 feet in length, ran from Leschi Park to Newcastle via the Mercer Slough, connecting with stages from Robinson's Landing on Lake Sammamish and other inland ports.[5] A charge of 50 cents

[5] *The Marine Digest,* May 24, 1941, p. 5 says he was Quartermaster.

[4] Later Dieckhoff was general superintendent of Pacific Coast Engineering Company.

[5] George W. Tibbetts erected a hotel and store on his farm. In 1882 he established a stage line from Seattle to Lake Washington, then by boat to Belmont and Lake Sammamish and from there by stage to North Bend, operating in connection with the Columbia & Puget Sound Railroad. (*History of Seattle*, 1905, p. 667).

XANTHUS AND CYRENE

       WILLIAMSON COLL. P.S.M.H.S.

INLAND FLYER

ACME

(opposite page) C.C. CALKINS

      KIRKLAND

was made for a round trip on the run. The WIN-NIFRED supplemented this business and Anderson was soon able to branch out. He added the 68 foot propeller steamboat QUICKSTEP about 1894 and extended the operations to Madison Park.

Anderson followed the recognized policy of building steamboats in the winter and spring, operating them on the lake during the summer season, and then selling them in the autumn. His steamers ACME and CITY OF RENTON were built by J.V. Johnson who had come to Seattle in 1888 and recognized Seattle's need for another boatyard on the shores of Lake Washington. Johnson had learned his trade on the St.Lawrence River at Clayton, New York, where he was born. He had served in the army under General U.S. Grant during the Civil War, enlisting when he was 17. Johnson spent a number of years in Wisconsin and Minnesota after the war, working at carriage making and boatbuilding.[6]

Johnson's CITY OF RENTON was built for service between Renton and Leschi with Johnson's son Mark as the operator. It was operated for a short time but then sold to the Bothell Transportation Company to run between Madison Park and Bothell under the name CITY OF BOTHELL. The ACME serviced Leschi Park and Madison Park. It, too, was sold to the Bothell Transportation Company after one year for the Bothell-Madison Park run. It operated on that run with the same name, CITY OF BOTHELL.[7]

During the 1890s Anderson built the steamers LADY OF THE LAKE,[8] which was sold to Bellingham interests, and then the steamer LESCHI, sold after one season to the U.S. Government. James Colman, of the Colman Dock Company, approached Anderson about purchasing his fast propeller yacht CYRENE,[9] and later, Anderson purchased Colman's second yacht XANTHUS as well. With this vessel Anderson invented his popular Sunday lake excursion around Mercer Island in 1903. This venture blossomed and grew, lending stability to Anderson's future business endeavors for the remainder of his life.

Anderson was said to have transferred more boats from the Sound to Lake Washington via the Black River than any other man. The Black River was only three miles long. The Indians called it Mock La Push, meaning river with "two mouths." The work had to be done in the spring when the river rose. It demanded extreme care and a great amount of physical labor. Anderson proved himself cautious and skillful in this undertaking. The procedure entailed running the boat

JAMES M. COLMAN

COLMAN FAMILY

via the Black River which ran between the Cedar and Duwamish Rivers. It was in this sense that the Indians believed it had two mouths.

Anderson fast became an acknowledged expert on boats for Puget Sound and its lakes. He inspected a vessel in Portland for the Bellingham Transportation Company. While in Oregon, he discovered the famous steamboat INLAND FLYER, then without machinery.

Anderson purchased the INLAND FLYER at small cost from Joseph Supple, a Portland shipbuilder, and sold the hull to Joshua Green and LaConner Trading & Transportation Company. He equipped the vessel for Green and under her own power delivered her to Puget Sound.

[6]Matson, "Leschi Park Shipyard," *The Sea Chest,* Vol. 13, p. 126. In 1888 there was no direct access to the lake from Elliott Bay via the water. Boatbuilding was important on the lake shores as a major and necessary means of transportation. Canoes were also employed to carry passengers across the lake in the early days of settlement.

[7]There were three CITY OF BOTHELLs. The first was the Ex-CITY OF RENTON, the second was the Ex-ACME, and the third was the Ex-MAY BLOSSOM.

[8]Built after the QUICKSTEP burned. Anderson also acquired the steamer EFFORT, operating between Bellingham, Point Roberts, Lummi Island and Blaine until 1898 after which it ran between Olympia, Shelton and Tacoma. (*History of Seattle,* 1905, p. 423.)

[9]The CYRENE was built by Matt Anderson at a boatyard on the site of Colman Dock for J.M. Colman who wanted to help create jobs at the yard. (Ibid.)

Following the Portland venture, Anderson purchased a steel hull for the sternwheeler MERCER for lake service. After the MERCER, he had the launch RAMONA and the steamboat FORTUNA[1] built. The URANIA was the last vessel constructed for Anderson at a yard two blocks south of Leschi Park. It was launched March 31, 1906.

LAKE WASHINGTON SHIPYARD

In 1901, Captain George Bartsch, first captain of the first ferryboat on Lake Washington, the KING COUNTY, joined with Captain Harry Tompkins in selecting a site for a new Lake Washington shipyard. They chose Houghton, now a part of Kirkland, as the ideal spot. The steam scow SQUAK had been built at that site for Captain J.C. O'Connor by Edward Lee in 1884, as was the EDITH, built by E.J. Easter in 1886.[2]

The yard is remembered as consisting of a single 10' x 12' shanty where 12 men, a horse and a wagon were employed. The workers brought their own tools and launched the boats they built during the flood season on the lake. Bartsch and Tompkins modernized their facilities with a mule-powered windlass and a marine way capable of handling vessels up to 125 feet in length.

In 1904, Bartsch and Tompkins organized the B & T Transportation Company to operate the DORO-THY built at their yard in 1903, the EMILY KELLER built in 1902 and renamed WILDWOOD, and the GAZELLE built in 1898 by Edward Lee. The tug SUCCESS, built in 1869 at Port Blakely, completed the fleet. The firm continued to run the county's KING COUNTY ferryboat between Madison Park and Kirkland for a substantial fee of $140 per month.[3]

In 1906 Jacob Furth, the same financier who had helped out Joshua Green and his partners, sent for Anderson and suggested that Anderson consolidate all of the steamboat services on Lake Washington. At the time, there were three operations—the B & T Trans-

[1]*The Marine Digest,* 5/24/1941, p. 5. FORTUNA measured 81 gross tons, 106.9 feet L.O.A. She operated the Mercer Island run for years and was fondly remembered for her chime whistle, tuned personally by Anderson. He filed off bits of the whistle's pipe, testing it for sound until it suited him. The whistle was later transferred to Anderson's SIGHTSEER.

[2]McDonald and Hemion, "Lake Washington Shipyard," *The Sea Chest,*, Vol. 11, p. 130.

[3]The KING COUNTY was launched March 8, 1900 at Madison Park. Captain Bartsch towed log booms with the GAZELLE on the lake when he was not busy skippering the KING COUNTY. Some say that was most of the time due to a very limited ferryboating business.

portation Company, the Anderson Steamboat Company, and the Interlaken Steamboat Company. [4] Anderson responded to Furth's offer by incorporating the Anderson Steamboat Company and absorbing the Anderson and B & T fleets. Anderson became president of the new company and Captain Tompkins became vice president.

Anderson also consolidated the Lake Washington Shipyard belonging to Bartsch and Tompkins and named it the Anderson Shipyard. The first vessel built there was the ATLANTA launched May 28, 1908, [5] for the Anderson Steamboat Company.

New management brought about some definite changes, such as increasing the crew from 25 to 30 men and making an active bid for orders from clients in addition to Anderson's lake fleet. In those early years they built the yacht RAINIER for Andrew Hemrich of Rainier Brewing Company.

The yard's facilities were limited to basic equipment. A shack housed the sawmill; another small building contained a marine engine employed to haul craft out of the water and replace mule-power previously used. Atlanta Park, also owned by Anderson, was behind the yard, and was a favorite picnic spot. There was a dance pavilion that was later pressed into service as the yard's pipe shop. The GAZELLE gave up her steam boiler to supply steam for the yard.

In a former employee's description of the launching of the ATLANTA, he told of the muddy road leading from the ferry building to the plant. Draymen bringing supplies would often find themselves stuck in the road and workers would knock off, hike through the woods and boost the wagon out of the ruts by hand. [6]

GROWTH OF EASTSIDE COMMUNITIES AND FERRY FLEETS

Anderson Steamboat Company and the Lake Washington Shipyard prospered for years under the captain's guidance. They helped build up the various lake communities and districts, always providing service ahead of public need. These companies were recognized as early influences in the development of the entire lake area.

During those early years of expansion, Anderson built the TRITON, AQUILO and ATLANTA[7] as additions to the steamboat fleet. These vessels were busily employed during the Alaska-Yukon-Pacific Exposition of 1909, running excursion tours from Leschi Park and

[4]Competition on the Leschi-Bellevue run. Anderson absorbed the company after 1909, taking over two boats, the WILDWOOD and the L.T. HAAS.

[5]87 gross tons and 95 feet L.O.A.

[6]McDonald and Hemion, "Lake Washington Shipyard," *The Sea Chest,* Vol. 11, p. 130.

[7]Captain Bob Matson, nephew of Captain Anderson was quizzed for the reason for these exotic names. Answer: Anderson had already acquired the XANTHUS and the CYRENE and decided to keep the Greek mythology trend by continuing to name his vessels for the gods. It couldn't hurt.

Madison Park to the fair. It was a 30 minute trip made popular by a 25 cent fare.[8] Anderson operated 12 boats on the lake that summer.

Under public pressure from the East Side, King County concluded a survey in 1900 and agreed to build ferry slips at Madison Park and Kirkland. The ferry KING COUNTY of Kent was considered a jinx. She had struck a mud bank at Madison Park when launched.[9] That jinx was to be felt by the county itself.

The county began its operation by cutting rates in half and the KING COUNTY was making four round trips daily between Madison Park and Kirkland. The county was in direct competition with Anderson's boats. Several years later, the Port of Seattle decided to enter the competition since they, too, were operating ferryboats at an unprofitable margin on the West Seattle run. These operations would prove to be costly experiments for the taxpayers. King County reputedly lost $100,000 per annum with its lake fleet. The debate of private enterprise versus public ownership had begun. The controversy raged on Lake Washington.

[8]Ralph Johnson writes in *The Sea Chest*, Vol. 3, p. 93, "I rode the lake boats often because you could do it for a quarter, whereas a steamboat on the Sound ran you a dollar or more and I didn't have much money in those days."

[9]Built by the Moran Brothers of Seattle but launched at Madison Park.

149

Anderson built the ferry ISSAQUAH in 1914 as his biggest and most elaborate steamer. Captain Anderson was the first *private owner* to build a ferryboat in this region. The ISSAQUAH was one of the first ferries designed and constructed to carry automobiles and passengers in the Pacific Northwest. She carried 40 cars and 600 passengers on the Leschi-Mercer Island-Newport route originally, and required only a crew of six.[1] She had a hardwood dance floor on the upper deck and catered to crowds on moonlight excursions. The vessel carried a price tag of $50,000.

King County commissioners were irritated, to say the least. They sued Anderson Steamboat Company for $10,000 for running the steamboat URANIA to public docks just ahead of their ferry and picking up all the passengers. The raging legal battles between the county and Anderson discouraged clientele, too. By 1916, Anderson Steamboat Company had tied up 11 idle boats.

This slack trade, however, was made up in increases of business at the Anderson Shipyard. In 1914, the yard built the steamer BAINBRIDGE for the Eagle Harbor Transportation Company and the U.S. Lighthouse tender ROSE at a site on the East Waterway.[2]

The county ferry LESCHI was operated on Lake Washington by Anderson. It was a peculiar example of a "manufactured" ferryboat. A steel sidewheeler, the LESCHI was cut and tacked at East Waterway in Seattle then taken apart and trucked to Taylor's Mill on the lake. There the hull was reassembled under the direction of J.F. Duthie, a future shipyard owner. Cabins and decks were built of wood cut at the mill.

Two young men were introduced to ferryboating aboard the LESCHI while it was operated by John Anderson. Harold Graham was oiler with chief engineer Walter Shaw, and Bob Matson served as A.B. topside.[3]. These two men went on to excel in their fields, the former as chief engineer, and the latter as a ferry captain. The LESCHI proved to be long-lived, operating on the lake until January, 1950, when transferred to the Vashon-Fauntleroy Ferry District.

The ferry LINCOLN was a ferry constructed for King County at Anderson's Shipyard. The LINCOLN, 580 tons, 147.3 feet in length and 43 feet in beam, was designed to carry passengers and automobiles. She replaced the county ferry WASHINGTON of Kirkland on the Madison-Kirkland run while the WASHINGTON continued to serve standby for a time. The WASHINGTON was transferred to the Seattle-Vashon Heights-Harper route inaugurated on Puget Sound in 1919.

LAKE STEAMER AQUILO

TRITON

[1]This route connected with a road to Lake Sammamish, Fall City, Preston, Issaquah, North Bend and Snoqualmie. (Grant, *History of Seattle,* 1891, p. 423). It is unlikely that the ISSAQUAH ever carried her full capacity of automobiles.

[2]This formed part of the Duthie Shipbuilding Yard during World War I.

[3]Bob Matson and Harold Graham have been resourceful guides to the authors of this manuscript.

THE FIRST ISSAQUAH

COUNTY FERRY LESCHI

CAPTAIN BOB MATSON

LINCOLN

The WASHINGTON was found on the Vashon route in her later years. During the last days of Puget Sound Navigation Company's operation, Vashon commuters formed their own ferry district and operated the decrepit WASHINGTON until the State of Washington assumed control of the fleets.

As a result of the First World War, there was an acute shortage of ocean ships. Anderson turned his energies to shipbuilding, since the publicly-owned ferries had virtually put his company out of business. He sold his interests in Anderson Steamboat Company and resigned the presidency. He turned his efforts toward reorganizing the Anderson Shipbuilding Corporation. He established a modern wooden shipbuilding plant at Houghton where he built four ocean-going ships for France. The yard had been made available for more business with the opening of the Lake Washington Ship Canal in 1916.

That same year, Captain Harry E. Tompkins left the yard to operate the Bremerton-Port Orchard and Bremerton-Manette ferry routes with Anderson's URANIA and the SWAN. The SWAN was the former CITY OF BOTHELL (Ex-MAY BLOSSOM).

About 1918, Anderson leased the shipyard to N.C. Price Construction Co. The plant became nationally acclaimed as one of the most advanced and progressive steel and wooden shipbuilding plants in the country. They built noted merchant marine and government vessels.[4]

[4]In 1919 the yard made its first conversion of a steamer into an auto carrier. This vessel was the FORTUNA which remained a single-ender but cars drove through from one end to the other. She landed bow-on at Roanoke, backed out and turned around to cross the lake to Leschi, where she turned again and backed into the ferry slip to allow cars to drive off over her stern. This called for a skilled captain and an engineer who was adept at responding to signals.

In February of 1919, Anderson was appointed King County Superintendent of Transportation, having charge of the county's ferry fleet. He held that position three years with jurisdiction over the county's two ferryboats on Fauntleroy-Vashon route and the fleet of the lake. The county continued to suffer losses, though, and conditions finally regressed to the point that the lake community was forced to take action.

The Port of Seattle Commission recognized the wisdom of leave-taking from the ferry operations business and unloaded all of their vessels, including the West Seattle ferries, on the King County Commissioners. The Port Commission had owned several ferries and linked their operations with the fleet on Lake Washington. Municipal ownership had proven to be such a costly endeavor for the taxpayers that the county was soon forced to retire as well. Political constituents were up in arms with the state affairs and in a surprise move, March 14, 1921 at midnight, the county abruptly terminated West Seattle service. The AQUILO,[5] the last vessel on that route, was returned to her Lake Washington duties.

King County ferry services (and certificates) were offered for lease and John Anderson resumed command of the lake fleet and routes, operating these under the name of Lake Washington Ferries. Captain Tompkins returned to Anderson's fold as manager of the Bremerton runs while simultaneously, King County leased the Sound operations to Kitsap County Transportation Company, then headed by Lyman D. Hinckley[6]

Captain Anderson reputedly treated his crew members well, although he was known to watch the direction of every dollar passing through his company. A column in *The Marine Digest,* January 27, 1923, states that the employees of Lake Washington Ferries were provided life insurance by Anderson as evidence of his appreciation for their "loyalty, cooperation, and continued service." As of December 22, 1922, all of his employees were insured for $500 each, to be increased $100 every year for each succeeding year's service to a maximum of $1,000. New employees were eligible after three months and the entire cost of the insurance was borne by Anderson as long as the ferryworker remained in his employ. This was a progressive attitude on the part of an employer in 1922.

Today one can only speculate about the interesting problems that arose in the relationship between Captain John Anderson and the King County Commissioners. Anderson had been a leader and developer of an adequate and noteworthy ferry system for the Lake Washington communities. Under pressure of citizen groups, King County had forced him out of business, but later turned again to Anderson to lease and operate their ferries. There was a negligible amount of commuter business on the Lake, hardly enough to warrant such a tussle over nickels and dimes. But the commissioners recognized that politically influential and affluent citizens were residents of the east side of the Lake. They were eager to please them. Ill will and emotional scenes continued to plague the private versus municipal association throughout its existence; it was evident in a variety of ways. The following editorial appeared in *The Marine Digest's,* May 9, 1925. Jackson B. Corbet, Jr., editor and publisher of *The Digest* at that time, was a close friend and business associate of John Anderson.

"THE COUNTY FERRIES

"It is hard to refrain from smiling at the perturbation in Seattle caused by Captain John L. Anderson's suggestion that King County equip one of its Lake Washington ferryboats with diesel engines. Captain Anderson leases the county's fleet on the lake and finds himself up against a tough problem.[7] Paved roads now connect all shores of the lake with Seattle, thereby giving the boats a competition that has cut heavily into their patronage. At the same time the cost of fuel oil has gone up. The paved roads, however, seem to be the chief factor. Captain Anderson's lease has seven years to run, but he has the privilege of terminating it without cause simply by giving written notice.

"These details, however, are beside the mark. The amusing thing is the perturbation caused by Captain Anderson's suggestion that one of the lake ferryboats be equipped with

[5]In 1920 King County had altered the AQUILO's bow to allow her to serve the ferry slip of the West Seattle run. She was then capable of carrying 2 cars on the rounded bow but did not on the West Seattle run. ("Lake Washington Shipyard," *The Sea Chest,*, Vol. 11, p. 130).

[6]The Seattle-Vashon Heights-Harper run was started by King County August 16, 1919. The run was leased to Kitsap County Transportation Company for a period of 12 years on December 8, 1921. The WASHINGTON was returned to King County in July, 1940.

[7]The fleet needed attention due to the age of the vessels. The WASHINGTON was 17 years old, the AQUILO was 16 years, the LINCOLN was 11 years, the LESCHI was 12 years and the ATLANTA was 17 years old.

diesel engines, a job that would cost about $70,000. The suggestion has become a subject of conference.

"There is little or nothing to confer about. If King County is going to persist in remaining vessel-owner, it must be prepared to expend great sums from time-to-time on its fleet. Private owners have to do it, even in routes where there is no competition from paved roads. Such expenditures are as inevitable as taxes.

"Our opinion is that King County got into very deep water when it embarked in vessel-ownership. If it is going to remain in business, it must pay the bill. It will find that with its fleet deteriorating and becoming passe, it is now in the beginning of expenditures that will make $70,000 look small. It would be better for all concerned—for the general taxpayer and for those who live on the routes served by its vessels—if the county could find some way to dispose of its fleet."

Battles would continue to be waged from both sides for at least another 15 years. In a sense, both sides were the losers.

JACKSON B. CORBET, JR.

ANDERSON WATER TOURS

At the suggestion of the Seattle Chamber of Commerce about 1922, Captain Anderson embarked on a plan that met with remarkable success. He was, in fact, said to have based the financial well-being of his lake enterprise on the success encountered by excursions. Traffic across Lake Washington in those early days was negligible but Anderson might have as many as 300 people daily aboard one of his excursion vessels. He introduced summer daylight cruises of Seattle's salt and fresh water. Elliott Bay, Salmon Bay, Lake Union and Lake Washington connected with the interesting passages through the Lake Washington Locks and the Lake Washington Ship Canal. The cruises were established under the name of Anderson Water Tours. At first he employed the steamer ATLANTA[8] for these outings.

By 1934 these water tours had met with such overwhelming success that Anderson decided to operate a bigger boat for the tours, even though the region's economy was noticeably depressed. He had purchased the steamer VASHONA four years earlier from the Vashon Island Navigation Company and early in 1935 sent it to Lake Washington Shipyards[9] to undergo conversion as a "daylight steamer." Tours could be made regardless of weather due to the newly enclosed cabins with windows that could be raised or lowered with ease. Her furnishings were custom-built in Seattle and seating accommodations provided occasional chairs for comfort. The vessel's house was entirely rebuilt. Other reconstruction work transformed the steamer into a luxurious carrier with capacity for 300 people. The newly decorated vessel was christened SIGHT-SEER and embarked on summer service of two trips per day, morning and afternoon. In the summer of 1936, her second year of operation, she experienced heavy patronage from tourists from New York, New England and Pennsylvania. Additionally, there was a large number from Europe, New Zealand and other foreign regions.[1]

The SIGHTSEER operated as an excursion boat until 1962 with time off during World War II. Anderson recognized that most of his money on Lake Wash-

[8]ATLANTA was the first vessel built in Anderson's Lake Washington yard at Houghton.

[9]Lake Washington Shipyard Company was then owned by Seattle capitalist, Charles A. Burckhardt, with Paul E. Voinot as director and general manager, Charles E. Taylor as general superintendent, and A.R. Van Sant as purchasing agent and office manager for the corporation.

[1]*The Marine Digest*, May 23, 1936, p. 5.

ington had been made, not by providing ferry service, but by providing pleasure cruises and sightseeing tours. During the summer of 1957, the SIGHTSEER operated on a cross-lake run once again in an experimental route to relieve traffic congestion from the Mercer Island Floating Bridge.[2] The venture which lasted 4 days failed miserably due to the lack of walk-on passengers, thus ending boat service to Bellevue permanently.[3]

THE FLOATING BRIDGE CONTROVERSY

It seems that John L. Anderson could not avoid conflict with the King County Board. Resuming its monthly luncheon meetings after the summer vacation of 1929, the Maritime Association assembled in Seattle at the Frye Hotel, Thursday noon, with a heavy attendance. The Association was concerned about the threat of county dominance to private maritime interests. They appointed a committee to investigate the newly proposed Mercer Island Bridge project. Association president, C.J. Stewart, announced these appointments: Chairman, George R. Cary, Puget Sound Tug & Barge; Clarence H. Carlander, Puget Sound Freight Lines; Captain J.R. Jones, Standard Oil Company; J.L. Burnside, Williams Line; Captain J. Howard Payne, ferry operator; Captain L.J. Hall, Alexander & Baldwin; and W.G. Rogers, Yamashita Shipping Company.

Page one of *The Marine Digest,* September 28, 1929, gave a detailed account:

"The bridge question was brought up by Captain John L. Anderson, owner of the Lake Washington Ferries and president of the Kitsap County Transportation Company. The proposed bridge will connect Seward Park and Mercer Island.

" 'I am not opposing new construction of the bridge between the park and the island,' said Capt. Anderson. 'The construction of such a bridge seems to be inevitable and it might as well be built now. But there are several things to be considered as regards the type of bridge. I for one would hate to see anything done that would spoil the beauty of the lake, now a great scenic asset of the city. Again, the problem of navigation must be considered. Renton at the south end of the lake is rapidly coming to the front as the industrial center. Shipping to and from that place is increasing and it is now apparent that Renton

is to be an important center in the waterborne trade. Indeed the volume of Renton shipping is larger right now than I have ever expected. Care must be taken as regards the proposed bridge. From the scenic viewpoint I am opposed to making a fill for the proposed bridge. The bridge should be a pier structure.'

"Capt. C.B. Warren pointed out that more industrial plants are being established in Renton and that the shipping of that place is bound to grow. Another large Union Oil tanker, he said, had gone into Renton this week.[4] Capt. J. Howard Payne of the Independent Ferry Lines also discussed the growth of Renton as a shipping asset, and moved the association appoint a committee to investigate the bridge project. President Stewart later announced his appointments for the committee."

After the stock market crash of October 28, 1929, the bridge topic was tabled for future discussion. County relations with Anderson continued to be strained throughout the next decade. In 1939 the bridge project was once again pursued by the King County Board of Commissioners.

"On the theory that the contracts entered into by the former King County Board are not binding on its successors in office, the King County Commissioners last week cancelled as of January 1 [1939] the lease under which the Lake Washington Ferries for years has operated county-owned vessels on that body of water. The lease has still nine years to run. The move of the present County Board caused a sensation in waterfront circles."[5]

John L. Anderson was determined to fight the cancellation of his lease to the bitter end. The State Highway Department, with the strong support of King County Commissioners, planned to bridge Lake Washington with a highway built from concrete scows anchored end to end. The structure and its approaches were to be financed with a grant of $3,794,400 from

[2]Prior to construction of the Evergreen Floating Bridge.

[3]The SIGHTSEER became the excursion boat COLUMBIA QUEEN in the late 1960s on the Columbia River and homeported at the Tri-Cities in Eastern Washington. She sank at Pasco the summer of 1970 without chance of salvageable recovery.

[4]Tankers were going into Renton about every two weeks, fuel barges made more frequent trips there. The Shuffleton Steam Plant and the Puget Sound Power & Light Company had plants in Renton.

[5]*The Marine Digest,* December 24, 1938, p. 1.

the Federal Government's Public Works Administration and by the sale of $5,020,000 in public bonds. Anderson maintained that there was no public demand for the bridge and that the department had no public mandate from the voters.

The bridge bonds were to be retired by means of a toll collected on each auto and truck that crossed the bridge. It was estimated that 3,000 vehicles would have to drive across the bridge every 24 hours in order to meet payment of the bonds as they fell due. People found it hard to believe that such high volumes of traffic would cross the bridge. There was also concern about crossing the bridge when the pontoons began wallowing in the heavy seas which were by no means unknown on the lake. Wind storms gusting to 90 miles an hour were not unlikely on Lake Washington, particularly in the late fall and early spring.

King County Commissioners guaranteed that the County would cover the cost of maintenance and operation of the bridge until it was on a basis whereby the tolls began to meet bond interest and redemption. The County acted *without* voters' mandate or referendum.

The Marine Digest's editorial comment, December 12, 1938, once again had something to say about Anderson and King County:

"...Years ago it [King County] owned and operated ferries on Lake Washington. It lost such huge sums of the taxpayers' money in that operation that the taxpayers were on the point of revolt. The Board then leased the boats to the Lake Washington Ferries, headed by Captain John L. Anderson. The present lease still has a number of years to run, but the present County board evidently believes in going to the limit on the screwy trail. It has adopted a resolution cancelling the lease as of January 1, next, and it plans to operate the ferries until the bridge monstrosity is completed and it will then abandon the water routes on the lake. The present board has cancelled the lease on the ground that one County board cannot bind a subsequent County board. Well, if this is true, then the present board cannot bind its successor in the matter of guaranteeing the bridge's maintenance and operation pending the day when 3,000 machines will cross the bridge each 24 hours."[6]

[6]Captain Anderson said the same thing, essentially: "If the commissioners can cancel a lease with me, then a future board can cancel the agreement made by the present board to guarantee the upkeep

Washington
TOLL BRIDGE AUTHORITY

LAKE WASHINGTON BRIDGE
SEATTLE
TACOMA NARROWS BRIDGE
TACOMA

and operation of the proposed new bridge." (*The Marine Digest*, December 12, 1938, p. 4).

On behalf of Lake Washington Ferries, Anderson filed a tentative claim for $213,000 "Anticipated Profits" against the Washington State Toll Bridge Authority for recompense when the bridge was built and opened for operation. "We are not going to step out of the picture and let the county take us over without a fight. We have been strictly neutral and have played the game fairly during all this lake bridge controversy. And we have not violated the lease in any way."[7]

Anderson further stated that the County would have to settle with him a $100,000 personal investment in the lake ferries. These ferries were the WASHINGTON, LESCHI, LINCOLN and the passenger launch and ferryboat MERCER. The county board had ignored Anderson's petitions for vessel improvements earlier due to their heavy losses within the ferry operation and Anderson had undertaken the upgrading on his own to ensure their continued operation.

The case was finally settled out of court two months later. The Lake Washington Ferries Company was to continue to operate their boats for two years under the lease arrangements of King County. When the bridge was completed, Anderson was to surrender his certificates of operation in the services for the East Seattle passenger run and cease all operations; in return, Washington Toll Bridge Authority would pay Anderson $35,000. That sum, stated Anderson, would nearly cover his "items of capital investment I have made in the ferries."[8]

The County Commissioners agreed that when the bridge was completed, the County would neither operate nor permit anyone, through private enterprise, to operate the vessels relinquished by Captain Anderson. The County, however, did retain the right to operate a service on the Kirkland-Madison Park route.

The abandonment of the Medina-Roanoke route, as proposed, would result with the unemployment of 35 crew members. Captain Anderson petitioned the court with a claim against the Washington Bridge Authority for wages for one year for these men. Such a claim could be legally allowed only by act of the Washington State Legislature. Captain J.M. Fox, head of the Ferryboatmen's Union, would eventually press the claim for compensation for the crews.

The Mercer Island (Lacey V. Murrow Memorial)[9] Floating Bridge opened July 2, 1940. There was little doubt that the traffic volume generated by World War II civilian and military personnel was sufficient to meet payment of the bonds.

Captain Anderson died May 18, 1941. His death did not interrupt the service of his ferries or tours. The operation continued under the capable management of Captain H.E. Tompkins who had been a close friend and business associate since the early 1890s. It was fitting that Anderson's flag, unfurled at half-mast aboard his ferries, would announce the sad news of his death to the lake communities he had served faithfully and well.[1] Another age had passed; another era was at an end. Anderson had served as the cohesive link in the development of a fine ferry fleet in the Puget Sound region.

The automobile influenced drastic and permanent change in the form of floating bridges. It proved its might with political persuasiveness during the 1930s. Ferryboats did not escape this influence. When change occurred, ferries were altered to accommodate or they simply disappeared from their routes. In the case of Lake Washington, permanent structures replaced the ferries. The Kirkland-Madison run continued to be served by the ferry LESCHI with the City of Kirkland appointing operators. The venture could not be managed by the small community and in 1950 all efforts were abandoned. The opening of a second floating bridge, The Evergreen Point, secured the permanent termination of ferryboats on the lake, at least for another 35 years.[2]

[7]Ibid.

[8]Ibid., p. 4.

[9]This first floating bridge was dedicated to State Dept. of Highways Director Lacey V. Murrow. It is popularly called the Mercer Island Floating Bridge. The bridge was designed by Homer Hadley of Seattle.

[1]J.L. Anderson had numerous marine associates as the list of pall bearers demonstrated: Kenneth Colman, Captain Alex M. Peabody, George H. Lent, Philip Macbride, Joshua Green, Leslie Knight, Captain H.E. Tompkins, Captain J. Howard Payne, Bert S. Murley, Clarence H. Carlander, A.H. Wenck, Paul E. Voinet, Charles A. Burckhardt, F.R. Singleton, E.L. Franks, Jackson B. Corbet, Jr., Captain B.P. Kunkler, Alpheus Byers, Henry L. Pinney, Samuel J. Hunes, A.E. Todd, Hugh Martin, S.R. Franklin, Walter Lynch, Alfred J. Westberg, Frank D. James and W.P. Sprague.(The Marine Digest, 5/24/1941).

[2]A brief attempt was made in November 1950 when SHEARWATER, a passenger only motor vessel was placed on the Madison Park-Kirkland run by Lynn Campbell and Joseph Boles. Their operation, too, ended because of lack of patronage after about a month's trial.

COMPETITION HEATS UP

Captain John L. Anderson was a perfect match for Charles E. Peabody and Joshua Green of Puget Sound Navigation Company, as the competing head of the only other major ferryboat company on Puget Sound. At the time of Anderson's purchase, the Kitsap County Transportation Company was already a significant competitor of the navigation company. Because of service to smaller communities profits were not comparable. Anderson had the vision and the motivation to alter this dilemma.

In 1925 all of Western Washington was changing rapidly. The automobile forced roads to be built; bridges to span waterways and government responsibilities to be acknowledged. No other single form of transportation or machinery had done that. Independent companies either accepted the challenge and expanded their enterprises or they were simply overridden by those who could.

John Anderson had enjoyed a long and continuing success as a pioneer steamboat and ferry operator on Lake Washington when he accepted the presidency of Kitsap County Transportation Company. Few individuals on Puget Sound had proven themselves to be such a constructive and progressive factor in the development of Northwest water transportation. Anderson opened a 30-mile lake to settlement and growth for the prosperous communities of the East Side. He fought hard battles with county and state officials. Then he turned his efforts toward revitalizing the Sound's Kitsap County routes.

The stories have not been uncovered revealing the thoughts and impressions of Peabody and Green when Anderson assumed the presidency of their major opposition on the Sound, but one can guess that the event did not go unnoticed, nor did it pass with tempered comment. It is pointless to speculate whether Puget Sound Navigation Company attempted to purchase Kitsap County Transportation Company when its owner Lyman D. Hinckley died. Records do not show such efforts, nor do the memoirs of Joshua Green refer to the 1925 sale.

It was just as well that they did not pursue the purchase. Joshua Green was leaving Puget Sound Naviga-

tion Company, he had already begun to purchase stock for his future bank. Charles Peabody was dead within one year of Anderson's ascendency.

Competition between Puget Sound Navigation Company and Kitsap County Transportation Company had deep-rooted histories of conflict. Joshua Green was involved in a number of steamboat wars during the first decade of the 1900s with the Kitsap County Transportation Company, owned by Warren L. Gazzam and operated on the routes of H.A. and O.L. Hansen and Captain A. Hostmark. The steamboat war on the Poulsbo run became a matter for public debate in the Christmas Day issue of the *Navy Yard American,* 1909:[1]

"…Last week we set forth some of the plans of Mr. Greene [sic] and revealed to the public what we believe is the real purpose in attempting to drive the KITSAP[2] and other boats for that run.

"After having planned with himself, as detailed in our last issue, Mr. Greene called in his associates and advisors. Certain offers were first made to the owners of competing boats, but failing to make terms, orders were issued to get off the run—orders as preemptory as were ever hurled from a dictator's throne.

" 'You are ordered to get off this run,' says Millionaire Greene.

" 'But, Mr. Greene,' says Mr. Gazzam, 'we have built up that run; it's our child, so to speak; we are contented with it; we charge the same fare to haul people, and the same

[1]Quotation taken from article entitled, "Get off This Run, Says Millionaire Greene." The article states that these words were used in a "conference," but it does not include its time, place or the circumstances surrounding the meeting. One cannot be sure that the editor is not paraphrasing or even imagining the words which were spoken within the conference, but it at least serves as a reflection of the views of some residents of Kitsap County and the manner in which they visualized Mr. Green's character during the confrontation.

[2]Steamboat built in Portland, Oregon for W.L. Gazzam.

rate to haul freight, to Poulsbo that you charge to Bremerton. You have ten times the traffic and make ten times the money on your line than we make on ours, but we are satisfied to serve our people."

" 'You and the people be d'd,' says Greene. 'If you don't get off that run I'll put you off. I can buy those people away from you at the rate of two for a quarter, and I'll do it, too.'

" 'But,' says Mr. Gazzam, 'I have sold property to personal friends and many to whom I am under obligations to maintain the service I have been giving. Mr. Greene, I'm bound to stand with Hostmark and the Hansens; every dollar they have on earth is invested with me.'

" 'What do I care about Hostmark and the Hansens? My name is Joshua Greene. I own more boats than any other man on the Sound. I have some cheap boats and must have places where I can use them. I can break you, for the people will ride with me to save the cut I will make on the fare. I can afford to lose for a whole year if necessary, for what I lose on one run I make up on another. Gazzam, there's no use for us to talk further. You must sell out unconditionally or I'll ruin you, for I'll follow your boats wherever they go.'

" 'Greene,' replied Gazzam, 'we'll never sell our boats and abandon our people on that run under any such conditions.'"

Green delivered the INLAND FLYER, formerly on the Bremerton run, to serve the Poulsbo route and added the LYDIA THOMPSON to carry freight, reducing fares to two-for-a-quarter. He ordered Gazzam not to land the Kitsap County steamers at Colman Dock.

Protests were also raised in the same article about the construction of an approach to the dock frequented by Green's steamers in Bremerton and owned by Mr. Bremer. The City of Bremerton built the approach to the dock with public funds. The editor preferred that those funds be used to build a city-owned and operated dock—"one that ladies can walk upon in the rain without wading in the water and mud."

In 1910, Gazzam placed the steamer KITSAP of his White Collar Line on the Seattle-Bellingham run, strictly outside of his precious Kitsap County territory.

The fares to Bellingham dropped as low as 25 cents. Competition was stiff and the races were common, leaving passengers confused and unhappy with the schedules for both companies.

As a calculated task of retaliation, Puget Sound Navigation placed the 79-foot BAINBRIDGE on the Kitsap Company's run to Bainbridge Island. Accusations and legal threats were tossed from side to side. Both companies were prepared to "see the battle through." Until, as Joshua Green retells in his memoirs, he realized that the low fares to Bellingham were cutting into his returns on the Vancouver, B.C. run. Passengers were paying the steamboat fare of a quarter to Bellingham and transferring to the Great Northern Railway train to Vancouver. The P.S.N. boats were running nearly empty after the Bellingham stop and were forced to abandon the Vancouver route entirely in 1910.

Both companies continued to operate vessels to Bellingham until Gazzam grew tired of the fight and returned the KITSAP to Bainbridge Island service. Six of the thirteen years that Gazzam spent in the steamboat business were spent at war with Green, the Puget Sound Navigation Company and its subsidiaries. Green was always telling him that he was ruining the ferry business on Puget Sound by teaching his patrons to demand such speed. "The little KITSAP used to run to Bellingham alongside the CHIPPEWA, and could beat her, too," declared Gazzam.[3]

ANOTHER REGIME

Captain Anderson brought the Kitsap County Transportation Company a world of experience and a constructive spirit. He had had some previous, less direct contact with Kitsap County operations when he sent his top associate, Captain Harry E. Tompkins, to operate the Bremerton-Port Orchard and Bremerton-Manette ferry routes with Anderson's URANIA and the SWAN in 1918.

Kitsap County Transportation Company had contracts for the operation of King County's ferries on the Vashon-Harper-Vashon Heights run. The public sector, not private enterprise, was responsible for the construction of the first explicitly designed *diesel*

[3] "Island Ferry Problem Recalls Old Battles," *Bremerton Daily News Searchlight*, December 30, 1935. Perhaps Gazzam and Green were physically improved by their years in the steamboat business. Gazzam had been diagnosed with terminal tuberculosis at the age of 20 but lived to be 97, while Joshua Green lived to be 105 years old.

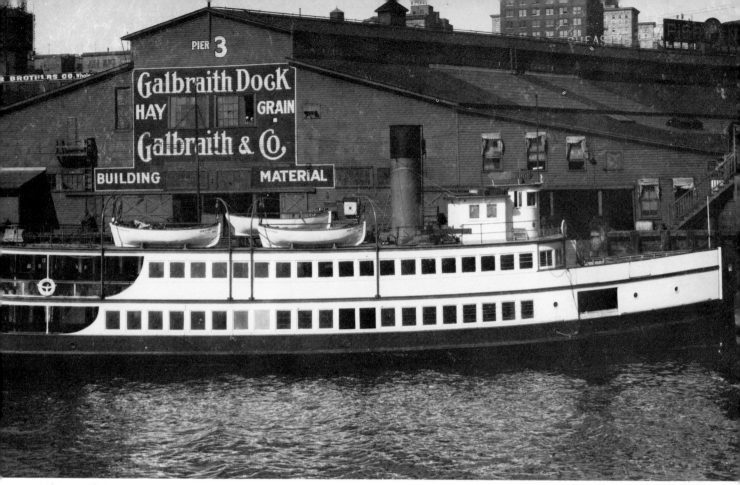

BAINBRIDGE

VASHON ISLAND   *CAPT. R. MATSON*

automobile ferryboats on Puget Sound.

In a letter written by William O. Thorniley to Bob Gordon, Burton, Washington, dated August 4, 1972, he comments:

"...The ferry VASHON ISLAND, built at McAteer Shipyard in Seattle in 1916, was the first new diesel-powered automobile ferry to appear on Puget Sound. She was designed for King County by Captain O.D. Trieber who supervised her construction.

"As ferryboats go she was an unusually trim craft. She was 119 feet in length, had a beam of 35 feet and was 10.7 feet in depth of hold. She was powered with a 250 hp Atlas True diesel.

"As soon as she was ready for operation she was placed on the Des Moines-Portage run, making four round trips daily with two extra trips on Sundays. She was licensed to carry 400 passengers and could handle about 30 cars if they were mostly Fords. Twenty would be a good load for today's [longer] cars.

"She continued on this route until well after the establishment of ferry service to Vashon Heights. In the early 1920s (?) she was taken to Lake Washington and renamed the MERCER a few years later [1928].

"With the completion of the Floating Bridge in 1940 she was laid up in the lake but in 1941 she was sold to the Los Angeles Harbor Department for use between San Pedro and Terminal Island. She was towed south by tug

GOLIAH and renamed the ISLANDER. On her way back to Puget Sound, incidentally, the GOLIAH brought up the venerable San Francisco Bay ferry SAN MATEO.

"When the bridge between Terminal Island and San Pedro was completed in 1965 the ISLANDER [Ex-VASHON ISLAND], now nearly half a century old, was converted into a fishing barge and located off the Long Beach breakwater. As far as I can find out she is still going strong."[4]

The letter is accompanied by a newsclipping entitled, "Little Girl Christens Vashon Island Ferry—Real Champagne at Ferry Launching." "King County's new $40,000 ferryboat, the VASHON ISLAND, was launched at 5 o'clock this afternoon at the McAteer Shipbuilding Company's yard on the Duwamish waterway. As the craft moved down the ways she was speeded by a bottle of something that fizzed and cost $5, broken across her bow by Margaret Case, 12-year-old daughter of I.H. Case, president of the Vashon Commercial Club and editor of the *Vashon News*.

"When hope had flown and it seemed as if the VASHON ISLAND must be christened with insipid soda water, John McAteer, president of the shipbuilding company, found a bottle of the desired fluid and his four day's search was ended."

The Port of Seattle had the automobile ferryboat ROBERT BRIDGES under construction in 1916 at the yard of J.F. Duthie & Co. for operation on the West Seattle crossing. Its launching followed the VASHON ISLAND. She measured 100' x 28' as a double-ender, designed by Lee & Brinton, and was propelled by a two-cycle Southwark-Harris diesel engine of 225 hp connected to a propeller at each end of the ship. She was fitted with passenger accommodations on the main deck only. No cars were carried.

By April 1925, Kitsap County Transportation

STEAMER BREMERTON

Company had doubled their service between Seattle and Vashon Heights and Harper by transferring the ferry WASHINGTON[5] from her usual landing at Marion Street, downtown Seattle, to the Fauntleroy landing,[6] thus affording the vessel five round trips daily and more on weekends. The steamboat BREMERTON (Ex-KITSAP) was transferred to the Marion Street-Vashon-Colby route, making three round trips per day. The WASHINGTON handled automobile and other vehicular traffic as well as foot passengers. The BREMERTON carried foot passengers only.[7]

Announcement of improved Vashon service followed the signing of the supplementary contract by the transportation company and Anderson's old friends, the King County Board of Commissioners. King County still owned the route, the landings and the ferryboat WASHINGTON, leasing the service to Kitsap County Transportation Company under a contract already several years old.

Anderson moved rapidly and launched the company's second ferryboat, the KITSAP, in June 1925.

[4]The ISLANDER was a total loss by fire on December 25, 1974.

[5]On the Marion Street route, the WASHINGTON required one hour for the run to Vashon Heights, but the Fauntleroy run required only 17 minutes. Transfer resulted in a reduction of vehicular rates. The BREMERTON's run from Marion Street required 45 minutes.

[6]Kitsap County Transportation Company built the new dock and ferry slip at Fauntleroy.

[7]Fire destroyed the steamer BREMERTON and badly damaged the Kitsap County Transportation Company's steamer RELIANCE at a mooring on Lake Washington in November 1926. The fire apparently started on the BREMERTON. The RELIANCE was saved from destruction by the Kirkland Fire Department. Loss was estimated at $65,000 and was covered by insurance.

Typical of Anderson, the boat was built and launched in a gala affair at Lake Washington Shipyards, the yard he had originally founded. She received the 35th Washington-Estep full-diesel engine to be installed in a vessel. The KITSAP's engine was the largest built thus far. It was constructed according to A.C. Estep's design:[8] a 600 horsepower, full diesel, four-cycle plant. It was 14 feet high and 35 feet in overall length.

Miss Elizabeth Byers, daughter of Alpheus Byers, a trustee and general counsel for the Kitsap County Transportation Company, was the KITSAP's sponsor. She broke a beribboned bottle on the vessel's bow, dedicating it to a successful career. The new ferryboat was 158.9 feet long, 49 feet broad and of double-ended construction. She was said to be ''square-built'' in order to use all possible space on the lower deck for automobiles. Six lanes of cars could be carried, compared with four lanes on the ordinary ferryboat.[9] The passenger deck was the same width as the lower deck and nearly as long, accommodating an estimated 1500 passengers. Her unique style was designed by Captain John L. Anderson.

Anderson demanded that the vessels he built include Washington State products as far as possible. The KITSAP was no exception, with a Washington-Estep diesel propelling her at 14 miles an hour and hull and woodwork throughout built of winter-cut Wash-

[8]An interview in *The Sea Chest*, Vol. 11, p. 91, with Mr. A.C. Estep states: ''During my life I manufactured engines for 25 years and was in the marine engine business in one form or another for nearly 50 years. They have been most enjoyable. I think, however, the greatest pleasure occurred every time I went out on a trial ship when one of my new engines was put through its paces for the first time. What a thrill! When I went down in the engine room and looked along the line of cylinder heads I could see all those rocker arms, rocking forth and back as they opened and closed the valves with perfect timing. And then in the pilot house out in Puget Sound where we would plow up a white frothy furrow. Other vessels passed by, also powered with engines from our factory. It was wonderful to say to myself, 'I designed those engines.' '

[9]*The Marine Digest*, 6/27/1925, p. 10, 15.

ington fir by local labor. All equipment was purchased in Seattle.

After the launching, the KITSAP was towed from the shipyard to Smith Cove, Pier 40, where the Port of Seattle's crane was used to install the new engine. The ferryboat entered the Fauntleroy-Vashon Heights-Harper run by the middle of the following week, carrying twice as many cars[1] as her counterpart, the WASHINGTON, which she replaced on that run.

THE PUBLIC APPROACH

Captain Anderson was a diplomatic spokesman for his company. He approached the small communities to be served by his ferries when major announcements occurred. He shared his excitement and enthusiam. His audiences at banquets and openings often numbered between 600 and 700 people; his announcements had far-reaching effects on these growing communities.

Anderson came into the foreground in Puget Sound shipping about the time Puget Sound Navigation Company was undergoing internal changes in administration and management structure. There is no doubt that their public image suffered for a time from this inner turmoil. Charles E. Peabody died in 1926; Joshua Green resigned the presidency in 1927. At the time of Peabody's death, his third eldest son, Alexander Marshall Peabody, was already making plans to return to the Pacific Northwest to become involved with the Navigation company's operations. Ira Bronson, a temporary president, was appointed to train and assist the young ship captain for his future role as Puget Sound Navigation's president.[2] He would assume the office in 1929.

Alexander Peabody, as vice president and secretary of the corporation, began to participate as the public spokesman for the company in 1927. Even by the late twenties the public, unfamiliar with this Peabody, played a game of "wait and see" when it came to choosing sides between the ferry companies. They wanted to know who would make the best offer of transportation service.

Anderson was a more familiar figure within the communities and maritime associations. His public announcements were always aimed directly at the clientele who would benefit most from his ferry service. In this manner, he gained the confidence of his patrons and an allegiance to his company.

For instance, in July 1927, Anderson announced the contract for construction of a fast 200-foot ferryboat with accommodations for 1000 passengers and 90 automobiles. Construction was to begin within two months and on completion, would operate on the Seattle-Bainbridge Island run. Equipped with a new 800 to 1000 hp Washington-Estep diesel, the new vessel would reduce the running time between Seattle and Bainbridge from 45 minutes to 25 minutes. Announcement of these plans was made before a crowd of 600 people from the Kiwanis Club of Bremerton and the Chamber of Commerce of Bainbridge Island. They met in Foster Hall at Fletcher Bay. Anderson spoke of the cooperation of residents of the island in the development of ferry service across the Sound and the assistance given his company when there was not enough business to support it.[3]

The ferryboat Anderson spoke of was the BAINBRIDGE. It was launched from Lake Washington Shipyard in 1928 and immediately pressed into service. In 1930, the same yard launched yet another ferryboat of similar design for Anderson. This one, named the VASHON, represented an investment of $250,000 and ranked the largest vessel of her type in Northwest waters.[4]

The KITSAP and the VASHON operated on the Fauntleroy-Vashon Heights-Harper run, while the BAINBRIDGE served the Seattle-Port Blakely run. These three ferryboats were considered major contributors to the development of Vashon Island and Bainbridge Island.

Prior to the advent of automobile ferries, island

[1]The KITSAP carried 90 to 100 cars.

[2]Captain Alexander Marshall Peabody was named for his paternal great uncle who had sailed Black Ball packet ships across the Atlantic; Alex earned his deep-water master's certificate crossing the Atlantic. Peabody trained as a youth on sailing vessels and was captain of the freighter EASTERN CLOUD of the Barber Line in the early twenties. His vessel participated in a triangular trade carrying case oil and general merchandise from New York to Japan, China and the Philippine Island ports, loading Oriental goods for European ports where goods were discharged and European products loaded for New York.

[3]*The Marine Digest,* 7/30/1927, p. 10.

[4]*The Marine Digest,* 8/8/1930, p. 14

VASHON

farmers were restricted to markets primarily on Puget Sound. Many of these routes could only be reached by steamer. Ferryboats brought auto trucks from fish canneries, egg dealers and fruit wholesalers to the island fishermen and farmers. The products of both islands now entered the foreign export trade of Seattle and Tacoma. The movement of strawberries by refrigerated ship to the United Kingdom and Continental Europe was one of the striking features of the Sound's export trade. It was automobile ferries in the 1920s that made it possible for the islands to participate in these exports.[5] It was highly unlikely, though, that the Frenchman, enjoying his bowl of breakfast berries, realized that they had been carried by a ferryboat on Puget Sound.

Anderson, like Puget Sound Navigation Company, was also aware of the impact of automobile tourism on the Peninsula, although he seldom advertised this feature to the extent that his competitor did. In an editorial of *The Marine Digest*, July 10, 1926, Jackson Corbet writes:

"...Tourists who have visited many sections of the country declare that no other body of inland water on this continent can be found automobile services that approach the Puget Sound lines equipment, efficiency and energy. The news of this will spread over the nation and bring the automobile pleasureseekers to the Inland Sea in increasing numbers each year. In addition to that, however, the automobile ferry services are ena-

bling many of the smaller communities on the Sound to grow on a safe and substantial basis. They are binding all the Sound communities closer together commercially, socially and mutually.

"Our great Inland Sea led the nation in war-period shipbuilding. It showed the way. Our Puget Sound transportation companies fill the same roll in the development of the automobile ferryboats."

There was yet another incident that occurred in the fall of 1926 to widen the broadening gap between Puget Sound Navigation Company and Kitsap County Transportation Company or White Collar Line. The crack steamer TACOMA serving the navigation company on the Seattle-Tacoma run collided in the fog with the ferry KITSAP in late October. The impact tore a hole in the side of the TACOMA at the waterline and further served to rekindle the flames of competition between these two rivals.

[5]Ibid.

WASHINGTON ROUTE, INC.
WHIDBY ISLAND TRANSPORTATION CO.
117 CANADIAN NATIONAL DOCK
SEATTLE

CAPTAIN F. G. REEVE

THE WASHINGTON ROUTE

As the 1920s progressed, Anderson began strengthening his company's formal affiliations and associations with other Sound shipping companies. In some cases, there was outright purchase; others were less formal corporate agreements, and still others were subsidiary companies that absorbed smaller operations and shorter routes through trades and investments. Kitsap County Transportation Company maintained fast steamboat services to Poulsbo, Brownsville and other county ports. Near the end of 1927, Anderson and associates purchased the Eagle Harbor Transportation Company and its spotless steamboat BAINBRIDGE to obtain rights to the certificate of the Seattle-Winslow (Eagle Harbor) run. The SPEEDER was included in this purchase. It was this route that would create one of the greatest focal points for contention between Kitsap County Transportation Company and Puget Sound Navigation Company. The route today is the most heavily traveled ferry crossing in the nation.

In May 1928, the Kitsap company effected a merger by which it became the holding and operating corporation of the interests of Captain F.G. Reeve and associates of the Washington Route and the Whidby Island Transportation Company. Captain Reeve, president of both companies, had ranked for nearly 25 years as one of the constructive contributors to Puget Sound transportation. Reeve's maritime career began as a youthful deckhand and continued until he ceased working for others at the age of 26 and became a vessel owner. His reputation stood as a steamboat owner who gave service that commanded the confidence of the communities served by his vessels.

The Washington Route, Inc. operated the steamboats F.G. REEVE and KINGSTON from Seattle, Chico, Silverdale and other way points on the Peninsula and Bainbridge Island. The Whidby Island Transportation Company operated auto ferries WHIDBY and

CLATAWA and the steamboat ATALANTA in the Seattle, Everett and Whidbey Island route.

F.G. Reeve was born in Dudley, England August 22, 1878, and came to the United States two years later. His family first settled in Buffalo, New York, then moved to Detroit, Michigan, and in 1888, they moved to Seattle. A short time later the family relocated at Sheridan, Port Washington Narrows[6] where Reeve received his schooling at Tracytown schools in that county.

Reeve left school to join the fleet of Puget Sound as a deckhand on such famous old vessels as the ELIZA ANDERSON, WASCO, MOUNTAINEER, and the GRACE. At 16, he began mining in the Kootenay country of British Columbia. There he earned $3.50 per day, nearly three times the wage of a deckhand in 1894 on the Sound.

Reeve returned to the Sound several years later and worked in the steel construction department of the newly built navy yard at Bremerton. By working

[6]Kitsap County.

166

hard and saving most of his money he was able to enter business for himself in 1904. He joined with Captain William Johnson and Gene Stewart to organize the Washington Route. With their combined resources, they bought the steamboat NORWOOD from Captain Chance Wiman and associates. The Washington Route maintained a reliable service for the patrons of the Seattle-Chico-Silverdale route.[7] When the firm was incorporated in 1906, Captain Reeve was appointed president and Johnson and Stewart sold out their interest. During the first three years of the Washington Route, Reeve had served as mate of the NORWOOD until he obtained his master's papers and took command.

The Washington Route bought the CHICKAREE about 1906 and maintained two vessels. The company bought the INLAND FLYER from Joshua Green in 1910, built the steamboat WASHINGTON in 1914 and the steamer F.G. REEVE in 1916. The WASHINGTON[8] was sold in 1917 and Reeve bought the FLORENCE K., trading that vessel the following year to Anderson for the speedier ATALANTA. The KINGSTON was a chartered carrier.

In the summer of 1922, Reeve added to his holdings by acquiring the controlling interest in Whidby Island Transportation Company. He immediately placed a contract with the Martinolich Yard on Vashon

NORWOOD AND ATHLON

Island for a fine new steam ferryboat—the WHIDBY. It was launched the spring of 1923. The ferry business between Whidbey Island and Everett grew to such extent that Reeve added the converted autocarrier CLATAWA[9] to the run in 1924.

[7]Stops on this route included Bremerton, Waterman, Pleasant Beach, Fort Ward and South Beach. They made up to three round trips daily with steamers, primarily because there were no roads connecting these communities.

[8]The WASHINGTON was sold to B.C. interests for her boiler only.

[9]The steamboat CLATAWA was converted to an autocarrier at the King & Winge Shipyard in Seattle.

PRIVATELY-OWNED AUTOMOBILE FERRYBOATS

The Whidbey Island route was an important focal center for the development of autocarriers on the Sound. Sound Ferry Lines, Inc. had good reason to boast their foresight in 1919. Captain O. Joyce, vice president and general manager of the Sound Line personally designed and placed an automobile ferryboat in operation between Mukilteo and Whidbey Island that year. Captain Joyce studied the trend of Puget Sound navigation a number of years, particularly while in the towboating business,[1] and reached the conclusion that the automobile carrier was the real factor of the future. His conclusions proved to be correct. His ferry, along with the VASHON ISLAND and the ROBERT BRIDGES, were the forerunners of a vast fleet that followed.

Joyce's first autoferry was a modest venture. Built by Willis Nearhoff at Clinton in 1919, the WHIDBY[2] was launched as a gas-powered, drive-through ferryboat, only 59 feet in length. It was for the Mukilteo-Phinney Spit-Greenwood run on Whidbey Island. The WHIDBY's maiden voyage was August 10, 1919. The month before, on July 10, 1919 the Central Ferry Company, owned by W. Nearhoff, launched its small steam ferry CENTRAL, 31 tons, measuring 60.2' x 18.5' x 4.8'.[3] Her maiden voyage was not until August 26, 1919. Captain Willis Nearhoff built the CENTRAL for new service between Clinton and Everett. The CENTRAL was powered with one of two steam engines from the former Sound freighter RAPID TRANSIT. The other engine was later placed in the CENTRAL II.

Captain Willis Nearhoff was born and raised in Indiana and learned the boatbuilding trade on the Wabash River. He and his wife moved to Seattle in 1900 where he built two cruisers behind his house in the Fremont district. He worked at boatbuilding in Vancouver, B.C., Mill Creek, B.C., and Ketchikan, Alaska. For a time he and his family lived on Camano Island where fishing supplemented their income and their diet.

After working in a Seattle shipyard during the tremendous shipbuilding era of World War I, Nearhoff struck out on his own. He bought a scow, a couple of horses and a steam tractor and moved to Whidbey Island. There he logged and started a mill at Clinton with boatbuilding in mind. With a pile driver and mill's donkey engine, Nearhoff built his boatyard and docks. There were a number of skilled tradesmen on the island with inherited knowledge of boatbuilding design and construction. By employing their talents and labor, and using the virgin timber of the island, Nearhoff began to build ferryboats.

References indicate that the WHIDBY was in service for the Sound Ferry Lines on the Port Gamble-Shine run of Hood Canal starting June 1, 1923.[4] When the Whidby Island Transportation Company was controlled by Captain Reeve, service was conducted on a far grander scale than previously enjoyed by the residents of Whidbey Island.

Captain Reeve's steam ferryboat, the new WHIDBY, was considered a genuine success. Christened May 16, 1923, by 11-year old Gretchen Lovejoy[5] at Martinolich's Yard in Dockton before a launching crowd of 200 people, the WHIDBY entered operation June 24 on the Everett-Langley-Clinton route. It is said that old timers remarked on the vessel's graceful lines and shallow draft, giving passengers' comfort the first consideration in her extensive accommodations.

A clam bake and dance held at Langley in honor of the WHIDBY celebrated the inauguration of five round trips daily to the mainland. The larger WHIDBY was a single-ended ferry. She was designed to carry 400 passengers[6] and 25 to 35 cars. The vessel measured only 114.2 feet x 30.5 feet. Her Colvin[7] boiler and 500 horsepower Nafin & Levy triple expansion engine gave

---

[1]Captain O. Joyce organized the Sound Ferry Lines with his brothers, Alfred R., Clarence J., Arthur and Percy. Captain Joyce was born in Minnesota in 1885 came to Seattle in 1894 with his family and as a ten year old, he was a deckboy on steam and sailing vessels of the Sound. Joyce entered Everett towboating in 1910, operated purse seiners 1911-1914 and returned to towboating during the years 1914-1919. (*The Marine Digest*, 7/31/1926).

[2]Not to be confused with the larger and later built steam ferry WHIDBY launched in 1923 by Captain Reeve.

[3]The CENTRAL and WHIDBY were built from the same design even though the WHIDBY was gas-powered and the CENTRAL was steam-powered.

[4]Leithead, Robert C., source.

[5]Daughter of Captain B.H. Lovejoy, secretary of the Whidby Island Transportation Company.

[6]The WHIDBY was a small ferry by today's standards to be carrying 400 passengers but Coast Guard regulations even today do not limit the number of passengers on *ferryboats* by the size of the vessel. The number of passengers is limited by the number of life jackets on board. See *Laws Governing Marine Inspection*,, Chap. 15, 46:451, "Number of Passengers Allowable."

[7]*The Marine Digest*, 5/19/1923. Seabury type. The WHIDBY had a propeller wheel designed by L.H. Coolidge and carried an elevator forward for use at Clinton which was not then equipped with a ferry slip.

LANGLEY STEAMER ON WHIDBEY ISLAND   *RALPH WHITE*

her a speed of 13 miles per hour.

The first week of business was far ahead of expectations. Stage service to Coupeville by way of the ferry landing had been established, making two round trips daily.

The WHIDBY was originally commanded by Captain B.H. Lovejoy; Stanley Hunziker was mate and Ben Short was in charge of machinery. Captain H.B. Lovejoy, father of B.H. Lovejoy, was the previous owner of the Island Transportation Company, predecessor of the Whidby Island Transportation Company. The Island Company had been operating steamers to Whidbey Island points since 1906 when they bought the steamer FAIRHAVEN for that purpose. The confidence and cooperation of the people of the island district had been enjoyed for years and the Lovejoy ancestors were founding families of Whidbey Island settlement at Coupeville.[8]

Captain Reeve began to intermingle the operations of his two companies, the Washington Route and the Whidby Island Transportation Company, in the autumn of 1923 by placing The Washington Route's KINGSTON and ATALANTA on the Seattle-Coupeville run. The Washington Route's steamer CLATAWA was converted into a ferryboat in 1924[9] for Everett-Langley run to assist on the Whidbey run but she was sold within one year to Sound Ferry Lines to inaugurate services between Edmonds and Port Ludlow on the Olympic Peninsula.[1]

[8]The original Lovejoy home is restored today at Coupeville.

[9]*The Marine Digest,* 2/16/1925, p.10.

[1]The establishment of this ferry service was celebrated on an equally grand scale, May 2, 1925. All business was suspended in Edmonds that afternoon. Businessmen and residents gathered at the ferry dock for a band concert. The entire assemblage boarded the CLATAWA for Port Ludlow where they dined and danced until midnight. Passenger and express bus service on the peninsula, connecting with Port Ludlow, was provided by the Wolverton Auto Bus Company. The Yost Auto Company provided transportation between Seattle and Edmonds.

GAS WHIDBY

                CAPT. R. MATSON

ORIGINAL CENTRAL

                LIESEKE COLL.

GAS WHIDBY UNDERWAY

                CAPT. R. MATSON

CENTRAL

                LIESEKE COLL.

FERRY CENTRAL II, HALCYON AND FERRY PIONEER
                CAPT. R. MATSON

STEAM FERRY WHIDBY LATER BECAME THE ROSARIO

LEGAL CONTROVERSY

In the fall of 1924 Puget Sound maritime groups were waiting with keen interest a decision by Judge Wilson of Thurston County.[2] His ruling would determine whether Sound ferryboats were under the jurisdiction of the Washington State Department of Public Works or the commissioners of the counties in which the vessels operated. The suit arose in a controversy between the Whidby Island Transportation Company and the Central Ferry Company, the latter owned by Willis Nearhoff. This decision and the resultant legislation would have a bearing on the future course of operations of the Sound's ferry fleets, workers' strikes throughout the 1930s, and the eventual ownership of the total enterprise by Washington State in 1951.

The Whidby Island Transportation Company contended that Sound ferryboats were under state jurisdiction, while Central Ferry felt that they were under county control. Both companies operated their ferries between Snohomish and Island Counties. Philip D. Macbride represented Whidby Island Transportation Company while Lloyd Black of Everett and Lloyd Hatfield of Island County were attorneys for Central Ferry.

The Washington State Territorial Legislature of 1854 had passed a law empowering county commissioners to license ferryboats operating in the ''lakes and streams'' in their respective counties. By an act passed in 1869 amending the 1854 law, the legislature authorized county commissioners to establish and alter routes on ferries ''within and bordering on their respective counties.''

In the early twenties, the State Highway Department had petitioned the State Supreme Court to issue a Writ of Mandamus ordering the State Department of Public Works to exercise jurisdiction over a ferryboat on the Snake River in Eastern Washington. The court decided against Public Works' jurisdiction in that case because the old territorial law had not yet been repealed. It held that county boards long had had jurisdiction in such cases. The act creating the Public Service Commission, later known as the Department of Public Works, made no reference to ferries.

In 1924 the State Attorney General ruled that the territorial acts referred only to ferries on lakes and streams. The Whidby Island Company and the Central Company were involved in a dispute over rates before the Department of Public Works. The Island County commissioners had decided to wield whatever power they possessed and proclaim jurisdiction over *all* ferries serving their county. The commissioners issued an order that the ferry companies should file their rates with the county. Public Works countermanded the order on the basis that counties had no jurisdiction over ferryboats in private ownership over *salt* water. It was Nearhoff who carried the case to court. No matter which way the court was to decide, each party was prepared to appeal, so that the scope of the word ''ferryboat'' would be established and defined for all time.[3] This decision was greatly needed since everything that could carry a vehicle across the Sound or Strait was called a ferryboat.

QUEEN: FERRYBOAT OR NOT?

[2]Many of the court cases involving ferry and steamboat routes were taken to Thurston County since the State capitol at Olympia is located within that county and these cases usually involved state departments and statutes.

[3]*The Marine Digest,* 9/27/1924, p. 8. ''For instance a certain type of steamship is called a steam schooner. Looking at one of those vessels, the observer can easily determine where the ''steam'' is justified. But he can find no justification for the ''schooner'' half of the name. The so-called steam schooner and the real schooner have only one thing in common. Both float. So does a certain soap.''

Ultimately, Judge Wilson ruled against the Central Ferry Company and their jurisdiction of Island County, as follows: [4]

"This case involves the right of the Department of Public Works to exercise jurisdiction over steamboats plying between Whidbey Island and Seattle, operated by the petitioner and which are claimed by the petitioner to be ferries within the meaning of the law. The petitioner relies almost entirely upon the case of State Ex Rel Allen v Public Service Commission 111 Wash., 294, to sustain his position that the department has no jurisdiction over his business.

"I am of the opinion that the facts in this case disclose a condition which is not controlled by the Allen case. The boat operated by the petitioner has not been operated under the supervision of the county commissioners or in conformity to any other or version of the statutes regulating ferries in this state, and his operations and business conducted by him do not fall within that class of operations. The petitioner is undoubtedly operating as a common carrier and should be subject to all the provisions of the public service act in this state and should be governed accordingly."

The wars that raged during the 1920s between ferryboat companies were often fought with legal action and court cases. Where once individuals raced steamboats with daring, skillful masters, competing for public attention and fares, transportation companies of the twenties raced one another for control of routes, rates and lawful domination. Bureaucracy had interjected itself. It became a necessity to hire a good lawyer as well as a good captain or general manager. Steamboat racing continued, but stricter government controls, larger, more cumbersome autocarriers, and the dominance of routes by major companies tended to eliminate spirited competition for speed. Attention was focused away from the thrill of the race. Audiences looked to the courts for battles.

Court cases created yet another, newer need. Public relations and advertising professionals began to appear within the industry. Corporate heads, already encumbered with business, legal action and management competitiveness turned to these officials to strengthen patron and employee rapport. Public relations men like William O. Thorniley did this effectively with imaginative advertising campaigns and sales programs. His efforts were reliably tested when court cases called upon the community served to select the "best" company service. Promotion, good will and regular service proved to be strong points in favor of the successful company.

PUGET SOUND NAVIGATION STEPS IN

Looking forward to a busy tourist season in 1925 Whidby Island Transportation Company planned to place a ferryboat in operation between Mukilteo and Clinton to augment their Everett-Whidbey service. Whidby Island Transportation Company was operating in direct competition with Nearhoff's Central Ferry Company. Final arrangements were made for a landing and construction of a ferry slip at Mukilteo. Dock work at Clinton was already underway. Captain Harry Ramwell purchased 25 percent interest on the Whidby Company in late summer, 1926.[5] By December of that

CAPTAIN HARRY BARRINGTON

[5] *The Marine Digest,* 9/11/1925, p. 7. Ramwell was a successful Everett entrepreneur who owned among other businesses, three docks and the busiest section of the Everett waterfront. P.S.N. already owned 25% of the stock of the Washington Route as early as 1913, according to the *Report of Investigation of Earnings,* May 1947. In 1929 P.S.N. dismantled the WASHINGTON (Ex-FLYER) and turned the engines and boilers over to the Whidby Island Ferry Lines, Inc. (organized in 1926 with 360 shares authorized at par value of $100 each) in exchange for 25% of the company's stock. That same year Whidby Island Ferry Lines built a terminal at a cost of $9,000, issuing stock to secure payment thereof. P.S.N. acquired a total of 270 shares, giving it an interest of 75% of the company. The confusion of ownership is related to the similarity of names: Whidby Island *Transportation* Company and Whidby Island *Ferry Lines.* It probably confused the owners as well, since P.S.N. ultimately wound up with the entire operation!

year, Captain Ramwell and Puget Sound Navigation Company had purchased all the ferry interests on Whidbey Island belonging to Whidby Island Transportation Company. Ramwell became president and Captain Harry Barrington became manager of the new Puget Sound Navigation Company subsidiary, Whidby Island Ferry Lines.

On Saturday morning, December 4, 1926, the WHIDBY entered new service between Mukilteo and Columbia Beach (Clinton). The ferry BEELINE[6] replaced the WHIDBY on the Everett-Langley route. Captain Bart Lovejoy commanded the BEELINE and Captain Russel Taylor was master of the WHIDBY, with J.A. Green as purser.[7] The Whidby Island Transportation Company continued to run the steamer ATALANTA from Seattle to Whidbey Island points and the Whidbey stage (bus service) out of Everett.[8] This arrangement continued until the Washington Route and Reeve's Whidby Island Transportation Company were acquired by Kitsap County Transportation Company in 1928.

CENTRAL IV WAS RENAMED AND OPERATED AS THE CITY OF MUKILTEO (below)

BUSES PROVIDED COACH SERVICE TO FERRIES LIKE THE BEELINE ON WHIDBY

[6]Crosby renamed the GLORIA (Ex-FLORENCE K), c. 1903, BEELINE.

[7]The WHIDBY retained her former engineers, George C. Leach, chief, and Charles Stahl, assistant.

[8]Captain O. Swenson was skipper of the ATALANTA.

174

Hold-on, the story grows even more complicated.

Captain Willis W. Nearhoff disposed of his Mukilteo-Whidbey route and the Central Ferry Company by selling his interests in May 1927 to Puget Sound Navigation Company who in turn had acquired the certificate for the Port Orchard-Bremerton ferry run from the Horluck Transportation Company. Nearhoff bought Horluck Transportation Company and operated boats on the Port Orchard-Bremerton-Mannette passenger run. He died soon after leaving Whidbey Island. The management of the firm was left to his 23-year old daughter, Mary Lieseke.

Mrs. Lieseke and her family still own and operate the Horluck Transportation Company in Port Orchard, running passenger vessels to Bremerton. Their newest vessel, the SPIRIT OF '76, was built by Nichols Bros. on Whidbey Island in 1976 and is employed in charter service, as well as commuter runs.

Still a popular run, this Bremerton service was especially busy during World War II carrying Navy Yard workers. Mary Lieseke bacame a licensed master at that time and ran her own vessels with the assistance of her son. Today the company owns a tugboat and five passenger vessels. The family also owns a marine railway in Port Orchard for boat repair.

MARY LIESEKE, PRESIDENT, HORLUCK TRANSPORTATION COMPANY, 1983

THE JOYCE-PAYNE INTERESTS

In 1927 Puget Sound Navigation Company awarded a contract to P. Manson & Son to begin construction of the Keystone Landing near Fort Casey on Whidbey Island.[9] Two steel bridges were built by Wallace Equipment Company for the landing. That summer the navigation company inaugurated a new route between Keystone and Port Townsend, placing the ferryboat MOUNT VERNON on that run.[1] The MOUNT VERNON was formerly operated by the Sound Ferry Company on the Edmonds-Port Ludlow run.

Sound Ferry Lines was owned jointly in the late twenties by the Joyce-Payne interests and Puget Sound Navigation Company. The company was ordered "dissolved" and assets sold as a result of a legal dispute between two factions of ownership.[2] It became the Edmonds-Olympic route of Puget Sound Navigation Company in September 1928, with the reorganized route including ownership of the newly completed ferry QUILLAYUTE running from Edmonds to Port Ludlow.

[9]*The Marine Digest*, 4/16/1927.

[1]Captain Bush Leighton and Chief Engineer J.B. Sweet were the MOUNT VERNON's officers. The Keystone-Port Townsend ferry route was sold by P.S.N. to Olympic Ferries, Inc. in 1947. This company was organized by Captain Oscar Lee, H.J. Carroll and A.C. Grady. The motor ferry FOX ISLAND was purchased by the new firm from the Horluck Transportation Company and placed in command of Captain Lee. The route had not been used since 1943 and it was necessary to construct new landing slips at Keystone due to heavy storm damage.

[2]Newell, *Marine History of Pacific Northwest*, p. 381.

CAPTAIN J. HOWARD PAYNE

SOUND FERRY LINES TERMINAL   *PEABODY FAMILY*

Captain Joyce was one of the fathers of Puget Sound ferryboating when he created the Sound Ferry Lines with four of his brothers in 1919. The little WHIDBY had been their formal initiation into the business. The company established headquarters in Edmonds about 1923. Joyce was joined by Captain J. Howard Payne in the mid-twenties and by 1927, Payne was president of the ferry line.

Howard Payne was an industrious fellow. Born in Denver, Colorado in 1889, and relocating in Seattle with his family in 1897, Payne completed grammar school in 1904. He joined a steamboat crew when he was 15, working aboard the LYDIA THOMPSON for a year and then on a couple of ocean steamships. He returned to shore to complete his high school education. He then shipped as quartermaster with Captain "Dynamite" Johnny O'Brien on Alaska Steamship Company's liner VICTORIA.

Payne returned to Seattle in 1910 and joined Puget Sound Navigation Company again on the express steamer INDIANAPOLIS as mate under Captain Howard Penfield. He was transferred as mate to the

SIOUX in 1911 on the Seattle-Everett route and at the age of 24 was promoted to the SOL DUC's command on the Seattle-Port Angeles-Victoria run in 1917.

In June 1918, Payne left the ferry company's employ to join the U.S. Shipping Board as training ship master of the former Puget Sound Navigation Company's steamer CHIPPEWA. By 1920, Payne was the Washington district manager of the Sea Service Bureau of the U.S. Shipping Board. He held this position until an early retirement from that office in 1927 when he undertook the presidency of Sound Ferry Lines,Inc.

In 1927 the fast and modern $150,000 ferryboat QUILLAYUTE was under construction and near her launching date by the Sound Line. She was christened April 30 by Seattle Mayor Bertha K. Landes at Winslow Marine Railway, Eagle Harbor. Mrs. Rose Littleton of Lake Crescent, the owner of the Rosemary Lodge, had bestowed the QUILLAYUTE's name.[3]

The QUILLAYUTE was of single-end design, 160 feet long, a 52 foot beam, drawing 13'9''. She had twin six-cylinder Washington diesel engines of 750 hp that propelled her at a tested speed of 14 miles an hour or 12.5 knots. She had a capacity for 60 automobiles and 500 passengers.

Mrs. Landes and the launching party were the guests of Captain James Griffiths aboard his power cruiser SUEJA III; 500 Seattle guests were carried by the steamboat BAINBRIDGE to Winslow; 200 residents of Edmonds came on the ATALANTA and guests from Port Ludlow and the Olympic Peninsula were present. The Seattle mayor, selected by the Edmonds City Council as the sponsor, broke her beribboned bottle of Quillayute River water over the prow. The QUILLAYUTE entered service on the Edmonds-Port Ludlow route.

The QUILLAYUTE was advertised as solely a product of the Pacific Northwest. Lumber for the hull and cabins came from the Port Ludlow Mill of Charles R.

McCormick Company. Hardware was purchased from Pacific Marine Supply Company of Seattle. Oakum, spikes, nails, ship felt and other chandlery was furnished by Walter C. Bryant & Company of Seattle. The steering gear (compressed air pneumatic type) with pilot house control and the Viking semi-diesel auxiliary engine were built by the Markey plant. The engines were Washington-Estep. Even the composition flooring was manufactured and installed by Seattle's own J.S. Ransome & Co.

After all the legal haggling and arguments with Puget Sound Navigation Company over the Whidbey Island routes and other potential runs, Captain J. Howard Payne joined forces with Captain John L. Anderson. The events that followed prepared the way for the famous Black Ball Line to emerge within less than a decade as the single, uncontested major controller of the ferry business on Puget Sound.

[3]Miss Littleton won a $50 prize for submitting the best name in the Sound Ferry Lines' contest.

A view of Lake Crescent. On the shores of this lake and Lake Sutherland are situated a number of excellent summer resorts with first class appointments.

fast Diesel Ferry *"Ballard"* with spacious , inviting dining room and comfortable ob- tion room, operates between Ballard and Ludlow four round trips daily.

OLYMPIC LOOP HIGHWAY with its moun- forest and ocean scenery, invites the motorist.

early morning start may be made by taking the A.M. trip from Ballard. Or if more convenient the leroy-Harper Ferry may be used. This ferry is ted by the Kitsap County Transportation Co. e Main 3039 for schedule and rates.

SCHEDULE
Automobile Ferry "Ballard"

Leave Port Ludlow	Leave Ballard Dock (Seattle) Near Gov't Locks
4:00 A. M.	6:15 A. M.
8:30 A. M.	11:00 A. M.
1:30 P. M.	4:00 P. M.
6:15 P. M.	8:45 P. M.

Car No. 28, on First Ave., connect with Bus at 24th Ave. and St. for Ferry.

RATES

	Single Trip	Round Trip
ger Fare	$0.60	$1.00
nder 2,800 pounds	2.00	3.50
ver 2,800 pounds	2.25	4.00

Vehicle Rates Include Fare of Driver

ormation regarding Commutation rates and rates on Trucks, of Purser or Telephone Main Office.

he Ballard OLYMPIC Route

LARD-LUDLOW FERRY CO.

J. HOWARD PAYNE, President

ffice, 117 Canadian Nat. Dock   MAin 3039
SEATTLE, WASHINGTON

The Ballard OLYMPIC Route

FERRIES AND FREIGHT: TRANSPORT AND COMMERCE

Ferries play an integral role in the commerce of several counties of western Washington. The ferry system provides a two-way movement of raw materials and consumer goods, adding up to over a million and a half tons of cargo, transported on 200,000 commercial vehicles carried aboard ferries every year. Ferries are a vital link in supplying residents of Puget Sound islands such as Bainbridge, Vashon, Whidbey, the San Juans and the Olympic Peninsula with food, petroleum products, household goods, heavy equipment and construction materials which are trucked via ferries.

Once the little vessels of the Mosquito fleet carried such commerce on pallets and hand trucks, longshoring the cargo aboard with muscles, cranes and Barlow elevators. Wagons and later, trucks, awaited their arrival at the other end of the run to off-load cargo and carry it to its final destination. Over a period of twenty years the automobile and the development of highways and traffic resulted in numerous vehicular ferry routes. The routes were consolidated and rearranged as traffic increased, population and economic centers grew, and highway networks changed.

The major industry of the Kitsap Peninsula is federal defense installations. Logging and lumber products are the most important activities on the Olympic Peninsula, and in certain parts of both peninsulas and the Sound's islands agricultural development is substantial. Water transportation has always served as the commercial avenue between the peninsulas, the islands and the heavily populated eastern shores of Puget Sound. As long as there have been passengers, freight, or motor vehicles, water craft has sustained their vital needs.

Automobile ferries were immediately recognized for their potential in the transport of tourists and passengers to the hinterland of this beautiful state but the transport of commerce was not so quickly pursued aboard ferryboats. A number of the popular old steamers were "semi-retired" to carrying freight and some passengers, like the SOL DUC, the FAIRHAVEN, and the SIOUX and IROQUOIS. Freight continued to be carried in much the same manner as in the Mosquito Fleet days until trucking companies began to emerge, utiliz-

ing the growing system of highways. The ferry lines soon realized that transport of the entire auto truck and its cargo was not only easier but it was less expensive, reducing the number of deckhands needed to handle freight. Customers for the most part were pleased since the transport network became a consolidated system, providing door-to-door pick-up and delivery of goods. The ferry companies initiated trucking efforts within the western side of the state and were responsible for its growth and modernization until the early forties when state regulations began to deter existing "monopolies" and assist in the introduction of a greater number of trucking companies on the Sound.

K.C.T.C. JOINS P.S.F.L.

Early in 1927 the Kitsap County Transportation Company and a major Sound freight carrier, Puget Sound Freight Lines, formed a new corporation known as the Ferry Dock Company, leasing the Grand Trunk Dock[1] for a number of years. The passenger and freight carriers of both companies made Grand Trunk Dock their terminal and homeport and the rundown pier and its offices became an active shipping center on the Seattle waterfront.

The Ferry Dock Company was headed by Captain John L. Anderson as president. Captain F.E. "Ed" Lovejoy, president of Puget Sound Freight Lines was vice president and Philip Macbride was secretary-treasurer. The company made extensive improvements. They constructed a ramp from the ground floor to the second floor that gave their passengers quick access to the overhead bridge at Marion Street.[2]

Anderson was a friend of the Lovejoy family of Whidbey Island and familiar with the ferry operations to that island. He had a strong competitor in Captain Alex Peabody and the Puget Sound Navigation Com-

[1]Located north of the Colman P.S.N. Dock, today the property is a parking and holding area for the Washington State ferries at Colman Dock.
[2]This walkway exists today, crossing from Colman Dock to First Avenue. It was built by the railroad in the fall of 1909. *The Sea Chest*, Vol. 3 and 4, p. 15.

pany, and the ambitions of Captain Lovejoy would do a great deal to bolster Anderson's own competitive nature.

Puget Sound Navigation Company, or the Black Ball Line (the title restored to P.S.N. by its new president), was strong not only for its established passenger and auto transportation system, but also for its freight haulage and highway and wharfage connections. The Black Ball Line owned the piers and roads servicing their docks in most of the communities they served, as well as the property and terminals located at those piers.

Much of this property had been acquired through the deals and company consolidations initiated by Charles Peabody and Joshua Green. The partners involved with the formation of Alaska Steamship Company began their venture by forming the Pacific Wharf Company and gaining control of the pier at Port Townsend. This became a part of Puget Sound Navigation's holdings. The 1929 records show that they also owned the Colman Dock Company which held the

lease to Colman Dock issued by owner J.M. Colman; the Neah Bay Dock Company owning the wharf and hotel at Neah Bay; the Peoples' Wharf Company owning the wharf at Port Angeles which was capitalized on the books at $25,420.10 but had no value set for leases of property upon which the wharf was erected; the Victoria Dock Company, Ltd. owning and operating the dock at Victoria, B.C. used by Puget Sound Navigation and its vessels (the land upon which the dock stood was owned by P.S.N. but the foreshore water rights were leased from the Canadian Department of Marine and Fisheries); the terminal for Whidby Island Ferry Lines at Mukilteo and the Citizen's Dock at Bellingham.[3] There were numerous other property holdings, crossover ownerships and stock investments that gave the Black Ball Line a finger in every pie.

In 1924 Bremerton Auto Freight, Inc. was organ-

[3]*Report of the Investigation of the Earnings, Property, Operations, Rates, Services and Facilities of the Puget Sound Navigation Company*, prepared by Harold E. Jones, Department of Transportation, State of Washington, May 1947.

CAPTAIN F.E. LOVEJOY

ized to operate motor freight business between Seattle and Bremerton via the Navy Yard Route ferries and between Bremerton and Port Orchard via highway.[4] In 1926 Puget Sound Navigation Company acquired 60 percent of the Bremerton Freight stock and spent a total of $10,500 in connection with this company. Puget Sound Navigation Company turned over two trucks to Bremerton Freight and a permit from the Department of Public Service.[5]

In 1928, with Captain Alex Peabody at the helm, Puget Sound Navigation Company issued its first bonded indebtedness, totaling $750,000. This was evidenced in the form of a first mortgage from Pacific National Bank, Seattle, as trustee. All physical property of the company together with its Department of Public Service certificates were pledged. Proceeds were intended for use in the acquisition of subsidiary companies' capital stocks and construction of new vessels. That same year, the Black Ball Freight Service was organized to operate in the local cartage service of Seattle, Bremerton, Port Angeles and other cities served by the company's ferries. Black Ball Freight picked up freight and hauled it to ferry terminals, running freight-carrying trailers aboard the ferries. At the destination the freight was distributed by the same company in local cartage service.

Alex Peabody eliminated the use of hand trucks from freight handling in 1928 and introduced trailers and trucks to his ferry system. The Barlow marine elevator had already had a significant impact on freight handling, and the navigation company had been one of the first to install them on vessels and at Colman Dock. The Black Ball Line was distinguishing itself from other passenger steamer and transportation lines by purposefully seeking to develop *profits* from the handling of freight with equal attention to passenger transport.

In the decade of the twenties, Puget Sound Freight Lines created an impressive record for hauling freight and cargo, particularly on the South Sound. This was due in large part to the efforts of the company founder and president, Captain F.E. Lovejoy. Captain Lovejoy was a member of one of America's most distinguished maritime families. He was born into Maine seafaring stock. His forefathers were shipowners and masters with distinguished credentials, and his grandfather and father were pioneer Pacific Coast shipowners.

Lovejoy's grandfather, Captain Howard Bentley Lovejoy,[6] was well-known as the master and part-owner of the bark CHALCEDONY, engaged in carrying ice from Sitka, Alaska to San Francisco in the 1850s. He often sailed between the Northwest and the Bay City and it was in this manner that he became interested in Whidbey Island in 1852. His son, Howard Bartlett Lovejoy, was born in San Francisco in 1854. The old New England navigator decided to establish his permanent residence at Coupeville, Whidbey Island. There he raised three sons, Captain H.B. Lovejoy, Captain L.B. Lovejoy, and E.O. Lovejoy.

Captain F.E. Lovejoy, son of H.B., was born at Coupeville in 1888 and was raised on the island. At fourteen years of age he moved to Seattle for further education. He spent the summer of 1904 as a flunky on the steamboat FAIRHAVEN. He was paid $25 a month by the Puget Sound Navigation Company subsidiary, LaConner Trading & Transportation Company.

The following summer he worked aboard the

[4]Ibid. Horluck Transportation Company still owned the certificate for boat operation between Port Orchard and Bremerton.

[5]Ibid. Similarly, C.F. Deppman, owner of the remainder of the stock, donated equivalent assets and in both cases paid-in surplus was credited. P.S.N. acquired the remainder of the stock in 1927.

[6]Also the grandfather of Captain B.H. Lovejoy of the Whidby Island Transportation Company. Biographical material from *The Marine Digest*, 8/9/1924, p. 5.

DODE on the Sound and the L.T.HAAS on Lake Washington. One of his high school projects was carving the nameboard for the pilot house of the CAMANO built in 1906 by his father.

Lovejoy joined the CAMANO crew as deckhand. Owned by the family's Island Transportation Company,[7] the little vessel operated between San de Fuca on Whidbey Island and Seattle via Everett without sleeping accommodations or galley. The hands ate breakfast before boarding at six o'clock in the morning; they ate dinner when they returned at 11:30 at night. They consumed a cold lunch with coffee heated on the high-pressure cylinder head.

F.E. Lovejoy worked this schedule aboard his father's boat 21 straight days, then slept for three days. He had lost 14 pounds, but he did return to the CAMANO working an easier schedule.

Lovejoy worked on several steamships, traveling to Southern California and the Arctic, each time returning to Whidbey for a couple of months' tour of duty with Island Transportation. By the age of 21 Lovejoy was a licensed mate and the following year, 1910, he became a licensed master. For the next three years he commanded vessels of his father's fleet. He also purchased five acres of land on Whidbey Island and interspersed his sea duties with farming.

In 1916 he supervised the building of the CHACO. Upon her completion he assumed command of the vessel for that year. He became manager of the Elliott Bay Drydock Company but left the shipyard in 1918 for appointment as master of the tugboat PROSPER of the Puget Sound Tugboat Company. He oversaw installa-

tion of the equipment of the steam schooner H.B. LOVEJOY that same year at the Ballard Marine Railway. Following the LOVEJOY's completion, F.E. raised and beached the old German steamship MARIECHEN which had been submerged in Smith Cove waters many years. That fall he accepted appointment as navigating officer of the U.S. Shipping Board's training ship under the command of Captain J. Howard Payne. The year 1918 proved to be a very busy one for Ed Lovejoy.

Lovejoy shipped as mate on Puget Sound Tug's PIONEER until 1919 when he operated the freighter CHACO again under contract from Sound Freight Lines,[8] the vessel's new owner. He was paid $500 per month as captain and was expected to pay the rest of the crew from this stipend, as well.[9] Within a few months, Lovejoy personally chartered the vessel with an option to buy and making a success of the venture, purchased the CHACO in 1920. He placed her in the Seattle-Olympia route via Tacoma. Besides these Puget Sound Freight Lines' interests, as the company was called, Captain Lovejoy was also part-owner and a director of the Puget Sound Motor Freight Company, operating a large auto truck freighting service within southwestern Washington, connecting with Olympia.

By 1917 another aspiring youth had graduated from the University of Washington with a degree in mechanical engineering. World War I delayed his plans and Clarence Carlander found himself in the United States Army, serving first at Fort Worden[1] protecting the entrance to the Sound, and then as a lieutenant in heavy artillery in France. He returned to civilian life in Seattle in 1919.

Carlander found a berth at Seattle's Pier 4 as the office manager and bookkeeper for Sound Freight Lines which operated the CHACO and later the sternwheeler GLEANER carrying workers to and from Seattle shipyards. Ambitious Carlander was also agent for the Poulsbo Transportation Company and the West Pass Transportation Company, as well as dock cashier for Parr-McCormick[2] interests who leased Pier 4.

[7]Island Transportation Company was organized by H.B. Lovejoy, James Esary, Byers Brothers and others. The company built the CAMANO, CALISTA and FALCON and purchased the FAIRHAVEN from Green in 1906. They operated boats between Seattle, Everett and Whidbey Island points, as well as Seattle to Alki.
[8]Sound Freight Lines was organized by Captain J. Howard Payne, Ole Lund and George Coryell.
[9]The Sea Chest, Vol. 12, p. 87.
[1]Coast artillery assignment.
[2]Later became McCormick Steamship Company.

STEAM SCHOONER H.B. LOVEJOY BUILT IN 1918

LOVEJOY SUPERVISED BUILDING OF THE CHACO IN 1916

CLARENCE CARLANDER

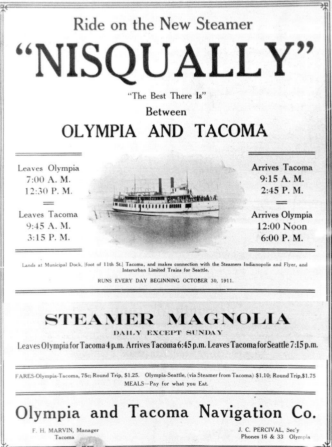

Ride on the New Steamer

"NISQUALLY"

"The Best There Is"

Between

OLYMPIA AND TACOMA

Leaves Olympia	Arrives Tacoma
7:00 A. M.	9:15 A. M.
12:30 P. M.	2:45 P. M.
Leaves Tacoma	Arrives Olympia
9:45 A. M.	12:00 Noon
3:15 P. M.	6:00 P. M.

Lands at Municipal Dock, (foot of 11th St.) Tacoma, and makes connection with the Steamers Indianapolis and Flyer, and Interurban Limited Trains for Seattle.

RUNS EVERY DAY BEGINNING OCTOBER 30, 1911.

STEAMER MAGNOLIA

DAILY EXCEPT SUNDAY

Leaves Olympia for Tacoma 4 p.m. Arrives Tacoma 6:45 p.m. Leaves Tacoma for Seattle 7:15 p.m.

FARES-Olympia-Tacoma, 75c; Round Trip, $1.25. Olympia-Seattle, (via Steamer from Tacoma) $1.10; Round Trip,$1.75
MEALS—Pay for what you Eat.

Olympia and Tacoma Navigation Co.

F. H. MARVIN, Manager
Tacoma

J. C. PERCIVAL, Sec'y
Phones 16 & 33 Olympia

Carlander became district operating manager for McCormick Steamship Company in 1924 and resigned that position in 1929 to become general manager of the Puget Sound Freight Lines. He had been stockholder and secretary-treasurer since 1924. Lovejoy had reorganized the company in 1924 in order to build the CAPITOL; Carlander and Philip Macbride joined the company at that time.[3] The CAPITOL and CHACO connected Olympia with Puget Sound Motor Freight's automobile freight trucks of southwestern Washington and Grays Harbor. Heavy freight traffic developed and steadily increased. Freight to Tacoma from Seattle was sold at $2 a ton and the crew was paid $2 a day.[4]

By the time Carlander joined Puget Sound Freight Lines as general manager he was well acquainted with the enterprise and its subsidiaries. These included Puget Sound Terminal Company, Puget Sound Freight & Ferry Company and the Percival Dock Company of Olympia. Carlander became general manager when the company took over the Merchants' Transportation Company[5] of Tacoma and other interests in 1929, giving it a fleet of 9 freighters. This was the largest single fleet of freighters in the history of Puget Sound.

THE LIFT-TRUCK FLEET

Puget Sound Freight Lines was instrumental in introducing some radical changes in handling of freight on Puget Sound. In 1928 Captain Lovejoy designed and commissioned the newly built freighter SKOOKUM CHIEF for lift-truck service, placing Elwell-Parker trucks in operation as an experiment. After one year of close observation, the operation was considered successful beyond all expectation. It proved to be economical and efficient under all freight handling conditions. The lift-truck system was very satisfactory for handling pulp, the principal commodity moved by the SKOOKUM CHIEF. Continued use demonstrated its efficiency under the store-delivery system for general merchandise. Lovejoy introduced store-door delivery to Puget Sound several years prior to his lift-truck systems. It was a wide departure from the accepted freighting methods but soon it met with general use in the larger Sound cities.

[3]Macbride became vice president and a director of P.S.F.L.

[4]*The Sea Chest,* Vol. 12, p. 87.

[5]A large freight account business to Tacoma was earlier controlled by the Merchant's Transportation Company. P.S.F.L. acquired Merchant's vessels: BELANA, SEATAC, F.H. MARVIN, V.P. HANDY through this sale.

The SKOOKUM CHIEF's installation consisted of a Barlow marine elevator, two Elwell-Parker lift-trucks and a number of wooden skips.[6] The mode of operation required that freight be piled on the skip in the transit shed. One of the gas electric trucks would run its platform under the skip, raise it a few inches off the ground and then carry the skip and load to the vessel. Once there, the marine elevator awaited the load at the level of the wharf floor. The truck would then run the skip onto the marine elevator platform and the elevator would descend to the freight deck. There the truck would carry the skip to the deck and set it in its reserved place. The freight remained on the skip. Other loaded skips were boarded in the same manner until the vessel's cargo was completed. The ship then proceeded on her rounds, following the same operation for discharge of cargo.

The latter detailed description may seem like a simple, commonly employed method of freight handling, but it should be recalled that this was the *beginning* of employment of these methods. The system was originally worked out for the handling of pulp movement from Shelton to Tacoma and then extended to general cargo, each ship taking two to three tons. The vessel was equipped with a heavy plank for use at the docks. The freight plank formed a necessary part of the vessel's equipment. With two lift-trucks in operation, the SKOOKUM CHIEF handled 139 tons of pulp in 56 minutes. Under the old system, using handtrucks and manpower, it required an hour to load 25 tons with four times the number of men.[7] The marine elevator, in use for over a decade on Sound ships by 1929, enabled the vessel to load regardless of tide conditions. Peabody introduced a similar system of lift-trucks for freight handling aboard the ferries in the early thirties.

[6] Wooden platforms with tops that resemble a large board sling. Each skip measures 6' x 5' and rests on two runners that hold the platform several inches above the floor. (These are similar to pallets or skids).

[7] *The Marine Digest,* 9/21/1929, p. 1.

HANDLING FREIGHT CAN BE A LIABILITY

In August of 1930 the Canadian Pacific Railway decided to participate in the Seattle-Victoria-Vancouver passenger business with sailings of their ships from the Grand Trunk Dock in Seattle as their American terminus. A part-time man was needed on the dock for a number of duties such as handling lines and daily record keeping. A University of Washington senior was found to fill that vacancy. It was a fellow by the name of J. Knox Woodruff. Thus began Woodruff's long association with the Puget Sound Freight Lines (and the Ferry Dock Company)—an association that would promote him one day to the position of executive vice president and a director of the company.

The freight line experienced similar problems encountered by the shipping companies and other public service businesses. A number of fire and storm disasters occurred throughout the years but the company always rebuilt and moved forward. In 1931 the Shelton wharf burned along with their truck and the customer's freight. The same year the Shelton oyster growers threatened a law suit to close the pulp mill. They claimed that the mill effluvium was damaging the oyster breeding beds.

Puget Sound Freight could ill afford to lose this major freight contract if the mill were to be closed. To an even greater extent, the small town of Shelton did not want to lose a major industry and source of employment, particularly at the height of the Depression. Public contributions were solicited to buy out the oyster farmers. The freight line donated $5000[8] of their badly needed corporation funds to further the recovery cause. That same year the SKOOKUM CHIEF was leaving Hammersley Inlet with a full load of pulp and ran ashore on a rock that opened a hole in her bottom. The pulp was off-loaded to a barge. A soft patch closed the hole sufficiently to allow the ill-fated vessel to limp into the shipyard for repairs. Repair costs totaling $9000 were covered by insurance.[9]

Puget Sound Freight Lines incorporated passenger service into some of their freight runs. The MOHAWK, obtained through a consolidation with the San Juan Island Transportation Company,[1] was unprofitably operating on the Bellingham-San Juan-Seattle route. The schedule was inconvenient, requiring the passengers to spend a night in Seattle while awaiting the return trip the following morning. Hotel lodging was expensive so Puget Sound Freight altered the schedule to accommodate a one-day, round trip for the islanders. Traffic noticeably increased but Puget Sound Navigation Company's Anacortes-Sidney run of auto carriers proved to be too strong a competition and Puget Sound Freight abandoned these efforts quickly.

The company's principal freight routes as of 1932 were:[2]

"Shelton-Olympia-Tacoma. In Olympia they operated over the Percival Dock[3] while in Tacoma the Milwaukee Dock was their terminal. The warehouse at both locations had been somewhat reconstructed so the deck of the wharf was level with the bed of the truck.

"Seattle-Tacoma-Olympia with the run Seattle-Shelton through Tacoma. In connection with these routes they had truck connections at Olympia for Grays Harbor and from Shelton via truck to many towns on Hood Canal.

"Seattle-Bellingham-Anacortes-San Juan Island and Seattle-LaConner. These runs hauled canned salmon south from the canneries, pulp from the mills and lime from Roche Harbor, as principal commodities. . . . all the day-to-day needs were also found on vessels such as fresh produce for the stores, hardware for the mills, dry goods and so on."

[8] *The Sea Chest*, Vol. 12, p. 92.

[9] Ibid.

[1] Lovejoy took over the semi-diesel freighter SEAL (c. 1939) operated by Wayports Transportation Company from Seattle to Port Townsend. R.M. King was the owner. He also acquired his father's company, the San Juan Island Transportation Company and the steamer MOHAWK (Ex-ISLANDER, c. 1921). These vessels and firms merged into the Puget Sound Freight & Ferry Company in 1928. Newell, *Marine History of the Pacific Northwest*, p. 382.

[2] *The Sea Chest*, Vol. 12, p. 93.

[3] The original Percival Dock was built by Captain Samuel W. Percival, retired sailing master, shipowner, general mercantile store owner who settled in Olympia in 1850, establishing his store and one of the first sawmills built at Tumwater Falls. He built Percival Dock in Olympia in 1860 and five years later built the second Percival Dock, relocating it to its present location.

Sixteen year old John Cushing Percival was directed by his father to take charge of the dock in 1877 and he managed the wharf affairs and served as Olympia agent for the Pacific Steamship Company, The Chicago, Milwaukee & St. Paul Railway, the Great Northern Railway and the Canadian Pacific Railway.

Percival Dock was sold to P.S.F.L. in 1926. It had already served as the major support dock for early day steamers of many years, the center of freight and passenger activities as well as their supply of wood and water. Percival Dock is owned today by the City of Olympia. "John Cushing Percival," *The Marine Digest*, 4/3/1926.

P.S.F.L.'s BELLINGHAM

In the late twenties Puget Sound Freight Lines formed a partnership with Kitsap County Transportation Company to purchase the steamer GENERAL FRISBIE, formerly a San Francisco-Vallejo ferry. She was renamed the COMMANDER upon her arrival in Seattle and was placed by the new company on the Seattle-Bremerton run June 6, 1931 under the Washington Route's certificate then held by Kitsap County Transportation Company.

Puget Sound Navigation did not take kindly to this turn of events since the Navy Yard Route to Bremerton had always represented their most lucrative business.

The companies settled their differences in the State Supreme Court.[4] The COMMANDER was allowed to make six round trips daily plus an additional two trips with the HYAK. This service was granted the Washington Route certificate on the basis that "...no reason exists for refusing to permit improved service to these points whose traffic justifies greater service.... There is a need for additional service at Bremerton and as both companies serve Bremerton, both companies possess the right to improve that service.... The problem, as presented by this voluminous record and briefs, seems much involved. We think, however, that the foregoing considerations are decisive in favor of the Washington Route and call for the upholding of the decision and order of the department (of Public Works)."[5] The COMMANDER continued on the run as a thorn in the side of the Black Ball Line until bought out in 1935.

[4] It is interesting to note the comparative speed with which the state court judicial system made decisions in those days. The Washington Route petitioned the Dept. of Public Works for an altered certificate in April 1930. The case was tried in Thurston County Court that year and appealed to the State Supreme Court, receiving their decision almost exactly one year to the day of the original certificate application.

[5] "Washington Route Decision of the State Supreme Court," *The Marine Digest*, 4/11/1931, pp. 3, 4, 7.

S.S. HYAK

THE COMMANDER, COMPETITION FOR BLACK BALL

BLACK BALL FREIGHT

During the years of company development and the concurrent improvement of highways and auto trucks, Puget Sound Freight was able to gather a number of permits to conduct operations over highways. Certificates of necessity governing trucks were just coming into being, so sometimes "unlikely" methods such as showing a truck haul when a freight boat was overloaded or out-of-commission were employed to "convince" the Washington Department of Public Service to award them a certificate. It presented an unusual situation for the Department because they did not normally grant certificates to one company for more than one method of competitive hauling, such as trucks *and* freight boats. The interstate and intrastate truck regulations allowed the grandfather clause to be applied a number of times in favor of the freight line. The company exercised this priority on several truck routes that would prove to be of great importance in the coming years.

In 1928, an associated freight trucking company was formed, known as Marine Auto Freight Lines, Inc. Transfer services of the region were pooled into this company headed by Walter Eyres and principals Bill Baxter and Joe Daw of Lloyd's Transfer. Marine Auto Freight managed the trucking of commodities carried over the auto ferries of the Black Ball Line as well as outside orders not related to ferry transportation. This was an aggravated source of competition for Puget Sound Freight Lines, especially in the early thirties when it functioned in a similar capacity. Puget Sound Freight continued to work in close association with Kitsap County Transportation with their subsidiaries operating ferryboats. Black Ball already had a valuable network for freight handling and movement.

On June 28, 1928, Marine Auto Freight's corporate name was changed to Black Ball Freight Service. R.J. Acheson, traffic manager for Puget Sound Navigation Company, purchased Black Ball Freight Service in March 1936 and continued to work in close association with Puget Sound Navigation Company. Despite the similarity of name, Black Ball Freight Service was never a subsidiary of Puget Sound Navigation Company or the Black Ball Lines.

Labor disputes of the mid-thirties forced Puget Sound Freight to remove the MOHAWK from her run.

The company acquired the Citizen's Dock[6] at Bellingham at the time and numerous other consolidations and changes were made, leaving Puget Sound Freight Lines with very little water freight competition while Black Ball concentrated on ferry operations and the transportation of independent trucking freight.

Trucks were making definite inroads on every route that could possibly be served, especially since it was growing easier for the truck to deliver to the customer's door rather than the local dock. The complexion of Puget Sound's towns was rapidly changing and growing away from the waterfront as their populations expanded and their businesses flourished. The twenties and thirties proved to be a time of rapid expansion for the Northwest. Humble little communities found that they could no longer depend on the steamer to deliver sufficient quantities of goods to sustain their welfare. The steamer's personal convenience for townspeople was eliminated, too. Those tiny communities which had depended on the Mosquito Fleet were fast fading from the scene and they turned to roads and overland travel as a source of transport if they even managed to remain intact as a town. Young people were moving away from the agricultural communities to the large cities in search of employment. With this permanent relocation, they helped alleviate the persistent demands for way stops once patronized by the steamers. Terminals were built at the major ports of call.

Puget Sound Freight Lines survived the Depression with difficulty. The SKOOKUM CHIEF burned to the waterline with a full load of pulp, a highly flammable commodity, January 16, 1935. Insurance covered her loss and Captain Lovejoy and his son, Howard, then a student of naval architecture at the University of Washington, drew up plans for a new vessel.

The WARRIOR emerged in 1936 according to Howard Lovejoy's design. She had a double-tunnel stern and a shallow draft to serve the Shelton mill and other ports of limited water depths. Her 200 horsepower Atlas Imperial diesels were installed below deck to afford an unobstructed interior for freight. A 10-ton Barlow elevator and two Elwell-Parker lift-trucks could accommodate the vessel's maximum 500 tons of freight on pallets. She was considered the most modern and efficient vessel of her kind in the nation.

As the Depression years wore on, Puget Sound Freight Lines offered the SEAL, ATALANTA, TOURIST and MOHAWK for sale. The CHIMICUM, V.P. HANDY

and CAPITOL were very small and could function with handtrucks only. Fire struck the CAPITOL in 1937. The vessel burned and sank in deep water without loss of life. At least it was one less freight boat to worry about at the time.

Captain "Ed" and his trusted engineer, Al Solibakke, visited Astoria, Oregon to inspect the steel L.P. HOSFORD[7] which had been built in 1931 for the Portland-Astoria run. After her purchase, the vessel was towed to Lake Washington Shipyard from which she emerged in rejuvenated form in 1937 as the INDIAN. Her bow had been closed in and the house from the TOURIST was added.

Business steadily improved for the line as American involvement in World War II neared. Pulp haulage continued to climb as the mills stockpiled for an anticipated boom in production. The freight boats carried other commodities such as canned goods, lime and lime products, petroleum products, feed and mill products, steel, cement, copper ore and copper concentrates, liquor, empty cans, fresh berries, dynamite, dried peas and beans.[8] They could haul almost anything anywhere—and did.

V.P. HANDY

[6]Citizen's Dock was previously owned by P.S.N. interests. In an agreement between the two companies, P.S.N. transferred the Citizen's Dock and the freighters TOURIST and ALOHA, previously running in the Bellingham trade, to P.S.F.L. in exchange for their guarantee to remain out of the ferry passenger business. Walter Green, freight manager for the Black Ball's Bellingham office, returned to company headquarters in December 1935 following the signing of this agreement with P.S.F.L. and the closure of the P.S.N. freight operations there.

[7]Which was for sale by the Harkins Transportation Company of Astoria.

[8]*The Sea Chest*, Vol. 12, p. 97.

FREIGHTER INDIAN

Captain Lovejoy was 51 years old when he suffered a fatal heart attack in 1940. The company he had built was a strong one, operating a fleet of eight of the most modern freight carriers to be found in the country. Their trucking business was expanding; it is this portion of the firm's interests that today comprises the majority of freight handling. A fleet of 200 tractor trucks and over 400 trailers now carry the "P.S.F.L." logo.[9]

Captain Ed Lovejoy had trained a crew of people who would continue in the paths he had blazed. Among these were Howard Lovejoy, his son, now chairman of the firm; Clarence Carlander, a former Seattle port commissioner; George Foss, senior vice president and retired vice chairman of the board; and J. Knox Woodruff, vice president and director. Captain Lovejoy enjoyed the loyalty and respect of his many captains, engineers and deckhands without whom no company would prosper.

The F.E. LOVEJOY was built in 1945-46 at Reliable Welding Works, Olympia, 800 tons capacity. It was retired by Puget Sound Freight Lines in 1971 and oper-

ates today in Alaskan trade as the DENALI. It is the last self-propelled freight vessel built by Puget Sound Freight Lines.

Puget Sound Freight Lines serves the public today in a manner established by the Lovejoy family of Whidbey Island. Their ventures into ferryboats and passenger steamers has ended but they remain one of the few companies in private ownership that traces its lineage directly to an early Puget Sound steamboat line.

Conversion of Puget Sound Freight Lines marine operations to tugs and barges began in 1960. They have been 100 percent a tug and barge operation since retirement of the F.E. LOVEJOY freight carrier. Today they operate four tugs and seven barges with a total capacity of more than 13,000 tons, moving more tonnage by water than ever before. Thomas E. Lovejoy, great-grandson of Captain H.B. Lovejoy, is the president and chief executive officer of Puget Sound Freight Lines.

[9]Ibid.

INCORPORATED UNDER THE LAWS OF

THE STATE OF NEVADA

№ 301

Shares 71

PUGET SOUND NAVIGATION COMPANY

CAPITAL STOCK $2,000,000—FULLY PAID

This Certifies that _____ W. B. FOSHAY CO. _____ is the owner of

Seventy-one ------ Cancelled in new ------ Shares of the Capital Stock of
Certificate No. 376

Puget Sound Navigation Company

transferable only on the books of the Corporation by the holder
hereof in person or by Attorney, upon surrender of this Certificate
properly endorsed.

In Witness Whereof, the said Corporation has caused this Certificate to be
signed by its duly authorized officers and to be sealed with the Seal of the Corporation
this 7th. day of August, 1929 A.D. 19

SECRETARY

PRESIDENT

SEAL — PUGET SOUND NAVIGATION COMPANY NEVADA

FOSHAY COMES TO TOWN

Historians will debate the degree to which a single individual can persuade or influence epoch changes. A study of small isolated environments on Puget Sound reveals interesting individuals and their roles in the tide of regional development. While major events rocked the stability of social and economic structure in the late twenties, the ferry fleets of Puget Sound were overcome by the appearance of a powerful individual. Their operations would never be the same; in the case of some companies, they would eventually cease to exist.

Seattle's waterfront community was astounded in 1929 when a newcomer, the W.B. Foshay Company of Minneapolis, came on the scene. Mr. Foshay intended to make his mark on the Sound and Alaskan marine circles. That is precisely what he did.

W.B. Foshay offered to purchase the Puget Sound Navigation Company, Puget Sound Freight Lines and Kitsap County Transportation Company. He first turned his persuasive talents upon Alex Peabody. He pointed out that his recent purchase of Northland Transportation Company was running successfully to Southeastern Alaska and he had a new vessel, the W.B. FOSHAY (1200 tons) under construction at Lake Washington Shipyards.[1]

Here was a peculiar situation to be faced by the ferry and freight corporations. Most of these companies had been created from limited resources, one or two vessels, and family management and leadership. Each had achieved much-deserved respect on the Sound where the owners, as well as the crew members, lived and worked. Their fleets were growing and service had improved as routes were refined.

A number of corporate consolidations had already produced stronger companies and more stable alliances. One may presume that they were witnessing profit increases, yet competition had risen steadily, too. Legal battles fought and won on both sides had reduced corporate reserves and had frazzled their nerves. Rumblings of labor organization were overheard and employers had reason to be concerned. There was no instant cash available for new construction of vessels, new equipment or new terminal facili-

ties; but the public clamored for all of these. Should the ferry companies at least consider Foshay's offer?

HOLDING ON

Captain Peabody had demonstrated that he was ready and willing to take control of the Puget Sound Navigation Company. Although considered a young man at age 32, Peabody was experienced and toughened in the shipping business. He had been at sea a number of years, sailing aboard square-riggers and rising to the position of master of ocean vessels for an international shipping line. Alexander Peabody was admittedly the chosen son of Charles to assume leadership of the company his father had founded. The third son in a family of eight boys, Alex headed the Puget Sound Navigation Company with pride and distinction. His strong family lineage was a constant reminder when he reinstated the trade name "Black Ball Line" for his ferry fleet. Peabody intended to do justice to his family, his company and himself with fortitude, imagination and a resoundingly astute business sense. He would not avoid competitive challenge. He did not hesitate to tell Mr. Foshay "NO" under any terms. The contest of wills was just beginning.

Foshay had a good idea. Consolidation of all ferry and freight companies could have improved route service. An injection of substantial capital could have helped modernize and streamline the Puget Sound Fleet. Costs and, therefore, rates, could have been reduced with more efficient vessels, one administrative body and a single pool of experienced crew members upon which to draw. Labor organizations would have had an easier time if they had attempted to negotiate with only one major company instead of three. W.B. Foshay demonstrated potential to become a very powerful individual.

Foshay's grandiose dreams became conjecture when Peabody pointedly refused his offer. Nevertheless, he made an attempt to acquire a sizeable amount

---

[1] W.B. Foshay had also acquired large public utility properties in Ketchikan, Alaska.

of stock in the navigation company. Peabody, Lawrence Bogle and E.T. Stannard, vice president of Alaska Steamship Company, formed a new holding company to operate the line and fight Foshay.

The Marine Digest, November 16, 1929, provided a detailed account of transactions for the marine community:

"In a deal involving approximately $3,000,000, the control of the Puget Sound Navigation Company of Seattle was taken over by the recently organized Founders Syndicate at the annual meeting of the navigation company's stockholders in its Colman Dock headquarters last Tuesday. The Founders Syndicate is headed by E.T. Stannnard of New York, vice president of Alaska Steamship Company.[2] The new syndicate voted 11,000 shares out of the total of 21,000 shares.

"Captain Alexander M. Peabody, vice president and secretary of the Puget Sound Navigation Company for a number of years, was elected president of the company, succeeding Ira Bronson, resigned. H. Arthur Rust of Seattle and Tacoma was elected vice president and treasurer and C.V. LaFarge of Seattle, secretary.

"New directors chosen, follow: W.T. Ford, secretary and auditor of the Alaska Steamship Company and the Copper River & Northwestern Railroad Company, Morgan corporations; J.H. Bloedel of the Bloedel-Donovan Mills Company; William Calvert of the San Juan Fishing & Packing Company; Lawrence Bogle, Seattle attorney; and Mr. LaFarge. Mr. Bogle was elected chairman of the board of directors. Directors re-elected follow: Captain Peabody, R.R. Pierson, Mr. Rust, and George Roberts.

"...The syndicate is composed of the founders of the navigation company and their associates."

The Founders Syndicate held 53 percent of the company's 21,000 shares. The Foshay interests cornered only 2,369 shares. Foshay found power among the navigation company's investors. He would be an immediate problem to them for only a short while.

APPROVALS AND ARRANGEMENTS

Kitsap County Transportation Company and Puget Sound Freight Lines were more receptive to Foshay's ideas. In the greatest single deal in local Puget Sound shipping, the W.B. Foshay Company of Minneapolis purchased these two companies and their subsidiary, Ferry Dock Company, in May 1929. Captains Anderson and Lovejoy met with representatives of the Foshay interests and closed the deal involving 23 vessels owned and operated by these companies and the Ferry Dock Company that operated the Grand Trunk Dock under a long term lease.

In the case of both the Kitsap County Transportation Company and the Puget Sound Freight Lines, no changes were made in personnel. Captain Anderson continued as the president and general manager of the Kitsap company and Captain Lovejoy continued to direct the affairs of the freight lines. The two companies annually handled an estimated 1,000,000 passengers, 125,000 automobiles, and heavy freight movements on Puget Sound routes.[3]

Foshay assured the corporate leaders that purchase of these properties would mean unlimited financial resources for their future development. He said that he was a strong believer in the destiny of the Northwest and Alaska and visited Seattle a number of times to become fully familiar with local conditions.

Wilbur Burton Foshay was an entrepreneur in the strongest sense of the word. His business career began with the New York Central Railroad where he was employed in various capacities. He spent several years with the United Gas Improvement Company at Tarrytown, New York, and later at Hutchinson, Kansas and Dodge, Iowa with local electric, gas and water companies. He then joined the Electric Bond & Share Company of New York who eventually sent him to the Pacific Coast. It was through contacts in this position that he became manager of the Northwestern Electric Company of Portland, Oregon.

Foshay returned to Minneapolis in 1915. There he organized the W.B. Foshay Company for the purpose of owning and managing utilities and industrials in that region. The substantial growth of his company over the following 12 years confirmed his confidence in the

[2]The Alaska Steamship Company, in addition to their familial associations with P.S.N., most likely felt pressure from Foshay in their Alaskan operations what with his ownership of the Northland Transportation Company.

[3]*The Marine Digest,* 5/11/1929, p. 1.

"security and fair returns offered by investments in sound business enterprise when properly managed."[4]

Foshay was unable to attend the launching of the $500,000 steel motorship W.B. FOSHAY at Lake Washington Shipyards in July 1929. It was christened by his daughter, Miss Julianne Foshay. Washington Iron Works built the vessel's diesel engines and Allan Cunningham's plant manufactured her electric-driven auxiliary deck equipment. Virtually all of the $500,000 invested in the vessel remained in Seattle.[5] So did the unpaid bills.

THE INDEPENDENT: CITY OF VICTORIA

Even though highway networks on the Sound threatened to end watercraft passenger transportation for all time, the evolution of the automobile ferry actually created a resurgence of interest in this field. The spring of 1928 witnessed the debut of yet another new ferry corporation, the Edmonds-Victoria Company. It was organized by Herbert Fleishhacker of San Francisco, H.F. Alexander, D.E. Skinner and Henry G. Seaborn. They purchased the steel passenger steamer ALABAMA[6] and renamed her the CITY OF VICTORIA.

Appointment of Captain Cyprian T. Wyatt[7] as master of the CITY OF VICTORIA was announced in 1929 by Captain J. Howard Payne. About the time of the sale of Kitsap County Transportation Company to Foshay, Captain John Anderson joined forces with Payne to form the Independent Ferry Company to operate the Edmonds-Victoria Route and charter with option to buy the CITY OF VICTORIA. The vessel was acclaimed to be the largest and fastest automobile ferry steamship operating under American Registry[8] on Puget Sound. Making two round trips daily from Edmonds to Victoria, the steamship had 100 staterooms for the accommodation of those returning at night. A number of staterooms were arranged in suites, fully equipped with hot and cold running water and bath. A spacious glass-enclosed observation room was built on the forward cabin deck at the Todd plant to provide an unobstructed view of Puget Sound and the Strait of Juan de Fuca while enroute. Fresh flowers adorned all the rooms and the passengers were quoted as having a most enjoyable ride.

Captain William E. Mitchell joined the Independent Ferry Company in 1930 as manager of the operating department of the ferry line. Captain Mitchell had enjoyed maritime prominence for a number of years as the former general manager of the largest inland water

CAPTAIN WILLIAM E. MITCHELL

fleet in America, the Puget Sound Navigation Company and the Navy Yard Route.[9]

[4] The Marine Digest, 7/6/1929, p. 5.

[5] The Marine Digest, 8/2/1929, p. 26.

[6] ALABAMA formerly owned by the Baltimore Steam Packet Company. Captain Alexander J. Zugehoer and Chief Engineer S.G. Clifford brought the CITY OF VICTORIA from the East Coast via the Panama Canal in 1928 for the new owners.

[7] Chief mates were George Barrell and Bush Leighton, chief engineer was S.G. Clifford, chief steward was J.P. Fitzpatrick, purser was George W. Esary. Company agent at Edmonds was Reuban Hauan, port steward was Claude Stryker.

[8] This acclamation was made specifically as rebuttal to the Canadian PRINCESS ships on the Sound which were larger than the CITY OF VICTORIA. This vessel's dimensions were 293.8 x 54 x 16, of 1,938 tons, driven by a triple-expansion (24.5, 40, 47 x 42) four-cylinder engine of 3,400 hp. Steam was at 160 pounds pressure from the two return tube boilers. Newell, *Marine History of the Pacific Northwest*, p. 381.

[9] P.S.N./N.Y.R. included the following ferries at the time of Mitchell's management: OLYMPIC, CITY OF ANGELES, PUGET, MT. VERNON, PIONEER, SEATTLE, CITY OF BREMERTON, KITSAP II, TOURIST, BAILEY GATZERT, and the motor freighter ALOHA.

EDMONDS-VICTORIA COMPANY'S CITY OF VICTORIA

CAPTAIN CYPRIAN T. WYATT, MASTER OF CITY OF VICTORIA

Mitchell worked for Joshua Green and his associates from 1898 onward, beginning as deckhand and rising to general manager of the two corporations. His record in that service included eight years as master of the express steamship H.B. KENNEDY, later the ferryboat SEATTLE.

Mitchell was born in Coupeville in 1879; his parents were pioneers who settled permanently in that island community in 1866. His father, Emerson Mitchell, spent the early years of his life in shipbuilding in Bath, Maine. He came west during the California Gold Rush in 1849 and explored the Northwest regions for future settlement six years later. The elder Mitchell entered the lumber trade and worked for Puget Sound Mill Company owned by Pope and Talbot.

Captain Mitchell left the family farm on Whidbey

at age 17 in 1896 for a job as cabin boy on the steamboat LYDIA THOMPSON operating between Seattle and Bellingham. He worked the same route in the same capacity on the WASCO.

As cabinboy, deckhand and night watchman he became familiar with many of the Puget Sound routes. He served the Seattle-Everett route on the ALBION, the Seattle-Bellingham and Seattle-LaConner run on the FAIRHAVEN, the Seattle-Navy Yard Route on the CAPITOL CITY, PORT ORCHARD and the STATE OF WASHINGTON. He was later mate on the FAIRHAVEN, INLAND FLYER and the ATHLON. He was appointed master of the ATHLON in 1901. He commanded other vessels of the Navy Yard Route which was then headed by H.B. Kennedy. In 1909 he began eight years' service on the H.B. KENNEDY as her first master.

Mitchell came ashore to manage the Navy Yard Route for H.B. Kennedy. In 1920, after the merger of the Route with Puget Sound Navigation Company, Mitchell became manager of these two allied lines.[1] After Joshua Green's departure from the navigation company, Mitchell perhaps felt less loyalty to the owners and was likely to have been interested in new business challenges. The Independent Ferry Company offered just such an interest.

FERRY RATES
SOUND FERRY LINES, Inc.
Edmonds, Washington

Edmonds-Kingston Route

	S.T.	R.T.
Passenger fare	$0.25	
Autos under 2500 lbs.	1.25	$2.00
Autos over 2500 lbs.	1.50	2.50
Motorcycles	.75	1.25
Auto Trailers	1.25	2.00

Port Gamble-Shine Route

Passenger fare	$0.25	
Autos under 2500 lbs.	1.00	$1.50
Autos over 2500 lbs.	1.25	1.75
Motorcycles	.75	1.25
Auto Trailers	1.00	1.50

Thru Rate—Edmonds-Kingston, Port Gamble-Shine

Passenger fare	$0.50	$1.00
Autos under 2500 lbs.	2.25	3.50
Autos over 2500 lbs.	2.75	4.25

Edmonds-Port Ludlow Route

Passenger fare	$0.75	$1.25
Autos under 2500 lbs.	2.25	4.00
Autos over 2500 lbs.	2.50	4.50
Motorcycles	1.50	2.50
Auto Trailers	2.00	3.50

Vehicle rates include fare of driver.
(Over)

Captain J. Howard Payne and Captain Joyce were seeking additional ferry interests in the midst of W.B. Foshay's purchases and consolidation. They initiated automobile ferryboat service with the LIBERTY in the Ballard-Ludlow route. The company owned Washington Certificate Number 14[2] for the operation of the steamboat NARADA between Seattle and Port Ludlow, via Kingston and other points. An amendment extended the service to cover the ferry route between Ballard and Port Ludlow.

Puget Sound Navigation Company filed suit instantly. The contention was that the amendment allowed a duplication of its ferry service between Edmonds and Port Ludlow. Thurston County Court barred the company from operating the new service. An appeal to the State Supreme Court sent the case back to the State Department of Public Works with instructions to determine whether Ballard, as part of Seattle, formed a territory not served by the existing routes. The order by the Department once again granted the Joyce-Payne application permission to operate. The steam ferry LIBERTY[3] initiated the service in 1930. Simultaneously, plans were announced for the construction of a new automobile ferryboat with capacity for 500 passengers and 60 automobiles. Their terminal was originally located at Grand Trunk Dock with the Ferry Dock Company. Payne made arrangements to move the terminus to Ballard once the Department's order was final.

The impact of Black Friday, October 28, 1929, when the American stock market plunged to the bottom, was felt around the world. Reverberations echoed across Puget Sound as the W.B. Foshay Company folded with the market. Stock of Kitsap County Transportation Company and Puget Sound Freight Lines had been deposited with a Seattle bank in trust, to be given to the Foshay interests when all payments were completed. The Foshay company could not meet their payments and the stock was returned to the owners.[4] Legal matters were not resolved for a number of years but the dreams of a great floating empire had vanished in one day.

Early in 1930 a Seattle and Alaska group headed by G.W. Skinner, H.G. Seaborn and William Semar took over Foshay's Northland Transportation Company. They completed delinquent construction payments on the W.B. FOSHAY and renamed her the NORTHLAND. She was placed with the NORCO in weekly service to Alaska.

---

[1]F.E. Burns, preceding general manager of P.S.N., retired to other business interests in Seattle.

[2]Payne and Joyce bought the Ludlow-Kingston Transportation Company owned by Otto Lorenz who held the freight and passenger certificate for the Seattle-Kingston-Port Ludlow route.

[3]Capacity for 250 passengers and 25 autos. The LIBERTY belonged to K.C.T.C.

[4]A bank employee of the time reports that the payments already made for the stock by W.B. Foshay were not returned. He had bought the companies with an option and these payments were considered payment thereof.

NEW FERRYBOAT VASHON

Contracts had already been signed for the construction of the new ferryboat VASHON with Lake Washington Shipyard. Anderson was hard-pressed to meet payments for the vessel. He and the Kitsap County Transportation Company managed to make financial arrangements which would allow for its completion, but the company's strength was further strained by this venture.

The Depression era and labor unrest were suddenly upon the ferryboat fleets of Puget Sound. The next decade would drastically alter the major transportation system of the Pacific Northwest. Mr. W.B. Foshay had merely set the scene.

AN ERA OF LABOR RELATIONS AND STRIFE

"A Waterfront Carol"
(By William O. Thorniley and Jack Piver)[1]

You may work day and night,
You may wear out your sight,
And develop new lines on your phiz,
You may worry and figure,
You may live on the trigger,
In an effort to salvage your biz.

But your taxes will take
A chunk of your cake,
And that cut ain't the end of it, boy;
For, of what you have left,
You will soon be bereft
By a strike of the guys you employ.

The Marine Digest

You may think the strike's o'er,
On sea and on shore;
And again turn thots to your biz.
You may seek added dollars
To stop kicks and hollers,
As the wrinkles grow on you phiz.

When a brick hits your head
You'll find the strike isn't dead
And more and more dollars you'll waste.
For the strikers will say
As they ask for more pay
The agreement is not to their taste.

The Shipping Register

It is difficult to envision the Northwest region's dependence upon ferry service until that service ceases and all subsequent disruptions of normal activity become evident. The region has had numerous, but unwelcomed opportunities to feel the full impact of this situation over the last fifty years. "Waterlocked" residential, agricultural and recreational areas have been virtually isolated from metropolitan centers like Seattle and Tacoma while ferryboat companies (and later the state) and the unions stood immobile. Both sides firmly held to opposite lines of thinking.

In a five year period, from 1934 to 1939, ferry service was interrupted by five strikes. Consequently, a severe loss of island crops and commuter inconvenience forced a general arousement of public wrath against labor-management disagreements. In the case of health care of the 1930s, as one example, ill or injured people were best advised to leave their island homes because of the limited availability of medical assistance on the small islands and the unpredictability of ferry service. Planes and helicopters were not as readily available as today. Small battalions of pleasure boats and union-sanctioned steamers attempted to fill the yawning gap in service.

Dangerous public outcries were further heard when undependable service was coupled with rising rates in an already sorely depressed time. Companies petitioned for Washington State Public Service permits to raise fares as a compensatory means of retrieving higher wages and fuel charges. Documents are scarce outlining the actual profits of ferry companies, but they are assumed[2] to have been negligible during the Depression prior to the war materiel build-up and the increased patronage of the Navy Yard Route. The public took an active and vocal interest in the management and labor relations of the ferryboat fleets on Puget Sound.

An investigation of the history of labor movements within the Sound's floating highway industry is an awkward research study due to the scarcity of documentation and unbiased accounts. Memories, dimmed by the unpleasant events and the general hard times, challenge the present-day historian to find an objective view of the circumstances and present it to readers unemotionally. [This study has primarily been limited to oral recollections with the exception of a few written investigation reports of arbitration boards and several dissertations prepared by university students

[1] *The Marine Digest*, 1/4/1936, p. 7. Thorniley wrote half of the poem one week in *The Digest* and Piver answered the second half the following week in the San Francisco *Shipping Register*.

[2] Based on interviews conducted by the authors with former administrators of the Black Ball Line, their bankers and Kitsap County Transportation Company officials.

which were also based on information gathered in private interviews. Those interviews were with individuals who formed the upper echelons of both sides of the arguments.]

The Board of Arbitration, headed by Chairman William A. Gaines of Seattle, did, however, reveal some evidence indicating the financial condition of the major companies directly associated with the inlandboatmen's unions and their demands. Chairman Gaines' findings were submitted in a statement that is part of the permanent arbitration record:[3]

"The financial statements of the operating companies prove to the satisfaction of the Chairman that no excessive profit has been derived from the operation of these vessels. On the contrary, some of the companies show losses for the past years, one of the larger companies sustaining a loss of $621,000 including depreciation [K.C.T.C.] in four years; another company has sustained a loss of $60,000 in the last two years [P.S.N.?]. To add to the present operating expense an amount necessary to meet the demands of the unions would be disastrous to both parties in this case, in that it would mean the abandonment of routes and laying up of boats. Such action would result in the reduction of service to the people living in Puget Sound country, in both freighter and passenger lines, and would certainly mean the complete loss of employment to many men now working. This agreement is to run approximately one year, and at the termination of the agreement should the boat industry show an appreciable increase, the manner is afforded this document for the men to press their requests for shorter hours and increased wages, and the writer believes that the operators will cooperate in carrying out such a program under normal business conditions."

The impact of a depressed economy and the rising costs and labor contracts forced one company to sell out to the Puget Sound Navigation Company, thus initiating major private consolidation of the entire ferry fleet under the Black Ball flag. Captain Alex Peabody was then to head the largest inland fleet in the world and a regulated monopoly of the Sound's ferry transportation just six years after becoming president of the company. This position was not without its pitfalls and

heartaches. But it was the impact of this monopoly that provoked public awareness, coupled with rising rates, which ultimately led the governor of the State of Washington to order purchase of the ferry fleet on Puget Sound.

Three unions represented ferryworkers on the Sound in the 1930s: the Inlandboatmen's Union of the Pacific; the Masters, Mates and Pilots Organization; and the Marine Engineers' Beneficial Association. The Inlandboatmen's Union was the largest of the three and seems to have taken the leadership in labor negotiations. Formation of the unions and their influence on the formation of the Sound ferry fleets is the story at hand.

A YOUNG MAN FROM THE WINE COUNTRY

In the early thirties the waterfront witnessed the arrival of an intelligent, capable and goodlooking young man, Captain John M. Fox. Just 29 years old, Fox had been provided $500[4] working capital by the California Marine Council of San Francisco Bay, including the Ferryboatmen's Union and the Masters, Mates and Pilots, San Francisco Division, and the Marine Engineers Beneficial Association. Fox had been selected to represent both the Ferryboatmen's Union and the Master, Mates and Pilots in the Puget Sound region. After his outstanding performance in labor relations in the Bay Area, he was charged with organizing the Puget Sound ferryworkers.

The proposed organization of Sound workers was viewed as a plus for the Bay Area unions seeking yet higher wages and further advances that were said to be stalemated by the significantly lesser conditions on the Sound.[5]

John Fox was an inspiring and articulate man. He had turned to the sea and sailing ships at age 14 and was proud to have sailed on the bark JOHN ENA as second mate. As a small child he had witnessed the San Francisco earthquake in 1906 and the fire that followed. It left deep impressions, and as an adult, he spoke occasionally of the abhorent looting that followed it. Fox had worked in the vineyards of the Sonoma and Napa

[3] *The Marine Digest*, 11/1/1935, p. 4, published the total statement.

[4] Shrader, *The Black Ball Line*, Edmonds Printing Co., 1980.

[5] This was farsighted thinking on the part of unions in the Bay Area to recognize that their efforts were significantly handicapped with the menace and threats of poorer working conditions in other ports. It suggested to them that they should organize coastwise; therefore in 1930, this policy of coastwise organization was adopted.

CAPTAIN JOHN M. FOX

Valleys, testing grapes for their sugar content. He grew to be a wine connoisseur and claimed that California wines were some of the best in the world.

Captain Fox had been master on several ship tenders in the Bay Area and worked in Florida fishing commercially for sharks. He returned to San Francisco holding an inland and coastwise master's license, but like many others during the Depression, accepted a job on deck.

Fox moved his wife and small daughter to Seattle early in 1931 and settled permanently. He wasted no time opening a union office at Second and Cherry, the heart of Seattle's maritime district. He began to familiarize himself with the waterfront crews and the ferryboat routes. He was a good speaker and crew members listened while he collected his facts and reiterated them in public speech with a genuine aptitude for reasoning and persuasiveness.

Unlicensed men in Puget Sound ferry crews worked 12 hour days at that time and deck officers worked as long as 18 hours a day. Crew members were granted days off once a month, only when there was no work to do. This time off never exceeded four consecutive days unless the crew member simply quit. Sick leave was nonexistent. Most crewmen agreed that the work on ferries was not exceptionally strenuous and that the food was fairly good. The hours, however, were determined by schedules and weather conditions; employment was prescribed by company management.

Chairman Gaines of the 1935 Board of Arbitration had comments on the working conditions of the ferryboatmen:[6]

"Since 1929 the country has been in the throes of the longest depression in history, and to the credit of the employers, they have endeavored to keep up wages, shorten the working week, without reduction in force. In fact since the start of the depression several of the companies have changed from the single crew operation to the double crew operation, thereby increasing the operating costs of such companies very materially.

"The men who are employed in this service are fortunate in one respect, at least, they have had steady employment while thousands of citizens are unable to find employment of any kind and have been compelled to go on the dole. Many of the men employed in the industry have their meals and quarters furnished them and their wages represent a net return on their labor. The employees of the ferries are able to be at home with their families every day.[7] The Chairman at one time had a public interest in one of the ferry companies; has traveled on the ferry and passenger boats extensively; known several of the men personally, and until this hearing came up was of the opinion that they were fairly well satisfied with their jobs and steady employment. I am still of that opinion."

Chairman Gaines' comments might be misconstrued to sound almost patronizing, but an appropriate perspective of the attitudes of the day compared with the present is important. It does seem, however, that the standard of wages at that time for the industry were miserably low and employers needed to be prompted to improve them. Able seamen on ferries received $55.25 per month; firemen and unlicensed engine room employees (oilers and wipers) received about the same. Able seamen on freight boats were getting $45 per month, working 12 hour days, while truckers (so-called for the hand trucks they pushed) received only $39 a month. Tugboat hands received

[6] *The Marine Digest*, 11/9/1935, p. 4.

[7] This was a major incentive for roaming seafarers to work for the ferry system on Puget Sound.

$40 a month, putting in a 12 to 14 hour shift. Overtime pay was nonexistsent in any of these positions.[8]

THE M.E.B.A.

Even though the workers seemed ripe for militant organization under these conditions and wages, it has often been said that this attempt to organize along the coast took more courage than common sense. The Depression was beginning to attack the Pacific Northwest in severe shock waves, creating a lethargic stranglehold among the workers who had begun to appreciate just holding onto a job with plenty of work to do. Fox and the Marine Council forged ahead in the task of combining the isolated and discontented workmen into an economically forceful group. It was soon apparent that the employers took a dim view of labor organization among their crews, forcing organizational work to be carried on in secret. The union would be well established before fully exposing itself and making demands on the companies.

Fox hit upon the approach that organizing the licensed officers first would open the doors further to organization of non-licensed employees. The officers were the natural leaders of the crews and for the movement. Fox sought them out socially to press his influence as their equal. He worked through their fraternal organizations such as the Marine Engineers Beneficial Association (M.E.B.A.) which at that time was primarily a brotherhood and service-oriented group.

M.E.B.A. No. 38 of the Northwest was first organized in Seattle on April 18, 1883 with 21 members. Robert Moran, founder of steel shipbuilding and a future mayor of the City of Seattle, was elected the first president. In 1885 practically all the members being employed, it became impossible to collect a quorum to hold a meeting, and the association was abandoned. The organization formed again at Port Townsend in 1888. It returned to Seattle in 1889 and has continued in steady operation through to the present day. The association moved into a three story brick building in 1920. By 1926 their small membership managed to make the final installment on the building's mortgage.

David W. Miller was the first business manager of Local No. 38 taking that position in 1922. He had been one of the veteran members of the Seattle association, having joined it in 1897. He served as president for five years and attended national conventions as the local delegate for a number of years. He was vice president of the national association of the M.E.B.A. for several

DAVID W. MILLER OF THE M.E.B.A.

terms and turned down the national presidency because he did not want to move away from Seattle and the Pacific Northwest.

Miller had had a varied background of employment ranging from the meat packing business and salmon canneries to the chief engineer's job on the Stimson Mill Company's tug TILLICUM, the Grays Harbor tug GENERAL CUDAHY,[9] the steamer CITY OF EVERETT and the steamship NORTHLAND, operating between Seattle and Southeastern Alaska. About 1917 he became a marine salesman for the Standard Oil Company[1]. Eventually he opened a marine machinery and supply business with V.S. Jenkins as his partner. He sold out to Jenkins during 1921 and became the business manager for the M.E.B.A. in January 1922. He held that office until his death in 1931 at which time that position was filled by William Peel.

The financial secretary of Local No. 38 was a native son. William Mortimer Coombs, known as ''Mort'' on the waterfront, was born in 1862 in a house at the corner

[8] Fox, ''A Glance Back and Looking Ahead with the Inlandboatmen of Puget Sound,'' pamphlet, 1939, pp. 2-3. Some personal sources recall that the wages were higher for ferry workers in 1935 than those given here. Fox may have confused them with tug crew wages.

[9] The first oil burner on Grays Harbor.

[1] Miller must have been one of their first marine salesmen because diesel boats were still a rarity on the Sound in 1917.

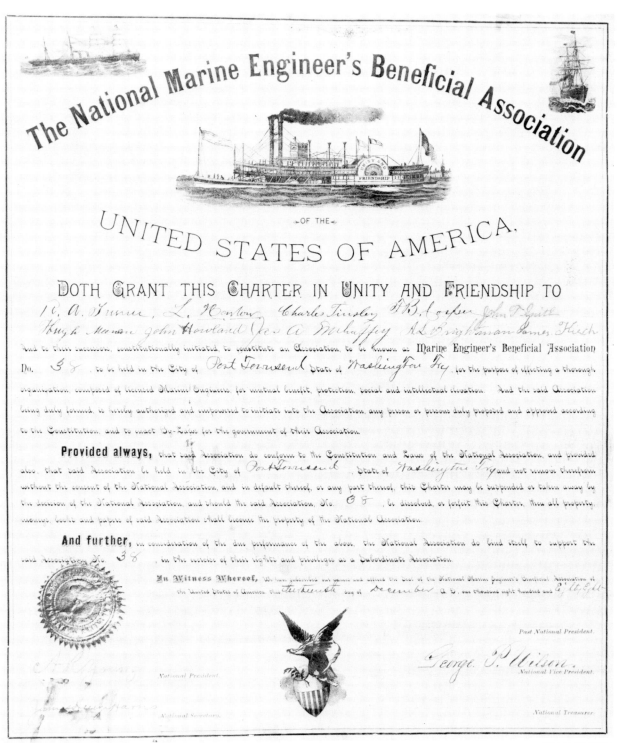

NATIONAL CHARTER FOR MARINE ENGINEER'S BENE-
FICIAL ASSOCIATION

GRAHAM COLL.

of Cherry Street and First Avenue, Seattle. He was the son of pioneer Judge Samuel F. Coombs. Four of his uncles were master mariners.[2] At the age of 18, Coombs entered the plant of the Washington Iron Works, serving four years apprenticeship as a machinist.

Coombs went to sea as oiler of the AL-KI in 1885 and then served as oiler of the steamship OLYMPIAN and as first assistant on the tugs BLAKELY and RICHARD HOLYOKE. He was licensed as chief engineer in 1886 and shipped as oiler in 1888 on the steamer PREMIER, leaving her to work as watertender on the steamship MEXICO.

Coombs entered his own business with Captain Elmer E. Libby in chartering the tug YUKON for operation in Sound towing. When the charter with the YUKON expired, he returned to the PREMIER and held that berth as second assistant until the vessel sank in a collision with the collier KEEWEENAH.

Coombs became the first assistant engineer on the

WILLIAM MORTIMER COOMBS

Seattle fireboat SNOQUALMIE in 1892, but within a year had transferred to the steamship CITY OF TOPEKA. In 1896 he was appointed chief engineer of the WILLAPA, flagship of the Alaska Steamship Company, then operating on the Alaska routes. Throughout the following years he worked as chief and first assistant engineer on a number of steamships operating out of San Francisco and Portland. He served as second assistant for the Oceanic Steamship Company when their new steamship SIERRA was brought to the West Coast. This trip was followed by a round trip to Australia on the SIERRA.

On January 1, 1909, Coombs was elected financial secretary of the M.E.B.A. Local No. 38, Seattle, and held that position until his death at age 72 in 1934.

At no time prior to 1930 did Local No. 38 have more than 50 members. This small membership minimized their efforts and diminished their progress toward influencing the working conditions for ferryboat employees. Only engineer officers with licenses from the Bureau of Navigation and Steamboat Inspection were allowed to join M.E.B.A. Their manager and financial secretary were well-liked and respected men within the maritime community; and this may have contributed to some difficulties when the organization tried to interject itself into labor negotiations with the long-time familiar waterfront employers.

DEBATES, DEBACLES AND ARBITRATION

By December 1, 1931, Captain John Fox saw through the successful charter of the Masters, Mates and Pilots Association by the national organization. Designated Local No. 6, this union was an affiliate of the American Federation of Labor, representing the licensed deck officers of the Puget Sound inland waters. The Ferryboatmen's Union was chartered the following April, representing all unlicensed employees of the Sound's inland waters. This included all unlicensed personnel of the deck, steward and engine departments.

These charters were like waving a red flag in front of the employers. They, too, were organized, calling themselves the Waterfront Employers. The ferry companies threatened dismissal of all union employees. Union organization only became more intense with this move, in an effort to gain substantial strength before the employers carried out their threats. In the early summer of 1932, Puget Sound Navigation Com-

[2] Uncles were Captains William Boyd, George Boyd, Theodore Arey and Frank Parker.

NATIONAL ORGANIZATION

of MASTERS, MATES AND PILOTS of AMERICA

Faith is a Living Power

TO ALL

WHOM IT MAY CONCERN, KNOW YE THAT

The National Organization of Masters, Mates and Pilots of America

By virtue of the authority vested in it, having been duly petitioned and reposing a special trust and confidence in the following named Brother Masters, Mates and Pilots

NAMES

C.M.McLennan	H.H.Owens	L.H.Stevens	P.D.Motzer
L.E.Fowler	L.Crowley	W.Boyd	C.H.Weyrich
H.J.Williams	F.V.Kasch	R.C.McMurren	B.P.Leighton
A.F.McClellan	C.Demsky	D.Jensen	E.Mehus
T.E.Sumner	A.O.Rindal	P.Jensen	J.R.Shaw
C.F.Lampman	T.B.Coffelt	H.F.Wilson	J.M.Fox

hath granted this **Charter** or **Warrant**, *authorizing them to organize, constitute and*

pany fired five members of the Masters, Mates and Pilots Association. The union, still in its infancy, was called upon to test its strength and prove its right to exist. The issue was crucial to their future if they were to impress prospective members of their economic effectiveness and ability to endure in the face of the employers' might.

Confronted with this direct attack, the Masters, Mates and Pilots were not yet strong enough to respond with a strike. They decided their only alternative was to boycott the Black Ball Line.

The two unions, Ferryboatmen's Union and the Masters, Mates and Pilots, having affiliated with the Washington State Federation of Labor, appeared at the annual convention of that body and requested that it place the Puget Sound Navigation Company on its unfair list. This was an unprecedented situation in that the unions were asking all union members to boycott a company when members of the union were still on the job. There was no strike. It was further embarrassing to the Federation that Puget Sound Navy Shipyard workmen (and mostly union members) commuting between Seattle and Bremerton were compelled to ride unfair boats.

But the Masters, Mates and Pilots were a resourceful group, calling upon their own talents to resolve the issue. Jointly, these two unions chartered the old steamer MONTICELLO and operated her between Seattle and Bremerton for the convenience of the Navy Yard workmen using an all union crew. This operation continued for eleven months without state route certificates. Finally in July 1933, the unions had won a partial victory and the boycott was lifted. It is interesting to note that at the end of June 1933, President Roosevelt announced a new naval construction program prepared to expend $238,000,000 for new warships. Half of the work was to be performed in private yards, leaving the remainder to such facilities as were located at the Bremerton Naval Shipyard. This was a promising sign to employers, workers and ferry operators alike. Several of the five discharged members of the Puget Sound Navigation Company were reinstated; however, the company refused to grant outright recognition of the union as a collective bargaining unit.

Indicative of the lack of recognition for these budding unions and their boycott is the fruitless effort to research newspapers and journals of the day. There simply is not much information available. Apparently, it was considered of no local news value, causing only minor inconvenience to commuters or island shippers.

Manitou Beach - Agate Pass Ferry Assn.

CLUB FERRY SCHEDULE

Summer 1933

MOTOR FERRY QUILCENE

Operated for

Benefit of Club Members by the

**Manitou Beach-Agate Pass
Ferry Association**

Club membership entitles members to the use of the facilities of the club upon payment of the club dues of $1.00 per year.

R. M. Hitchcock,
Sec'y-Treas.

Claude Arnold,
President

It is quite astounding that under such conditions the union accomplished a very slim victory.

Shortly following the lifting of the boycott, the federal government eased the situation of union recognition with the passage of the National Recovery Act. In section 7-A of the Act, the rights of workers to organize and bargain collectively was established. In the face of this, the employers had no choice but to cease opposition to the unions' existence, thus relieving some of the former issues under vehement argument.

The west coast employers met union organization with owner organization through the auspices of the Washington Shipowners' Association. This became a strong and powerful lobbying and negotiating body that continued to face the battles squarely on behalf of the Pacific's inland boat owners. In 1934, a local arm of this society, known as the Waterfront Employers' Association, were represented publicly with statements accusing the International Longshoremen's Association and the Masters, Mates and Pilots of forcing a closed shop on shipowners and destroying the freedom of choice for the individual marine employee.[3] A strike had evolved through the efforts of these two unions when they tied up all ocean and coastwise shipping on the Pacific Coast for weeks. The ferry fleets were not directly affected on Puget Sound but ferry employers were acutely aware of the threat that such a strike would result from future labor relations. *The Seattle Daily Times,* May 23, 1934, published a front page article in which the Seattle Chamber of Commerce asserted that Seattle was losing a million dollars a day during the longshoremen's strike.

It was against the setting of this coastwise strike that on May 29, 1934, the Ferryboatmen's Union of Puget Sound voted its first strike against the Puget Sound Navigation Company, the largest ferry fleet on the Sound. Public sentiment against marine employee strikes was already running high and the public did not distinguish clearly between inland marine employees and ocean-going employees.

The strike was called on the eve of Memorial Day weekend, traditionally one of the most heavily traversed times of the year for island ferry traffic. The demands of the Ferryboatmen's Union included a six day week and no wage decreases. Captain Alex Peabody met the union's demands by hiring non-union crews to man the vessels. The first scheduled run affected by the strike was only four minutes late leav-

3 *The Seattle Times,* May 18, 1934.

ing the Seattle dock. The strike-breakers were protected by 25 policemen and 20 deputy sheriffs on the
company's Colman Dock.[4]

The Seattle strike was organized by C.W. Deal,
general manager of the Ferryboatmen's Union of the
Pacific, homeported in San Francisco. Deal was one of
those responsible for Fox's appointment to the region.
In all, there were 120 strikers organized in the Puget
Sound area in 1934. At 11:00 P.M., 12 strike-breakers
attempted to enter Edmonds ferry dock but were set
upon by 20 strikers and promptly fled. Strikers thus
prevented the operation of the Edmonds, Port Ludlow
and Port Gamble runs. Regular schedules were maintained, though, on the Seattle-Bremerton, Seattle-Port
Orchard, and Alki-Manchester runs. The Seattle police
guards did not succumb to the strikers and kept these
routes open to operation by strike-breakers. The
strikers finally boarded the Seattle-Bremerton ferry at
Bremerton and convinced the workers to walk off the
job there.[5]

This strike has been uniquely identified in the
Sound's history as the only one that ended in an
unqualified victory for the Ferryboatmen's Union. The
public was informed on May 31, 1934 that the strike
was over and that the Black Ball Line and the Navy
Yard Route had agreed to a contract specifying no
wage reductions and a six day week. It was also one of
the shortest ferry strikes on record in the area; it lasted
only three days.

The contract was of short duration; it went into
effect June 1, 1934 and expired December 1, 1934.
Union officials today have explained that the reason
for this short-term contract was so that they could
renegotiate their demands every few months since the
working conditions were in need of major improvements. Union officials felt it was more important to
take little steps each time and achieve some victory,
than to propose radical changes all at once and risk all
chance of winning. Following termination of the contract in December, the union asked for modifications
in the terms of contract provisions, reflecting higher
wage scales and shorter work days. Arbitration was
agreed to when a settlement could not be reached and
all matters were submitted to the Board of Arbitration.

The Gaines Arbitration Board was composed of
three members appointed by the unions: Captain John
M. Fox, Earl Gunther and Charles E. Nelson, and three
members appointed by the Washington Shipowners'
Association: Captain Harry E. Tompkins, Clarence E.

CAPTAIN HARRY E. TOMPKINS

Carlander and Charles R. Lonergan. These men represented Kitsap County Transportation Company, Puget
Sound Freight Lines and Puget Sound Navigation Company, respectively. The seventh member, who was to
act as chairman, was appointed by the other six members. This position was filled by W.A. Gaines of Seattle.

The Board hearings commenced in late July 1935.
Testimony submitted by both sides was heard through
October 1935. At the conclusion of this testimony, the
Board discontinued open hearings and started execu-
tive sessions.

The major issues reviewed were the union
demands:

1) Maximum hours were to be a consecutive eight
hour day up to 13 hours in a 24 hour period, averaging
actual work time during that period between 3 and 9½
hours. Between working periods the men amused
themselves aboard the boat by eating, sleeping, playing cards or other entertainment. Regardless of the
hours of actual work, they were paid a full 13-hour day.

2) Overtime pay meant time worked in excess of
regular assigned hours and the balance was absorbed

---

[4] *The Seattle Times,* May 29, 1934.

[5] Smith, *A History of Labor Relations in the Puget Sound Ferry
Boat Trade,''* University of Washington Thesis, c.1950.

by time off. The union amendment demanded time-and-a-half pay for any time worked in excess of eight hours on days on or days off and during watch below.

3) Minimum call: Any employee called to work was to receive at least one-half day's pay. The union demanded a full day's pay if called to work.

4) Wages at that time ranged from $226 per month for a master's rating, to $65 per month for the lowest paid in the steward's department. The average wage was about $100. The union demanded substantial increases in several classifications, some of them as high as $50 per month additional.

5) There were no existing provisions in collective bargaining contracts for seniority protection. The union now proposed that one be inserted into the contract. Primarily it addressed promotion by use of seniority.

The Gaines Arbitration Board decided practically all of the issues against the union. In as much as most of the issues discussed ended in deadlock between union representatives and employers, the chairman was hard-pressed to make all the decisions or simply leave them undecided. His judgements were said to have been controlled by the companies' ability to pay wages. In those days of sorely depressed economy, it was wiser to remember that reasoning during arbitration, since it may have been the only sensible approach to take. Indeed, the chairman's assumption that one or all of the companies would fail if they were pressed harder by the employees, was proven correct within a very short time. Nevertheless, the seeds of workers' benefits and rights were planted with the employers who would eventually experience better times in some cases and the workers would stand in line for a "piece of the action." The days of tyrannical entrepreneurs and "capitalists" who had created gigantic monopolies were breathing their last in the Northwest shipping industry. The maritime unions had worked hard to establish their toehold. When the economic picture improved, they would reap the benefits along with the employer.

Employers and union officials agreed to uphold the decision of the arbitration board before the meetings and hearings began; but when the award was finally handed down, the union was dissatisfied and bitterly attacked it, charging that the Board had exceeded its authority and had improperly exercised the powers granted it.[6] Many of the criticisms expressed through this written charge were based on the differences in judgement, rather than substantiated assertions that the Board had abused its power or that the employers had presented false financial information. In retrospect, it is very likely that the companies' financial figures were truly as dreary as they appeared.

The union's retort to Chairman Gaines' remarks about the owners' right to a fair return on their investment follows:

"... The employees are not stockholders in the companies by which they are employed. They do not receive dividends nor do they participate in management. They do not share in the companies' profits. They ask only a living wage, and, by every canon of social justice, such a wage should not depend upon the contingency that the companies should suffer no loss. A business, which cannot afford to pay a living wage, has no right to prey off the community; has, in fact no right to existence."[7]

The total effect of the unions' reasoning was to convince the union members that the award was illegal. The unions refused to be bound by the award and in retaliation, voted a strike against the Puget Sound inland ferry and freight fleets on November 2, 1935. Events that occurred in the following two weeks changed the total complexion of history within the Sound fleets and aroused such public wrath that the early groundwork was laid for the eventual ownership by Washington State.

THE STRIKE OF '35—ONE TO REMEMBER

Events moved swiftly in the Sound ferryboat and steamboat world the afternoon and evening of November 14, 1935. "Coming like a bolt out of the blue," the Puget Sound Navigation Company purchased the stock and vessels of the Kitsap County Transportation Company and its subsidiaries, including the Washington Route and the Whidby Island Transportation Company. Kitsap County Transportation was believed to have an interest in the Ballard-Ludlow Ferry Company, but it was not included in the transaction. Captain John L. Anderson was a major stockholder and director of all the Kitsap operations as well as the Lake Washington Ferries. His lake fleet was not affected by the sale; he continued to own it until his death.[8]

[6] *Analysis of Award,* submitted by the Joint Steering Committee of the Masters, Mates and Pilots, Local No. 6 and the Ferryboatmen's Union of the Pacific, Puget Sound Division, 1935.

[7] Ibid, p. 1.

WINSLOW

An audit performed by the state of Washington in 1947[9] shows that as early as 1933 the Black Ball Line was considering the purchase of Kitsap County Transportation Company. That year, Black Ball was shown to have authorized a stock increase to 25,000 shares par value of $100 each, totaling $2,500,000. The report states: "It was anticipated that 3,500 shares of this authorized stock would be used in the acquisition of capital stock of Kitsap County Transportation Company, a transaction under consideration." The industry was acutely aware of the considerable financial difficulties experienced by the Kitsap company at the hands of bankruptcy of the W.B. Foshay Company in 1929 and the commitments which had been undertaken at the time for the construction of the ferry VASHON in 1930.

The sale of Kitsap County Transportation Company to Puget Sound Navigation Company was precipitated by the strike called at 1:15 P.M., Thursday, November 7, by the Masters, Mates and Pilots and the Ferryboatmen. They tied up nine vessels of the Puget Sound Freight Lines, the ferryboats VASHON and BAINBRIDGE. Operation of all vessels of the Kitsap company was halted with the exception of the steamboat WINSLOW and the ferry HIYU, the latter operating between Bainbridge Island and the Kitsap peninsula (Fletcher Bay to Brownsville) and the express steamer COMMANDER of the Washington Route. All the vessels of the Whidby Island Transportation Company and the Ballard-Ludlow Ferry Company were also tied up. Captain Peabody of the Black Ball Line is said to have warned union official Clyde Deal that the Kitsap County Transportation Company could not

withstand the strike because it was already on the brink of going out of business.[1]

Soon after the strike against Kitsap County Transportation was called, it was rumored that they were folding. Peabody is said to have approached Philip Macbride with an offer of cooperation but was refused. Nothing changed until Monday, November 11, when, under an emergency agreement, the steamship COMMANDER and the steamer VERONA returned to service for the Washington Route's Seattle-Bremerton run. By Tuesday, November 12, officers and crews of the Puget Sound Navigation's TOURIST and ALOHA had walked out. Until then, the Black Ball fleet had not been struck. That same day the crews tied up the navigation company's freighter COMMANCHE, the ferryboat IROQUOIS and the steamer SOL DUC. The union announced that the tie-ups were due to a "hot cargo" issue and that a strike had not been officially called on those vessels.

Wednesday, it was announced that the Ballard-Ludlow Ferry Company and the striking marine unions had entered into a conference. Captain Lovejoy, head of the Puget Sound Freight Lines and the Washington Shipowners' Association, remarked that Captain Howard Payne, head of the Ballard-Ludlow Company, had thus automatically withdrawn from the owners' association; his proposition to the unions was not in accord with the other owners. The association intended to stand on the Gaines' Arbitration Board findings and insisted that the award be observed. Captain Payne expressed his dissatisfaction with Captain Lovejoy's handling of the strike situation and that his own withdrawal was to end an "inconsistent position."[2]

By Wednesday afternoon, the Puget Sound Navigation crews of the ferries QUILCENE and QUILLAYUTE walked out when the vessels docked in Edmonds. The Ballard-Ludlow Ferry Company's ferryboat BALLARD had been allowed to continue

---

[8] The company was later dissolved when the Lake Washington bridges were opened. Captain Harry E. Tompkins, original general manager and partner of Anderson continued to administer the lake fleet for its duration.

[9] *Report of the Investigation of Earnings, Property, Operations, Rates, Services and Facilities of the Puget Sound Navigation Company.*

[1] Shrader, *The Black Ball Line.*

[2] At that time Payne was embroiled in a battle with P.S.N. who was fighting his application to reduce ferry rates on routes of the Ballard company competing with P.S.N. The navigation company's operations on those routes had not been affected by the strike.

BALLARD

operations to serve the Olympic Peninsula dairy farmers as an emergency measure and as a result of Payne's negotiations, the BALLARD remained in operation pending the strike settlement.

Thursday of that week, the unions gave permission for the VERONA (referred to as the "Wobbly" boat) to begin service between Fauntleroy and Vashon Heights, supplementing the emergency service of the VIRGINIA V which was also making stops at Vashon Heights in addition to her regular calls. That same day Philip Macbride called Peabody with a proposal offering all of the Kitsap County Transportation Company capital stock to Puget Sound Navigation Company, including that of its subsidiaries, if they would assume the liabilities amounting to about $140,000.[3] Peabody accepted the offer and his company promptly took over the colorful steamers, well-built ferries and the important island and peninsula routes of the White Collar Line.

With this sale, an era closed forever, taking with it independent little steamer companies, the heated competition for routes and fares, and the competition to build bigger and better ferryboats. Captain Alexander Peabody, whether he desired it or not, found himself in virtual control of a ferry fleet monopoly on Puget Sound. He owned the largest and most modern ferry fleet under the American flag.

With the impending sale of Kitsap County Transportation Company to Puget Sound Navigation Company, Captain John Fox announced to his union brothers that they had no choice but to extend the strike to all ferries of the navigation company's fleet. All of the crews walked off their jobs, tying the vessels to the pier on their last run. Ferry service was at a standstill.

The strike continued for 33 days.

During the third week, the Washington Navigation Company of Tacoma, Skansie Brothers, was granted the right to reorganize its financial structure under federal bankruptcy law. The state had recently ordered that company to refund Pierce County $126,000 in subsidies paid in the previous three years, on the grounds that the county commissioners had no legal right to pay subsidies. County attorney Harry H. Johnston opposed reorganization of the company as endangering the county's claim of thousands of dollars. The Washington Navigation Company was then operating ferries to Gig Harbor, Vashon Island, Fox Island, McNeil Island and Longbranch. Their vessels had not been struck by the unions.

The 1935 marine workers' strike was the first strike to totally interrupt service on Puget Sound for a prolonged period of time. This one was felt deeply by the commuting and traveling public and they let their sentiments be known. It followed closely on the heels of the 1934 strike and even worse, people still recalled the ocean and longshoremen's strike of two years before when most shipping was tied up or hampered severely. Roads did not adequately provide service to their communities; people could not get to work in a time of severe need and heavy competition for existing job opportunities; local medical service was strained. People around Puget Sound were unexpectedly reminded of their continued dependence on water

---

[3] The 1947 State Audit shows that P.S.N. acquired 2,983 shares of Kitsap County Transportation Company, being the entire outstanding issue of common stock for a total consideration of $394,150, represented by a cash amount of $245,000 and 1,491-1/2 shares of the $100 par value common stock of P.S.N. At the same time there was outstanding 500 shares of Class "A" 6 percent cumulative preferred stock. This stock was held by John L. Anderson, 150 shares; Harry E. Manson, 125; and the Citizens Utilities Company (Foshay associates), 225 shares. As of 1947, Anderson's widow continued to hold 1,146 shares of P.S.N. stock acquired through this sale of Kitsap County Transportation Company to P.S.N. It was not until 1942 that as a result of various stock redemptions only 500 shares of Kitsap County Transportation Company preferred stock in the amount of $500 (owned by Citizens Utility Company, 250 shares; Manson Construction Company, 100 shares; and the estate of J.L. Anderson, 150 shares) was acquired by an exchange, share for share, of P.S.N. common stock, sufficient shares for that purpose being held by Kitsap County Transportation Company When this transaction was made, Kitsap County Transportation Company became a wholly owned subsidiary of P.S.N. Philip Macbride sold his intersts to P.S.N. in 1935, disassociating his interests with ferryboats forever. He later joined the Pacific American Fisheries Company of Bellingham and continued to practice law.

*THE VIRGINIA V TODAY SERVES AS THE LAST OF THE
SOUND'S MOSQUITO FLEET*

THE INFAMOUS VERONA

transportation and commerce. The holidays were soon approaching; the strike was simply not a festive occasion for anyone.

In general the newspapers tended to side editorially with the employers, expressing their distrust of the unions involved. Not only were newspapers experiencing their own threats of labor organization among their employees, but paper suppliers and distributors were handicapped by the ferry strike. Everyone concerned, including ferry workers, feared that these strikes might become a bad habit on the part of the unions. The pictures painted by the newspapers were grim.

Legislation dealing with strikes and labor negotiations was almost non-existent in 1935. *The Marine Digest,* expressed a need for legislative action through Jackson Corbet's editorial, November 16, 1935:

"... The State is strict with the vessel owner. Before he can operate in any Puget Sound route, he must get a certificate of necessity from the Department of Public Works. The Department then fixes his passenger and freight rates, passes on his schedule and otherwise supervises him. The vessel-owner cannot withdraw from service at his own sweet will; he cannot walk out on his customers and leave them high and dry. Before he can withdraw from the route, he must first get the Department's permission, and permission is granted only after an investigation. But the vessel owner's employees can quit or strike of their own volition.

"The strike that began on Puget Sound routes last week is bringing this whole problem to the front. It is becoming painfully clear that if the public welfare is to be safeguarded adequately, the control of the State Department of Public Works must be extended to include officers and crews of the vessels in question. The Department that regulates and supervises the vessel-owners should also regulate and supervise the wages and working conditions. Because of the detailed data it has on the vessel-owner's business, it is in an ideal position to do justice to the men and the employer and to conserve the public welfare. Discontinuance of service, by the operators, without permission of the department, is now outlawed. Then, and only then, will the welfare of the people be safeguarded.

"If this reform cannot be brought about, the people might as well repeal the law giving the State Department control over Puget Sound vessel-owners. A mere strike turns that control into a howling farce."

Labor negotiations broke off, ending in a deadlock, during a strained Thanksgiving holiday. Captain Lovejoy announced on behalf of the Shipowners that they were withdrawing all offers of concessions made to the striking unions. Thereafter, the Shipowners would stand on the award of the Gaines' Arbitration Board and would resume operation of their vessels only on the basis of that award.

Major developments during the previous week led to this announcement. The unions had decided not to allow the ferry KALAKALA to handle freight to and from the Bremerton Navy Yard. The KALAKALA was permitted to continue to carry Navy Yard workers who lived in Seattle since many of these people were union members, too. The federal government expressed concern with the strike situation. The Shipowners decided to press this advantage.

Under an arbitration agreement signed by the Washington State Governor Clarence D. Martin in Olympia December 10, 1935, a truce was declared in the Puget Sound ferryboat and steamboat strike. The issues were again to be submitted to arbitration. Governor Martin's success in bringing about the truce and the resumption of services in the Puget Sound local routes was highly appreciated by the traveling public and the communities of the inland sea. "Capital is entitled to a fair return on its investment and the working men are entitled to a fair wage and a decent standard of living," stated the Governor to the members he appointed to this new board of arbitration.[4] Members appointed were the Rev. Dr. Samuel L. Divine, pastor of the Mount Baker Park Presbyterian Church of Seattle; Mrs. Pearl D. Wanamaker of Coupeville, member of the state legislature from Island County; and Superior Judge Timothy A. Paul of Walla Walla County, who was chairman.

Puget Sound was not optimistic about the New Year—1936, if this *Digest* editorial was any indication of their feelings:

"The waterfronts of the Northwest were glad to see the Old Year go. Like 1934 it was a

---

[4] *The Marine Digest,* 12/12/1935, p. 5.

period of strikes and turmoil that did no good for anyone, least of all for marine and waterfront labor. It was about as bad as 1934 when the protracted longshore strike and shipping tie-up brought virtually every Northwest community to the verge of ruin. In 1935 we had the strike of oil tanker officers and crews, the widespread strike of the men employed on the Sound ferryboats and other Sound carriers, and as the year ended we had the strike of the coastwise fleets, resulting in the tie-up of more than two score vessels.[5] The coastwise strike is still in full progress. The ferryboat strike is suspended pending a decision by the Governor's arbitrators. They are due to give their decision January 20. What then?

"For more than a year and a half the entire Pacific Coast has been beset with one strike after another. There have been regularly called strikes. There have been unsanctioned localized strikes against some particular ship or ships, the latter strikes being known as 'job action.' As a result of this, the whole Coast has been set back years.

"To make matters worse for the shipping interests, new tax has been piled on new tax. We have reached the point where between strikes and taxes, the shipowners don't know where to turn. Labor wants more money. Tax collectors want more money and shipping concerns are now between the devil and the deep blue sea.

"One thing stands clear and distinct in all this confusion and turmoil—the utter incapacity, futility and worthlessness of President Roosevelt's labor department. To the general public its mediators have been a joke; they never get anywhere, and if they do make a decision, it is merely another one of those things. The public response now is 'Oh yeah?'

"... We have entered 1936. What is it going to bring? More turmoil, more upheavals, more privation, more economic losses, more official sidestepping and negligence? No one can tell. But if the people of the Pacific Coast don't wake up and assert themselves, their cities and communities will show a drop in population in the 1940 census that will stagger them."

On the whole, the unions were not satisfied with the Paul Arbitration award[6] but having just undergone a long and costly strike, with the need of recruiting additional union members, the unions accepted the award. It remained in effect through October 1936. No action was taken by the unions throughout the winter of 1936-37.[7] In May 1937, the unions requested modifications which provoked lengthy negotiations that ended once again in total deadlock. On May 27, 1937 a strike was called by the Inland Boatmen's Union of the Pacific,[8] formerly known as the Ferryboatmen's Union

[5] On December 21, 1935, coastwise trade was almost at a standstill when 33 steam schooners were tied up in Pacific Coast ports as a result of a strike called that day. Crews of the vessels walked out when the Shipowners' Association of the Pacific Coast refused their demands for a six hour day in port and $1 an hour overtime. The crews of these carriers worked on a monthly basis, handling cargo while in port. Theretofore, they had been employed on an eight hour basis with 70 cents an hour overtime. The vessels were medium sized steam freighters operating in the interstate ocean traffic of Washington, Oregon and California. The employers pointed out that the conditions of their businesses at that time did not enable them to grant the men's demands. The companies insisted they were already operating on a very slender margin and all of them were merely "getting by."

[6] The award included the following decisions: 1) Granted an increase of $5.20 per month to ordinary seamen, able-bodied seamen, ship's truckers, stevedores and the lowest paid men in the steward's department. Increase was received by 360 men or 60 percent of the total employed. It was retroactive to December for non-licensed men. 2) A minimum wage scale was established: able-bodied seaman, $85.80 per month (unions asked for $121); ordinary seamen and ship's truckers, $80.60 per month (unions asked for $116); lowest paid men in the steward's department, $70.20 per month (unions asked for $101). The award increased the payrolls of the companies involved a total of $15,000 per year. Union demands, had they been granted, would have meant an increase of $300,000 including the substantial raises for licensed crew members. *The Marine Digest*, 2/1/1936, p. 5.

[7] There was a strike that fall of 1936 of all Pacific Coast marine and longshore unions from the Mexican border to the Canadian border, but it did not interrupt ferry service on the Sound. It did affect freight haulage for the ferry and freight boat companies and aroused the further animosity of the Northwest public. U.S. Government statistics show that one-half million Americans were involved in sit-down strikes between September 1936 and May 1937.

[8] In 1936 the Ferryboatmen's Union, under the leadership of C.W. Deal, changed its name to the Inlandboatmen's Union. In August 1937 the union became affiliated with the Congress of Industrial Organization (CIO). This placed Captain John Fox in the unusual position of being an official in both the A.F. of L. through the Masters, Mates and Pilots and the C.I.O. These two unions continued to cooperate in labor negotiations despite their different national affiliations. From time to time, Fox was asked to resign from one affiliation or union due to his dual roles, but he consistently refused to do so.

but now encompassing tugboat workers, as well. They tied-up all the ferryboats and passenger carriers on Puget Sound. The union asked for shorter hours and higher wages.

Early in the week, the Ballard-Ludlow Ferry Company signed with the union and several smaller concerns followed suit. The Lake Washington Ferries also agreed to meet union demands after King County commissioners consented to increase ferry rates. The county still owned the lake franchise and leased the operation to John Anderson and his company.

The strike was raging full bore against Puget Sound Navigation Company and all of its vessels. Even the Navy Route was tied up this time, including the world-famous streamlined KALAKALA. Nearly 1200 Navy

Yard workers were prevented from reporting for work. The Navy supplied transportation for its own personnel, but for the most part they could not accommodate civilian employees.

Previously, the strikes had occurred in the fall and winter months, but this time it hit the region at the summer season. Vashon Islanders could not get their berry crops to market except via the inadequate Washington Navigation's ferry to Tacoma and the steamer VIRGINIA V of the West Pass Transportation Company. Bainbridge Island service was completely cut off except for the operation of a chartered yacht.

Four hundred men had walked off 25 passenger and auto ferries and steamers on Puget Sound the day before the heavy Memorial Day traffic. They struck for an eight or nine hour day and a 20 percent increase in wages. It was estimated that employers lost 10,000 or 12,000 ferry fares due to the loss of the holiday travelers.

Midway through the strike the county commissioners gave their permission to operate the chartered ferryboat WASHINGTON on the Fauntleroy, Vashon Heights and Harper run. That became the only Black Ball route in service. It was estimated that Vashon farmers were losing $200 a day with the lack of transportation for the strawberries that were rotting in their fields. The islanders organized a protest meeting and demanded, through a committee representing them, that the county or state furnish emergency service. As the strike continued, the committee urged the state to permanently operate Puget Sound ferries as an extension of the Highway Department. Mayor Dore of Seattle concurred. The state responded that it was in no position to take over the ferry industry, primarily because it had no ferries to offer and furthermore, it owned no ferry terminals or docks. The majority of these were owned by Puget Sound Navigation Company.

The unions offered to furnish crews for any ferries which they considered seaworthy and were owned by anyone other than the Black Ball Line. But the WASHINGTON, under lease by King County to Captain Anderson on Lake Washington, was the only spare vessel available within the region, and to bring some from the outside was unthinkable in terms of time and dollars.

In a desperate effort to return all vessels to service,

Governor Martin proposed that the strikers return to duty under the old conditions with regard to hours but with the promise of substantial wage increases, up to 30 percent. The State Department of Public Service would then conduct an investigation into the proposal that if the shorter hours and higher wages were due the men, the Department would allow the navigation company to increase its fares to set off the increased prices.

Captain Peabody pointed out that the Governor's plan for settling the strike would add up to $175,000 a year to the expenditures of his company and that the company had made a profit of only $60,000 in 1936. Peabody's earning figures were taken from the audit of company books conducted by the State Department of Public Works. The Governor's plan would put the Black Ball Line $115,000 a year into the red. Peabody asked that the controversy be submitted to an impartial board of arbitration with the immediate resumption of service.

Peabody quoted Judge Paul of the former arbitration board who had written that the ferry business on Puget Sound "is losing industry, severely hit by the evolution of transportation through automobile and highway construction." If the company were allowed to raise its rates 10 percent to allow for the proposed increases in wages and changes in working hours, as the Governor suggested, Peabody felt it would be a "very dangerous procedure and unjust to the traveling public. The rate increases would discourage consider-

FERRY WASHINGTON   *CAPT. R. MATSON*

able travel. We might then have to resort to further increases, which would put up fares so high that the industry would perish."[9]

The union accepted the governor's proposal but they objected to the close association between wage and the necessary increase in rates. They stated that they did not like to be included in the controversy over rates and that that was a matter between the companies and the State Department of Public Works. Labor did not wish to have any part in such a determination.

Relations between the employers and the employees were stretched further and further and a timely settlement of the strike seemed elusive. Settlement was obscured by the bitter remarks dealt from both sides. The public, caught in the middle, was disgruntled. A number of individuals were convinced that the strike would result in the state taking charge of the ferry system. Public pressure was directed this time not only at the strikers who had forced this inconvenience upon them but at Peabody and his company for refusing the governor's strike settlement proposal and a 10 percent rate increase. Peabody replied that his definite refusal would actually save the ferry riders and the voters over $275,000 a year, which he estimated were the ultimate demands of the union if their conditions were accepted.

Twenty nine days after the Sound ferry strike was called, it ended. Peabody had at last agreed to the governor's proposal of June 9. That proposal provided that the issues be submitted to a governor-appointed board of arbitration. The Unions had been reassured that provisions would be made for at least a nine-hour day and certain wage increases. They were willing to risk yet another unfavorable arbitration award.

The award carried out the governor's promise and added an additional $2.50 per month in wages for most positions, in addition to the increase already guaranteed by the strike settlement. The nine hour day provoked the controversy of payment of overtime in time off or as suggested by the company, in cash at the regular hourly rate. Due to standards already established by other industries, the company was ordered to pay time-and-a-half.

As a result of this award, ferry rates were raised and the increased costs ($175,000) were passed on to the ferry-riding public. The union officials seemed satisfied with their bargain; the ferry company had passed on its costs and preserved its profits. The public was left with the bill. Never happy, the public directed their gibes at the politicians in Olympia who had suggested this absurd solution in the first place.

WAR CLOUDS BEHIND THE EIGHT BALL

By 1937 Nazi Germany and England were very close to war; China and Japan were already battling one another; and the United States was moving closer to a direct involvement. War production was building and with that came signs of strength to the economy on the west coast. Recovery from the Depression was gradual and hard-won. The Wall Street stockmarket declined that year signaling a serious economic recession for the United States but once again Northwest industry was slow to feel its effects. Optimistic signs took precedence and as business improved, commuter ferry traffic increased. With more jobs and greater family income, came a heightened interest in recreational activities, thus the ferry company began to profit in both directions.

A study by the Department of Public Service produced figures that triggered the reduction of the percentage granted for increases in ferry rates of the Black Ball Line. They were to be allowed to cover the costs of increased wages and shortened hours only. Very little information is available regarding the study but the Public Service Department's decision was upheld and rate reductions went into effect November 1, 1937.[1]

The award by the arbitration board and Department of Public Service was to extend through May 31, 1938, and on that date, was extended through May 31, 1939. In early May 1939 the unions notified Puget Sound Navigation Company that they wanted certain amendments to the contract. The negotiations revealed a number of demands relating to hours, wages and working conditions. When negotiations failed to bring agreement between company and union, union members voted overwhelmingly to strike. This time notice was delivered to the company and the public. The strike was set for August 2, 1939.

It is fascinating to realize the progress that had been made in a few short years by reviewing the demands of the Inlandboatmen's Union:[2]

1) Approximately $10 per month increase in wages for deck and engine room departments;

[9] *The Marine Digest*, 6/19/1937, p. 1.

[1] Ibid. 10/23/1927, p. 5.

[2] Smith, *A History of Labor Relations*.

220

2) Eight hour day in deck and steward's departments;

3) 10 cents per hour increase for overtime rate;

4) Wipers on certain of the larger ferries;

5) One week's vacation with pay and one week's vacation without pay;

6) Uniforms furnished and laundered by the employer for the steward's department;

7) Elimination of half-day shifts;

8) General understanding of the working conditions in all three departments;

9) Dismissal wage for employees who lose their jobs because of reduction in service.

Captain Peabody refused to consider any of these requests on the grounds that the company had no means of meeting the resultant higher costs. He emphasized that the company had not paid dividends to stockholders for years. He offered to allow the old contract to be renewed.

The governor and W.T. Guerts, federal mediator of the Maritime Labor Board, tried to bring the parties together before the strike deadline. The unions reportedly made several concessions and expressed a willingness to submit their negotiations to a board of arbitration, but Peabody would not agree to it unless the proposal submitted to arbitration included a 26-month freeze on wages. The unions were not willing to consent to inclusion of such a condition.

The public's anger was aroused beyond control with the impending strike as the deadline approached. They had no reason to believe that it would be settled quickly. This would be the third time in five years that the island residents had been cut off from the mainland. In mass protest, 200 Vashon Islanders swarmed aboard the ferry VASHON armed with axes, clubs and rocks in an attempt to seize the vessel on its final run before the strike began.[3]

On August 3 the Ferry Users Committee demanded that the men return to work. They issued the ultimatum that the employers must discharge crews permanently if they failed to return. The committee threatened the operator with cancellation of his certificate of public necessity if he failed to renew service.

The strike situation took a peculiarly difficult turn as the Ferry Users Committee began to make headlines in the major Seattle newspapers on an almost daily basis. Negotiations were no longer just a forum between employer and union. A third party, the public sector and patrons whose service had been inter-

rupted, added their conditions and demands.

The following ultimatum from the Ferry Users Committee appeared in the *Seattle Daily Times* on August 3 addressed to employers and employees of ferry routes:

"Let us remind you, and every man in your employ, that the only reason you have the right to operate on Puget Sound at all is because you are given that right by the State of Washington acting under its sovereign power. The state has delegated to you performance of its own duties ... Neither you, nor your men ... have any right once you have entered into this public employment, to drop it because of some difference between yourselves; to do so is virtually a strike against government and everyone knows this may not be done."

In the present, while the ferry system is operated by the state of Washington, this issue of strikes against government and its degree of legality is a continually controversial issue between unions and the state legislature, the court system and particularly among the public sector.

The union worked to maintain a good public image without yielding to public demands. The union chartered the county's ferry WASHINGTON, printed schedules and called themselves the Eagle Harbor Transportation Club or The 8-Ball Line. Union members traded off working shifts for which they were paid a nominal fee to replenish the family coffers during the strike. The WASHINGTON made four daily trips to Winslow from Seattle's Colman Dock. Their motto was "We run WHEN and IF and AS we can." It wasn't much more than that.

As a means of further soliciting the goodwill of the public, the union advocated legislative action to dissolve Peabody's "ferry monopoly" by proposing that ferries be operated by the state highway system, assuring the public that this was the only means of securing stability for the industry.[4] Merle Adlum, former head of the Inlandboatmen's Union of the Pacific remarked in an interview in 1982 that the union later changed its position regarding the state's control of the ferry fleets.

[3] *The Seattle Daily Times*, August 2, 1939.

[4] A letter in possession of Captain Fox shown to Virginia B. Smith, author of *A History of Labor Relations*, verified this position of the union. The letter could not be found at University of Washington Archives, Captain John Fox Collection.

They recognized, perhaps too late, that it might be more difficult to deal with a government agency concerning labor relations than it had been to deal with private enterprise. Suddenly under state ownership the demanding public had become the employer. Public relations had been neatly exchanged.

Many are sorely reminded of the animosity and resentment which occurs during a strike period between management and employees and just among the employees. The issues are never black and white or right or wrong and the effects of such a situation is interpreted separately for every individual. The ferry strike of 1939 was no exception; in fact, rarely does a retiree not have a personal story to relate about it.

Captain Peabody filed libel charges against the unions, contending that they had publicly accused him of "bad faith, dishonesty, threats and coercion, and unfair labor practices."[5] The union responded to this accusation by filing a complaint against the company with the National Labor Relations Board. The battle was bitter and emotions on both sides taxed the endurance of employee and employer alike. When the strike finally ended, 23 days after it had begun, and arbitration ensued while the men returned to work, it was those personal relations that were the hardest wounds to heal. Inflamed by public sentiment and outright participation, neither unions nor the company ever fully recovered from this long series of strikes.

During the war years the country experienced a bonding together to protect the homeland and fight to ensure freedom around the globe. Labor relations became secondary issues. The ferry service was an integral part of carrying workers and freight throughout the war period. Captain Peabody was lauded for reducing rates to an all time low to accommodate those passengers and the supplies that his ferries shuttled across Puget Sound.

The compromises of the 1939 strike resulted in the company meeting many of the demands of the union, including an eight hour day, a week's paid vacation, overtime increases and a $2.50 per month average increase (instead of $10) in wages for deckhands and engine room employees. The contract remained in effect by renewal and with minor alterations through 1944. That year a strike was quietly avoided by submitting the union proposal to arbitration early. It was not until after World War II had ended that another ferry strike occurred on Puget Sound.

The die was cast in the thirties for eventual government ownership of the ferry system and within a dozen years of the 1939 strike the state of Washington owned and operated most of the routes of the famous Black Ball Line. Had it not been for the intervention of World War II, the take-over may have occurred sooner.

[5] *The Seattle Daily Times*, 8/6/1939.

One Gorgeous Ferry
Serving 17 Communities
•
SUPPORT THIS SERVICE
•
Get Behind the

"The 8-Ball Line"

We run WHEN and IF
and AS we can
•
Today's Odds
Morning Line — 35 for 1
Afternoon Line ⎰Remain
Evening Line ⎱ the
Night Line ⎱ Same

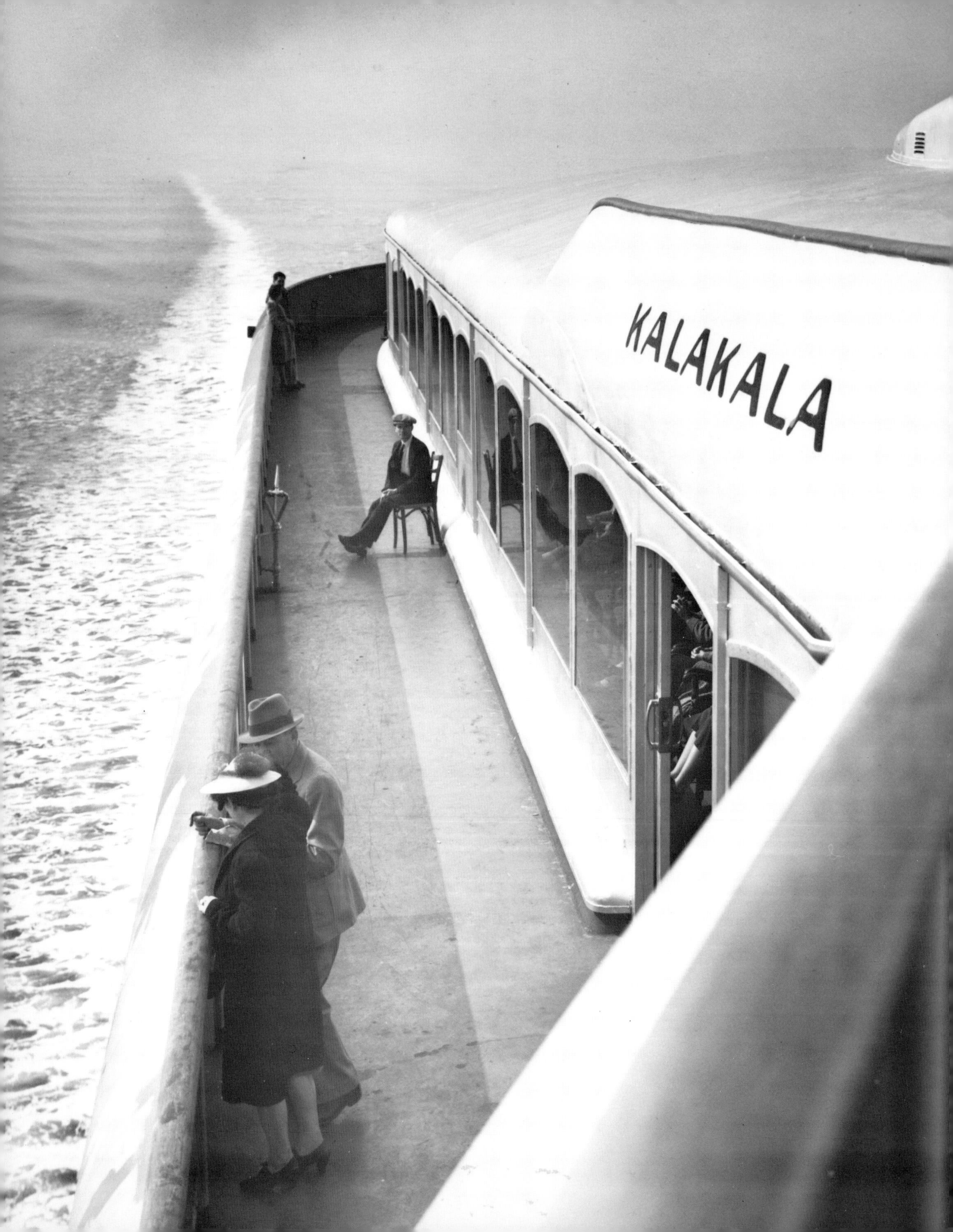
KALAKALA

A STREAMLINED SUPER FERRY

The auto ferry on Puget Sound was developed to an extent previously unknown in other waters. It was here that forethought and timing combined to provoke a revolution in the design and engine power of ferryboats. Sound ferry companies were thinking *big* long before their dreams became realities.

As early as 1925 the Puget Sound Navigation Company announced the proposed construction of a tremendous and costly ferry that would have a motion picture theatre with seating capacity for 1,000 persons. Joshua Green, president of the company, told the press it would cost $300,000 to build the vessel. The new ferry, designed by Seattle naval architects, would virtually be a moving picture theatre afloat. Contracts were to be made with leading distributors by which the latest films of great artists would be exhibited. The new ferryboat would be available for any of the Sound routes for charter, but probably the most popular one would be the Seattle-Bremerton run.

"Moving picture theatres have been operated aboard overseas and inland vessels but the ship we will build probably will be the first designed with a moving picture theatre included in the plans and specifications," declared Joshua Green.[1] "There will be an elevated stage which will permit an unobstructed view from any part of the theatre. A large orchestra will be employed at all times to furnish music during the voyages of the ship in the Puget Sound ferry routes. The vessel is being built with the moving picture theatre the main feature and there will be no stanchions to obstruct the view. All the latest pictures will be exhibited and special musical programs will be given by the ship's orchestra. The new ferryboat will be 200 feet long, 48 foot beam, and if our present plans are carried out will be built of steel.

"She will have a capacity of 100 automobiles and will be able to maintain a speed of 13.5 knots. . . . The new vessel will have a total capacity of 1,500 persons and 1,000 of these can occupy seats in the theatre.

". . . The new ferry will be a daytime boat, which will exceed in attractiveness and accommodations any vessel of her type on the Pacific Coast. . . . there will be space for dancing and entertainment. The new fer-

ryboat will be one of the fastest on the Sound. It is expected to have her ready for service by the opening of the tourist season next summer."[2]

A ferry even remotely similar to this description did not appear on Puget Sound until the summer season a decade later. When it did emerge, Joshua Green no longer had a direct association with the management or planning of the Puget Sound Navigation Company, nor did he ever take credit for his contributions to the marvelously unique vessel that resulted in 1935.

Speculation has it that the scheme for a new ferryboat announced by Green in 1925 was purely a promotional ploy, mixed with a handful of imaginative skullduggery. Competition at the time was fearsome and Green is reputed to have been a great prankster as well. Captain John Anderson had just purchased the Kitsap County Transportation Company that year. The launching of his fine new wooden ferryboat, the KITSAP, was scheduled for later that spring. Green was not one to idly sit by and watch his major competitor take the limelight. No further mention of Green's "fantasy ferry" was ever made.

Captain Alex Peabody, a man of practicality and staunch demeanor, was a dreamer, too. In September 1933 the young ferry company president announced the purchase of the ferryboat PERALTA from San Francisco Bay. It was to enter the Seattle-Bremerton route and assist in carrying the gradually increasing numbers of Puget Sound Navy Shipyard commuters.

The PERALTA was formerly operated by the Key Route in the Bay and was one of the largest ferryboats in existence on the Pacific Coast. She was 256 feet long and had accommodations for 2,000 passengers and 115 automobiles. The craft was towed by the Seattle tug CREOLE[3] up the coast one week after her sale to Black Ball Line on October 12, 1933.

If Captain Peabody was a superstitious mariner, he

[1] *The Marine Digest,* 11/21/1925, p. 1.

[2] Construction of this vessel was to be limited to only seven months and the shipyard contracts had not yet been awarded. Joshua Green left town for a visit to California the same day this announcement was made.

was a brave one also, to have purchased the PERALTA. Many San Franciscans were convinced that she was jinxed, at least on the Bay. This Oakland-built ferry, vintage 1927, and her identical sister ship the YERBA BUENA[4] were the finest ferryboats introduced in the San Francisco-Oakland route of the Key System. The elite of their type, they were the last steam ferries built on San Francisco Bay. According to an appraisal by Richard Sachse, civil engineer, these turbo-electric ferries were valued at $972,599 in a first lien. A second lien appraised them at $1,740,672 as of July 20, 1929.[5]

The ferries PERALTA and YERBA BUENA were constructed entirely of steel and were advertised by the Key System as "fireproof and unsinkable." No doubt it was a declaration they would live to regret. They sported a new feature for Bay ferries by carrying ballast tanks forward and aft which were used to trim the double-ended vessels.[6] As the passengers crowded the forward end of the ferry to disembark, the ballast tank aft was filled to balance the ship.

Every attention was paid to details to ensure the passengers' comfort. The turbo-electric engines were not efficient fuel conservers, but they did provide for an exceptionally smooth ride. Decor and trim was elegant aboard the ferries and the ballast tanks reduced the wariness of unsteady passengers aboard ship.

Unfortunately the ferry PERALTA was prone to a series of expensive dock rammings within her first year of operation. These were only preliminary to major tragedy that struck this ill-fated ferryboat on the Bay.

February 17, 1928, as the PERALTA was approaching the Oakland side with a full complement of 4,000 commuters, small waves began to break over the bow. Throngs of passengers, eagerly collecting forward to await the ferry's docking, became slightly aware that the crashing waves were becoming larger. Many crowded forward to get a better look, peering over the bow just as a giant breaker smashed over the forward end and rushed amidships. Thirty panic-stricken observers were swept overboard. Five perished in the icy waters of the Bay.

The PERALTA's crew was instantly accused of negligence. It was charged that the forward ballast tank had been filled rather than the one aft. However, the investigation that followed did not find them guilty since the weight of the crowded foredeck may have lowered the freeboard into a trough that preceded the PERALTA's bow wave. That may have been magnified by the existing tide rip that afternoon and the

swell of a passing steamer. Due to insufficient evidence, the crew and all charges were dismissed from court and legal custody. The ballast tanks were never used again. The PERALTA narrowly escaped total exclusion from service on San Francisco Bay when unhappy memories forced many commuters to avoid the posh ferryboat.

Fortune was not destined to shine upon the PERALTA. On May 6, 1933, a spectacular fire consumed the Key System ferry terminal at Oakland where sat the magnificent PERALTA at her moorings. Her fireproof steel construction trapped and intensified the heat of the flames as they spread throughout the ferry. Above the waterline, the vessel was a total loss. The hull escaped fire with relatively minor damage, but the smouldering ruins of the cabins were a vivid reminder to Bay residents that the PERALTA's existence there was doomed.

That year the Northwest's Black Ball Line purchased the hull and had it in tow for Puget Sound. Peabody viewed this opportunity as a fortuitous development of circumstances and snatched up the PERALTA for a song at the height of a depressed economy and labor unrest.

Captain Peabody is said to have considered several designs for the reconstruction of the PERALTA. From the start he was interested in an excursion-type vessel like the CHIPPEWA and the INDIANAPOLIS had once been but with more modern accommodations for automobiles. He was particularly adamant that her speed for the Seattle-Bremerton run be at least 17 knots. The vessel would be single-ended to aid in achieving this speed even though the vessel would dock bow-on in Seattle, but would have to back into

---

[5] The steam tug CREOLE, owned by Puget Sound Tug & Barge Company for nearly a decade, was sold at the time of this tow to the Harbor Tug & Barge Company of San Francisco (1934). Jurisdictional disputes among the Coast's maritime unions delayed the tug's departure from Seattle with a 13-man crew representing five different unions.

[4] The YERBA BUENA served out her days on San Francisco Bay until 1957, when she was scrapped after serving the U.S. Govt. from the start of WWII.

[5] "Plan for Readjustment" for the Key System Company, appraisal prepared by Richard Sachse, July 20, 1929. (Bancroft Library).

"The Key System's earnings are insufficient to meet its fixed obligations, let alone to pay dividends on any of its stock."

[6] Both ends of the vessels were identical to the last fitting and the resultant confusion of this within and without the shipyard was eliminated by painting "San Francisco End" and "Oakland End" on opposite ends of the ferries.

PERALTA   SAN FRANCISCO MARITIME MUSEUM

PERALTA AFTER FIRE   WILLIAMSON COLL. P.S.M.H.S.

KEY SYSTEM FERRY BOAT "YERBA BUENA." INTERIOR OF UPPER CABIN. CONSTRUCTED BY THE MOORE DRY-DOCK COMPANY. OAKLAND. CALIF., APRIL 26. 1927.

the Bremerton slip in order to off-load cars. It was felt that even with turn-around time added at each end of the run, a faster speed could be achieved without the drag of an idle propeller on the forward end.

A diesel direct drive was selected for the converted PERALTA in the summer of 1934. Puget Sound Navigation Company had already converted the ferry CHIPPEWA from steam to a Busch-Sulzer diesel in 1932—the first ferryboat to have this make of engine.[7] The Busch-Sulzer company sent an experienced engineer from their firm, Helmuth W. Schmitz, to Seattle to witness the CHIPPEWA's installation. He liked the region so much that he stayed with the Black Ball Line.

Based on Black Ball's experience with the CHIPPEWA's 2,200 shp engine which had been in service 23 months without missing a day, and with a record of over 10,000 trouble-free hours, they selected a 3,000 bhp Busch-Sulzer 10-cylinder single-acting unit of the same type. Helmuth Schmitz stayed on to install the new engine and to become a naval architect for the company.

Alex Peabody called for an entirely new superstructure arrangement for the PERALTA, requiring capacity for 110 cars and a passengers' seating capacity of 1,500 on the upper deck. The beam overall was to be reduced from 70 feet to 56 feet, 6 inches, which would still allow for three lanes of cars on either side of the engine room casing.

Peabody was propelled by his exuberant and imaginative ad manager, Bill Thorniley. Thorniley convinced Peabody to name the new ferry KALAKALA rather than WILLAPA after Puget Sound Navigation Company's first boat. KALAKALA, pronounced Kahlock-ah-lah, means ''Flying Bird'' in Chinook jargon, the intertribal language of Northwest Indians and fur traders. Thorniley was a student of Chinook and made an effort to name all Black Ball ferries, and later, Washington State ferries, after appropriate Northwest Indian names.[8]

The KALAKALA became immortal for her unique superstructure design. She was launched as the world's first completely streamlined vessel; she bore more similarity to a DeSoto than to the majority of the automobiles of the day that she would carry. Full credit should be extended to Alex Peabody for desiring and influencing such a modern design;[9] to Helmuth Schmitz for creating a functioning engine casing and installation plan; to the Boeing Company engineers who studied the steel superstructure, tested the func-

BILL THORNILEY AND CAPTAIN MANGAN WITH GUEST

tion of the design against wind velocities and other restricting speed factors and helped create the impressive structure that provoked reminders of aeroplanes;[1] to Lake Washington Shipyards and Puget Sound Navigation's marine superintendent, James E. Murphy, for devising construction methods and producing such a vessel; and to William O. Thorniley who aggrandized all of their achievements internationally, winning reknown for his company and the ferry it had produced. The *world* was rocked by favorable impressions of this popular technical maritime achievement and instantly newspapers and magazines recorded the event of its launching and trial run.

[7] Story recalled by Walter Green.

[8] Those vessels already bearing Northwest Indian names or regional names were not altered. See Appendix for listing of Chinook ferry names and definitions.

[9] In an interview with Mrs. Alexander Peabody and Laurence Peabody on February 27, 1983, Mrs. Peabody stated that Captain Alex, her husband, showed her early KALAKALA drawings in late 1932 and she personally redrew the superstructure lines to her own satisfaction and the present configuration.

[1] Those engineers and designers, if any, involved with the reconstruction must have been moonlighting. None of the KALAKALA's design or construction was performed in the official capacity of the Boeing Company. It may have been rumor.

"The vessel is fully streamlined in accordance with the latest practices in aero-dynamics. Strikingly unusual in appearance and coated in shining aluminum paint, she will at a distance resemble a mammoth aeroplane skimming over the surface of the water. The flying bridge on either side of the wheelhouse has the appearance of modified wings and a low tapered stern accentuates the illusion. In order to fully carry out the streamline design, the running lights are cleverly housed in the sides of the flying bridge and the range light is carried on a mast which disappears from sight during the daytime and is electrically controlled from the wheelhouse. Lifeboats, carried on the main deck, are completely inset and are equipped with a special launching gear.

"The steel construction on this ship is quite unusual as the ship itself. A unique method of electric welding gives great strength and has made it possible to do away with unsightly rivet heads and other objectional features common to ordinary steel construction. Gracefully rounded I-beams have been used in place of the conventional angle irons and many other innovations have been introduced in her construction to give the new vessel rugged strength as well as a pleasing appearance. From stem to stern the graceful curves have replaced angles and flat surfaces.

"Not only is this vessel notable as the first streamlined ship to be built, but she will rank as the largest and fastest ferry ever to ply Puget Sound. The KALAKALA, 276 feet long, has a beam of 55 feet 8 inches, and a draft of 13 feet. She is 21 feet 6 inches in depth of hold and has a freeboard of 10 feet and is designed to carry 2,000 passengers and 110 automobiles. She has three large observations rooms; one on the first passenger deck forward and one forward and one aft on the sun deck. Between these two upper observation rooms is an observation type dining room with a seating capacity of over one hundred. The central portion of the dining room contains a double horseshoe counter, while the tables are arranged in each corner. The dining room furniture is all of metal and the tables and counters have hard rubber tops, trimmed in stainless steel. The galley is furnished in metal throughout and all cooking is done electrically.

CAPTAIN ALEX PEABODY AND JIM MURPHY WORKED CLOSELY ON THE CONSTRUCTION OF THE KALAKALA

"On the main passenger deck amidships are the passenger cabins, with a seating capacity of over seven hundred. The ladies lounge, aft, which is being fitted out in harmonizing shades of tan and brown, will have a seating capacity of 100. A total of 500 deep upholstered chairs will be used in furnishing the ferry. Under the seat of each of these chairs is a special case containing a regulation life preserver. In two spacious compartments just below the automobile deck, yet well above the waterline, is located the tap room and the men's lounge. Just off the men's lounge are the shower and locker rooms, designed primarily for the Navy Yard workers who may want to clean up and change clothes enroute. These facilities, however, are available to anyone who may want to use them.

"All passenger cabins, lounges and observation rooms are provided with a special type of controlled ventilation, giving complete air conditioning at all times. The interiors of all observation rooms, lounges, etc., are of steel, finished in pleasing shades of polychrome sprayed lacquers. A different color scheme is used in the draperies and decorations of each room. Indirect lighting is provided throughout. All decks in the passenger cabins are covered with a special type of rubber tile and all windows are of plate glass in bronze frames.

"Two large murals are now being painted by S.A. Cookson, Seattle marine artist, for the cabins of the KALAKALA,[2] one of the Black Ball Liner of over a century ago and another of the fast Black Ball packets of the clipper ship era.

"The elimination of fire hazard has been given unusual consideration[3] in the building of this new vessel and she is 97.75 percent steel construction. Even the wheelhouse, which heretofore has always been of wood, is now built of non-magnetic metal. The ship is equipped throughout with a new design of firefighting apparatus unlike anything yet to appear on shipboard. Eight watertight bulkheads make her virtually unsinkable.[4]

"Some idea of the size of the ship can be gained from the fact that it is 412 feet around the promenade on the sun deck. The hull, designed by Hibbs, McCauley & Smith and built in 1927 by the Moore Shipbuilding Com-

[2] One of these hangs today inside the terminal at Colman Dock.

[3] Note that they did not claim that it was "fireproof" as had the Key System.

[4] The ballast tanks of the PERALTA had been permanently removed.

pany of Oakland, California, is of unusually fine lines. She is powered to make the trip from Seattle to Bremerton in forty-five minutes.[5] The main engine is a 10-cylinder, 2 cycle, 3,000 horse power Busch-Sulzer diesel, the largest ever to be installed in a ferry. The foundation of this engine is over one hundred feet long and contains one hundred tons of steel. Turning at a speed of 230 revolutions per minute the engine will drive a single screw propeller 8½ feet in diameter. The main engine is without auxiliaries of any kind, the entire 3,000 horse power being used for propulsion. A speed of 18 knots is indicated. All pistons are visible through large plate glass ports, making it possible to see just what condition they are in at all times. The auxiliary engine is a 4 cycle, 8 cylinder, 600 horse power Busch-Sulzer Diesel and is directly connected to a 400 kilowatt generator which supplies the auxiliary equipment through the latest type of central, dead front switchboard. The auxiliary engine is more powerful than the main engine of many well known Puget Sound ferries. All auxiliary units are electrically operated and can be started and controlled at the switchboard. Aboard the ship are a total of 112 electric motors. When the ship is in port, the auxiliary engines may be stopped and electricity supplied through shore lines. Both engines are fresh water cooled and the temperature of either engine can be controlled to a fraction of a degree. Steam heating for the entire ship is produced in a cleverly designed boiler, utilizing waste heat from both engines. A booster boiler is also provided for extreme cold weather.

"The wheelhouse of the KALAKALA contains navigating equipment of a type never before used on a vessel in this class of service. She is equipped with a Hyde electric-hydraulic steering gear, which is not only supersensitive, but is also the fastest steering device known. The wheelhouse will be connected with the engine room with an automatic electric telegraph, the first of its type to be used on inland commercial vessels. Communication between the wheelhouse and the stern of the vessel is maintained by telephone.

"The construction of this vessel is going forward under the direct supervision of James E. Murphy, Marine Superintendent, and Helmuth W. Schmitz, Naval Architect, of the Puget Sound Navigation Company. Both men are widely known in marine construction circles and have taken an active part in the building of several outstanding ferries.

"Captain Wallace Mangan, who will command the KALAKALA, is one of the most colorful characters in Puget Sound shipping. He has been employed as a Master of vessels of the Black Ball Line and associated companies for over thirty years. Almost without exception this entire period has been spent on the Seattle-Bremerton-Port Orchard route. During this time he has made over fifty thousand round trips in this route without a single mishap to a vessel under his command.

"The first automobile ferry to the Olympic Peninsula was established in 1921. The famous old sternwheeler, BAILEY GATZERT, which carried about 25 cars, was operated over the same route which will be served by this new vessel. In the space of fourteen years this remarkable development in inland passenger and automobile carriers has taken place. This development is a direct result of increased interest in the Olympic Peninsula and the Puget Sound country as an outstanding vacation area.

"Also, during recent years, there has been a marked tendency on the part of citizens of Seattle and other large centers of population to establish residences in desirable suburban localities nearby. With the development of faster and better cross-Sound transportation this tendency has manifested itself in the building of summer and all-year-round homes on the west side of Puget Sound. The KALAKALA is being built in anticipation of an even greater interest in this area as well as the development of the Puget Sound Navy Yard as the great naval base of the Pacific.

"The original Black Ball Line was established in 1816 to give regular service between New York and Liverpool. During the famous clipper ship era some of the fastest ships to fly the American flag flew the houseflag of the Black Ball Line.

"For the past six years, Captain Alex M. Peabody, son of C.E. Peabody, has been in charge of the destinies of the Black Ball Line. Under his administration the delux automobile ferry has been developed and four of these fine ships are in operation on Puget Sound, the IROQUOIS, CHIPPEWA, QUILCENE, and ROSARIO. Just as the Black Ball Line of a century ago led the field in marine transportation, so the Black Ball Line of today is a long step in advance of the times in bringing about this remarkable vessel, the silver winged KALAKALA."[6]

---

[5] About the same length of time that it takes today.

[6] This transcript was taken from the original press release written and distributed by William O. Thorniley. It was found in his files without title.

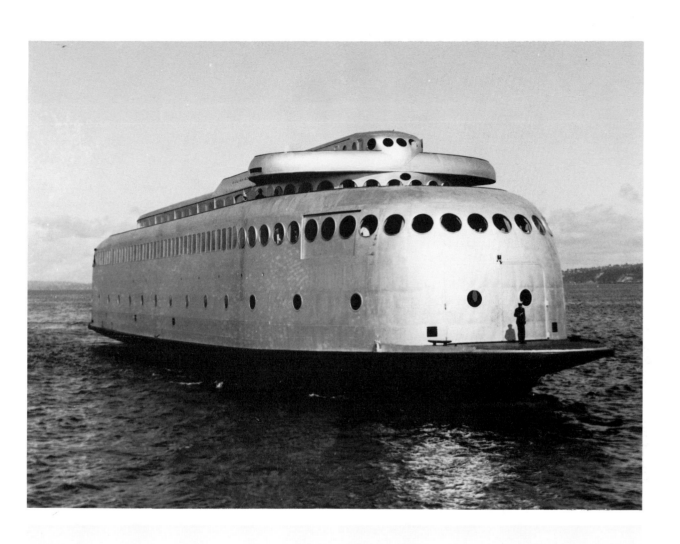

236

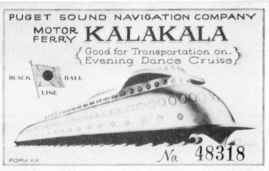

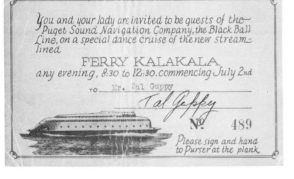

You and your lady are invited to be guests of the—
Puget Sound Navigation Company, the Black Ball
Line, on a special dance cruise of the new stream-
lined

FERRY KALAKALA
any evening, 8:30 to 12:30, commencing July 2nd

to   Mr. Tal Guppy

Tal Guppy

No. 489

Please sign and hand
to Purser at the plank

239

THE WORLD AT HER FEET . . . WELL, JUST ABOUT

After the news of the KALAKALA's advent was published during the fourth week of May 1935, column upon column appeared in the newspapers of port cities and countries around the world. Photographs of the streamliner accompanied the articles and it is doubtful if any vessel yet built in the United States has surpassed the tremendous media coverage received abroad as well as at home. William Thorniley gave much credit for the successful publicity to his secretary, Kathleen Roemer. He claimed that she personally helped make the KALAKALA the most-photographed ferry in the world.

Perhaps it was just a streak of good fortune for the PERALTA, or it may have been the futuristic aspects of her design that made the KALAKALA internationally famous but it was William O. Thorniley who was present to take advantage of her distinctive lines. It may have been a rather slow news week for the newspapers the summer of 1935 and the marine industry had not yet been hit with the shocking strike that would follow in the autumn. Internationally, Germany was setting the stage for another major world war; China and Japan were at war. At home, President Franklin D.

Roosevelt signed the Social Security Act; George Gershwin's *Porgy and Bess* was introduced to the stage; jazz was becoming popularized as "swing;" the motion picture "*Mutiny on the Bounty* starring Clark Gable and Charles Laughton was released and the S.S. NORMANDIE crossed the Atlantic in 107 hours and 33 minutes. The British were perfecting radar for detecting aircraft. The world was in a state of flux, like a calm tide ebbing in and out. It might be said that the KALAKALA was a technological wonder, novel enough to appeal to all the sea-related world. Carrying people rather than ammunition, KALAKALA was a social rather than a military advancement that grasped the attention of the world.

Coming like a breath of fresh air to the depression weary residents of Puget Sound, *The Marine Digest* writes of her: "As she glided out from Colman Dock, her 3,000 h.p. diesel engines purring softly,[7] bedlam broke loose on the waterfront. Plants and ships pulled down their whistle cords, filling the harbor with a deafening uproar. She answered the salute with her

---

[7] The KALAKALA's engines did not purr. It was more like a KA-BOOM de KA-BOOM! KA-BOOM de KA-BOOM!

own whistles and then flung to the warm July breeze the silken folds of the Stars and Stripes and the black and red banner of the Black Ball Line of the Puget Sound Navigation Company.''[8] More than 100,000 people are said to have trained eager eyes on the streamlined vessel's trial run, July 2, 1935.

Construction of the KALAKALA had gone forth with little fanfare and with the secretiveness of a new weapon. There is little doubt that the owners and planners had a very good time playing with her design. The design did raise complications for construction methods previously untried, as well as for mounting her enormous engines. Paul E. Voinot, general manager of the lake yard, was credited for working out the details of streamlined construction.[9] The work took as much time to accomplish as the construction of a new wood ship of similar size.

The KALAKALA inaugurated her regular summer schedule that year, making six round trips daily between Seattle and the Navy Yard city. Summer evening cruises departed from Colman Dock at 8:30 P.M. and arrived back there at 12:30 A.M. She carried her own eight-piece ''Flying Bird'' orchestra headed by Joe Brown. The orchestra became a popular feature of a number of ship-to-shore national radio broadcasts. Equipped with a loudspeaker system, there was dancing on three decks during the evening and the ship's famous horseshoe counter served light luncheons. Alcoholic beverages were not sold aboard ship.

The evening cruise passengers did not much care where the streamliner carried them. To avoid additional Coast Guard regulations for charter vessels, the KALAKALA's crew maintained routes covered by Black Ball certificates for the evening excursions. They might circle around Vashon Island heading down the West Pass to Manchester and return up the East Passage to Seattle. Sometimes they ran the Seattle-Bremerton route or took a turn around Bainbridge Island. A few times they took a jaunt down to Tacoma and back to Colman Dock. The music had a soothing rhythm and the company was fine so no one gave much thought to their destination on a summer's evening.

Always jolly, Captain Wallace Mangan was at the helm and standing ready to assist the KALAKALA's passengers. Mangan had served as master of every important vessel of the Black Ball fleet.

Mangan was born in Missouri in 1874, and moved west with his parents in 1879 to Guemes Island in Puget Sound. His father became the postmaster there

CAPTAIN WALLACE MANGAN

and owner of the store and dock. Wally Mangan began his maritime career as a deckhand, fireman, purser and mate at age 16 aboard the IOLA. Then he fired the sternwheeler, MARY F. PERLEY, but tiring of the heat of a fireroom, he returned to the deck. He served on a number of historic steamboats[1] on the Sound and became mate of the Puget Sound Navigation Company vessel FAIRHAVEN. His commands as master included the H.B. KENNEDY, later converted to the ferry SEATTLE, which he commanded as well. Mangan was master of most of the larger and faster diesel ferries that followed the SEATTLE in the fleet and was appointed Commodore of the Black Ball Line by Captain Peabody. He was reputed to be not only a successful mariner but a master poker player, possibly a skill well worth having in ferryboat command.

[8] *The Marine Digest,* 7/6/1935, p. 1.

[9] Paul E. Voinot entered the U.S. Naval Academy in 1916 and was called to active duty in the war zone waters of the Atlantic the following year. At the end of WWI he returned to Annapolis to graduate from that institution in 1919. He resigned the Navy in 1923, joining the Lake Washington Shipyard. A short time later he was appointed manager and then director and general manager. By the time of the KALAKALA's construction, Voinot had established himself as a successful Pacific Coast shipyard executive. Voinot and Peabody were close friends.

[1] These vessels included the EDITH, GREYHOUND, FLYER, STATE OF WASHINGTON, as deckhand. He commanded the FAIRHAVEN, ALBION, SEHOME, PORT ORCHARD, PERDITA, TOURIST, BAILEY GATZERT, CITY OF BREMERTON, CHIPPEWA and TACOMA.

*MRS. CHARLES PEABODY AND CAPTAIN MANGAN
WITH MODEL OF KALAKALA*

The Mangan family tradition grew to include commanding Black Ball ferries. Captain W.H. Mangan's brother, Jerry W. Mangan, skippered vessels for the line for a number of years, as did Captain Wally's two sons, Captains Gregory W. and Jerry W. Mangan. All four of these men commanded the express ferry CHIPPEWA. To follow one's father's profession may have been common in other American communities, but in the newly-settled Pacific Northwest, the Mangan tradition was something of a rarity. It was particularly unusual that they all commanded the same vessel.

We wonder today how the jovial Captain Wally Mangan, purported to be an excellent candidate for Santa Claus, managed to maintain his constant good humour. Serving the same Navy Yard Route more than 37 years, changing vessels but not the run, Captain Mangan made six round trips a day on the KALAKALA, followed by the evening cruise five nights a week until 12:30 A.M. in the summertime. Working 28 days per month, the crew must have looked forward to the 31-day months of the calendar and winter schedules that afforded them more time off.

Captain Mangan's unblemished record of 30 years' service without a vessel mishap under his command was marred aboard the KALAKALA. In November 1936, in the drizzling rain and misty fog that clouded the channel, the KALAKAKA and the CHIPPEWA collided off Fort Ward in Rich Passage on the Seattle-Bremerton run. Both vessels proceeded to their destinations but the CHIPPEWA limped into Bremerton with a gaping 40-foot hole on her starboard side, aft, above the waterline. In Seattle, it was evident that the KALAKALA's pilot house was damaged and dents appeared in her steel side, starboard above the waterline.

The passengers on both boats were uninjured when the ferries struck and all donned life belts after the crash. Five automobiles aboard the CHIPPEWA were totally demolished.

Then in 1938 the KALAKALA made a resounding mark on Colman Dock. At six o'clock in the evening the streamliner was warping into the slip with 1,200 passengers waiting to disembark when she struck the pier with a blow that was said to have jarred the machinery used in raising and lowering the ramp. The ramp fell just as the passengers started across it. Several persons slipped from the ramp and others were pitched forward off the ferry by the press of the crowd. Ten people were injured, including the KALAKALA's second mate, Fred Boyd. Was the PERALTA's spirit still present?

In the official inquiry that followed, Captain Mangan maintained that his vessel collided with the pier because of the concentration of weight forward, causing the propeller aft to tilt and lose thrust. He said he was convinced that the collision did not cause the ramp elevator failure. Mate Fred Boyd corroborated the captain's testimony with his own dramatic story of the scene on the deck at the time:

> "About 1000 feet out from the pier, where we're suppose to reverse, I noticed the vibration was not what it should be. I noticed that the propeller wheel was slipping through the water, sucking up air. We had about 300 Navy Yard workers forward. I told 'em, 'You'd better hang on, boys! We're coming in pretty fast and it looks like we might hit something!' We hit the dock a glancing blow, sheered off, hit the wing on the south side of the slip... I heard the piling crackle, but there was no visible damage."[2]

The similarities to the PERALTA's catastrophe in Oakland Bay were coincidental ... KALAKALA no longer had the "unsinkable" ballast tanks that had been blamed for the first accident. However, for those who were faint of heart, it was probably too much to bear.

Within one month after belting Colman Dock, the KALAKALA demonstrated her impartiality to communities by shearing off piling in Bremerton. It was described as a "very routine accident."

The KALAKALA, anxious to prove her worth and make amends in 1941, rescued two men from a capsized boat. Caught in the swells of a passing ferry off Duwamish Head, Melvin Seeley and Ray Briscoe were overturned in their 14-foot fishing boat. Their rescue was made with the cooperation of two other fishermen in a nearby boat and the crew of the KALAKALA, Seattle-bound on a five o'clock trip from Bremerton.

Captain Louis Van Bogaert, the KALAKALA's relief skipper, saw the overturned boat at dusk. The other two fishermen had sighted the men in the water, still clinging to the sides of their rowboat. They pulled them from the cold water into their overcrowded craft while Captain Van Bogaert sent three of his crew over the side in a lifeboat to assist.

[2] Unidentified newsclipping found in Louis Van Bogaert's scrapbook, dated 9/27/1938.

SEATTLE TIMES DRAWING BY ALAN PRATT

CAPTAIN LOUIS VAN BOGAERT

The rescue was witnessed by 1000 Navy Yard workers on the ferry, when Seeley and Briscoe were taken aboard the ferry. As the KALAKALA docked a few minutes later in Seattle, an aid squad awaited their arrival. The victims were soon reported in fine condition at a nearby hospital but they expressed their disappointment at the loss of their day's catch when the boat overturned.

CHANGING COMMAND

Captain Wally Mangan retired from the Black Ball fleet in 1941 after a half-century of service. His most recent command aboard the KALAKALA had been particularly troublesome but prestigious. Captain Louis Van Bogaert[3] was assigned to Mangan's former duties. Van Bogaert had served on steamers since 1904 and joined the Puget Sound Navigation fleet November 10, 1909 as lookout on the ROSALIE under Captain Sam Barlow. He held master's papers by 1915 and gained a widespread reputation for the many rescues he performed as commander of the IROQUOIS on the Seattle-Port Townsend-Port Angeles-Victoria run. He had served as the KALAKALA's alternate skipper for less than one year when this appointment came. He suc-

ceeded Mangan as Commodore of the Black Ball fleet of 22 ferries.

But the KALAKALA was impartial in mishaps to her masters, too. In 1943 she rammed a railroad car barge. The same year she went aground off Bainbridge Island under the command of Captain Ole Rindal. Her auxiliary engine had given out and the large craft swung inshore. Before the end of the decade, she had stalled off Alki Point with a broken crank shaft and clobbered Colman Dock again.

It was not that the vessel was unseaworthy for she was remarkably buoyant. She was battered and beaten at every turn but she proved that she was ''unsinkable'' as proclaimed. KALAKALA skippers grew to regard the federal inquiries as a fringe benefit for time-off.

The ''Silver Swan'' was aground again in 1951 with another engine failure. Then she collided with a tugboat and sank it off of Victoria in 1957. The vessel was apparently impartial to owners, too, because Washington State Ferries suffered just as many mishaps on behalf of the KALAKALA as had her previous owners.

The 1960s were off to an uproarious start when the piston overheated and went off with a *BANG* in the engine room. Within the month she collided with the ferry ILLAHEE, sending her California contemporary to drydock. By the mid-sixties, she twice had demolished ferry slips at the new Washington State Ferry Terminal, old Colman Dock. But through all of this, the KALAKALA was a survivor. She even escaped the 1964 fire at Todd Shipyard where she was moored for repairs.

''Unsinkable'' and ''fireproof'' were her namesakes.

SHE WAS A SHAKER

KALAKALA was known far and wide for her teeth-shaking vibration throughout her service on the Sound. From the day she was relaunched the quaking and rattling was obvious but at first her passengers were just too polite to notice. Later this problem was slightly alleviated by the opening of the aft end of the ferry, which was sealed with steel doors while underway. The opening allowed the wind to ''whoosh through the vessel'' rather than aerodynamically flow around it. It is likely, though, that the vibration was mostly provoked by the incorrect alignment of the

---

[3] Scrapbooks kept by Captain Van Bogaert and loaned to the authors by Puget Sound Maritime Historical Society revealed a number of personal stories about the Sound's ferry fleets.

KALAKALA's engine at the time of installation, a factor that could never be satisfactorily corrected.[4]

In 1956 the state replaced her four-blade propeller with a five-blade to smooth out the ride. She was tightened, reinforced and rebored a number of times but passengers continued to grin tightly, holding their teeth in place while they experienced a rattling good ride for the price of a single fare.

Due to all the excitement of bumps and jumps, the tossled commuters developed a variety of affectionate names for the streamliner: ''Silver Slug,'' ''Silvery Beetle'' and ''Galloping Ghost of the Seattle Coast'' were names of common reference. An Indian suggested ''Chqueesem Cuss't'' or in loose translation, ''Shake 'Em Up Very Much to Beat Hell.'' Seattle's Scandinavian community dubbed her ''Kackerlacka,'' which means cockroach. This was purely a phonetic resemblance, of course, casting no aspersions on the superstructure of the vessel.

KALAKALA's unorthodox appearance provoked the purists of steamboating heritage to grumble that she looked like a ''pregnant whale.'' The KALAKALA received no end of complimentary remarks.

Bill Thorniley claimed that there were times he was busier trying to get the newspapers not to write about a KALAKALA happening than he was getting them to write something favorable. Like, for instance, the ceremonial cruise, when the honor party was escorted back to shore in small craft and left the ''Flying Bird'' to wing it ashore at the end of a tow line. Grumble, grumble, grumble . . . must be the fault of bad press.

But amidst all the crushing accidents, verbal abuse and commuters' disenchantment with their rollicking rides, the KALAKALA did a good job. She was big, if clumsy, and when World War II ignited, the KALAKALA exchanged moonlight cruises for thousands of Navy Yard workers, vehicles and supplies. She was bestowed with the title ''Workhorse of the Sound'' during the war. Making six trips a day between Seattle and Bremerton, KALAKALA carried nearly 5000 passengers daily.

Social problems arose for the KALAKALA's crew when she carried so many tired workers and sailors. Many of the passengers looked forward to rest and relaxation at the end of a hard day; they would have a beer and play some poker which was occasionally cause for arrest. There were others who had the idea that a good time could be had by breaking and burning the ferry's furnishings and throwing life preservers

overboard. One youth was tossed in jail for imperiling the vessel's operation with mock engine room signals; cars could have been caught crossing the ferry's ramp while the ferry reversed. Those were trying times, but once again the ''Silver Bullet'' managed to survive.

WASHINGTON'S TOURISTS

KALAKALA's outstanding advantage was her attraction for tourists. By 1941, just six years after her world-shaking appearance, the streamliner had already carried more than 6,000,000 passengers. Throughout 32 years of Puget Sound service she continued to be the visitors' pet.

In the summer of 1942 Puget Sound Navigation Company introduced the KALAKALA to the Seattle-Victoria run, weekends only. She ran between Victoria and Port Angeles in the summers of 1946 and 1947, and again in 1955 through 1959. This greatly enhanced her

[4] Captain Alex Peabody's younger brother, Larry, spotted this engine mounting problem in the late thirties at the time of a serious accident. Attempts to eradicate the condition were begun then.

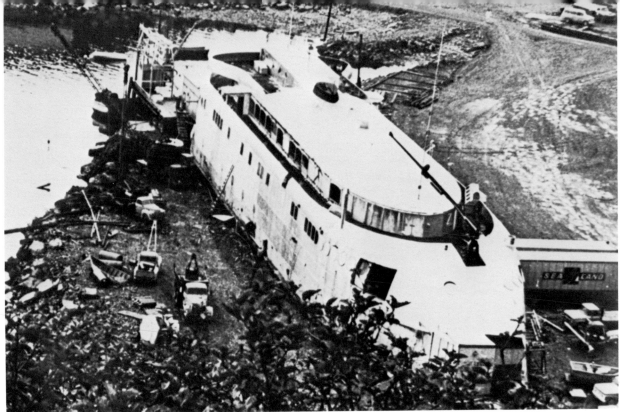

tourist appeal. When people came to Puget Sound they wanted to ride the KALAKALA.

Washington State Ferries relegated the streamliner to standby service for winter months in the early sixties, but used her constantly throughout the summers. Only the Seattle Space Needle rivaled her international flair during Seattle's World Fair, 27 years after her introduction. According to ferry officials, they received more letters of inquiry about the KALAKALA than any other ship in their service. She was also a favorite for special excursions.

The KALAKALA's service on Puget Sound did not end until 1967. Exorbitant maintenance, fuel and engine costs, combined with her reduced capacity for the car deck from 115 vehicles to 65[5], forced the all-steel vessel into retirement that year.

KALAKALA was sold to American Freezerships for $100,000 and towed to Kodiak, Alaska. There she remains today, placed on the stationary grid as a crab processing plant. Hard times have fallen on the succession of seafood processors who have owned the KALAKALA at Kodiak. In February 1983, she was found on the auction block of the U.S. Marshall. Flexible indeed, the mighty KALAKALA, Ex-PERALTA, has survived through to the present, "unsinkable," and "fireproof," wondering at her fate.

KALAKALA MET HER FATE AS A SEAFOOD PROCESSING PLANT AT KODIAK, ALASKA

KALAKALA AT BREMERTON

[5] Attributed to larger automobiles.

SAN FRANCISCO FERRIES COME NORTH

San Francisco boasted the world's largest ferry fleet in 1929 when the great Southern Pacific Railroad merged its auto ferry fleet with the Golden Gate Ferry Company, Ltd. Combined, the newly formed company known as the Southern Pacific-Golden Gate Company, owned 29 vessels, most of them double-ended ferryboats. The Puget Sound Navigation Company in Seattle owned 27 vessels[1] in 1929 but only 19 of those were auto ferries. The Sound company was still in the process of converting its old steamers to ferries and acquiring ready-built ones from the other local companies through mergers and take-overs. Puget Sound Navigation Company had yet to build any auto ferries from start to finish, but they had acquired several original Sound-built ferries from their amalgamation of the Crosby Direct Lines, Inc., the Whidby Island Transportation Company, the Nearhoff interests, and the Sound Ferry Lines.

Puget Sound's ferry fleet gradually emerged over the years from the passenger boats of the Mosquito Fleet. The scarcity of trains and passable roads influenced the substantial popularity and commercial use of the natural waterways. The introduction of automobiles in the first decade of this century and their ever-increasing use persuaded the passenger steamer owners in the early twenties to rapidly adapt to vehicular ferries or get out of business.[2] Successful business in the Northwest has often been based on giving the people what they want, not necessarily what they need. A good many fortunes were made using that philosophy.

San Francisco's ferry network was decidedly different. It was well planned for the most part, highly organized and coordinated with other existing forms of transportation and construction; it was also well-financed in the beginning. Railroads controlled the major transportation systems of the Bay City for many years. In conjunction with the trains, connections across the Bay were accomplished with double-ended ferryboats as early as the 1860s.[3] The ALAMEDA of 1866 had been planned as a single-decked vessel, but financier William Ralston suggested a second deck. The EL CAPITAN, appearing in 1868, closely followed the ALAMEDA's design; both vessels had upper decks

featuring enclosed passenger cabins under clerestories. Roof-covered promenades on either side prevented rain from soaking passengers who strolled the upper deck. The ALAMEDA set the pattern on which future San Francisco ferryboats were based. Upper deck extensions would later be added as upper deck ramps to connect with the terminal ramps.

The Central Pacific and the Southern Pacific introduced more double-ended ferries to the Bay in the 1870s, beginning with the conversion of the lavish river steamer CHRYSOPOLIS, circa 1860, to a railroad car ferryboat in 1869[4] with a carrying capacity of four freight cars of the time. The vessel was renamed OAKLAND with this conversion. The Southern Pacific also built the car ferry[5] THOROUGHFARE on the ways at Block 9[6] at the foot of Second Street, San Francisco, in 1869-1870. The railroad ferries served to connect train

[1] The fleet for P.S.N. included:

CITY OF BREMERTON-cf; INDIANAPOLIS-p; IROQUOIS-cf; CHIPPEWA-cf; TOURIST-ft; SEATTLE-cf; KULSHAN-p; OLYMPIC-cf; WASHINGTON-p; PUGET-cf; SOL DUC-p; TACOMA-p; COMANCHE-p; CITY OF ANGELES-cf; ALOHA-ft; CITY OF BELLINGHAM-cf; MOUNT VERNON-f; PIONEER-f; WHIDBY-f; CROSLINE-f; AIRLINE-f; BEELINE-cf; CITY OF MUKILTEO-f; CENTRAL II-f; QUALLAYUTE-f; CLATAWA-cf; CITY OF KINGSTON-cf

cf: converted to ferryboat; p: passenger only; ft: freighter; f: built as a ferry.

[2] Joshua Green wrote in his memoirs *The Green Years* that he finally left P.S.N. in 1927 because the steamboat business was "rapidly degenerating into the ferryboat business anyway." p. 115.

[3] The first steamboat in San Francisco Bay was the 37 foot side-wheeler SITKA, imported by sailing ship from Russian Alaska in 1847 and a number of other steamers shuttled to many points on the Bay. Brown, "San Francisco Bay Ferries," *Sea Breezes Magazine*, Oct. 1957.

[4] *Personal History and Reminiscenses of Henry Root, 1845-1921*, published privately. Manuscript found at Bancroft Library, U.C. at Berkeley. Root claims the conversion year was 1869 but most sources cite 1875. Root may have confused this history with another vessel or government documentation may not accurately reflect all alterations and dates. See also, Kemble, "Chrysopolis," *American Neptune*, Vol. 2, Nov. 4, 1942.

[5] "Car ferry" refers to railroad cars, not automobiles.

[6] Block 9 was bounded by Townsend, King, Second and Japan Streets. Ibid.

commuters and transport baggage for train passage. Most did not carry the railroad cars.

On the UKIAH, however, train cars were actually switched aboard the cargo deck of the ferry;[7] but for the most part, early ferries carried a rail down the center of the main deck. Baggage carts carrying aboard the baggage and the U.S. mail, were pulled by gasoline tractors down this rail.[8] The primary reason many of these ferries were double-ended (two pilothouses and rudders and propulsion on each end) even though they were passenger carriers on both decks, was to avoid turning the vessels around and backing them into the slips. It required more time to negotiate this turn and demanded strict and skilled maneuverability in a ship-crowded bay. Double-ends also facilitated the loading and off-loading of baggage carts.

These California double-enders were particularly adaptable as auto carriers when the need arose in the Twentieth Century. It was not until 1908 that a philosophical change in the design approach for Bay ferries occurred. The MELROSE was then built primarily to carry automobiles. She was followed by a second THOROUGHFARE in 1912, built for the same purpose. The companies continued to build luxury passenger ferries, including the turbo-electric twins, HAYWARD and SAN LEANDRO, launched by the Key System in 1923, and even later, the YERBA BUENA and the PERALTA in 1927.[9] The interior decor on these ferries reflected the gracious appointments in harmony with the railway owners' Victorian tastes. The ferries that were displaced when these newer passenger ferries were built were relegated to carrying motor cars. That duty apparently reflected a social stigma attached to the outdated ferries.

The automobile began influencing changes in those attitudes; one individual, Harry E. Speas, grew impatient waiting to get his car aboard the Northwestern Pacific boats crossing to and from Sausalito and San Francisco. His frustrations culminated in the formation of the Golden Gate Ferry Company which would specialize in the handling of autos on this run. His financial backers owned the Rodeo-Vallejo line on the northern bay and sent their new steamer AVEN J. HANFORD to inaugurate the run in 1922. When the first diesel-electric ferry, the GOLDEN GATE, entered the Golden Gate run, its terminal was not at the Ferry Building, home of the Southern Pacific ferries, but at Hyde Street Pier,[1] near Fisherman's Wharf.

More diesel-electrics were added, all slightly over 200 feet in length and built of wood. These vessels were the GOLDEN WEST, 1923; GOLDEN STATE, 1926; GOLDEN BEAR, GOLDEN SHORE and GOLDEN POPPY, 1927; and the GOLDEN AGE, 1928. The Golden Gate company acquired former Key System vessels and adapted some as auto carriers, renaming them the GOLDEN COAST, GOLDEN ERA, GOLDEN WAY and GOLDEN DAWN.[2] The AVEN J. HANFORD was converted to diesel and renamed GOLDEN CITY in 1927. Soon after, she collided with the steamship NEWPORT and sank, a total loss.

Rivalry between the Golden Gate company and the Southern Pacific grew fierce. Southern Pacific decided to cater to automobiles again about the same time as their competitor did. They acquired three steam autoferries built with steel hulls and wood superstructure. These ferries were still on the ways at the Bethlehem Shipbuilding Corporation, San Francisco, under construction for the Six-Minute Ferry Company. They were the 230 foot sisters SHASTA, SAN MATEO and YOSEMITE. Southern Pacific introduced them to the East Bay runs along with modern auto facilities built at the Oakland and Alameda piers. Then in 1924, Southern Pacific added three more boats, the EL PASO, NEW ORLEANS and the KLAMATH. These too, were built of steel. Southern Pacific also acquired Monticello Steamship Company in February 1927 which included the ferries CITY OF SACRAMENTO, CALISTOGA and NAPA VALLEY.

The Golden Gate company remained ahead of the Southern Pacific in auto service so the railway built six diesel-electric sisters in 1927. Three of these were the FRESNO, the STOCKTON and the LAKE TAHOE, all controlled by Southern Pacific. The other three, RED-

[7] This was much more prevalent in Europe than in the U.S.

[8] Information given by Captain Russel Taylor who worked aboard S.P. San Francisco ferryboats in 1917. Later these carts had wooden wheels with hard rubber rims that did not ride a rail.

[9] The Key System specialized in handling only passengers, no freight. Its trains were all electric from the start. The Key System considered S.P. ferries to be "cattle cars" because they handled baggage as well. Later, when Key signed a contract to handle Sacramento Northern Railway interurban cars and passengers, small hand carts were taken onto the tower deck with small hand luggage from Sacramento Northern electric trains. Richard E. Brown correspondence with authors, 1983.

[1] Today's home of the National Maritime Museum's historic fleet of ships including the ferry EUREKA.

[2] The former names of these ferries respectively were S.S. YERBA BUENA (I) (Ex-HARRY E. SPEAS), FERNWOOD, CLAREMONT and SAN FRANCISCO.

WOOD EMPIRE, SANTA ROSA, and MENDOCINO, went to their subsidiary, the Northwestern Pacific Railroad.

Competition and ferryboat races came to an abrupt halt when the Southern Pacific absorbed the Golden Gate company in 1928,[3] forming the Southern Pacific-Golden Gate Ferries, Ltd. All auto boats were pooled under the same houseflag and with 29 boats, the new company shifted vessels to runs according to the traffic demand. On any given run it was within their means to have a ferry leaving every three minutes.

Consolidated automobile ferry service on the Bay served eight routes and carried all auto traffic between San Francisco and Marin County and between San Francisco and the East Bay counties. More than 5,000,000[4] autos were carried in 1928 by this fleet of ferries. The Southern Pacific Railroad owned 51 percent of the stock in the ferry company. A Southern Pacific-Golden Gate Ferries brochure dated April 1929 stated, "The ferry transport of autos is greater on San Francisco Bay than anywhere else in the world, for no other major center of population is divided by such wide reaches of water as is the San Francisco metropolitan district."[5] The ferry routes were three miles in length.

Efficient auto ferrying on the Bay peaked just as the Depression gripped San Francisco. The Berkeley and Richmond runs were discontinued in 1936, followed one year later by the cessation of the Vallejo service. The Sausalito run expired in 1938 after the Golden Gate Bridge opened. The company breathed its last when, with the surrender of its operation in 1940, the LAKE TAHOE stopped making auto trips to the Oakland Pier. The Bay Bridge would henceforth suffice.

During the late thirties the ferries of the Bay experienced a quickly-extinguished flourish of interest for visitors and Bay residents. In 1939 the Golden Gate International Exposition at Treasure Island opened. Transportation was advertised with, "Ferries take you to Treasure Island, site of the Fair, for only 10 cents—much less than the cost of driving there."[6]

The Key System agreed to operate three of their ferries and lease five ferries from the Southern Pacific for additional operation and service. A letter dated September 14, 1938 addressed to W.P. Day, Vice President and Director of Public Works, Golden Gate International Exposition, San Francisco, from Lester S. Ready, Consulting Engineer, states that five ferries would be leased from Southern Pacific at a presumed cost of $150 per day for 300 days, or a total cost of $225,000.[7] "... $225,000 to Southern Pacific Company is for ferryboats which would otherwise be for sale... Presumably these boats would be in use by the S.P. Company in regular passenger service almost up to the time they are turned over to the Key System. There would seem to be some question as to the necessity of much reconditioning work, other than changing the ends on these boats."

Rent for the three Key System boats was to be only $130,000. The vessels would be the steamers HAYWARD, SAN LEANDRO and YERBA BUENA. "Present value for these boats would be somewhat limited as their use as ferryboats in the bay would cease with the rail operation across the Bridge were it not for the Exposition."[8]

[3] The year before W.B. Foshay attempted a similar consolidation of ferry companies on Puget Sound.

[4] Southern Pacific Golden Gate Ferries brochure, April 1919. It states that in 1928 ferries of the San Francisco-Sausalito run carried 1,172,108 automobiles. San Francisco-East Bay ferries carried 4,150,758 autos. There were 250 automobiles per 1,000 people in the Bay Area in 1928.

[5] Ibid. The president of the S.P.G.G.F. Company was S.P. Eastman, also the president of Atlas Imperial Diesel Company.

[6] Southern Pacific Railroad brochure, "Treasure Island on San Francisco Bay," 1939.

[7] *Report on Transportation Service to Golden Gate International Exposition 1939*, Sept. 1939, p. 80.

[8] Ibid. p. 113.

COMMUTERS FROM EAST BAY ON THEIR WAY TO WORK, WALKING UP MARKET ST., SAN FRANCISCO, IN THE EARLY 1930s. IN THE BACKGROUND IS THE HISTORIC FERRY BLDG., WHERE FERRYBOATS BEGAN AND ENDED CROSS BAY JOURNEYS.

THE CHRYSOPOLIS WAS REBUIT AS THE OAKLAND FOR SAN FRANCISCO BAY

FERRYBOAT BAY CITY

SAN FRANCISCO'S YOSEMITE WAS REBUILT AND
OPERATED AT THE TURN-OF-THE-CENTURY ON
PUGET SOUND

SOUTHERN PACIFIC AUTO FERRIES SANTA ROSA AND
FRESNO

LUXURIOUS COMMUTER FERRY YERBA BUENA IN
DRYDOCK

RAIL CAR FERRIES ON SAN FRANCISCO BAY

KLAHANIE WAS THE FORMER GOLDEN AGE

THE SHASTA AND THE SAN MATEO ON SAN FRAN-
CISCO BAY

CLARENCE BELL COLL., TRANSPORTATION INSTITUTE

FOR SALE

7 Automobile and Passenger Ferry Boats, now on San Francisco Bay

STEEL HULL—OIL BURNING

Steamships	Auto Capacity	Passenger Capacity	Vehicle Clearance	Length		Width		Brake Horse Power	Tonnage	
				Keel	Deck	Beam	Guards		Gross	Net
City of Sacramento	103	2,027	11' 6"	298' 0"	308' 0"	50' 0"	67' 4"	2,600	3,016	1,829
Calistoga	103	1,526	9' 6"	298' 2"	308' 5"	45' 0"	65' 0"	2,600	2,680	1,516
Napa Valley (1)	85	1,528	11' 6"	231' 2"	242' 0"	48' 7"	62' 5"	2,600	2,189	1,289
El Paso	70	450	11' 8"	234' 0"	246' 0"	44' 10"	63' 6"	1,230	1,953	926
Shasta (2)	62	2,200	11' 6"	206' 0"	230' 0"	42' 0"	63' 6"	1,230	1,782	1,120
Yosemite (2)	62	1,400	11' 4"	206' 0"	230' 0"	42' 0"	63' 6"	1,230	1,782	1,120
San Mateo (2)	62	1,175	11' 6"	206' 0"	230' 0"	42' 0"	63' 6"	1,230	1,782	1,120

(1) Similar in type to Calistoga. (2) Sisterships; similar in type to El Paso.

For Information
C. F. Fennema, General Manager,
65 Market Street, San Francisco, California
Southern Pacific Golden Gate Ferries, Ltd.

ALEX PEABODY RECOGNIZES ADVANTAGES

Peabody had an eye for a good business venture. His KALAKALA had proven to be a financial success. He had snatched up the unwanted California ferry PERALTA for a mere $6,500,[9] invested about $300,000 in engines, equipment and streamlined superstructure, and had launched his innovation with a fanfare that rocked the maritime world. Puget Sound's Black Ball achieved a place in American history that would compliment its predecessor company of East Coast packet ships. With his reputation well cemented, Alex Peabody approached local financiers and the Sound's Pacific National Bank to assist him in further expanding his fleet and upgrading its service.

War clouds gathered over Europe and the Pacific, while Puget Sound Naval Shipyard and the Naval Torpedo Station at Keyport hired more and more civilian employees. Both of these yards were served by the Black Ball Line. Most of the workers commuted from Seattle. The local economy was showing signs of the same improvement and Peabody took this opportunity to approach the bank.

Pacific National Bank, known as the "Boeing Bank" granted Puget Sound Navigation Company a sizable loan to purchase and refurbish six newly-retired California ferries. Heavyweight backers and the company's fine reputation probably served as collateral. Peabody headed for San Francisco to purchase the "Golden" fleet.

His purchase included six of the diesel-electrics of wood construction that had comprised the core of the original Golden Gate company fleet, namely the GOLDEN WEST, GOLDEN STATE, GOLDEN BEAR, GOLDEN POPPY, GOLDEN SHORE and GOLDEN AGE. With the exception of the GOLDEN WEST, all had been built between 1926 and 1928 in the Bay Area. Peabody is said to have paid $150,000 for the six ferries and soon after, sold the GOLDEN WEST to the San Diego & Coronado Ferry Company due to her age and smaller size. The other ferries were towed to Puget Sound.

Designed for the rough weather crossings at the Golden Gate with a freeboard of nine feet, these vessels were considered to be excellently suited for any route on Puget Sound. Each ferry had a speed of 12 knots, a capacity for 70 contemporary automobiles and overhead clearance "sufficient for the highest truck." Accommodations for approximately 500 passengers were provided and each ferry was said to have a modern marine-view room.

CAPTAIN LOUIS VAN BOGAERT

Tugs of the Puget Sound Tug & Barge Company were hired to bring the ferries up the coast in November 1937. The GOLDEN BEAR, in the tow of the tug ACTIVE, was the first to depart. It was a good thing that the company did not believe in bad omens.

The tug and ferry met a wild storm off the Oregon Coast. Nearing Empire, Oregon, the towline parted, sending the ferry adrift. Tremendous waves battered and wrecked the GOLDEN BEAR's house. The masterly seamanship of the ACTIVE's Captain W.J. Sorman enabled the tug to run alongside the ferry and safely remove the crew of seven in spite of the raging storm.

Captain Louis Van Bogaert, experienced ferry captain and soon to be the Black Ball fleet commodore, was in command of the GOLDEN BEAR for the trip north. The U.S. Coast Guard Cutter PULASKI was called to the scene and with her aid the ACTIVE succeeded in getting a line on the runaway ferry. They towed the GOLDEN BEAR into Empire, Oregon.

The GOLDEN BEAR's hull had escaped damage but her superstructure was a shambles. The storm subsided and the tug and half-a-ferry finished the journey

[9] Faber, "KALAKALA Wins Dock Battling Record," *Enetai*, 2/18/1983, p. 8.

WRECK OF THE GOLDEN BEAR

safely to Puget Sound where the GOLDEN BEAR was escorted to Lake Washington Shipyard for repairs or reconstruction. With some optimism the company announced that the vessel's new name would be CHETZEMOKA. W.C. Nickum and Sons were preparing plans to rebuild the ferry as a single-ender similar to the CHIPPEWA. The shipyard survey soon revealed that repairs were impractical. Her Ingersoll-Rand engines were later put into the KEHLOKEN. The hulk became an unnamed cement barge which, while unloading cement for the Bremerton Navy Yard, capsized and sank. When salvaged, the hull had a pronounced twist and was unusable. It was towed to Vancouver Island and sunk as a breakwater on a logging boom ground.

Undaunted by the same storm but following on the heels of it, the tug COMMISSIONER towed the GOLDEN STATE safely into Black Ball's West Seattle moorings. There she was prepared for initiation into service as the KEHLOKEN at the yard of Winslow Marine Railway. Eighteen days of repair included renewing part of her house and alterations to passenger entrances. The KEHLOKEN was to be placed on the Seattle-Eagle Harbor run, replacing the diesel ferry BAINBRIDGE.

After a lengthy voyage through stormy seas, the ferry GOLDEN AGE arrived undamaged in tow of the

GOLDEN BEAR   *KNIGHT MARITIME MUSEUM*

COMMISSIONER. Tug and tow ran into violent weather off the Oregon Coast and put into Coos Bay for several days. The GOLDEN AGE was christened the KLAHANIE which means "great outdoors." KLAHANIE was permanently assigned to the Seattle-Indianola-Suquamish route, replacing the ferry SEATTLE.

The remaining two, the GOLDEN SHORE (renamed ELWHA) and the GOLDEN POPPY (CHETZEMOKA), were towed north uneventfully. The newly commissioned tug NEPTUNE of the Puget Sound Tug & Barge Company made good time with the GOLDEN SHORE while the tug ACTIVE towed the other vessel.

261

KLAHANIE (EX-GOLDEN AGE)

KLAHANIE AGROUND ON MUD BANK

KEHLOKEN (EX-GOLDEN STATE) (left)

263

CHETZEMOKA (EX-GOLDEN POPPY)

ELWHA (EX-GOLDEN SHORE)

GOLDEN STATE BOARDED UP FOR THE JOURNEY NORTH. THE GOLDEN FLEET THAT ONCE SERVED SAN FRANCISCO BAY WOULD SERVE PUGET SOUND FOR MANY YEARS TO COME.

ENETAI (EX-SANTA ROSA)

WILLAPA (EX-FRESNO) (upper right)

*WILLAPA AFTER CONVERSION BY P.S.N. FOR THE BRE-
MERTON RUN*

QUINAULT (EX-REDWOOD EMPIRE)

NISQUALLY (EX-MENDOCINO)

KLICKITAT (EX-STOCKTON) (left)

ILLAHEE (EX-LAKE TAHOE)

KLICKITAT (EX-STOCKTON)

CITY OF SACRAMENTO AND THE NAPA VALLEY (MALAHAT)

KAHLOKE (EX-CITY OF SACRAMENTO)

271

MALAHAT (EX-NAPA VALLEY)

STEAM FERRY SHASTA

RIVER QUEEN (EX-SHASTA)

J.E. MURPHY, MARINE SUPERINTENDENT, P.S.N., PREPARED THE CALIFORNIA FLEET TO COME NORTH

By the summer of 1940, the Black Ball Line had over 300 daily sailings, showing increased service between Seattle and Suquamish with the KEHLOKEN; between Port Angeles and Victoria with the ferry OLYMPIC; between Anacortes and Sidney with the ferries CROSLINE and BAINBRIDGE; and between Mukilteo and Columbia Beach with the ferry VASHON. Service between Seattle and Bainbridge also improved. By this time, Puget Sound Navigation Company was maintaining 13 routes: Seattle-Bremerton, 15 round trips daily; Seattle-Manchester, 7 round trips; Seattle-Indianola-Suquamish, 6 round trips; Fauntleroy-Vashon-Harper, 12 round trips; Edmonds-Kingston, 7 round trips; Seattle-Eagle Harbor, 14 round trips; Fletcher Bay-Brownsville, 9 round trips; Mukilteo-Columbia Beach, 24 round trips; Port Townsend-Keystone, 7 round trips; Seattle-Port Townsend-Port Angeles-Victoria, 1 round trip; Anacortes-San Juan Islands, 4 round trips; Anacortes-Sidney, 2 round trips.

Even with this busy schedule service was not yet adequate for Puget Sound. In preparation for the constant growth at Bremerton due to Navy Yard activities, Captain Peabody bid $330,000[1] for six more diesel-electric ferries of the defunct Southern Pacific-Golden Gate Ferry Company. The bid was subject to court approval because of the former San Francisco company's bankruptcy proceedings.

A Brazilian company submitted a bid for the same amount, but withdrew that offer when it failed to provide an adequate performance bond. Seattle's bid was then raised by a dollar in order to dispel any question regarding the highest tender received. Acceptance of the Peabody bid was strongly urged before the court by Rear Admiral E.B. Fenner, commandant of the 13th Naval District and the Puget Sound Navy Shipyard at Bremerton. He stressed that improved transportation facilities were needed in the Seattle-Bremerton service to increase the production levels of the yard. These ferries would carry workers as passengers and haul much-needed supplies, too.

The six vessels purchased by Black Ball in this bid were each of 2,470 gross tons, diesel-electric with steel hulls measuring 265 feet in length. Each would accommodate 75 vehicles. These vessels and their respective Sound Indian names were: FRESNO (WILLAPA); LAKE TAHOE (ILLAHEE); STOCKTON (KLICKITAT); MENDOCINO (NISQUALLY); SANTA ROSA (ENETAI); and REDWOOD EMPIRE (QUINAULT). Of these six ferries, four remain in operation in the Washington State Ferry fleet in 1983: ILLAHEE, NISQUALLY, QUINAULT and KLICKITAT. The KLICKITAT was remodeled and overhauled in 1982 by Tacoma Boatbuilding Company.

Once again the first of the newly-purchased fleet to journey north was battered and torn in a wild nor'wester four miles off Humboldt Bay, California in mid-August 1940. Seas raked the vessel's upper deck, seams opened and the ferry was taking water. The COMMISSIONER, towing the LAKE TAHOE, removed her crew of seven men. The towline parted in the gale but the tug succeeded in picking it up again. U.S. Coast Guard Cutter SHAWNEE stood by to assist. The ferry REDWOOD EMPIRE, towed by the tug ACTIVE, was following the LAKE TAHOE up the coast. Both vessels were dropped by their tugs at Cape Flattery where they mustered their own power to enter Seattle, the LAKE TAHOE having sustained only minor damage in spite of her near-demolition. The tugs returned to San Francisco for another pair of ferries for an uneventful tow north.

Involving an expenditure of about $600,000, the ferries SANTA ROSA (ENETAI) and FRESNO (WILLAPA) were rebuilt for operation on the Seattle-Bre-

---

[1] P.S.N. financing came from National Bank of Commerce.

[2] 2,800 h.p. Busch-Sulzer diesel engines. All of the four diesel-electrics were rebuilt and modified to increase horsepower.

CAPTAIN CHARLES F. FRESE, P.S.N. MASTER OF LAKE TAHOE ON VOYAGE NORTH

merton run. Direct-drive diesel power plants[2] were installed in place of the original diesel-electric equipment, purportedly increasing their speed from 11 to about 17.5 knots. These two vessels became single[3] rather than double-enders. Reconstruction work increased their seating capacity to 1,500 persons. With completion of the ENETAI and the WILLAPA, ferries then sailed approximately every 35 minutes on the Seattle-Bremerton run.

The QUINAULT (Ex-REDWOOD EMPIRE) and the ILLAHEE (Ex-LAKE TAHOE) were completely reconditioned and the ILLAHEE's engines were rebuilt. They entered the Seattle-Bremerton run temporarily as double-enders while the WILLAPA and the ENETAI were undergoing reconstruction for that run. By 1941, four Black Ball vessels were crossing the old Navy Yard Route for a total of 26 round trips daily. These ferries were KALAKALA (still the flagship), CHIPPEWA, WILLAPA and ENETAI. When the WILLAPA and the ENETAI entered the route in 1941, the ILLAHEE was shifted to the Seattle-Suquamish run and the QUINAULT was handling the Seattle-Manchester route.

The STOCKTON and MENDOCINO arrived on the Sound in April 1941. They were renamed NISQUALLY and KLICKITAT and underwent alterations similar to the ILLAHEE and QUINAULT. When they were placed in service, the Black Ball fleet numbered 19.

During the summer of 1941 in an effort to assist ferry commuters, especially those involved in the defense program, the State Department of Public Service approved a ten percent reduction in the cost of the 10-day, 20-ride passenger fare of the Puget Sound Navigation Company. The company voluntarily put this rate schedule into effect; one which was of special importance to the several thousand daily commuters in the Bremerton run. The fare on that route was reduced from 22.5 cents per commuter ride to 20 cents.

The other fares cut on the 10-day commutation tickets were the Seattle-Manchester, reduced from 17.5 to 16 cents; Seattle-Suquamish-Indianola, cut from 20 to 18 cents; Fauntleroy-Vashon, from 10 to 9 cents; Fauntleroy to Harper, from 15 to 13.5 cents; Vashon to Harper, from 10 cents to 9 cents; Seattle-Bainbridge, from 16.5 to 15 cents; Edmonds-Kingston, from 15 to 13.5 cents; and Mukilteo-Columbia Beach, from 10 to 9 cents. By the summer of 1942 the Black Ball fleet was able to transport over 21,000 cars and 280,000 passengers daily.

Routes were altered during this time as were the newly-acquired ferryboats. The State Department of Public Service ordered the establishment of a new ferry route from Point White, on the southern extremity of Bainbridge Island, to Bremerton.

Puget Sound Navigation Company was granted permission October 1, 1941 to shift its franchise from the Fletcher Bay-Brownsville route directly to the Point White-Bremerton run. This change was made to accommodate Navy Yard workers living on the island. The following month the company succeeded in purchasing the franchise from the Washington Navigation Company (Skansie Brothers) for the operation of ferries between Point Defiance, Tacoma and Tahlequah, Vashon Island.[4] The Black Ball Line had been operating the ferry route between Fauntleroy and Vashon Heights at the north end of the island for a number of years. Ferries CHETZEMOKA and KEHLOKAN were on this run and now service would be doubled with the addition of the south end crossing from the island.

Puget Sound Navigation Company was awarded a contract on a bid for the Narrows crossing in 1942.

---

[3] Single-enders had proven to be faster ferries. The single-ender came head on into the congested Seattle harbor and backed into the outer terminal.

[4] Another temporary run by P.S.N., Utsalady to Crescent Harbor, Whidbey, with VASHONIA. Emergency war service of Austin Co. building Whidbey Island Naval Air Station. Operated 3 months.

This run was from Titlow Beach (6th Avenue, Tacoma) to Point Fosdick, Kitsap Peninsula. The company operated the SKANSONIA and the DEFIANCE, but the state continued to own these two ferries.

THE LAST OF THE STEAM FLEET HEADS NORTH

Peabody had one more major purchase to make in California. This was for the two steam ferries SHASTA and SAN MATEO, circa 1922. He also purchased the NAPA VALLEY,[5] a steam ferry which was later renamed the MALAHAT on Puget Sound. A mysterious fire swept through and destroyed that vessel's upperworks while berthed at night in Bremerton in 1943, but the structure was completely rebuilt. The MALAHAT was sold by the Black Ball Line for scrapping in 1956; she had not been included with the fleet sold to the state. The MALAHAT was ultimately destroyed by another fire while awaiting break-up at the scrapyard in Portland, Oregon.

Violent weather caused some delay in towing the SHASTA to Seattle. Puget Sound Tug & Barge's ocean tug GOLIAH, under the command of Captain Ray Quinn, safely delivered the SHASTA to the Black Ball mooring in West Seattle. The GOLIAH returned south with the Lake Washington ferry MERCER (renamed the ISLANDER) in tow for delivery to Los Angeles. There she would be operated by the Los Angeles Harbor Department between San Pedro and Terminal Island. After delivering the MERCER, the GOLIAH headed up the coast for San Francisco to pick up the SAN MATEO and head for home.

With their tall black stacks, stained glass clerestory windows and pleasing chime whistles, these two steam ferries created quite a stir on Sound waterfronts. They were a welcome reminder to Puget Sound residents of a bygone era that spoke of comfort with a touch of elegance. So popular did they prove to be that the SHASTA, fondly referred to by the regular passengers as the ROBERT E. LEE, did not retire from Washington State Ferries until 1959, age 37. She was sold to a Portland firm and opened as a restaurant.[6] The SAN MATEO continued in service until Labor Day, 1969. Today the SAN MATEO serves as the home of Northwest Seaport, a non-profit maritime historical center on Lake Union in Seattle.[7]

There is no explanation for the SHASTA and SAN MATEO retaining their California identities in lieu of Northwest Indian names. All of their southern predecessors had succumbed to the popular native names of the Northwest. About the time of their arrival in

Seattle, Bill Thorniley, Black Ball's advertising manager, became the company's dock superintendent. He succeeded R.H. Pierson, Black Ball veteran of 16 years who had joined the U.S. Army Transport Service as a captain. Thorniley's new duties were to monitor traffic and ships at the Line's terminals. Advertising would be carried on only as time permitted and because of the war effort, most advertising was curbed and highly regulated. Time was at a premium and perhaps it was felt by the management that serious business did not permit the pageantry and hoo-rah of renaming transferred ferries.

The YOSEMITE, third sister of the steam trio built by Bethlehem Shipbuilding Corporation in Oakland in 1922 for the soon-defunct Six Minute Ferry Company, was sold to a South American firm in 1940. She was renamed the ARGENTINA and traveled to that country under her own steam.

Captain Peabody bought a total of 15 ferries in San Francisco between 1933 and 1942. Of these 15, 11 were sold to Washington State Ferries in 1951 and 4 remain active in 1983.

(photo right) WM. O. THORNILEY AND CHARLIE LAFARGE

[5] The NAPA VALLEY had been built as a passenger steamer in 1915; she was 231 feet long.

[6] Briefly during 1959, the SHASTA ran excursions out of Portland under the name CENTENNIAL QUEEN, in commemoration of 100 years of Oregon statehood. The SHASTA is open for business as a restaurant in 1983, but it has been completely remodeled and engines removed. The restaurant is called The River Queen.

[7] When the SAN MATEO was retired in 1969, public sentiment and affection persuaded the Washington State Parks Department to seek designation of the vessel as a National Historic Site, as the last steam-powered ferry in the Northwest. Over $200,000 was spent reconditioning her steel hull and preparing her wooden superstructure for restoration. The State Parks was forced to abandon its restoration plans for the vessel in 1976 when budgets were cut and the vessel was transferred to Historic Seattle Preservation and Development Authority in Seattle. Quite a battle of towns and communities ensued prior to this transfer since several of them were interested in mooring and restoring the old ferryboat as a city attraction. While H.S.P.D.A. owned the vessel, an interpretive center was designed and restoration plans detailed. After two years the vessel was again transferred—this time to Northwest Seaport, a maritime association already owning and restoring several historic ships of national and Northwest acclaim. The vessel is presently moored at the South end of Lake Union, adjacent to the U.S. Naval Reserve Center and near the site of another former moorage for a retired ferryboat, the BALLARD, which became The Four Winds Restaurant. The BALLARD sank at berth a number of years ago when electrical power was shut off and her pumps failed.

ASBURY PARK

The Black Ball Line concluded the California additions to its fleet of adoptees in 1941 with the purchase of the CITY OF SACRAMENTO, formerly the twin-screw steamer ASBURY PARK of New Jersey. This boat, built in 1903, was brought to the West Coast in 1918 and pressed into service for the Monticello Steamship Company on the San Francisco-Vallejo run. That company was purchased by the Golden Gate Line about 1927 and the ASBURY PARK had already been renamed the CITY OF SACRAMENTO. The vessel did not come north until 1944 and in 1952-53 it was rebuilt as the motorship KAHLOKE and transferred to British Columbian registry for operation in the Black Ball Line, Canada.

The California ferries of the Puget Sound fleet were introduced at a time of great need. They were well-built and served a multitude of purposes during World War II in addition to their major function of carrying Navy Yard workers. Those workers were often reminded by circulars and handbills to keep "mum" on ferryboat trips regarding their work activities or

shipping procedures that they might observe while underway. Ferries, and the Black Ball Freight Service, associates of Puget Sound Navigation Company, carried torpedoes from the Naval Torpedo Station, Keyport. Ferry masters were required to maneuver their vessels through darkness and dense fogs with their "lights out" for security. Submarine nets crossed the shipping lanes of Puget Sound and ferryboat navigation became cumbersome under these circumstances. Crews were expected to manage the rowdy, over-crowded passengers who were tired and sometimes tipsy. Gambling raids aboard the ferries became a real chore for civilian and military police.

In late March 1942, the KEHLOKEN became the bearer of a sad company of individuals. All Japanese residents of Bainbridge Island—over 200 men, women and children, alien and American-born—were transported by that ferry to Seattle under the supervision of the U.S. Army. From there, they were sent by passenger train leaving immediately for the California relocation camps. These people were interned for the

278

CITY OF SACRAMENTO

duration of the war with Japan. They cooperated in expediting their evacuation. Many of them left their homes and farms in the care of Filipinos on the island.

Early in the war, the Black Ball Line boasted that their total passenger capacity was already capable of evacuating the entire population of the Seattle district in less than two days. The evacuation destination was not noted. By the summer season of 1942 the company was operating 23 modern ferries with a one-load total capacity of 22,567 passengers and 1,537 automobiles and trucks.[8] The fleet totaled 452 daily sailings in 15 different routes, amounting to a daily carrying capacity of 315,000 people and 22,570 motor vehicles. In 1940 there had been only 14 round trips daily between Seattle and Bremerton; two years later with ferries from California there were 28 round trips.

Additional docking facilities at both Colman Dock and the new Bremerton terminal were provided to enable peak commuting crowds to be handled with a minimum of inconvenience. Commuters had replaced the tourists; private automobiles were secondary to

military transports and shipments of war supplies.

The pace kept with the defense program expansion and the tremendous support of the war effort should be credited to the foresight and energy of the late Captain Alex Peabody and his associates. The Puget Sound Navigation Company benefited financially from the defense programs of World War II, but benefit should be coupled with the recollection that the company purposefully kept rates low and service reliable. The unions were wholly cooperative in this effort and the ferryboat crews were considered fairly paid for their labor. The Navy Yard at Bremerton depended in large part upon the schedules of the Black Ball Line. Peabody and his staff worked closely with Navy officials and responded to their needs. Looking to San Francisco for the vessels that had been replaced by bridges, Puget Sound found a solution to filling transportation needs during the war. The people of Washington accepted those "retired" ferries and are still making some of them work.

[8] Figures taken from *The Marine Digest*, 6/27/1942.

"Milestone"

While out for a stroll not long ago,
I sighted a ferry that I used to know,
One I hadn't seen for many a day,
And, as I paused to look, I heard her say:

"Tied up and alone—yes—here I lay,
In this dirty, stinking waterway.
For I've grown old and out of date,
And everyone seems now to hate
My doddering ways, my moans and groans,
When the joints crick in my weary bones.
Yes, everything that's part of me,
That seemed so fine when I put to Sea.

Now, in the Good Old Days, when ferries were few,
And the auto ferry was something new,
Then, old friend, my frame was tough,
And my iron heart sure had the stuff.
For they'd screw 'er down and give me steam,
Pull down the whistle and let 'er scream.
A short deep blast—we'd be on our way
A' makin' time across the bay
Across to here and across to there
Up and down, and most everywhere
Around the Sound (and the San Juans, too)
That ferries are run by a Black Ball crew.
But times have changed,
Runs and ships are rearranged,
There is no place for such as me
So says progress and the powers that be.
So I'm tied up here (I can't be sunk)
To just rot away, or be sold as junk.

But after all, I've lived my life
Thru weather fair, thru storm, thru strife.
But there's one little thing that gets my goat,
That certainly strikes a sour note,
It's that Southern Ship who has my place
With her larger decks and her faster pace,
That Frisco Hussy bedecked with paint
Who flips her stern across the Strait.
With this jealous weight upon my chest,
It'll be much easier for me to rest,
If, when one of these you sight and hail,
You'll give us a thot, who blazed the trail."

Poet Unknown.

280

BLACKBALLED: THE END OF THE LINE

Puget Sound Navigation Company's president was a man of visions for future transportation on the Sound. He foresaw a "main central crossing"[1] combining vessels and bridges where the main line would begin at the Seattle Marion Street terminal with boats crossing to Winslow on Bainbridge Island and bridges spanning Agate Pass and Hood Canal on the Olympic Peninsula.

This scheme, declared Peabody, would permit his company to eliminate the losing routes like long-haul service from downtown Seattle to Suquamish on the Kitsap Peninsula. It was easy enough to see, too, that the Seattle-Bremerton line, once the busiest route on the Sound for the war effort, would eventually become consolidated. The merchant interests of Bremerton considered that condition a threat to their prosperity.

Just who was this brash fellow with the grand plans?

Captain Alexander Peabody was an educated man, raised in a fine family of Seattle. He could be a hard-boiled taskmaster who had acquired a blustery stance from years at sea. He could also be as genuine and courteous as a tropical breeze.

Peabody had attended Cornell University for two years before he exchanged collegiate lodgings for a berth on a training ship of the U.S. Shipping Board in 1915. He served under one of America's finest sailing masters, Captain Parker, of the Barber Steamship Line. His vessel was the American-confiscated German RED JACKET,[2] a steel four-masted bark.

Alex Peabody was hired as an apprentice directly by the captain and was soon promoted to mate. Shipping papers and license were not prerequisites for sea duty during World War I. After one year on the bark, Captain Parker and mate Peabody were transferred by the Shipping Board to the freighter WESTERNER. After only one Atlantic crossing, however, Captain Parker retired from the sea. "Steam tea-kettles" were not for this aging sailing ship master. Peabody and the captain remained good friends.[3]

Alexander Peabody switched to the Robin Steamship Line of San Francisco and then to the fleet of Barber Steamship Lines, New York, having advanced from one berth to the next on the bridge. He received his master's papers and by 1922 he was captain of the Barber Line's EASTERN CLOUD, an unlimited ocean steamship built in 1919. The EASTERN CLOUD was a freighter that carried Oriental products to Europe, then proceeded to New York where she loaded case oil[4] and general merchandise for Japan, China and the Philippine Islands. A clipping found in a family scrapbook and dated 1922 reads:

"The EASTERN CLOUD, which arrived in port from New York on February 26, completed her third circuit of the world on her arrival at this port [U.S., unknown] under the command of veteran Admiral Line skipper Alex M. Peabody.[5] Her last circle took only five months and 25 days and the captain explains that he would have done better only the distance was too long for the time he had to do it in. He also says there is no truth to the

[1]Cunningham, "The State Had a Ferry Dream in 1951 . . . but, Sadly, It Never Came True," *The Seattle Times*, (no date shown on clipping).

[2]The RED JACKET was renamed MONONGAHELA and the 2,780 ton steel four-masted bark was sold to Charles Nelson & Co. in 1922 and journeyed to Puget Sound during that decade. She was eventually laid up with other Nelson ships on Seattle's Lake Union, and in 1931 was towed to Eagle Harbor just prior to the raising of the Aurora Bridge which would have permanently corralled her and other sailing vessels in the lake due to the height restrictions imposed by the bridge. In 1936 she was sold to the Maritime Agencies Co., Seattle, for $6,200 and was later converted to a log barge by a Canadian logging company at Vancouver. Newell, *Marine History of the Pacific Northwest*, pp. 440 & 448.

[3]Larry and Woody Peabody, younger brothers of Alexander, fondly recall the time that Captain Parker visited their home on Capital Hill in Seattle. These two youngsters were in awe of this lifelong ship master who could spin yarns by the hour. They have never forgotten his adept management of the consumption of chocolate cake. Captain Parker would cut the cake into bite sized pieces and shoot them into his mouth with considerable ease, flinging pieces from the end of his knife while he continued to mesmerize the boys with traumas of the sea. Larry and Woody practiced his trick for months and years, but never mastered Parker's form.

[4]One clipping states that the EASTERN CLOUD discharged 90,000 cases of oil at various Philippine ports before loading at Cebu and Manilla for Europe.

[5]Admiral Line was incorrect.

report that the crew suffered from cold as his vessel rushed through the Red Sea. The EASTERN CLOUD brought a full cargo of gasoline for discharge at Manila and Cebu and after discharging will load for Europe."

Captain Peabody left the Barber Line in New York to join the ship brokerage house of E.P. Farley & Co. of that city. New York was familiar territory for the Peabody family who had founded the original Black Ball Line in the early nineteenth century. In 1926 Alexander returned to Seattle to join the Puget Sound Navigation Company as its secretary and vice president. He was president and general manager by 1929. In 1942 he was summoned to New York again, forcing him to take a leave of absence from the ferryboat business and return to sailing ships.

WIND VESSEL WILL SAIL THE SEVEN SEAS

"Washington, July 15 (UP)

"Nelson A. Rockefeller, co-ordinator of the inter-American affairs, today announced the chartering of the Inter-American Navigation Corporation to purchase and build wooden sailing ships for western hemispheric trade.

"Vessels will be built in other American republics from loans of up to $10,000,000 supplied by the government's Reconstruction Finance Corporation, Rockefeller said.

"The corporation was chartered in Maryland, and Alexander M. Peabody of Seattle, was named president."[6]

Another article states:

" 'We will not only build and acquire, but operate wooden ships,' Captain Peabody said. 'They will be from 250 to 300 tons and will be sailing schooners with auxiliary power. One hundred ships at first will be placed on service and the fleet will be enlarged as soon as possible.'

"Captain Peabody will set up both a shipbuilding and operating organization. The vessels will ply from South and Central America to Gulf of Mexico ports. His first duties will be to assemble all seaworthy schooners in continental ports and return them to service. Then he will direct the building of auxiliary-powered schooners in shipyards in Cuba, Haiti, Dominican Republic, Nassau, Jamaica and Central and South America. The vessels will be built and manned by native crews.

"Captain Peabody estimated that there are at present about 20 schooners in United States ports that can be made serviceable for inter-American operation. The fleet will carry coffee, sugar, cocoa, and other South and Central American products to the United States, releasing steel ships for other wartime services. The vessels will increase waning stores of coffee now being considered for rationing."[7]

Peabody and his bride, Marie, moved to Washington, D.C. to take up his new duties. Peabody traveled the length of Central and South America in an attempt to identify shipyards and wood materials suitable for the construction of proposed schooners. There were few, if any, "acquirable" schooners by 1942; most had already been drafted by military forces if they were under American registry.

In February 1943 Peabody publicly stated,[8] "We have obtained sixteen freighters, both wooden and steel, on the East Coast. Three of them are in operation and the rest of the fleet will be in service by the end of January or early February. The vessels range from 250 to 1,000 deadweight tons. No sailing vessels have been acquired, and it is not the intention to operate anything but power vessels. No contracts have as yet been let for the construction of new ships." It was a scheme gone awry.

The Inter-American Navigation Company soon realized that the vessels they sought were not available and could not be built in the latitudes to the south at that time. Materials in Latin American countries were not readily available for construction of such ships. Moreover, the Axis submarine menace in the Caribbean and adjacent waters was greatly reduced by Allied military action and the demand for these supply vessels was minimized.

Captain Peabody had completed a 30,000 mile tour of South America, accompanied by Palmer Scott of the Palmer Scott Company, New Bedford, Massachusetts. They had traveled 20,000 miles by air and 10,000 miles by land, venturing almost as far as Cape

[6]*Yakima Republic,* July 15, 1942. Pacific Press Clipping Bureau, Seattle, Washington. (Alex Peabody met Nelson Rockefeller as a fellow student at Cornell University.)

[7]Unidentified clipping, probably a Seattle newspaper, found in a Peabody family scrapbook.

[8]"Pacific Ports Department," *The Log,* official organ of the Pacific Coast Association of Port Authorities, California Association of Port Authorities, Northwest Rivers and Harbors Congress, Transportation Club of Seattle, Seattle Industrial Traffic Managers Association. p. 72.

CAPTAIN PEABODY'S VESSELS: RED JACKET AND   PEABODY FAMILY

EASTERN CLOUD   PEABODY FAMILY

Horn, visiting different republics and conferring with businessmen. The captain often remarked that transportation by land at that time was nearly as crude as the aeroplanes.

With abandonment of the schooner construction program 18 months later, only routine work for the Inter-American Navigation Company remained at the nation's capitol. Peabody resigned the presidency to return to Seattle and resume the problems of his ferry fleet which was already greatly involved in war production schedules. He is said to have resumed his duties at the Puget Sound Navigation Company with pride and a sigh of relief.

Alexander's brother, Woody, and the reliable crew and managers of the company had faithfully held the fleet together in their president's absence. They had exercised some ideas of their own and decided to build two railroad car barges for the Bremerton service. Plans and specifications were prepared by H.C. Hanson, Seattle naval architect. The contract was let to Reliable Welding Company in November 1943. The barges were built at Olympia, the first welded steel barges of their type to be built on Puget Sound.[9] They replaced wooden car barges constructed 20 to 25 years before them.

It is hard to know if Alexander Peabody's respite from ferries prepared him for the strenuous battles that lay ahead.

[9]*The Marine Digest*, 11/13/1943, p. 1. The new barges were 265 feet long, 42 feet in beam, and 10 feet in depth. Each had three tracks capable of transporting a 15-car railway train. The first was delivered 2/1/1944 and the second 3/1/1944. The contract was the largest private order received by any Sound plant after the beginning of the war.

We are honoring a man today
Who, by grim determination
Could show the rest of us the way
To Success, through emulation.

By calendar he's still quite young,
Confessing to only fifty-three
But it's men like him to whom praises are sung
By folks like you and me.

There's a story they tell about this man
I am sure you would like to hear.
So I'll tell you about a little plan
He executed within this past year.

When a bull-headed Swede named Wallgren
Decided to buy the ferries
'Twas a cinch he would be foiled again
By Capn Peabody's vagaries.

For the Capn's a man, as we all know
Who stands for no man's guff
And when that man has bull to throw
The Capn calls his bluff!

"The ferries can't run on nothing per day
You'll have to raise the ante,
If you want the ferries, you'll have to pay,
Or call out the Vigilante!"

So they called out the Vigilante
And that was really tough
For the poor Vashon Islanders
Who already had enough.

Of course we know our Captain
Had already made his pile,
But he had to make things happen
To make the deal worthwhile.

You might call it a filibuster
For the deal is still on the cuff,
But we thought you'd like this story
About a guy who is really tough!

(Written on occasion of a luncheon for Captain Peabody, June 24, 1948.)

LOOKING AHEAD

Peabody, like most Americans, looked forward to the end of the war and the opportunity to implement some of his plans for the company. The passenger ferry IROQUOIS had grown tired after 19 years as an excursion ferry and Peabody was anxious to replace her with a modern vessel more suitable to his needs.

War surplus flourished with an abundance of vessels and engines and he was certain to find the parts he would need for a new ship. The U.S. Navy sold him five destroyer escorts for a total of $150,000 for the lot.[1] Peabody was primarily interested in their engines, General Motors diesels with less than 2,000 hours of operation. Each destroyer escort carried four engines.

The Navy ships were towed from Suisan Bay, California to the Black Ball boneyard in West Seattle where they were stripped of engines and driving motors. Four of the engines and appropriate gear were made ready for installation aboard the new Black Ball ferry under construction at Harbor Island, Plant "A" of Todd Shipyards Corporation, Seattle.

The M.V. CHINOOK, designed by New York City architects Gibbs & Cox, Inc., was touted as the "Queen Elizabeth of the Inland Seas," a title modestly bestowed by William Francis Gibbs, her designer. Construction was ordered July 22, 1946; the keel was laid December 17, 1946 and launching ceremonies were held Tuesday, April 22, 1947. Mrs. Alexander M. Peabody was the ship's sponsor. The vessel's successful trial runs were held June 15, 1947. Her maiden voyage, sailing from Puget Sound Navigation's Colman Dock, Seattle, at 11:45 P.M. to the new Black Ball terminal in Victoria, B.C., was June 25, 1947. The *Pacific Marine Review* wrote of the CHINOOK, "... the most modern and lavishly equipped vessel for automobile-passenger service yet built in America."

The all steel CHINOOK had spacious and luxurious passenger accommodations with 100 staterooms offering sleeping facilities for 208 people. Her automobile deck carried 100 cars. The wheelhouse was equipped with radarscope to provide "eyes through the night," a development of World War II. The CHINOOK was 318 feet in length.

Four pairs of the destroyer engines were scheduled as replacements for the Nelseco engines of the four steel double-ended electric ferries from California. Two of the ferries continued to carry the Nelsecos for ballast after the installation of the GMs. The remaining eight navy surplus engines were stockpiled.

Despite what Peabody's foes were soon to publicly state, the captain was an excellent manager and wise in the ways of warehousing for the future. Jackson Corbet of *The Marine Digest* once wrote of the company, "[it] is one of the best organized in American shipbuilding, and its fleet is operated with an efficiency that can challenge the severest comparison with any other transportation system in the country. No railroad has a finer record for regularity and reliability."

Peabody had proven that he could withstand the rigors of stockmarket take-overs, bleak depression, labor organization, lengthy strikes and unhappy commuters, boisterous soldiers and sailors, cranky machinery, outmoded steamboats, and yes, even politicians ... but he could not withstand the pressures of angry citizens and an organized public who decided that the ferry system would be better off in the hands of public agencies rather than private enterprise. It would be this public outcry that would influence the reputable banking houses of the Northwest to force the company stockholders to cast their votes to sell.

A series of unreconcilable events led to the purchase of the ferry system by the state of Washington in 1951. Alexander Peabody would be disappointed for the rest of his life. But he did not go down without a fight.

[1]Shrader, *The Black Ball Line*, p. 13.

THE M.V. CHINOOK WAS A LUXURY LINER. DESIGNED BY WILLIAM FRANCIS GIBBS, SHE WOULD REPLACE THE IROQUOIS ON THE SEATTLE-VICTORIA RUN IN 1947. ALL STEEL, SHE HAD 100 STATEROOMS AND SLEEPING QUARTERS FOR 208 PEOPLE. SHE CARRIED 100 CARS. SHE WAS EQUIPPED WITH RADAR TO PROVIDE "EYES THROUGH THE NIGHT."

LABOR AND RATES

At the outbreak of World War II the ferry workers' unions had achieved the eight-hour day, recognition of seniority, and vacation time with pay. The unions and the company extended the contract terms uncontested throughout the war. "It was almost thought that the millenium had come to the waterfront and residents could look forward to a future of comparative peace and continuous service."[2]

The truce lasted only until April 1944, when the unions requested wage increases, a five day week, changes in seniority provisions and increases in vacation time. Arbitration was bound by the rules of the National War Labor Board which prohibited the granting of many of the provisions sought by the unions. The arbitrator did grant, however, the increase in vacation time. Ferry workers were to enjoy longer paid vacations.[3]

Even with lower rate charges, the Puget Sound Navigation Company was turning a fair profit throughout the war years due to the significantly increased commuter and freight traffic. Relations had eased between company management and employees. Everyone was fully occupied.

But by early 1947 the picture dimmed when the Black Ball Line offered a ten percent increase to the Inlandboatman's Union and the Masters, Mates and Pilots, as well as a forty hour week and a provision for further increases subject to arbitration. The company offered the Marine Engineers Beneficial Association the same ten percent increase and a renewal of the old contract. This was not acceptable to the engineers in light of the offers made to the other unions and a deadlock resulted. A strike was called for March 14, 1947.

This was the first strike called directly by the M.E.B.A. The engineers had always cooperated with the striking unions in the past, but the engineers did not enjoy the same benefits that other ferry union members had won such as seniority protection or a forty hour week. Seventy union engineers commenced the strike on schedule. Other ferryboat union members agreed to honor picket lines and stayed home.

One of these engineers recalls:

"The strikes of the thirties were so bitter and had so many facets that I doubt that anyone, even yet, can get a full story from participants. Unless there is documentation I would guess that much of it will never be told. The strikes, all of them, were lead almost

exclusively by the Inland Boatman's Union, with only the faintest of applause by Masters, Mates and Pilots. The MEBA was very divided and *I* think that far more engineers were supporting the companies than were supporting the strikers. This was especially true among the Kitsap County men.

"This changed very much after World War II when there was a huge increase in [MEBA] membership, and a totally changed attitude in the MEBA. There was a fierce contest for positions opening up in the MEBA union and all concerned were out to prove that they could get more for the men than anyone else. The companies paid the bills."[4]

For seven days, twenty-two ferries were tied up, stranding approximately 10,000 commuters. These commuters and their supporters organized themselves. Their groups were known as the Northwest Washington Community Council and the Ferry Riders Association. They demanded action from Governor Mon C. Wallgren, the MEBA, Captain Alex Peabody, the United States Conciliation Service and the State Toll Bridge Authority. During this strike the public was articulate in its condemnation of transportation strikes.

Commuters were confused, as is history, about who was to blame for the strike situation. Peabody was an excellent target with all the necessary accoutrements of cultural and community stature. Many were against the so-called "greedy" engineers who could not be satisfied or appeased. Several groups threw the blame at the governor and county councils who failed to provide emergency service and could not wrestle this vital transportation system away from private controls and maladies. Most travelers were convinced that the ferries were a bonafide part of the state highway system [hadn't those Black Ball tourist brochures convinced them of that?]. *No one* had the right to deny the public of their floating highways.

The governor suggested arbitration, but Peabody insisted on the right to address the public's ability to pay higher rates if the unions were granted wage increases. The unions were angry at the prospect of

---

[2]Smith, *A History of Labor Relations in the Puget Sound Ferry Boat Trade.*

[3]One week paid vacation after one year; two weeks paid vacation after five years or more of continuous service.

[4]Taken from memo to the authors from Harold Graham, chief engineer, April 1983.

tying wage increases to rate hikes and the bad image created by such a situation. Politicians were mutually uneasy because the gubernatorial campaign would present itself in 1948. This was sure to be an issue.

On the sixth day of the strike, with the public wrath fanned, the union and the company reached a compromise in the governor's office.[5] The engineers received substantial wage increases. A new collective bargaining contract was to have a no-strike, no-lock-out clause to be in effect for two years.[6] A sigh of relief could be heard all around. The compromise was the end of a battle, but the war raged on.

THE GREAT RATE HIKE

Captain Peabody had already sought to return ferry fares to pre-World War II rates plus ten percent to cover escalated costs and fewer passengers. Within a short period of time he sought another ten percent increase to cover the wage boosts. This request was granted conditionally by the state of Washington. Post-war commuters and their families were incensed by the rate increases. The cost of living was higher, jobs were difficult to find, and higher ferry fares were unacceptable.

On January 16, 1947 Paul Revelle, director of the State Transportation Department, announced that the state would allow a temporary increase in fares that would remain in effect only until a study could be presented for department review. The study was scheduled to take four months for completion.[7]

During the interim period the public was to be protected by a receipt-refund system that required the ferry company to issue dated receipts for which refunds would be granted if the transportation department ruled that the proposed increases were warranted.

Rate hearings regarding the permanency of the temporary increase were scheduled to start after May 15, the date earmarked for the conclusion of their investigations; 32 state inspectors and 13 state statisticians were involved.[8] The Northwest Community

[5]Those in attendance at the conference were Alex M. Peabody; Captain Harry I. Anderson, vice president of P.S.N.; Ward M. Toner, supervisor of Washington State Mediation Service; Harry H. Lewis and Albin L. Peterson of the U.S. Conciliation Service; H.L. Daggett, business agent; Mr. Rasmussen, secretary of the M.E.B.A.; and Governor Wallgren.

[6]A detailed account of this settlement is given in Smith's *A History of Labor Relations.*

[7]The published study has been used as research for this manuscript. It is entitled, *Report on the Investigation of the Earnings, Property, Operations, Rates, Services and Facilities of the Puget Sound Navigation Company.*

[8]Smith, *A History of Labor Relations,* pp. 77-78.

FELLOW COMMUTER

Be sure and sign the petition being circulated regarding ferry service. Your signature will help to get yourself a seat and a life preserver every time you ride. Let's prevent a catastrophe before it's too late. Let's all unite against being treated like cattle.

—This handbill paid for by Ferry Riders.

KILL THE
Steamboat Monopoly
~
PASS H. B. 364
~

This pamphlet contains the facts concerning the operation and effect of the monopoly created by the Steamboat Certificate Law (Chapter 248 1927 laws) based on the experience of the people of Bainbridge Island.

Presented by Manitou Beach-Agate Pass Ferry Association in their behalf.

Seattle office—810 American Bank Building—Phone EL 5206. This is a non-profit corporation organized by the people to obtain better transportation service for Bainbridge Island.

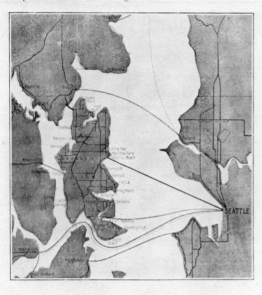

Retain This Receipt - It May Be Valuable

In accordance with orders of the State Department of Transportation the rates charged by the Puget Sound Navigation Company and now in effect are temporary, and if found excessive after investigation and public hearing by the Department of Transportation of Washington, this evidence of purchase may be used in establishing refund claims.

Puget Sound Navigation Co.

31423

Alex M. Peabody
President

AUTO AND DRIVER • ROUND TRIP

Route.....................Anacortes......Friday Harbor......

Void After December 31, 1947

Council, comprising 42 organizations, hired attorneys to represent their interests at the hearings.[9]

The Black Ball Line provided *free* boat fare for Islanders wishing to attend a hearing and "almost everyone took advantage of the offer. People who hadn't been to Seattle for months or years, made a trip to the big town. Some of them never went near the hearings, which were usually held in the Seattle Chamber of Commerce Building . . ."[1]

One columnist described these hearings as a drama entitled, "The People Versus the Black Ball Line." She went on to say that well-organized citizens armed with charts, statistics and photographs, would challenge the company and present their side. Then it would be the company's turn. Captain Peabody, who never backed down from a good wrangle, would counteract with data and figures which backed up his claim that the company was losing money.

"Captain Peabody was always the star of the drama. To my mind, he was very handsome, polished, and self-confident. Dressed in an impeccable blue suit, with a crisp linen handkerchief in his breast pocket, and wearing a jaunty bow tie, he would stride to the witness chair and take the stand. He would reply to the questions crisply and confidently. If he was unable to answer a question he would turn to one of his assistants, usually it was Charles LaFarge, and say, 'Make a note of that, Charley,' or 'Have you got that, Charley?' One afternoon he had Charley make so many notes that it became a good-natured rib at Charley's expense and he didn't show up for the next day's session. When someone asked the captain where Charley was, he threw back his head and laughed heartily . . .

"After World War II when traffic fell off and the Black Ball Line asked for a rate increase, we had a big public protest meeting in the Bainbridge High School's old gym. The captain strode into this meeting with his colleagues and faced a hostile audience. He was in rare, good form and to almost everyone present he seemed to be the 'villain.' He must have been aware of the feeling against him but it didn't faze him a bit. In fact, I think that he

[9]Attorneys were Hile, Hoof and Shucklin. Ibid.

[1]Warner, "Katydids," *The Bainbridge Island Review,* Dec. 5, 1942.

rather enjoyed trading punches with us. He won his rate increase but that was one of our last spats with the Black Ball Line and its dynamic president ... In his prime, Captain Peabody was a very classy fighter.''[2]

Peabody's concern for his company's financial well-being was matched by an equally prevalent concern for his fundamental philosophy that supported the advancement of private enterprise. Should a governmental agency be allowed to intervene between business and its clientele? Peabody was convinced that his company had been saddled with a confiscatory rate schedule that had resulted from his customers' political pressure upon the state and public officials. Public newspaper statements and hearings convinced him that the clientele had little or no regard for the future of his company and that they might exert influence to gain control of the ferry highways through the governmental act of condemnation. He feared that he might lose his company—not through sale, but by confiscation.

Court battles ensued throughout the summer and fall of 1947. Peabody threatened to tie up the ferries if the courts did not set aside the departmental order issued by Revelle, July 3, 1947:

1) Black Ball Line would be allowed a ten percent increase over the January (or pre-war) rates. This reduced the temporary 30 percent increase by two-thirds.

2) The company was ordered to make the appropriate refunds to all ferry patrons presenting valid refund coupons.

Peabody had not set aside funds for refunds; he spent those monies on wages and boat refurbishments. Commuters and government officials were indignant.

The question lurking in everyone's minds was whether state ownership was the solution to lower rates and better service. If Peabody chose to exercise his tie-up threat, the Northwest Washington Community Council[3] urged Governor Wallgren and the State Toll Bridge Authority to operate the ferries and to immediately begin exploration of ways to purchase the ferry network. Wallgren and his advisors were soon convinced that this group represented public opinion, and on August 4, 1947 he announced that the state might be ''forced'' to enter the ferry business.[4]

The ferry riders' associations remained confused and divided. It was this lack of united effort and cohesion that muddled the ferry ownership issue. Peabody squarely stated to the governor that the ferries were not for sale.[5] To demonstrate the economic situation of the system to Kitsap County residents, the company removed one ferry from the Bremerton-Seattle run. The company used poor judgement in this move because riders interpreted the removal as a show of might not a sign of company poverty. Actually, it was a more efficient and less expensive operation. The schedule was reduced from 25 to 22 trips on the Bremerton run, and one ferry was eliminated. In July 1950 the SHASTA ran as an extra on weekends on the Bremerton route for the summer. She was slow and unpopular.

A group of Vashon Islanders took strong initiative and organized a ferry district under legislative authorization, whereby, ''... if Black Ball's fare increase goes through, we think we can operate our own ferry more economically ...'' but ''... state purchase smells of creeping socialism.'' This indefinite sense of direction aroused the sentiments of nearly everyone living near Puget Sound.[6]

Superior Court concluded its hearings December 19, 1947 and directed the Black Ball Line and the Northwest Washington Community Council to file briefs within 20 days.

By the first of the New Year 1948, Puget Sound Navigation Company and the Inlandboatman's Union were faced once again with labor negotiations. Captain John Fox received a letter from Captain Peabody which, in effect, stated that the company was unable to meet shifting labor costs due to the inefficient rate schedules. ''We hereby give notice ... of our desire for a downward revision of wage costs to be made effective by reduction of wage rates and an increase in hours of employment paid in straight time rates.''[7]

Fox immediately responded that there was not a chance in the world that the unions would accept wage reductions or the loss of the 40-hour week but that on the basis of union study, ''... we think that Peabody got a helluva bum deal from the state when they only granted him 10 percent increase.''[8]

[2]Ibid.

[3]This group originated as a nucleus of Vashon Island shop owners, real estate brokers, professionals and influential residents who organized a caravan to Olympia to protest ferry rate increases. The caravan sparked similar community organizations around Puget Sound. Representatives of many of these groups met and organized the Northwest Washington Community Council.

[4]Gore & Shipman, *Commuters vs. Black Ball Line.*

[5]Shrader, *Black Ball Line*, p. 14.

[6]Gore & Shipman, *Commuters vs. Black Ball Line.*

[7]Ibid. p. 13.

[8]Ibid. p. 13.

On Saturday, February 14, 1948[9] the following letter was read before the meeting of the Washington Toll Bridge Authority. It was addressed to the Honorable Mon C. Wallgren from the Office of the President, Black Ball Line:

"Dear Sir:

"Puget Sound Navigation Company realizes that the intrastate ferry service so long furnished by it on Puget Sound is required by the communities served, but it is unable to continue at rates which are not producing income sufficient to meet operating costs.

"The company is in this situation through no fault of its own. It is required to operate under the direction and supervision of the Director of the Department of Transportation. The Director fixes the rates which may be charged and the service which must be given.

"The Director, recognizing that declines in traffic and increases in operating costs required increases in the rates established ten years ago, permitted an emergency increase of 30% effective February 15, 1947. Since that date these increased rates have been and are now being collected. On July 3, 1947 the Director entered an order determining that this increase was excessive, that the service could be furnished on an increase of 10% and that the amounts collected in excess thereof should be refunded. The company has been unsuccessful in securing relief from the court.

"The Director's order would require refunds to December 31, 1947 of approximately $652,000. If the company is forced to make refunds in this amount the operating loss for 1947 will be in excess of $200,000.

"Operating costs have increased substantially since September 1947 due in major part to the establishment as a result of a labor award, of a 40-hour week for all employees. Under conditions as they exist today, operations in 1948 at only the 10% increase in rates would result in an operating loss of over $1,000,000.

"The State of Washington, acting through the Director of the Department of Transportation, has ordered that the service must be furnished at rates not to exceed 10% in excess of those established ten years ago. The company is unable to finance the losses which would necessarily result. Therefore, it becomes the responsibility of the State of Washington to provide for the continuance of service. To make this possible the company offers to lease its vessels and facilities used in furnishing intrastate service to the Washington Toll Bridge Authority or other State Authority under terms and conditions which will insure the return of the property and the continuation of the company's organization. The company shall receive a fair compensation to be agreed upon and in addition, the amount necessary to pay the refunds ordered by the Director. The Director shall immediately undertake the responsibility of establishing rates and services which will enable the company to resume operations on a compensatory basis. The lease shall terminate on the establishment of such rates and services, or in any event within one year.

"If an arrangement as above suggested is not promptly consummated, the company will have no alternative other than to surrender its Certificate of Public Convenience and Necessity issued by the Department and abandon all service authorized thereby.

"This letter has been authorized by the company's Board of Directors.

"Very truly yours,

"PUGET SOUND
NAVIGATION COMPANY."

In response to this letter, interrogated by full discussion by the Authority, Revelle moved that Resolution #204 be adopted, rejecting Puget Sound Navigation Company's proposal on the basis that the determination of the Department of Transportation provided adequate revenue to the company to continue service at the rates prescribed by the Department. The Resolution was approved unanimously by the Toll Bridge Authority.[1]

Captain Peabody announced that the ferries would cease operation as of midnight on Sunday, February 29, 1948. Revelle emphatically insisted in his

[9] "Minutes of the Meeting of the Washington Toll Bridge Authority," Mon C. Wallgren Papers, 1948-49, T.B.A. & Ferries, Washington State Archives, Olympia.
[1] Ibid.

press release his assertion that, "I don't believe the Puget Sound Navigation Company can legally cease to operate without state's permission. As far as I am concerned, the company does not have that permission." Nor did the state know which agency within the state had the authority to grant that permission.

On February 24, the attorney general was presented a petition signed by 540 ferry workers of the Black Ball Line asking that the rate order be removed and thus publicly demonstrating their support for their employer. They stated their conviction that the 30 percent increase was essential.

The attorney general petitioned Thurston County Superior Court for a restraining order, prohibiting cessation of ferry service. On February 28 in review of the facts, the judge stated:

> "The company was not able to borrow any more money from the bank.[2] It has no money or means of securing money to pay for fuel or labor or maintenance, for each of which items it now owes a considerable amount. The evidence shows that there is a decided decline in travel between the points served by the ferry company as compared to travel existing at the time of the hearing before the Department."[3]

Peabody followed with the press statement, "It is with the utmost regret that the company is forced to discontinue its operation, as previously announced.... The Court has found ... that under the rates fixed by the Department of Transportation the company is unable to operate except at tremendous losses."[4]

And then, in the eleventh hour, the state's governor asked to meet privately with Alex Peabody and his counselors in Olympia. Alcoholic beverages were offered and refused; no common ground of discussion could be identified. Several of the old arguments were revived due to the presensce of Mr. Revelle. Governor Wallgren is said to have become confused with the dissention in the air and when asking for clarification of the issues under momentary discussion, Peabody became infuriated with Revelle's "misinterpretation" of the events and emphatically stated that his company would not be compromised nor would they give in for the sake of politicians. Peabody and his assistants left, returning to Seattle before the stroke of midnight when the captain gave the order to cease all operations. And it was done.

STATE SOLUTIONS: NOT A BED OF ROSES

A flurry of emotional scenes ensued as the politicians and the commuters realized too late that the Black Ball Line had intended to keep its word and walk out. Commuters were at first inspired by the challenge and the opportunity to rise to the battle. They offered friendly hands to stranded fellow citizens. Cabin cruisers and charter boats were pressed into passenger service while many people shared hotel rooms.

The Navy moved its shipyard workers by LST boats and on the whole, a substantial number of people took the Peabody retaliation in good humor.

But the lesions were beginning to widen particularly since freight could not be moved on inadequate power boats. Cross-Sound businesses recognized that they may be forced to wait several years to recover their losses at the hands of the ferry tie-up and the argument between citizen and state.

Inconveniences were burdening passengers, too, and medical assistance and emergencies were reaching dangerous levels. Moreover the fees charged for intermediary transport services were higher than those rates of 30 percent increase requested by Black Ball. Enthusiasm began to dwindle; commuters turned to government officials to voice their concerns and objections.

On March 6, six days into the tie-up, Governor Wallgren sent a telegram to the United States Maritime Commission. It read, "Washington State Toll Bridge Authority owns and operates ferry boats operating on Puget Sound. At present we are faced with a critical emergency due to fact one operator controlling most ferryboats has defied state government regulations and refuses to operate his ships.

"We have been endeavoring to secure boats to meet this emergency and have been negotiating with Moore Dry Dock Company, San Francisco, for the purchase of the ferry boat HAYWARD. Are advised they are not permitted to sell this ship for use by others without clearance from the Maritime Commission.

[2]Gore & Shipman, *Commuters vs. Black Ball Line,* p. 13, 16. On December 30, 1947, the Board of Directors authorized Peabody to negotiate a $2,000,000 bank loan to complete payment for the newly-constructed CHINOOK. In the Court proceedings the company attorneys stated that the company had sought additional loans for $1,000,000 in 1947 and $2,000,000 in January 1948 for operating resources. They stated no further loan funds were to be granted by the banks and the encumbered notes were already exhausted.

[3]Ibid, pp. 16-17.

[4]Ibid., p. 17.

"Because we are a state government making this request we hope you will agree to the sale of the ship by Moore Dry Dock Company to meet our problem. It is my understanding Moore Dry Dock Company also making request they be permitted to release ship to us."[5]

Moore Dry Dock had purchased five former San Francisco Bay ferryboats in September 1947 from the U.S. Maritime Commission for scrap. They were the ALAMEDA, SANTA CLARA, TAMALPAIS, CALISTOGA and the HAYWARD. In accordance with the terms of the government contract the dry dock had proceeded to scrap the vessels and March 6, 1948, only the TAMALPAIS was completely scrapped.[6]

The SANTA CLARA, ALAMEDA, and the CALISTOGA were in the process of being scrapped and were scheduled for total demolition within two months. Only the ferry steamer HAYWARD remained intact and the state's inspectors had deemed her suitable for operation as an automobile ferry on Puget Sound.

On March 8 Governor Wallgren received a proposal from Consolidated Builders, Inc., Portland, Oregon, and Nickum & Sons, Naval Architects and Marine Engineers, Seattle, for the construction of welded steel automobile ferries with main and auxiliary machinery from vessels in government war surplus.[7]

That same day a telegram arrived from San Francisco:

"Have two LSM's, 203 ft. long, 34 ft. beam, sea speed 14½ knots, powered with two diesels generating 3600 H.P., vessels equipped with loading and unloading ramps, so could be put on the beach and load and discharge automobiles without use of shore facilities. These vessels practically ready for sea, and believe with slight alterations can carry passengers as well as large quantity automobiles, deck averages 20 ft. wide, 200 ft. long, and think could be fitted for your purposes within two weeks. We ready to sell these for $60,000 apiece, San Francisco Bay . . ."[8]

This was a poignant reminder that the state did not own shoreside terminals or access roads for most ferry operations. The state was frantically thrusting for ways to resolve or at least reconcile this situation. The Washington Toll Bridge Authority called representatives from Jefferson, King, Kitsap, San Juan, Skagit and Snohomish counties to meet with the Authority on March 2. The ferry predicament was reviewed in great detail and the chairman stated that if it became necessary for the resumption of water transportation on the Sound, the governments would condemn some of the properties of the Puget Sound Navigation Company. State attorneys found that the state did not have this authority but that the counties were vested with the authority. The meeting was dismissed with the request that each county give consideration to the entire matter and advise the Authority of the degree of cooperation they would be willing to lend to the emergency.

Later that same day the executive session of the Authority reconvened and after "lengthy discussion" instructed H.A. Pebble[9] to contact Alex Peabody, et al, regarding whether or not said officials would give favorable consideration to the sale of *some* of the company's equipment and facilities to the state.

A special meeting of the Toll Bridge Authority was held March 11, 1948 and Mr. Pebble glumly reported on his meeting with Captain Peabody. Peabody and his attorneys had "declined to entertain any offer from the Authority for the purchase of any of the Puget Sound Navigation Company ferries or ferry facilities."[1]

[5]Telegram to Vice Admiral William W. Smith, Chairman, Maritime Commission, Commerce Building, Washington, D.C., from Mon C. Wallgren. Wallgren Papers, Washington State Archives.

[6]Letter to United States Maritime Commission, Washington, D.C., from Moore Dry Dock Company, Foot of Adeline Street, Oakland, California, dated March 6, 1948. Wallgren Papers, Washington State Archives.

[7]*Proposed FerryBoat for the State of Washington Toll Bridge Authority,* Consolidated Builders, Inc. & W.C. Nickum & Sons, 3/8/1948.

[8]Telegram from W.J. Mitchell, vice president, Meinton Co., Inc. Wallgren Papers, Washington State Archives.

[9]H.A. Pebble was the attorney for the Toll Bridge Authority. Taken from Minutes of the Meetings for Washington Toll Bridge Authority, 3/2/1948 and 3/11/1948. Wallgren Papers, Washington State Archives.

[1]Minutes of the Washington Toll Bridge Authority, 3/11/1948. On March 9, P.S.N. had resumed operations on many of its routes at rates 49% higher than the rate authorized by the Department of Transportation. While the ferries had been officially "tied up" numerous small vessels were pressed into emergency service while P.S.N. approached the counties for legal "bare boat charters" and "operating contract" agreements with the company. Most counties agreed to the plan, considering the emergency state of affairs.

The following resolution was adopted unamiously at that meeting:

"Resolution No. 250

"WHEREAS at all times since the State of Washington emerged from pioneer status, the residents thereof on the mainland abutting on Puget Sound and on the islands situated therein have suffered delays, difficulties and uncertainties in crossing the waters of Puget Sound, and

"WHEREAS the said residents, in the making of said crossings, have been subjected from time to time to excessive ferry rates and cessation of ferry service, all of which has been injurious to the economic conditions and welfare of said inhabitants and which has retarded the growth and development of the state in general and the Olympic Peninsula area in particular, and

"WHEREAS chapter 266 of the laws of 1945 authorizes the Washington Toll Bridge Authority to operate and maintain ferry service for the residents of this state, and

"WHEREAS said Authority now desires to operate and maintain for the people of this state the most efficient, adequate and economic permanent system of transportation of persons and vehicles across Puget Sound, which system, past experience has conclusively indicated, can be effected only through operation and maintenance thereof under public ownership and supervision;

"NOW, THEREFORE, BE IT HEREBY RESOLVED that the Director of Highways, ... is hereby authorized and directed to retain the consulting engineering firm of W.C. Gilman and Company of New York, N.Y., for purposes of making a complete traffic survey, etc."

The Director of Highways was instructed to retain naval architects from W.C. Nickum & Sons to furnish the Authority with preliminary plans for ferries and new facilities. The Authority had no funding for the enactment of these surveys or plans but the Highway Department was instructed to make use of funds budgeted under "usual functions."[2] All costs and expenses were eventually to be reimbursed by the Authority to the Department of Highways out of proceeds from the sale of bonds, "if and when issued and sold by the Authority for operation of ferries on Puget Sound or out of tolls and revenues derived by the Authority from such operations or out of any other fund which might hereafter in any manner become available for such reimbursement."[3]

It was this procedure that embroiled Governor Wallgren in scathing criticism by his gubernatorial opponent, the former governor Arthur B. Langlie who captured the full attention of the constituency, the legislature and eventually the State Supreme Court.

THE RACE FOR GOVERNOR

Arthur Langlie accused the State Administration of dealing "under the greatest cloak of secrecy (they) have apparently manipulated a deal whereby the State, at a price of approximately $6,000,000 is taking over the ferry system, the value of which and the utility of which is unknown to the public at large."[4] Langlie thought it possible that the public might save as much as $1,000,000 to $3,000,000 if the issue was publicly aired.

On October 6, 1948 Governor Wallgren addressed the Kitsap County Improvement Clubs, saying, "I was greatly surprised when an attorney from Spokane walked into my office and handed me a proposal from the ferry lines to sell them to the state. This was after they decided that the state meant business in the plan of entering the ferry business. Their first offer was $6,800,000. Then they came back with the offer of $5,975,000. We hired a New york firm to make an appraisal.[5] I don't want this appraisal made public because the newspapers would plaster it all over their front pages with misconstruction of its meaning.

"The bankers offered to put up $5,500,000 if the company would take $3,000,000 payment in bonds. I didn't think we should quibble over $475,000 on such a deal, so we got a firm offer from the company to sell for $5,975,000.

"The rates worked out by Gilman & Company for operation of the ferries under state ownership were a disappointment to me. They are only 11 percent lower than what you are now paying. But I am confident that there will be more traffic under state operation than they have estimated and the rates can be lowered. There is a provision for a reduction in rates after the

[2]Ibid. Resolution No. 36.

[3]Ibid. Resolution No. 206.

[4]"Statement by Arthur B. Langlie on Puget Sound Ferry Situation" dated 8/18/1948. Wallgren Papers, Washington State Archives.

[5]W.C. Gilman & Co.

Agate Pass Bridge[6] is completed. I hope there will be more traffic after the state takes over the ferries. Don't you think so?"[7]

There were a number of misconceptions in Governor Wallgren's plans for the state ferry system. In his public address on September 7, he asked, "... Will the ferry purchase saddle a debt on the taxpayers—will it cost them anything?

"The answer is it will not cost the taxpayer or the state one cent. The Toll Bridge Authority's resolution to purchase, and the bond indenture covering the specifications of the issue, provide that the entire cost of the ferries, their rehabilitation, operation, operating expense, depreciation, upkeep, and that of the docks and wharves, as well as interest on bonds and all other costs, shall be paid for in revenues derived from fares, and from fares only."[8]

Before the end of the year the State Supreme Court ruled that the state of Washington did not have the legal right to purchase the ferry system from Puget Sound Navigation Company through the sale of bonds. Governor Wallgren's re-election went down in defeat, also, and Arthur B. Langlie was returned to the Governor's Mansion for a second, nonconsecutive term.

The ferry issue had been a central debate of the recent campaign and both incumbent and opposing candidate, representing the major political parties, advocated acquisition of the ferry system and the subsequent removal of it from private ownership. Wallgren was willing to accept the purchase price from Black Ball Line while Langlie argued that the system could be more readily and economically acquired by condemnation.[9]

Langlie and George H. Boldt, legal council, considered Peabody's proposed purchase price a "hypothetical value of physical assets"[1] of the stockholders. The state was now willing to pay the fair market value of $100 per share for Puget Sound Navigation Company interests. The CHINOOK, the British Columbia Terminal facilities, and the certificates for international operations of the company, noted as "historically profitable" would be excluded from the purchase offer. Additionally, several other company properties, such as Pier 53 in Seattle and the freight barges would also be excluded from state ownership.

Langlie wholeheartedly believed that the ferry system across Puget Sound would only be necessary for another "six or seven years. The probabilities are great that within that time Puget Sound will be successfully bridged ... the necessity for maintaining most existing ferry routes will be removed and the ultimate cost of Puget Sound crossings will become a mere fraction of today's level of rates."[2]

Many, many residents of the state of Washington believed that Puget Sound could be crossed with an elaborate network of bridges; Peabody, too, believed this theory to an extent. He felt that the less lucrative ferry runs would easily be spanned by bridge, while the longer hauls would be more profitable and functional if served by ferry.

The issue of *where* to place those bridges soon arose. Which communities would be favored with a bridge that would automatically bring more tourists and more traffic? Environmentalists and residents of Bainbridge Island hesitated on this thought, remembering that the Mercer Island bridge introduced a tide of expansion that did not ebb. Bainbridge Island and Vashon Island might soon become brimming suburbs of Seattle. Most islanders dreaded such a thought.

An underwater tube from Alki was proposed but discarded with the feeling that people would be too afraid to use it. Bond writers would not finance it, some said.

[6]The Agate Pass Bridge was another point of derision between the gubernatorial candidates. Captain Peabody purchased the Port Gamble-Shine crossing certificate and ferries from Bertie Olson and replaced it with the more direct Lofall-Southpoint crossing. He planned to build privately the Agate Pass Bridge to make connection from the Olympic Peninsula via Winslow, Bainbridge, a more direct route to Seattle. Langlie spoke adamantly against this private ownership and Wallgren was not in favor of the idea. Peabody would have been forced to build his own highway, as well, to connect peninsula traffic to the bridge. This convinced Wallgren that the state must take the bridge seriously and interject government participation and ownership.

[7]"Report of Talk by Governor Wallgren before Kitsap County Improvement Clubs," Port Orchard, 10/6/1948. Wallgren Papers, Washington State Archives.

[8]"Not one cent will come from the general tax fund nor from any other tax fund. The purchase money will be furnished by private investors. Repayment will be made through fares collected from users—thousands of whom will be out-of-state tourists. In the final analysis the ferry system will be virtually a gift to the state." *Governor Wallgren's Ferry Address*, delivered 9/7/1948. Wallgren Papers, Washington State Archives.

[9]Letter to Smith Troy, Attorney General, from Arthur B. Langlie, dated 12/14/1948. Wallgren Papers, Washington State Archives.

[1]Letter to Captain Alex M. Peabody, Puget Sound Navigation Company, from George H. Boldt, dated 9/13/1949. Wallgren Papers, Washington State Archives.

[2]"Address by the Honorable Arthur B. Langlie on Puget Sound Ferry Situation," Arthur B. Langlie Papers, Washington State Archives, 1950.

The ferry issue was in a preposterous state of mass confusion. Langlie accused Peabody of trying to force the state to purchase all the company's property, regardless of its usefulness. The fact was that Peabody simply and unequivocably did not wish to sell his company to anyone or any entity. The captain argued that the ferry operations did not belong under government ownership because taxpayers would be forced to subsidize the operations. He doubted that bureaucrats would know how to run a fleet of ferries. Many years later Captain Peabody was still bitter that the ferry system had been forced out of private control.

It was a matter of philosophy with Captain Peabody. He felt that experienced maritime and business people knew a good deal more about ferry operations than government agencies and citizens' committees. But Peabody would never be a politician and at the time, he was even less a diplomat. He soon found that he was under fire from all directions. Republicans and Democrats, Baptists and Presbyterians, commuters balking at high fares and decrepit boats; and, most discreetly, the bankers who had financed his ventures in the past and now feared that his company was facing financial disaster—all were against Peabody's position. It was the lenders who finally knocked Peabody over and pressured him to sell to the state, pay off the bank loans and retire from business on Puget Sound.[3] And shortly, he did.

Arthur B. Langlie introduced legislation which would allow the state of Washington to purchase the Puget Sound Navigation Company and operate the inland ferry routes. The newly-elected governor's argument was:

"Wherever population has increased substantially in areas supported by waterborne traffic, a time has always come when more efficient substitutes for water traffic have been mandatory and the water ferries have disappeared. The water ferry era in transportation came to its close in New York many years ago. More recently we have all witnessed the same development in California when the San Francisco Bay and Golden Gate Bridges were completed . . ."[4]

And in a letter to Ernest Gribble, general manager of the Port of Olympia, the governor wrote,

". . . We feel that Kitsap County and all the territory west to the ocean cannot develop beyond its present stage so long as ferries con-

tinue to be the only method of transportation. Furthermore, we believe the elimination of ferries, if possible, is very necessary to the development of Seattle and the State as a whole.

"We fully realize the importance of navigation to all parts of Puget Sound and can assure you that any bridge or tube design will provide unrestricted passage for the largest ocean going ships to points south of Seattle. Before any structures can be constructed, permission to do so must be obtained from the U.S. Engineer after public hearings are held, thus giving further assurance against any undue hindrance to navigation."[5]

The governor felt that he was removing "the greatest obstacle to free enterprise development of the Olympic and Kitsap Peninsulas" by reaching a speedy and reasonable settlement of Puget Sound's "troublesome transportation problem."[6] There were to be no more arguments over fares, complaints about old vessels and poor service. There would be freedom from labor disputes and annoying strikes. The state residents would appreciate increased ferry traffic, tourism, introduction of modern ferries on selected routes and a comprehensive plan that would provide beautiful new bridges and tubes which would eliminate most ferry routes.

IT WAS OVER

Progress was imminent and with it would come the repeal of ferry traffic on the Sound, so said the governor and his many officials. Their constituency had another idea.

The State of Washington completed the purchase of the Black Ball fleet June 1, 1951. The state's motto was to become: "frequency of service, shortness of routes and smaller boats at lower fares." They would

[3]This statement was made by Ross Cunningham, former editorial director of *The Seattle Times,* and close associate of Wallgren and Peabody at the time of their dispute. Further evidence also exists within the papers of Langlie, particularly in a letter to Langlie dated May 29, 1950 from George H. Boldt, in which he reports his private conversation with one of P.S.N.'s bank leaders.
[4]"Address by the Honorable Arthur B. Langlie on Puget Sound Ferry Situation," Langlie Papers, Washington State Archives, 1950. [There are still ferries operating in New York Harbor in 1983.]
[5]Letter to Ernest Gribble, General Manager, Port of Olympia, from Governor Langlie, dated 4/14/1950. Langlie Papers, Washington State Archives.
[6]"Address of the Honorable Arthur B. Langlie on Puget Sound Ferry Situation," Langlie Papers, Washington State Archives.

complete the construction of the Agate Pass Bridge and consolidate ferry service. The best and most practical bridge crossing of the Sound was to be at West Point (Magnolia Bluff) to Murden Cove, Bainbridge Island (a distance of 3 miles), as compared to the ferry runs between Colman Dock and Winslow (8.5 miles) and Colman Dock and Bremerton (15.5 miles).

The state chose to pay the Puget Sound Navigation Company stockholders $100 per share, totaling $4,944,499. The sale price was approved by the majority of the stockholders at a meeting held December 30, 1950. Captain Alex Peabody, the major stockholder, abstained from casting a vote because he did not wish to persuade or override the other stockholders. Most of them were aware of his strong opposition to the sale but Peabody considered his decision a personal one; the desires and direction of the business proposition were not to be directly influenced by him.

Peabody never relinquished his opinion that ferry operation belonged in the hands of private enterprise and he felt this was in the best interests of the clientele, as well. But the stockholders saw no guarantee of success or even survival in the face of politics and bankers armed with liens; there was no hope that profits would ever be restored. Furthermore, the stockholders' involvement was not as deeply tied to a legacy of a New England seafaring family when the Black Ball flag proudly symbolized efficient, on-time passenger and freight service. They were not caught in the grasp of traditions and ties that had suffered the sinking of the CLALLAM. They had not shared in the profits and challenges during periods of economic growth for the company. Peabody held no grudges against his compatriots of the company who voted to sell, nor did he resent the financiers. The captain was primarily bitter with the State, the political maneuvers and an uncontrollable series of events that united to whisk from his control his lifeblood. The pleasures of his imagination, intelligence and business acumen, once challenged by adversity and subsequently rewarded with profits, had been thwarted. The Black Ball Line ceased to be a part of business on Puget Sound or American enterprise. Captain Alexander Marshall Peabody was no longer the same man in his own regard.

On May 31, 1951 all vessels of the Puget Sound Navigation Company fleet underway at sundown, halted for one minute in mid-course. The Black Ball flags were lowered for the last time on ships under American registry.

(l to r) H.C. STRASSBURGER, P.S.N. COMPTROLLER; JOSEPH C. MUCKLEY, SEA FIRST BANK; CAPT. ALEX PEABODY.

THE LEGACY: WASHINGTON STATE FERRIES

So it was that on June 1, 1951, the Puget Sound ferry fleet passed into ownership of the State of Washington. The fleet of vessels and their routes had become a recognizable part of the state transportation and highway system. Here were the boats and their runs that had sprung from family enterprises fifty years earlier when water was the only connecting highway link on Puget Sound. Some early day steamers had borne the names of those fathers, brothers, sisters, children and entrepreneurs who had developed transportation routes individually and collectively between the mainland, the islands and the peninsula.

The ferryboats that followed the Mosquito Fleet often carried the names of the Native Americans who first settled this land and utilized the waterways. Those early Americans demonstrated to the newcomers the reliability and freedom of water transportation on Puget Sound. Now the fleet of active boats had passed to the state government where it was to be controlled by the people who most frequently took advantage of this highway system.

Following the great hullabaloo and ruckus raised when state proceedings were underway to acquire the fleet from private hands, the act of transfer was peaceful and uneventful. There were gubernatorial reassurances to the citizenry that high fares would be reduced or eliminated once tourism had escalated to the point that operational costs could be lowered. For the moment, fares would remain at the Black Ball level.

The vessels were scheduled for upgrading and improved maintenance but ultimately they would be replaced with "modern ferries" that were fuel efficient. The governor admired Eastern-designed ferries that had meager passenger cabin facilities and on which automobiles were left on an open deck exposed to the weather. He proposed designs similar to the MV KULSHAN, which did not appear on Puget Sound until 1969. This type of ferry was to suffice for the runs that would not be replaced with magnificent bridges or underwater tubes. Governor Langlie predicted that the familiar large autocarrier would soon disappear from the Sound.

The ferry workers retained their right to belong to the maritime unions and they did not become typical state employees. Their pension programs, wages, holiday and vacation pay, as well as seniority, already surpassed the average state employee and their agent, Captain John Fox, was not about to relinquish these benefits.

The majority of the officers and crew from the Black Ball Line joined the Washington State Ferries, bringing experience and expertise to an otherwise uninformed state agency. Here were the men and women who knew ferries and routes, how to run them and where and when to use them. Many of the captains and engineers had followed their fathers or brothers into the trade and had known no other business in their lifetimes. Most had no desire to find another occupation. Like the sailor who is beckoned by the sea, the crew members of this inland fleet rarely looked elsewhere for jobs.

KULSHAN

The first year of state operation showed a balance sheet in the black.[1] Everyone was pulling together in this new venture of state management, and the attitude of "let's make it work" became an unspoken motto. The new general manager, Floyd J. McDowell, former vice president and general manager for James Griffiths & Sons, stepped into the formidable job of running an operation for the state with employees who had formerly worked for private enterprise. The majority of executive staff including C.R. Lonergan, traffic manager; Walter Green, assistant traffic manager; Jack

[1] "Annual Report, Washington State Ferries, 1951-1952," Governor Arthur B. Langlie's Papers, Washington State Archives.

*(l to r) CAPTAIN LYLE FOWLER, CAPTAIN "SPIKE"
EIKUM, CAPTAIN LYLE PETERSON, CAPTAIN HENRY
GRANDE*

CAPTAIN NICK TRACY AND FLOYD MCDOWELL

341 FOOT FERRY & TRAILER SHIP
FOR
BLACK BALL TRANSPORT, INC.
BUILT BY
PUGET SOUND BRIDGE & DREDGING Co.
HULL № 105
KEEL LAID JAN·12·1959

Embree, Peabody's secretary; Captain Harry Anderson, operating manager; M.O. Martin, assistant auditor; Captain Arnold F. "Spike" Eikum, port captain; John E. Sullivan, port engineer; and William B. Morrice, traffic manager, joined the Washington State Ferry management offices but not all of these men who had been close to Captain Peabody could adjust to state procedures. A few like Walter Green stayed just long enough to train replacements and went on to other ventures. The training was not easy for the newcomers when their predecessors had been reared with experience in the school of hard knocks, but bureaucracy would prove to be a new trade. Some ferry experiences and education simply had no application to this state-operated ferry industry.

R.J. and Lois Acheson organized a new subsidiary of Black Ball Freight Service, known as Black Ball Transport, Inc. Black Ball Freight had functioned as a coordinated service to the Puget Sound Navigation Company but it was not a subsidiary of the company nor was freight service included in the sale of certificates to the state.[2] The state courts had been emphatic in the ruling that the state was not to compete with commercial freight transport services nor were they

[2] R.J. Acheson began a career in transportation at Medicine Hat, Alberta with the Canadian Pacific Railway. He was 11 years old and served as a call boy. He became dispatcher in that district and moved to Seattle in 1924. On the Seattle waterfront he worked first as a freight checker for the Nelson Steamship Co., becoming general manager of that firm at Seattle. In 1932 he became traffic manager for the Puget Sound Navigation Company and four years later, purchased the Black Ball Freight Service. By 1951, the Acheson operation included 200 trucks and trailers employing 125 persons.

Lois Acheson assumed presidency and control of Black Ball Transport, Inc. upon the death of her husband in 1963. She holds that position in 1983 and has been a contributor to the research for this manuscript.

'BLACK BALL TRANSPORT'S SLEEK COHO FERRY OPER-
ATES ON THE PORT ANGELES-VICTORIA RUN

BOB AND LOIS ACHESON AT THE TIME OF THE COHO'S
LAUNCHING IN 1959

willing to operate the international ferry runs. Such service would be too complicated for the state officials to legally challenge it at the outset of their operation.

Black Ball Transport purchased the steamship IROQUOIS from Puget Sound Navigation Company in 1952 for conversion to a motor freighter. They also acquired the car barge service from the ferry company running between Seattle and Bremerton, Puget Sound Naval Shipyard and Ostrich Bay and Keyport, together with terminal facilities at Seattle, Port Townsend and Port Angeles.

The IROQUOIS underwent conversion from steam ferry to motor freighter and entered the overnight freight run between Seattle, Port Angeles and Port Townsend. Bob Acheson sought Captain Peabody's permission to incorporate a version of the famous Black Ball flag for their new company and a new but similar pennant appeared at the flag mast of the IROQUOIS.

In 1959 Black Ball Transport built the autoferry COHO at Puget Sound Bridge & Drydock Co., Seattle, for $3,000,000. She was designed by Philip F. Spaulding & Associates for the Port Angeles-Victoria ferry service, and operates on that run today. Black Ball Transport acquired shoreside and terminal properties from Puget Sound Navigation Company in 1951.

EVERYTHING HAD TO CHANGE

Several days after the official transfer of the ferry fleet to Washington State, a new houseflag consisting of an evergreen tree and a superimposed "W" was unfurled on the KALAKALA with wide press acclaim. Later the houseflag was replaced with the Washington State flag.

On the first day of state operation the new management circulated a memo stating that the docking signal would change immediately from the Black Ball "one long and two short" blasts, or, a warp and two woofs. The state changed it to one long and one short, and the experienced ferry workers were disgruntled by the order. Ferry skippers had built a tradition of distinction in the ways they sounded their ferry whistles. Most workers familiar with the vessels and the masters could identify the skipper by the characteristic manner in which he gave the signal for a landing. In the smaller communities like Clinton, Mukilteo, Edmonds and Kingston, most of the residents, too, were experts at identifying the ferries on the run by their frequent blasts.

The state's landing signal was said to have no color to it. It was grudgingly referred to as a "groan and a grunt." The Puget Sound Maritime Historical Society took matters into their own hands in 1958 and urged the state of Washington to return to the old signals. William O. Thorniley, a member of the Society, was quoted at length in the *Seattle Sunday Times,* March 9, 1958[5] on the history of ferry skippers and their whistles:

"One of the specialists on the whistle was Captain Harry Anderson,[4] now operating manager of the Washington State Ferries.

"Anderson skippered the famous sternwheeler BAILEY GATZERT between Seattle and Bremerton in the 1920s. The GATZERT had a particularly melodious 'five-chime' whistle that sounded five notes at once, and Anderson used to get as much music out of his whistle as did anyone on the Sound.

"Anderson blew a normal-length long, but the second short blast had a flutter to it. This was accomplished by skillfully manipulating the whistle cord up and down on the last short. That was sweet music.

"Captain Howard Penfield was master of the INDIANAPOLIS on the Seattle-Tacoma run. He had an opposite system of whistling. Penfield would wait until he got right up close to the dock and then blow a very short long, followed in quick succession by two very short shorts.

"The whistle on the INDIANAPOLIS was a deep bass that hit you in the pit of the stomach and rattled waiting room windows.

"Captain Wallace Mangan was the first master of the ferry KALAKALA. He blew the normal long and, then after a decided pause, he'd follow it with two shorts in sharp staccato.

"(Captain Louis) Van Bogaert, former commodore of the Black Ball Line, followed the Penfield system except that the first long was more nearly a normal-length long, and the shorts were more uniformly set apart. This kind of whistle required a taut whistle cord.

"Van Bogaert blew his last 'one long and two shorts' last September 19 [1957], despite

[5] Harvey, "Ferry Skippers were Artists at Warp, 2 Woofs," *The Seattle Sunday Times.*

[4] Captain Harry Anderson, a former Black Ball skipper, was operating manager of the Washington State Ferries from 1951 to 1960.

the fact that it had been 'outlawed' for six years. That was on the ferry CHIPPEWA coming into Seattle. That was his last trip before retirement, and other ferrymen dared him to blow the old signal.

"Captain Carl Stevens, now a Puget Sound pilot, was famous for his short whistles, which were well-spaced from the long.

"Another artist on the landing whistle in the days of the steamers was Captain T.E. Sumner, known as 'Big Ed.' He's now on the Seattle-Bremerton route.

"Sumner would start with just a little steam, let the whistle build up to full blast, then fade down again and follow it with two snappy blasts.

"I think one of the most colorful skippers on Puget Sound was Captain Samuel Barlow. Barlow's father was a British sailor who settled in the San Juan Islands in pioneer days and married a Lummi Indian princess.

"For well over 50 years Sam Barlow was the master of vessels which ran the dangerous waters of the San Juans. He never had a single mishap in all those years. Barlow was very deliberate and no one ever saw him excited.

"I think Barlow's landing whistle kind of reflected his character. The blasts were not only unusually long, but were set apart by lengthy pauses. Long before the last blast had left the whistle at some island landing, the first blast was echoing and re-echoing from the nearby shores."

In celebration of Maritime Day, May 24, 1958, I.D. "Bud" Birse, manager of Washington State Ferries, announced that TOOOOOOOOOOOOOT! TOOT! TOOT! would be reinstated as the official landing signal for the Washington State Ferries.

BLACK BALL LINES—CANADA, LTD.

Officers of the reorganized Puget Sound Navigation Company were Captain Alexander M. Peabody, president; H.C. Strassburger, vice president and secretary; E.A. Osborn, assistant secretary; I.D. Birse, traffic manager; Allen Bills, Seattle freight agent; and A.S. Bergeon, freight and passenger representative. R.R. U'Ren continued as Port Townsend manager, George Mock at Port Angeles, and Col. George Paulin as managing director

for Canada, with headquarters in Victoria.

Shortly before the transfer of ownership of the Puget Sound Navigation fleet to Washington State, Captain Peabody announced the formation of a Puget Sound Navigation Company Canadian subsidiary. Their plans included a new automobile ferry service between Horseshoe Bay (West Vancouver) and Gibson's Landing, B.C.

The sale to the state did not include all of the vessels of the Puget Sound Navigation fleet. The motor ferries BAINBRIDGE and QUILLAYUTE were transferred to Canadian registry and the BAINBRIDGE started on the Horseshoe Bay-Gibson run in August 1951. Later, in 1954, the QUILLAYUTE was placed in service across Jarvis Inlet from Earl's Cove, making five daily crossings. This was after completion of an additional highway built with funds advanced by Captain Peabody to the Provincial highway department.

Steam ferry CITY OF SACRAMENTO[5] was transferred to Canadian company ownership and the CHINOOK continued to serve on the Seattle-Port Townsend-Port Angeles-Victoria passenger run. The ferry VASHONIA was dismantled at Seattle before the sale to the state. Puget Sound Navigation Company had also retained one destroyer escort and its diesel electric power plant. It would later serve as machinery for the KAHLOKE.

The state sale contract with the Puget Sound Navigation Company included 20 terminals, 16 ferries, 1 destroyer escort, access roads built on Hood Canal, equipment and supplies. The state paid nearly an additional one-half million dollars for the Colman Ferry Terminal in Seattle. But with only three sound ferryboats and the Seattle-Port Townsend-Victoria route, Peabody carried his business and dreams to the north.

An article written by Fergus Hoffman for the business section of *The Seattle Post-Intelligencer,* August 26, 1959, sums up the Canadian operation:

"Some eight years ago [1951] the cruiser BLITHE SPIRIT was poking into some unlikely and remote recesses of the lower British Columbia coast. For days the skipper put her almost onto the beach as eager eyes measured unknown potentials.

"'For heaven's sake, Peabody,' the skipper finally asked, 'what are we doing this

---

[5] The MALAHAT was not placed in Canadian service but sold for scrap instead. The CITY OF SACRAMENTO was converted to diesel electric and renamed KAHLOKE under B.C. registry.

for—you can't see anything but trees.'

"But Captain Alex M. Peabody could see the forest for the trees. He could see ferry terminals, water routes, new highways, a growing population moving into the opening wilderness.

"And he could see the people using Captain Peabody's ferries.

"Peabody had a choice at the time. Washington State had taken over his Puget Sound Navigation Company's intra-state ferry routes. After half-a-century, the Black Ball flag was switched for the Evergreen State banner. But Peabody retained some ferries. His choice was to sell to the junkman or find new routes.

"That was when Black Ball Ferries, Ltd. was established as a wholly owned subsidiary of Puget Sound Navigation. A survey showed a reasonable return could be expected by serving B.C. points.

"So Peabody went to a Canadian bus company to sell it the idea—and his ferries. It could be a nice package, he pointed out.

"So Peabody wound up buying the bus company.

"He went to the province to sell British Columbia the idea of constructing highways to match ferry terminals.

"He wound up lending the province a million dollars to build the roads. Later, wanting paving, another half million was loaned.

"In eight years the changes have been enormous. Land values have increased, new people are flooding the land. Traveling with Black Ball, thousands of tourists see some of the Northwest Coast's best scenery.

"Work, imagination and investment:

"Yesterday, meeting in Seattle, the stockholders of the Puget Sound Navigation Company approved a 5 to 1 division of their common stock. Shares outstanding were increased from 38,458 to 192,290; par value was reduced from $100 to $20. Directors have indicated their intention to declare a dividend of 25 cents a quarter or $1 a year on the larger number of shares, an increase of 25 percent in the annual rate.

"Mentioning the increased asset value and earnings of the company, Peabody summed up the latest action:

" 'It is recognition of the patience and confidence of our stockholders during what has been, in effect, a pioneering venture since 1951.' "

The CHINOOK left the Port Angeles-Victoria run in 1955 and joined the KAHLOKE on the Horseshoe Bay-Nanaimo run that summer. Under the changed name of CHINOOK II, she served the Canadians.

Peabody started ferries on Horseshoe Bay-Bowen Island run for passengers only in December 1956. The boats began to carry cars after May 1958.

The ferries and passenger carriers of Black Ball, Ltd. and Canadian Pacific Railway were plagued with labor unrest in British Columbia throughout the 1950s. As in the United States, Canadians became dissatisfied with interrupted service and the annoyance to their lifestyles. The Provincial Government moved quickly to make amends, and following the practice of their neighbor to the south, moved to consolidate all ferries of the province into a publicly-owned system.

This time, Captain Peabody was amicable to a sale. The B.C. government paid Puget Sound Navigation Company $6,795,467 for five vessels[6] and all terminals in December 1961. The Captain was pleased with the deal and retired from the sea.

[6] Four of these were formerly under American registry: CHINOOK, BAINBRIDGE, QUILLAYUTE and KAHLOKE (Ex-CITY OF SACRAMENTO). The company acquired the Canadian-built steam ferry SMOKWA (built 1946) for additional Langdale service.

(following photos) BLACK BALL LINES, LTD. CANADA CAPTAIN PEABODY TAKES HIS FLEET NORTH

KAHLOKE

QUILLAYUTE RAN ON THE POWELL RIVER

THE BAINBRIDGE WAS REBUILT FOR CANADIAN
OPERATION

INTERIOR REMODELED ON THE BAINBRIDGE

MEANWHILE, THE STATE . . .

The State of Washington began to unearth and closely understand some of Captain Peabody's former problems in his attempt to operate an efficient and economical ferry system. Coordinating the structure of that system became a challenge to state officials.

The State of Washington has had seven general managers since the inception of Washington State Ferries in 1951. The general managers were originally hired by the Washington Toll Bridge Authority and with the dissolution of that department, by the Washington State Department of Transportation.[7] These general managers include, in respective order, Floyd J. McDowell, I.E. "Bud" Birse, Charles Prahl, J.P. Hogan, A.F. "Spike" Eikum, Richard A. Berg, and Nicholas H. Tracy.

Washington State Archives revealed an annual progress report for the Washington State Ferries covering the period June 1, 1951 to May 31, 1952.[8] Excerpts follow that demonstrate the state's attitudes and progress within the first year of operation.

"As of June 1, 1952, the Washington State Ferries have completed twelve months of operations and the following is submitted as a general summary of accomplishments during the past year.

"We assumed operation of the Puget Sound Intra-State ferry system as of June 1, 1951, at 2:00 A.M., following purchase from the Puget Sound Navigation Company of 16 ferries as follows: CHETZEMOKA, CHIPPEWA, ENETAI, ILLAHEE, KALAKALA, KEHLOKEN, KITSAP, KLAHANIE, KLICKITAT, NISQUALLY, QUINAULT, ROSARIO, SAN MATEO, SHASTA, VASHON, WILLAPA.

"We also secured, through a joint purchase agreement, from the King County Ferry District No. 1 and King County, the ferries LESCHI and LINCOLN. The LESCHI has been operated during a large portion of the last year. It was necessary, under this overall purchase agreement that we take over the ferry LINCOLN. However, it was not contemplated that the vessel would be operated and she was considered, from the standpoint of scrap value, as worth $5,000. However, the vessel was disposed of for the sum of $10,000.

"A somewhat similar situation prevailed in regard to the ROSARIO—taken over from the Puget Sound Navigation Company—as it was considered that the purchase price would be the same with or without the vessel. Due to her size and condition it was not planned that she be, nor was she, operated, except for a short intervening time during the summer of 1951 on the Seattle/Suquamish/Indianola route. There were extensive repairs required on this ferry, consequently she has not been, and will not be operated, but will eventually be stripped to provide valuable machinery and other parts for the ferries LESCHI and KITSAP, both of which have similar engines. The ROSARIO will eventually be disposed of at scrap value.

"The ferries CROSLINE and SKANSONIA were taken over from the Washington State Highway Department under Bareboat Charter as of June 1, 1951.

"Terminals

"The following terminals were purchased from the Puget Sound Navigation Company: Seattle (Fauntleroy), Winslow, Anacortes, Lofall, South Point, Orcas, Harper, Columbia Beach, Edmonds, Shaw, Lopez;

and the following leased from the owners indicated: Seattle (Colman Ferry Terminal) Puget Sound Ferry Terminals, Inc.; Bremerton, Bremerton Terminal Company; Friday Harbor, San Juan Agricultural Company; Kingston, The Port of Kingston; Mukilteo, The Port of Everett; Point Defiance, The Port of Tacoma

and the terminals at Vashon Heights and Tahlequah were purchased from King County.

"In addition temporary use was made of the terminals at Indianola and Suquamish—which route was abandoned September 28, 1951.

"Routes

"Under the terms of the bond financing, we are now operating the following routes:

---

[7] Under the original structure the Washington Toll Bridge Authority consisted of four members of the Highway Commission and the governor who chaired the committee. The TBA was dissolved and the Washington State Ferry System was placed under the state Transportation Commission, a seven member panel, governor appointed. The D.O.T.'s marine division is headed by an assistant secretary who is not politically appointed.

[8] Langlie Papers, Washington State Archives.

WINSLOW YARD: ENETAI, WILLAPA, SKANSONIA AND LESCHI

RALPH WHITE

Point Defiance/Tahlequah; Fauntleroy/Vashon/Harper; Seattle/Bremerton; Seattle/Winslow; Edmonds/Kingston; Lofall/South Point;[9] Mukilteo/Columbia Beach; Anacortes/Shaw/Lopez/Orcas/Friday Harbor

and in addition during the summer months, the Anacortes/Sidney, B.C. route; the latter necessary to provide better service to the San Juan Islands. These cover a combined total of 110.61 statute miles.

"In order to accomplish the financing for the purchase of the system it was necessary to comply with the recommendations and requirements of the consulting engineers that the Point White/Bremerton and the Seattle/Suquamish/Indianola routes—previously operated by Puget Sound Navigation Company at a substantial loss—be discontinued. The Point White/Bremerton route was aban-

doned as of May 31, 1951, and taken over by the Horluck Transportation Company with a small passenger service. The Suquamish/Indianola/Seattle route was temporarily operated during the summer of 1951 pending the elimination of the tolls on the Agate Pass Bridge and the route abandoned September 28, 1951, with the majority of the traffic moving over the Winslow/Seattle route.

"Traffic

"In order to accomplish maximum increases in traffic and eventual reductions in ferry rates, a substantial advertising-traffic sales program has been carried on and every effort has been made to make the vessels and

[9] Construction of the Hood Canal Floating Bridge to replace this ferry crossing was completed August 1, 1961. On February 13, 1979, a gale destroyed the bridge. The ferry crossing was reinstated until October 23, 1982 when a newer Hood Canal Bridge reopened to auto traffic.

terminals safe, clean, comfortable and efficient. As an indication of partial success in increasing traffic, a comparative summary of the twelve months one-way travel over the routes which we are operating is attached hereto.

"It will be noted from the above that there was an increase over the equivalent previous twelve months period of: 304,374 passengers; 173,325 automobiles; 21,346 trucks and other vehicles.

"It is our view that this traffic increase will be continued by providing proper ferry service and giving the ferry patrons the best possible and lowest-priced cross-Sound transportation we can furnish—consistent with our equipment and finances.

"Objectives

"Our operations are conducted with a policy of serving the greatest number of people and areas to the best interests of all concerned. Every effort is being made to operate the system in a businesslike manner, to provide ferry patrons with the lowest possible cost cross-Sound transportation and to give them safe, comfortable and efficient service with proper equipment and courteous and efficient personnel. It is our opinion that our general public relations are very greatly improved over those of the previous operation. A sincere effort is being made by all personnel to accomplish our objectives and it might be pointed out that our accomplishments to date have been made utilizing almost entirely the same personnel that the previous owners employed, but with an entirely different viewpoint toward maintenance, public relations, ferry rates and the interests of the traveling public.

"It is contemplated that the balance of the extensive rehabilitation and maintenance of our vessels and terminals, unless something unforeseen develops, will be absorbed out of our operation from our present—or possibly lower—rates. In the opinion of the operating personnel of the ferry system, a large amount of the rehabilitation work could not have been delayed much longer, and if the policy of the previous operators had been carried out, it is our feeling that all expenses of such rehabilita-

tion would have been passed on to the ferry riders thru increased rates—this having been the general practice in the past.

"We feel that our ferries with their white and green color scheme and greatly improved condition are an indication of our endeavors to provide comfortable, clean and safe equipment for the ferry traveling public.

"Labor Relations

"Our labor relations with the various Unions involved have been carried on during the past year in a harmonious manner and with the objective of sound operation, both from the standpoint of the ferry operation and the ferry personnel. On December 10, 1950, shortly before we purchased the system, wages were increased 10 percent by the Puget Sound Navigation Company. In accordance with the wage review clause of our vessel personnel Union Agreements, wages of such personnel were, after negotiations with the Unions involved, increased as of March 1, 1952 by 7½ percent. Both of these increases, together with the general increase in other operating costs due to higher prices of supplies, etc., etc., have been absorbed out of our operations. Current Labor Agreements expire December 31, 1952.

"Rates

"In view of our short term debt payment it is our opinion that lower rates will primarily result thru increases in traffic rather than further reductions in operating costs, in view of the fact that such costs generally in all types of business operations have been on a general increase and our intention to properly maintain vessels and terminals. However, our activities will continue with a view of operating at the minimum cost consistent with safety, proper maintenance of equipment and service to the ferry patrons.

"Conclusion

"If increases in traffic are continued as anticipated, there must necessarily be provided additions of modern vessels of sufficient size and capacity for proper handling of the traffic. Therefore, it would be advisable that immediate consideration be given to the construction of a standard ferry, or ferries, of the proper size and capacity to handle such traffic increases. Accordingly, a Marine Architect should be promptly employed to draw up plans for such standard type ferry to be used on the majority of the ferry routes. In view of the probable vessel costs under current conditions, it is recommended that new vessels be secured thru additional financing paid for over a 15 year period, as to endeavor to secure new vessels entirely out of current revenue would place an unfair burden on present ferry users.

"Full credit and sincere appreciation is given for the support and cooperation of the ferry personnel and the various departments and officials of the State of Washington in assisting us in our endeavors on behalf of the interests of all individuals and areas served by Washington State Ferries."

After the first year of successful operation by the state, the balance sheet began to appear in red ink. All of the letters once directed to the public relations staff of Puget Sound Navigation Company began to appear in the governor's office. This time, it was taxpayers' money that was being lost. If the system was to be subsidized by tax funds, should residents of Eastern Washington (not directly served by Puget Sound ferries) be forced to assist in that subsidy?

The discussion of building bridges continued to surface but the realities of such major construction all over the Sound grew dim. Talk of returning the system to private enterprise circulated, as witnessed by this contrite letter to the editor of the *Bremerton Sun:*

"I have just read in the Bremerton Sun that the answer to our cross-Sound transportation problem is to have regional transportation authority. I would like to say with the mess the state has made of the operation of the ferry system, they should give it back to private enterprise.

"Let us look at the record. The state bought the ferry system for $6,800,000. Now we are 38 million in the red, plus the fact we have paid $12½ million in subsidies. When the state was in the process of going into the red, they tried to sell the bonds on the open market. They couldn't sell them so they bought them themselves.

"Also they paid a commission to buy their own bonds. Peabody would not have done this, you can be sure. We have had subsidy studies, surveys, governor's committees and the worst service the state has ever known.

"If surveys would build bridges we would have bridges to Tokyo. I wonder if the state runs all their business like this.

"Please don't do anything for the ferry system until you check with Peabody. We just can't afford it and we will never have the needed bridges. What a boondoggle!"[1]

The Washington State Ferry fleet then began to grow. They have retained only four of the Puget Sound Navigation Company ferries over the years. These ferries are the ILLAHEE, NISQUALLY, KLICKITAT, and QUINAULT. They were widened eight feet and re-engined in 1957-59. The KLICKITAT had a second re-engine job in 1981 and wooden upperworks were all replaced with steel at Tacoma Boatbuilding Co., Inc.

"OLYMPIC-RHODODENDRON"

The State of Washington turned to Baltimore, Maryland for the purchase of two ferries that had been replaced by a bridge across Chesapeake Bay. The vessels were direct-drive diesels, named the GOVERNOR HARRY W. NICE and the GOVERNOR HERBERT R. O'CONOR. The NICE was renamed the OLYMPIC and the O'CONOR became the RHODODENDRON, named for the state flower. Both of these vessels remain under Washington Ferries' ownership in 1983.

"KULSHAN"

Built in 1954 at Moore Drydock Company at Oakland, California, the CROWN CITY first operated between San Diego and Coronado for the San Diego & Coronado Ferry Co. Replaced by a bridge, this ferry was sold to the state of Washington and towed north in August 1969. The vessel was a diesel-electric, double-ender, of all steel construction and was the only open-decked ferry in the Washington fleet. This design was the one most acceptable to Governor Langlie in 1951 but never proved to be popular with ferry riders on Puget Sound. It was sold for use in New York Harbor in 1982.

[1] Clipping from *The Bremerton Sun,* "Give the Ferries Back to Peabody." Letter submitted to the editor by Robert B. Stewart, Bremerton.

"THE EVERGREEN STATE CLASS"

The Evergreen State Class was the first commissioned, new ferries built for Washington State Ferries. Several of the war surplused diesel-electric engines of the destroyer escorts purchased by Captain Peabody were installed in these three new ferries.

The class was designed by W.C. Nickum & Sons and built in 1954, 1958 and 1959 at Puget Sound Bridge & Dry Dock Co., Seattle. The EVERGREEN STATE was launched first, with an auto capacity of 100 but her overhead clearance was insufficient to accommodate high trucks. This complication evolved when the state suddenly raised the height limit for trucks while the ferry was under construction. The low clearance problem was remedied with the second vessel, the KLAHOWYA. The TILLICUM used the KLAHOWYA's car deck design and a Navy war surplus engine, along with a rebuilt engine from a stationary power plant.

All three of these vessels remain in operation on the Sound in 1983.

"HIYU"

The HIYU, built at Gunderson Brothers Engineering Corp., Portland, Oregon, was built for Washington State in 1967. She was expressly designed to replace the old SKANSONIA on the Point Defiance-Tahlequah run. The HIYU, double-ended and equipped with pilot house controls, has two Caterpillar diesel engines—one pushes the ship and the other one pulls.

"SUPERFERRIES"

The Super Class, consisting of the ferries HYAK, KALEETAN, YAKIMA, and ELWHA, were all built for the Bremerton and Bainbridge Island routes. Constructed in 1967 by the National Steel & Shipbuilding Co. of San Diego, and designed by W.C. Nickum & Sons, Seattle, they are of all steel construction, double-ended, and equipped with four General Motors diesel engines, four electric generators and two drive motors. Each vessel is 382 feet in length and carries 2,600 passengers and 160 vehicles on the main car deck and two side decks referred to as the " 'tween" decks. These are located on each side of the main car deck and below the passenger cabin.

Superferries were the largest ferryboats yet built to operate on Puget Sound. They were followed by an even more stupendous class.

"JUMBO FERRIES"

At one time these were the biggest ferryboats in the world. The SPOKANE and the WALLA WALLA were built at Todd Shipyard in Seattle in 1972 for the busy Seattle to Winslow run. One was used in the San Juan Islands, but removed to the Seattle-Bainbridge run when Islanders complained of the strong bow waves and extreme numbers of people coming into these isolated island communities that had only spartan public accommodations.

Naval architects, Philip Spaulding & Associates, were responsible for these gargantuan carriers, 440 feet in length, 87 feet in breadth, and an 18 foot draft. Propelled at a speed of 18 knots by four main diesel electric engines, these vessels carry 2,000 passengers and 206 automobiles. Bearing Eastern Washington Indian names, these two ferries appear in photographs around the world.

"THE ISSAQUAH CLASS"

This latest class of ferry built on Puget Sound is the most controversial. Designed and built by Marine Power & Equipment, Seattle, the vessels are equipped with computer controls. This smaller ferry class, only 328 feet in length, carrying 1,200 passengers and 100 automobiles, was built for the shorter, inter-island runs and routes such as Edmonds-Kingston and Mukilteo-Columbia Beach. The Thorniley tradition of Indian names continues through to the present day. These vessels are named ISSAQUAH, KITTITAS, KITSAP, CATHLAMET, CHELAN and SEALTH. All of the vessels except the SEALTH were built between 1979 and 1982 and placed in commission on their respective runs. The SEALTH is predicted to remain in lay-up until early 1985, unacceptable to the state requirements due to legal controversy.

OLYMPIC

RHODODENDRON

THE EVERGREEN STATE

KULSHAN HAD AN OPEN CAR DECK

(opposite page, top) SEATTLE TERMINAL

FERRY KLAHOWYA

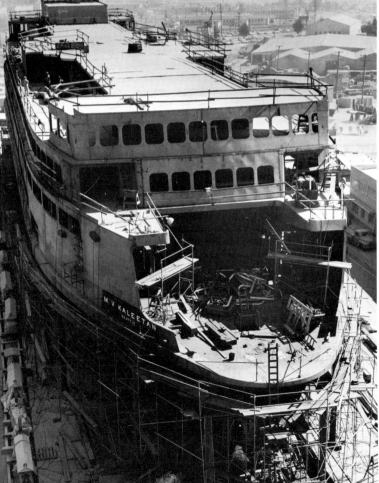

SUPERFERRY YAKIMA

KALEETAN UNDER CONSTRUCTION

YAKIMA

HYAK SUPERFERRY

HYAK IS EQUIPPED WITH FOUR GENERAL MOTORS DIESEL ENGINES

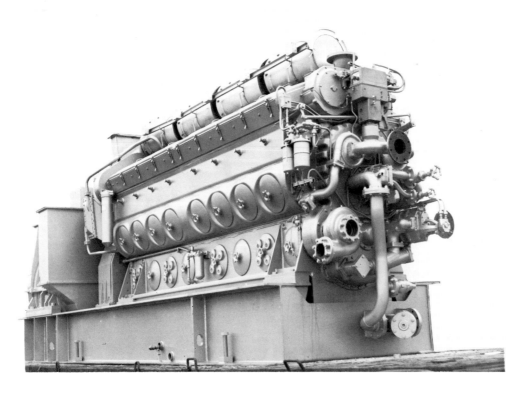

JUMBO FERRY WALLA WALLA IN THE YARD

HIYU, A CLASS OF ITS OWN

JUMBO FERRIES WALLA WALLA (left) AND SPOKANE (below) ARE THE LARGEST FERRIES IN THE UNITED STATES

THE ISSAQUAH CLASS HAS PROVOKED THE MOST RECENT CONTROVERSY FOR THE STATE FERRY SYSTEM

327

PROTOTYPES AND MODELS OF NEW CLASSES OF FER-RIES ARE COMMISSIONED BY THE STATE DEPART-MENT OF TRANSPORTATION. THIS IS THE ISSAQUAH CLASS.

ISSAQUAH WAS THE FIRST LAUNCHED OF ITS CLASS

KITTITAS

POSTSCRIPT

Visitors to Puget Sound will be hard-pressed to find many residents who believe that ferries will ever disappear from their scenery. Growing metropolises, Mount Rainier, evergreen forests and open countryside merge into focus from the deck of a Washington State Ferry. Energetic people with a purpose and a future are not likely to exchange ferries for underwater metros and traffic-crowded toll bridges. Where else in this world can one combine country living with city life, surrounded by majestic scenery, temperate climate, and service by efficient and modern marine transportation? Commuters and travelers, bus drivers, and truckers experience this venture by water every day of every year on Puget Sound. It's a legend of the past and a legacy for the future; it's an enjoyable retreat into the present.

KLICKITAT AND CASEY BAYLESS

REGISTER OF FERRYBOATS ON PUGET SOUND

ACORN (1924)
65' x 25' Diesel 75 HP
Owners: Olson Brothers; Olympic Navigation Co.
Sold

BAINBRIDGE (1928)
178' x 55' Diesel
Owners: K.C.T.C.; P.S.N.; Black Ball Ferries, Ltd.; B.C.
Government
For sale by B.C. Govt.

AIRLINE (a-ELK) (1921)
104' x 23' Diesel
Owners: Skansie Bros.; Crosby Marine Corp.; Crosby
Direct Ferry Lines
Scrapped 1931.

BALLARD (a-CITY OF EVERETT; LIBERTY) (1900)
155' x 30' Diesel
Owners: Seattle Everett Nav. Co.; Liberty Bay Trans.
Co.; K.C.T.C.; Ballard-Ludlow Co.; P.S.N.
Four Winds Restaurant-Sunk

BAILEY GATZERT (1890)
194' x 33' Steam Sternwheel
Owners: Columbia River & Puget Sound Navigation
Company; P.S.N.
Machine Shop 1926

BEAVER (1835)
101' x 20' Steam
Owners: Hudson Bay Co.
Destroyed 1888 on rocks at Vancouver Harbor
entrance.

BEELINE (a-FLORENCE K.; GLORIA) (1903)
97' x 26' Steam
Owners: Tacoma Ferry Co.; Crosby Direct Ferry
Lines; P.S.N.

CHETZEMOKA (a-GOLDEN POPPY) (1927)
227' x 44' Diesel Electric
Owners: Golden Gate Ferry; So. Pac. Golden Gate Ferries, Ltd.; P.S.N.; Washington State
Sunk under tow to California

CENTRAL (1919)
60' x 19' Steam
Owners: Central Ferry Co.
Abandoned 1950

CHINOOK (1947)
274' x 66' Diesel
Owners: P.S.N.; Black Ball Ferries, Ltd.
For sale by B.C. Govt.

CENTRAL II (1924)
60' x 24' Steam
Owners: Capt. Willis Nearhoff; P.S.F.L.; Berte Olson
Destroyed by fire 1931

CHIPPEWA (1900)
200' x 50' Steam-Diesel
Owners: Arnold Transit Co.; P.S.N.; W.S.F., Foss Tug;
U.S. Govt; Donald V. Clair
Destroyed by fire

CITY OF ANGELES (a-CITY OF LONG BEACH) (1906)
125' x 35' Steam (from Gas)
Owners: Chas. Fulton; Port Angeles Trans. Co.; P.S.N.
Scrapped Oct. 1938

CITY OF EDMONDS (1924)
56' x 20'
Owners: Sound Ferry Lines
Total loss by fire Sept. 1926

CITY OF BREMERTON (a-MAJESTIC; WHATCOM)
(1901)
167' x 48' Steam
Owners: Thompson Steamboat Co.; Alaska Steam;
P.S.N.
Scrapped 1939

CITY OF MUKILTEO (1927)
104' x 35' Steam
Owners: P.S.N.
Destroyed by fire Apr. 1932

CITY OF CLINTON (1921-22)
58' x 22'
Wrecked 1929 at Mukilteo; total loss

CITY OF SACRAMENTO (a-ASBURY PARK; b-
KAHLOKE) (1908)
297' x 50' Steam
Owners: Monticello Steam; G.G. Ferry; So. Pac.-G.G.
Ferries, Ltd.; Black Ball
Transferred to Black Ball Canada, 1951.

CITY OF SEATTLE (1888)
121′ x 33′ Steam Sternwheel
Owners: West Seattle Land & Improvement; Martinez
& Benecia Ferry & Trans. Co.
Located at Sausalito, Ca.

CLATAWA (1913)
86′ x 28′ Steam
Owners Alki Point Trans. Co.; P.S.N.; Olympic Naviga-
tion; Whidby Island Trans. Co.; Sound Ferry Lines;
U.S. Govt.
Destroyed by fire Nov. 1958

CITY OF STEILACOOM (1924)
110′ x 26′ Diesel 200 HP
Owners: Pierce Co.; Tacoma Ferry Co.; Washington
Navigation Co.
Sold to Webb Institute, California

COHO (1959)
342′ x 72′
Owner: Black Ball Transport Co.
Still operating

CITY OF TACOMA (1921)
124′ x 43′ Steam-Diesel
Owners: Tacoma Ferry Co.; Washington Navigation
Co.
Sunk at Yarrow Bay

COMMANDER (a-GENERAL FRISBIE) (1900)
184′ x 29′ Steam
Owners: Union Ferry Co.; K.C.T.C. & P.S.F.L., jointly
Upper decks: residence on Lake Washington; Hull:
floating salmon cannery, Alaska

CROSLINE (1925)
144′ x 48′ Diesel
Owners: Crosby Direct Lines; P.S.N.; Wash. State
Highway Dept.; Howard Risdon
Scrapped 1977

ELWHA (a-GOLDEN SHORE) (1927)
227′ x 44′ Diesel Electric
Owners: G.G. Ferries; So. Pac-G.G. Ferries, Ltd.;
P.S.N.; Washington State; San Diego-Coronado Ferry
Co.
Renamed SILVER STRAND (San Diego)

DECEPTION PASS (1924)
65′ x 24′ Diesel
Owners: Olympic Navigation Co.; Berte Olson
Scow 1981

ENETAI (a-SANTA ROSA) (1927)
243′ x 46′ Diesel
Owners: Northwestern Pacific; S.P.G.G. Ferries, Ltd.;
P.S.N.; Washington State
To San Francisco 1968

DEFIANCE (1927)
165′ x 48′ Diesel
Owners: Skansie Bros.; Washington Navigation Co.;
Washington State Dept. of Highways
C & H Seafood, 1981

EVERGREEN STATE (1954)
(Class includes TILLICUM and KLAHOWYA)
310′ x 73′ Diesel Electric
Owner: Washington State Ferries
Still operating

FOX ISLAND (a-WOLLOCHET) (1925)
89' x 32' Diesel
Owners: Washington Navigation Co.; Horluck Transportation; Olympic Ferries
To B.C. Govt. 1961

HARVESTER KING (1917)
97' x 21' Diesel
Owners: Puget Sound Potash & Kelp Fertilizer Co.;
Crosby Direct Lines; P.S.N.; Merchants Trans. Co.;
P.S.F.L. (Freighter: F.H. MARVIN)
Abandoned 1959

GIG HARBOR (1921)
116' x 37'
Burned June 1929

HIYU (1) (1924)
61' x 28' Gas, converted
to Diesel
Owner: Kitsap County
Transportation Co.
Abandoned 1968

GLEANER (1907)
144' x 40' Steam Sternwheel
Owners: Skagit River Navigation & Trading; Chartered
to Crosby Direct Lines
Sunk 1940

HIYU (2) (1967)
150' x 63' Diesel
Owner: Washington State Ferries
Still operating

HYAK (1967)
(Class includes YAKIMA, KALEETAN, ELWHA)
382' x 73' Diesel-Electric
Owner: Washington State Ferries
Still Operating

IROQUOIS (1901)
214' x 46' Steam-Diesel
Owners: T.T. Arnold Transit Co.; P.S.N.; Chicago & So.
Haven S.S. Co.; Black Ball Transport
Alaska fish processing plant

ILLAHEE (1927)
243' x 46' Diesel-Electric
Owners: So. Pac. R.R.; S.P.-G.G. Ferries, Ltd.; P.S.N.,
Washington State
Still operating

ISSAQUAH (1979)
(Class includes CATHLAMET, CHELAN, KITSAP, KIT-
TITAS, SEALTH)
328' x 78' Diesel
Owner: Washington State Ferries

INDIANAPOLIS (1904)
180' x 32' Steam
Owners: Indiana Transportation Co.; P.S.N.
Scrapped 1939

ISSAQUAH (1914)
114' x 38' Steam
Owners: Anderson Steamboat Co.; Rodeo-Vallejo
Ferry Co.
Hulk on beach, Sausalito, Ca.

KALAKALA (a-PERALTA) (1927)
165' x 53' Steam-Diesel
Owners: Key System; P.S.N.; Washington State Ferries
Fish cannery, Alaska

KITSAP (1925)
159' x 48' Diesel
Owners: K.C.T.C.; P.S.N.; Washington State; Oregon
Highway Comm.
Total loss under tow 1966

KEHLOKEN (a-GOLDEN STATE) (1926)
227' x 44' Diesel-Electric
Owners: G.G. Ferries; S.P.-G.G. Ferries, Ltd.; P.S.N.;
Washington State
Burned

KLAHANIE (1928)
227' x 44' Diesel-Electric
Owners: G.G. Ferries; S.P.-G.G. Ferries, Ltd.; P.S.N.;
Washington State
Moored on Duwamish River

KING COUNTY (1899)
116' x 33' Steam Sidewheel
Owner: King County
Sank May 1907

KLICKITAT (a-STOCKTON) (1927)
243' x 46' Diesel-Electric
Owners: So. Pac. R.R.; S.P.-G.G. Ferries, Ltd.; P.S.N.;
Washington State
Rebuilt. In operation.

KULSHAN (a-CROWN CITY) (1954)
242' x 65' Diesel Electric
Owners: San Diego-Coronado Ferry Co.; Washington
State; U.S.C.G.
Operated by Coast Guard

LINCOLN (1908)
147' x 43' Steam Prop
Owner: King County
Abandoned 1957

LAKE CONSTANCE
(a-RUBAIYAT; CITY OF
KINGSTON) (1923)
60' x 22' Diesel
Owners: Sound Ferry Lines;
P.S.N.; Berte Olson; Capt.
Wm. P. Thornton
Abandoned 1965

MALAHAT (a-NAPA VALLEY) (1910)
230' x 49' Steam
Owners: Monticello S.S. Co.; G.G. Ferries; P.S.N.;
Black Ball-Canada
Destroyed by fire

LESCHI (1913)
169' x 50' Steam Sidewheel; Diesel Screw (1931)
Owners: Port of Seattle Commission; King Co. Ferry
District; Washington State Ferries
Sold to fish cannery, Alaska, 1969.

MERCER (a-VASHON ISLAND) (1916)
120' x 36' Diesel
Owners: King County; L.A. Harbor Dept.
Fishing Barge

MOUNT VERNON (a-ROBERT BRIDGES) (1916)
101' x 31' Diesel
Owners: Port of Seattle; Crosby Bros., P.S.N.
Out of registry 1952

OLYMPIC (a-SIOUX) (1911)
175' x 39' Steam
Owners: P.S.N.; U.S. Army
Sold

NISQUALLY (a-MENDOCINO) (1927)
243' x 46' Diesel-Electric
Owners: Northwestern Pacific; S.P.-G.G. Ferries, Ltd.;
P.S.N.; Washington State
In operation

PIONEER (1921)
61' x 22' Diesel
Owners: P.S.F.L.; Berte Olson
Abandoned 1951

OLYMPIC (a-GOVERNOR HARRY W. NICE) (1938)
207' x 62' Diesel
Owners: State of Maryland; Washington State Ferries
In operation

PUGET (a-VASHONIA) (1908)
122' x 34' Converted to ferry in 1923
Owners: P.S.N.
Sunk 1951

QUILCENE (a-CITY OF BREMERTON; KITSAP II) (1916)
146' x 43' Steam
Owners: P.S.N.; U.S. Navy (barracks ship)
Floating machine shop; abandoned 1948

RHODODENDRON (a-GOVERNOR HERBERT R. O'CONOR) (1947)
226' x 63' Diesel
Owners: State of Maryland; Washington State Ferries
In operation

QUILLAYUTE (1927)
150' x 52' Diesel
Owners: Sound Ferry Lines; P.S.N.; Black Ball Lines-Canada; B.C. Government
Cannery

ROSARIO (a-WHIDBY) (1923)
147' x 38' Diesel
Owners: P.S.N.; Washington State Ferries
Abandoned; not on register 1980

QUINAULT (a-REDWOOD EMPIRE) (1927)
243' x 46' Diesel-Electric
Owners: Northwestern Pacific; S.P.-G.G. Ferries, Ltd.; P.S.N.; Washington State
In operation

SAN MATEO (1922)
217' x 42' Steam
Owners: So. Pac. R.R.; S.P.-G.G. Ferries, Ltd.; P.S.N.; Washington State Ferries
N.W. Seaport, Lake Union

SEATTLE (a-H.B. KENNEDY) (1924)
185′ x 44′ Steam
Owner: P.S.N.
Laid up in Alaska with power removed; burned 1968

SPOKANE Class (Includes WALLA WALLA) (1972)
440′ x 87′ Diesel-Electric
Owner: Washington State Ferries
In operation

SHASTA (1922)
217′ x 42′ Steam
Owners: So. Pac. R.R.; S.P.-G.G. Ferries, Ltd.; P.S.N.
River Queen Restaurant, Portland

STATE OF WASHINGTON (1889)
170′ x 31′ Steam Sternwheel
Owners: Pacific Navigation Co.; Pacific Coast Steam;
P.S.N.; Shaver Trans. Co.
Destroyed 1920

SKANSONIA (1929)
165′ x 50′ Diesel
Owners: Tacoma Ferry Co. (Skansie Bros & A.M.
Hunt); Washington Dept. of Highways
Retired 1969 on Lake Washington

TOURIST (a-SKAGIT CHIEF; PORT ORCHARD) (1907)
157′ x 28′ Steam Sternwheel
Owner: P.S.N.

VASHON (1930)
191' x 57' Diesel
Owners: K.C.T.C.; P.S.N.; Washington State Ferries
Sold to California interests; moored on Seattle
waterfront

WEST SEATTLE (1907)
160' x 48' Steam Sidewheel
Owners: West Seattle Land & Improvement Co.; Port
of Seattle; Lake Washington Shipyards; Treutle Marine
Ways
Abandoned

VASHONIA (a-RELIEF) (1930)
93' x 38' Diesel
Owners: Washington Navigation Co.; K.C.T.C.; P.S.N.
Dismantled 1951

WHIDBY (Gas) (1919)
58' x 22'
Owners: Joyce Brothers
Burned Mar. 1927 at Port Gamble

WASHINGTON (1908)
160' x 43' Steam
Owner: King County
Abandoned

WILLAPA (a-FRESNO) (1927)
243' x 46' Diesel
Owners: P.S.N.; Washington State Ferries
Returned to California

DEVELOPMENT OF PUGET SOUND NAVIGATION COMPANY AUTO FERRY FLEET

1907 TOURIST: Carrying a few cars on Navy Yard Route between 1910 and 1918.

1918 BAILEY GATZERT: Purchased on Columbia River for Navy Yard Route.

1921 CITY OF BREMERTON: Converted from WHATCOM auto ferry for Navy Yard Route.

1923 PIONEER: Purchased for Seabeck-Brinnon run.

1923 PUGET: Converted into auto ferry, Seattle-Port Ludlow route.

1923 CITY OF ANGELES: Converted into auto ferry, Anacortes-San Juan-Sidney route.

1923 MOUNT VERNON: Converted into auto ferry, Anacortes-San Juan-Sidney route.

1924 SEATTLE: Converted into auto ferry, Navy Yard route.

1924 OLYMPIC: Converted into auto ferry from SIOUX, Port Angeles-Victoria run.

1925 Steam ferry PUGET: Replaced with diesel.

1926 CITY OF BELLINGHAM: Converted from KITSP II, Bellingham-Victoria run.

1926 CHIPPEWA: Converted into steam auto ferry, Navy Yard Route.

1926 Steam Ferry WHIDBY: Purchased from Whidby Island Transportation Company, Mukilteo-Columbia Beach run.

1927 CROSLINE: Purchased from Crosby Direct Line Ferries, Alki Point-Manchester run.

1927 AIRLINE: Purchased from Crosby Direct Line Ferries, Alki Point- Manchester run.

1927 BEELINE: Purchased from Crosby Direct Line Ferries, Alki Point- Manchester run.

1927 CITY OF MUKILTEO: Purchased from Willis Nearhoff, Mukilteo-Columbia Beach run.

1927 CENTRAL II: Purchased from Willis Nearhoff, Mukilteo-Columbia Beach run.

1928 QUILLAYUTE: Obtained with combining of Sound Ferry Lines with Puget Sound Navigation Company, Edmonds-Kingston route.

1928 CLATAWA: Obtained with combining of Sound Ferry Lines with Puget Sound Navigation Company, Edmonds-Port Ludlow route.

1928 CITY OF KINGSTON: Obtained with combining of Sound Ferry Lines with Puget Sound Navigation Company, Port Gamble-Shine route.

1930 Ferry QUILCENE: Rebuilt from CITY OF BREMERTON, Seattle-Port Townsend run.

1931 Ferry PUGET: Altered to drive-thru ferry. Repowered with steam engine. Mukilteo-Columbia Beach run.

1931 Diesel-powered ferry ROSARIO: Rebuilt from Steam Ferry WHIDBY, Anacortes-San Juan-Sidney run.

1932 Steam Ferry CHIPPEWA: Rebuilt as diesel ferry for Navy Yard Route.

1933 INDIANAPOLIS: Bow altered to carry cars. Edmonds-Port Ludlow run.

1935 KALAKALA: Purchased from San Francisco and converted into auto ferry. Navy Yard Route.

Puget Sound Navigation Company

FLEET LIST

1901 - 1954

Vessels are listed in the approximate order in which they joined the fleet. The year in parentheses is the building date, while those following show years of service in a given capacity. If no year in parentheses is given, then vessel was built for company. Length and width are to the nearest foot.

NOTE: Unless otherwise noted, all vessels are steel hull, single screw, triple expansion steam engine, single stack.

1. ROSALIE [136 x 27] (1893) 1901-18 Passenger, wood hull, compound engine. Total loss by fire.

2. GARLAND [97 x 19] (1890) 1902-06 Passenger, wood hull, compound engine. Sold to Mexican interests.

3. PROSPER [84 x 19] (1898) 1902-05 Passenger, wood hull, compound engine. Converted into tug for Alaska Steamship Co.

4. ALICE GERTRUDE [131 x 26] (1898) 1902-07 Passenger, wood hull, compound engine. Wrecked.

5. LYDIA THOMPSON [93 x 23] (1893) 1902-10 Passenger, wood hull, compound engine. Sold. (b-tug MONITOR)

6. MAJESTIC [169 x 30] (1901) 1902-04 Passenger, wood hull. Altered, renamed.

   WHATCOM [169 x 37] 1904-21 Passenger, wood hull. Altered, renamed.

   CITY OF BREMERTON [167 x 48] 1921-38 Ferry, wood hull. Sold and scrapped.

7. EVANGEL [100 x 19] (1882) 1902-03 Passenger, wood hull, compound engine. Scrapped. (Machinery to SAMSON)

8. SAMSON [116 x 32.5] 1903-16 Freighter, wood hull, compound engine. Sold.

9. CLALLAM [155 x 33] 1903-04 Passenger, wood hull, compound engine. Wrecked.

10. UTOPIA [124 x 25] (1898) 1903-26 Passenger, wood hull. Scrapped.

11. GEORGE E. STARR [148 x 28] (1879) 1903-11 Passenger, wood hull, side-wheel beam engine. Sold to B.C. interests.

12. FAIRHAVEN [130 x 26.5] (1889) 1903-06 Passenger, wood hull, stern-wheel. Sold to Island Transportation Co.

13. INLAND FLYER [106 x 19] (1898) 1903-10 Passenger, wood hull. Sold to Washington Route. (b-MOHAWK)

14. RAPID TRANSIT [98 x 31] (1891) 1903-12 Freighter, wood hull, twin screw. Sold.

15. T.W. LAKE [95.5 x 25] (1895) 1903-05 Freighter, wood hull, twin screw. Sold to Merchants Transportation Co.

16. PORT ORCHARD [137.5 x 26] (1887) 1903-07 Passenger, wood hull, stern-wheel. Scrapped. Machinery to TOURIST. (a-SKAGIT CHIEF) (Owned jointly by P.S.N. and H.B. Kennedy).

17. ATHLON [112 x 20] (1900) Passenger, wood hull, compound engine until 1907, when triple-expansion. (Wholly owned by H.B. Kennedy, but operated by P.S.N. 1903-14, when sold to Liberty Bay Trans. Co.).

18. DODE [99 x 22] (1898) 1905-10 Passenger, wood hull. Wrecked. (a-schooner WILLIAM J. BRYANT).

19. BELLINGHAM [133 x 20] (1882) 1905-19 Passenger, wood hull, compound engine. Sold. (a-tug GENERAL MILES; b-WILLAPA).

20. PERDITA [103 x 23] (1903) 1905-08 Passenger, wood hull. Lengthened.

    PERDITA [143 x 25] 1908-11 Passenger, wood hull. Burned. (Machinery to COMANCHE).

21. STATE OF WASHINGTON [170 x 31] (1889) 1905-13 Passenger, wood hull, stern-wheel. Sold to Columbia River interests.

22. INDIANAPOLIS [180 x 32] (1904) 1906-38 Passenger. Sold, scrapped. (Bow rebuilt as ferry, 1933).

23. IROQUOIS [214 x 34] (1901) 1907-20 Passenger, two stacks. Sold to Great Lakes.

    IROQUOIS [214 x 46] 1927-52 Ferry, two stacks. (Returned from Great Lakes). Sold to Black Ball Transport, Inc.

24. CHIPPEWA [200 x 34] (1900) 1907-26 Passenger, two stacks. Converted into ferry, new upperworks.

CHIPPEWA [200 x 50] 1926-32 Ferry, two stacks. Repowered, new upperworks.

CHIPPEWA 1932-5l Ferry, diesel engine. Sold to Washington State Ferries.

25. WAIALEALE [125 x 27] (1886) 1908-28 Passenger, wood hull, compound engine. Sold, scrapped. (Pronounced: Wee-ally-ally). (a-Hawaiian sch. KAUAI; b-Hawaiian str. WAIALEALE).

26. TOURIST [157 x 28] 1907-29 Passenger, wood hull, stern-wheel. Remodeled. (Machinery from PORT ORCHARD).

TOURIST 1929-36 Freighter, wood hull, stern-wheel. Sold to Puget Sound Freight Lines. (As passenger vessel, owned by Port Orchard Route, then Navy Yard Route—jointly owned by P.S.N. and H.B. Kennedy).

27. H.B. KENNEDY [179 x 28] 1909-22 Passenger, 4-cylinder triple expansion, 2 stacks. Renamed. (Built for Navy Yard Route).

SEATTLE 1922-24 Passenger, 4-cylinder triple expansion, 2 stacks. Converted into ferry. (a-H.B. KENNEDY).

SEATTLE [185 x 44] 1924-39 Ferry, 4 cylinder triple expansion, 2 stacks. Sold.

28. CITY OF EVERETT [134 x 28] (1900) 1910-17 Passenger, wood hull, compound engine. Sold to Liberty Bay Transportation Co. Renamed. (b-LIBERTY in 1917; c-BALLARD in 1931).

BALLARD [155 x 30] 1943-45 Ferry, wood hull, diesel engine. Sold, became restaurant. (Engine to ROSARIO).

29. TELEGRAPH [154 x 26] (1903) 1910-12 Passenger, wood hull, stern-wheel. Sunk. Raised and sold. (b-OLYMPIAN).

30. BAINBRIDGE [79 x 12.5] (1908) 1910-11 Passenger, wood hull, gasoline engine. Sold. (b-SPEEDER in 1917).

SPEEDER 1935-38 Passenger, wood hull, diesel engine, 2 stacks. Sold. (Not operated by P.S.N.).

31. KULSHAN [160 x 32] 1910-38 Passenger. Sold, scrapped.

32. SIOUX [148 x 24] 1911-24 Passenger, 4-cylinder triple expansion engine. Converted into ferry, renamed.

OLYMPIC [175 x 39] 1924-41 Ferry, 4-cylinder, triple expansion engine. Sold to U.S. Army. (c-FRANKLIN S. LEISENRING).

33. FLYER [170 x 21] (1891) 1911-18 Passenger, wood hull. Rebuilt, renamed.

WASHINGTON [172 x 28] 1918-29 Passenger, wood hull. Sold, scrapped.

34. PUGET [115 x 24.5] (1908) 1911-23 Passenger, wood hull. (a-VASHONIAN). Converted into ferry.

PUGET [121.5 x 34] 1923-25 Ferry, wood hull. Repowered.

PUGET 1925-31 Ferry, wood hull, diesel engine. Repowered.

PUGET 1931-41 Ferry, wood hull, triple expansion engine (from WHIDBY). Sold.

35. SOL DUC [189 x 31.5] 1912-42 Passenger. Sold to U.S. Navy.

36. POTLATCH [150 x 27] 1912-28 Passenger. Sold.

37. TACOMA [209 x 30] 1913-38 Passenger, 4-cylinder, triple expansion engine, 2 stacks. Sold, scrapped.

38. COMANCHE [134 x 28.5] 1913-23 Freighter. (Machinery from PERDITA). Passenger accomodations added.

COMANCHE 1923-40 Passenger. Sold to U.S. government.

39. CITY OF ANGELES [128 x 21] (1906) 1916-23 Passenger, wood hull, twin screw. Converted into ferry. (a-gas engine CITY OF LONG BEACH).

CITY OF ANGELES [125 x 35] 1923-38 Ferry, wood hull, twin screw. Sold, scrapped.

40. ALOHA [80 x 22] 1916-24 Freighter, wood hull, diesel engine. Lengthened. (Built for Navy Yard Route, Inc.).

ALOHA [104 x 22] 1924-39 Freighter, wood hull, diesel engine. Sold, scrapped.

41. TRANSIT [63 x 22] (1916) 1917-18 Freighter, wood hull, gas engine. (Owned by Navy Yard Route). Sold. Lake steam auto ferry.

42. KINGSTON [93 x 24.5] (1901) 1919-24 Passenger, wood hull. (a-DEFIANCE). Sold to Washington Route, Inc.

43. KITSAP II [141 x 26] (1916) 1917-26 Passenger, wood hull, 4-cylinder, triple expansion, 2 stacks. (Owned by Navy Yard Route, Inc.). Converted into ferry, renamed.

CITY OF BELLINGHAM [141 x 26] 1926-30 Ferry, wood hull, 4-cylinder, triple expansion, 2 stacks. Rebuilt, renamed.

QUILCENE [146 x 43] 1930-42 Ferry, wood hull, 4-cylinder, triple expansion engine. Sold to U.S. government.

44. BAILEY GATZERT [194 x 33] (1907) 1918-20 Passenger, wood hull, stern-wheel. Altered into ferry. (Side-port loading of cars).

BAILEY GATZERT 1920-25 Ferry, wood hull, stern-wheel. Sold.

45. MOUNT VERNON [101.5 x 31] (1916) 1923-36 Ferry, wood hull, diesel engine. (a-double-ended passenger ferry ROBERT BRIDGES). Sold to Chuckanut-Interisland Ferry Co.

46. PIONEER [61 x 22] (1921) 1923-30 Ferry, wood hull, gasoline engine, no stack. Sold to Columbia River.

47. MORNING STAR [137 x 30] (1900) 1925-28 Freighter, wood hull, compound engine. Sold. (a-SHOE CITY; b-SUNBEAM).

48. WHIDBY [114 x 31] (1923) 1926-31 Ferry, wood hull. (Bought by Harry Ramwell and P.S.N.). Rebuilt, renamed.

ROSARIO [147 x 38] 1931-51 Ferry, wood hull, diesel engine. Sold to Washington State Ferries.

49. CROSLINE [144 x 48] (1925) 1927-42 Ferry, wood hull, diesel engine. Sold to Vancouver, B.C.

50. AIRLINE [104 x 23] (1921) 1927-38 Ferry, wood hull, diesel engine. Sold. (a-ELK until 1925).

51. BEELINE [97 x 26] (1903) 1927-39 Ferry, wood hull, compound engine. Sold. (a-passenger str. FLORENCE K.; b-ferry GLORIA).

52. CITY OF MUKILTEO [104 x 35] (1927) 1927-32 Ferry, wood hull. burned.

53. CENTRAL II [60 x 24] (1924) 1927-30 Ferry, wood hull. Sold.

54. QUILLAYUTE [150 x 52] (1927) 1928-51 Ferry, wood hull, twin screw, twin diesels. Transferred to B.C. registry.

55. CLATAWA [86 x 28] (1913) 1928-36 Ferry, wood hull, diesel engine. (a-passenger str CLATAWA, steam ferry CLATAWA). Sold to Agaton Olson. (b-U.S. Navy YFB 50).

56. CITY OF KINGSTON [60 x 22] (1923) 1928-34 Ferry, wood hull, diesel engine. (a-diesel freighter RUBAIYAT). Sold to Captain W.M. Thornton. (b-LAKE CONSTANCE).

57. WASHINGTON (1923) 1930-40 Ferry, wood hull, diesel, double-ended. Sold, scrapped. (Brought from Columbia River).

58. ALVERENE [60 x 14] (1912) 1931-32 Passenger, wood hull, semi-diesel. (Not operated by P.S.N.). Sold.

59. KALAKALA [265 x 53] (1927) 1933-51 Ferry, diesel. (a-tbn.-elec. PERALTA). Brought from San Francisco. Rebuilt by 1935. Sold to Washington State Ferries.

60. VASHON [191 x 57] (1930) 1935-51 Ferry, wood hull, diesel, double-ended. Sold to Washington State Ferries.

61. BAINBRIDGE [178 x 55] (1928) 1935-52 Ferry, wood hull, diesel, double-ended. Transferred to B.C. registry.

62. KITSAP [159 x 48] (1925) 1935-51 Ferry, wood hull, diesel, double-ended. Sold to Washington State Ferries.

63. HIYU [61 x 28] (1924) 1935-41 Ferry, wood hull, diesel, no stack. Sold to U.S. government.

64. HYAK [134 x 22] (1909) 1935-38 Passenger, wood hull. Sold, scrapped.

65. VERONA [113 x 23] (1910) 1935-36 Passenger, wood hull. Burned, sold.

66. MANITOU [106 x 23] (1917) 1935-43 Passenger, wood hull. (a-VASHON II). Sold, sunk in 1958.

67. WINSLOW [110 x 25] (1915) 1935-38 Passenger. (a-BAINBRIDGE, until 1928). Sold, scrapped.

68. F.G. REEVE [102 x 22.5] (1917) 1935-38 Passenger, wood hull. Sold.

69. SUQUAMISH [84.5 x 15] (1914) 1935-38 Passenger, wood hull, diesel engine. Sold. (Not operated by P.S.N.). (Later, fish boat TERRY to B.C. registry, 1949). (Then, c-AMBOYNA).

70. COMMANDER [184 x 29] (1900) 1935-36 Passenger, wood hull. (Not operated by P.S.N.). (Side-port loading for autos). Sold. (a-GENERAL FRISBIE).

71. ATALANTA [112 x 23] (1913) 1935-38 Passenger, wood hull, 5-cylinder, quad expansion engine. (Not operated by P.S.N.). Sold.

72. KEHLOKEN [227 x 44] (1926) 1937-51 Ferry, wood hull, double-ended, diesel-electric, 2 stacks. Brought from San Francisco (a-GOLDEN STATE). Sold to Washington State Ferries.

73. KLAHANIE [227 x 44] (1928) 1937-51 Ferry, wood hull, double-ended, diesel-electric, 2 stacks. Brought from San Francisco (a-GOLDEN AGE). Sold to Washington State Ferries.

74. ELWHA [227 X 44] (1927) 1937-44 Ferry, wood hull, double-ended, diesel-electric, 2 stacks. Brought from San Francisco (a-GOLDEN SHORE). Sold to San Diego. (c-SILVER STRAND).

75. CHETZEMOKA [227 x 44] (1927) 1937-51 Ferry, wood hull, double-ended, diesel-electric, 2 stacks. Brought from San Francisco (a-GOLDEN POPPY). Sold to Washington State Ferries.

76. GOLDEN BEAR [227 x 44] (1927) 1937-40 Barge, wood hull, no power. Sold. Wrecked, en route from S.F. to Puget Sound.

77. WILLAPA [242.5 x 46] (1927) 1940-51 Ferry, diesel. Brought from San Francisco. Sold to Washington State Ferries. (a-diesel-electric FRESNO).

78. ENETAI [242.5 x 46] (1927) 1940-51 Ferry, diesel. Brought from San Francisco. Sold to Washington State Ferries. (a-diesel-electric SANTA ROSA).

79. QUINAULT [242.5 x 46] (1927) 1940-51 Ferry, diesel-electric, double-ended. Sold to Washington State Ferries. (a-REDWOOD EMPIRE, from S.F.).

80. ILLAHEE [242.5 x 46] (1927) 1940-51 Ferry, diesel-electric, double-ended. Sold to Washington State Ferries. (a-LAKE TAHOE, from S.F.).

81. NISQUALLY [242.5 x 46] (1927) 1940-51 Ferry, diesel-electric, double-ended. Sold to Washington State Ferries. (a-MENDOCINO, from S.F.).

82. KLICKITAT [242.5 x 46] (1927) 1940-51 Ferry, diesel-electric, double-ended. Sold to Washington State Ferries. (a-STOCKTON, from S.F.).

83. CITY OF SACRAMENTO [297 x 50] (1903) 1941-52 Ferry, twin-screw, twin 4-cylinder, triple expansion. Brought from S.F. in 1944. (a-ASBURY PARK). Transferred to B.C. registry. (c-diesel-electric KAHLOKE; d-LANGDALE QUEEN).

84. MALAHAT [231 x 49] (1910) 1941-43 Ferry, 4-cyliner, triple-expansion. (a-NAPA VALLEY, from S.F., 1942). Fire, upperworks rebuilt.

MALAHAT [230 x 49] 1943-56 Ferry, 4-cylinder, triple expansion. Sold for scrapping.

85. SHASTA [217 x 42] (1922) 1941-51 Ferry, double-ended. Sold to Washington State Ferries.

86. SAN MATEO [217 x 42] (1922) 1941-51 Ferry, double-ended. Sold to Washington State Ferries.

87. VASHONIA [93 x 38] (1930) 1943-50 Ferry, wood hull, diesel engine. (a-RELIEF). Sold, scrapped.

88. CHINOOK [273.5 x 66] 1947-54 Ferry, diesel-electric, twin screw. Transferred to B.C. registry. (b-CHINOOK II; c-SECHELT QUEEN).

Two idle ferries owned briefly by Puget Sound Navigation Company were GOLDEN WEST (1923) 1937-38, and CALISTOGA (a-FLORIDA, 1908) 1941-41. They were sold without being brought to Puget Sound.

The above listing includes all subsidiaries to Puget Sound Navigation Company, such as Inland Navigation Company, International Steamship Co., Straits Steamship Co., Seattle-Poulsbo Co., Thompson Steamship Co., Navy Yard Route, Whidby Island Ferries, Inc., Crosby Direct-Line Ferries. No attempt has been made to segregate individual steamers into these companies.

Compiled May, 1958, for the Puget Sound
Maritime Historical Society.
Lloyd M. Stadum
Captain Louis Van Bogaert
Robert C. Leithead
Revised by Robert C. Leithead 3/30/1983.

KITSAP COUNTY TRANSPORTATION COMPANY

FLEET LIST

1905 - 1935

Unless otherwise noted, all vessels are wooden hull, single screw, steam-powered, 1 stack, passenger vessels. Length and width to nearest foot.

1. RELIANCE [118 x 20] (1900) 1905-26 In company when formed. Total loss by fire 1926.

2. SENTINEL [102 x 17] (1898) 1905-08 In company when formed. Sold.

3. ADVANCE [69 x 17] (1899) 1907-07 Sold.

4. BURTON [93 x 20] (1905) 1907-10 & 1911-23 Sold.

5. KITSAP [127 x 22] (1906) 1906-16 Built for company. Sold 1916. Renamed BREMERTON 1916.

   BREMERTON [127 x 22] 1918-26 Repurchased 1918. Badly damaged by fire 1926. Sold. (a-KITSAP).

6. HYAK [134 x 22] (1909) 1909-35 Built for company. Company absorbed by P.S.N. 1935.

7. FALCON [68 x 15] (1908) 1913-19 Sold. Gas-powered. (Later SCENIC of Vancouver, B.C.).

8. SUQUAMISH [84.5 x 15] (1915) 1915-35 Built for company. First diesel passenger ship in U.S. Absorbed by P.S.N. 1935.

9. KITSAP II [141 x 25] (1916) 1916-17 Built for company. 2 stacks. Sold to Navy Yard Route in 1917.

10. TOLO [109 x 17] (1906) 1915-17 Built as CAMANO. Purchased 1915. Collided and sank in 1917. Total loss.

11. VASHON II [106 x 23] (1917) 1919-31 Renamed MANITOU 1931.

    MANITOU 1931-35 (a-VASHON II) Absorbed by P.S.N. 1935.

12. VERONA [113 x 23] (1910) 1923-35 Absorbed by P.S.N. 1935.

13. LIBERTY [140 x 31] (1900) 1922-30 (a-CITY OF EVERETT). Converted to auto ferry LIBERTY in 1923. Sold to Ballard-Ludlow Ferry Co. 1930. (b-BALLARD in 1931).

14. HIYU [61 x 28] (1924) 1924-35 Built for company. Diesel-powered auto ferry. Absorbed by P.S.N. 1935.

15. BAINBRIDGE [110 x 25] (1915) 1927-28 Bought from Eagle Harbor Transportation Co. 1927. Steel hull. Renamed WINSLOW 1928.

    WINSLOW 1928-35 (a-BAINBRIDGE). Absorbed by P.S.N. 1935.

16. SPEEDER [79 x 12.5] (1908) 1927-35 Built as gas-powered BAINBRIDGE. Rebuilt as SPEEDER 1922. Purchased from Eagle Harbor Transportation Co. 1927. Diesel engine. 2 stacks. Absorbed by P.S.N. 1935.

17. KITSAP [159 x 48] (1925) 1925-35 Built for company. Double-ended auto ferry, diesel-powered. Absorbed by P.S.N. 1935.

18. BAINBRIDGE [178 x 55] (1928) 1928-35 Built for company. Double-ended auto ferry, diesel-powered. Absorbed by P.S.N. 1935.

19. VASHON [191 x 57] (1930) 1930-35 Built for company. Double-ended auto ferry, diesel-powered. Absorbed by P.S.N. 1935.

WASHINGTON ROUTE, INC. MERGED WITH K.C.T.C. IN 1928:

20. F.G. REEVE [102 x 22] (1916) 1928-35 Absorbed by P.S.N. 1935.
21. KINGSTON [93 x 24] (1901) 1928-33 (a-DEFIANCE). Sold.
22. COMMANDER [184 x 30] (1900) 1930-35 (a- GENERAL FRISBIE of San Francisco). Run by Washington Route 1930 and renamed. Absorbed by P.S.N. 1935.

WHIDBY ISLAND TRANSPORTATION CO. MERGED WITH K.C.T.C. IN 1928:

23. ATALANTA [112 x 23] (1913) 1928-35 Absorbed by P.S.N. in 1935.

K.C.T.C. TO P.S.N. 1935

Listed below are the thirteen vessels of the Kitsap County Transportation Company fleet which were absorbed by Puget Sound Navigation Company in 1935:

VASHON
BAINBRIDGE
KITSAP
HIYU
HYAK
F.G. REEVE
MANITOU
VERONA

WINSLOW
SUQUAMISH (not operated by P.S.N.)
COMMANDER (not operated by P.S.N.)
ATALANTA (not operated by P.S.N.)
SPEEDER (not operated by P.S.N.)

FERRY NAMES

Visitors to the Pacific Northwest are often tongue-tied with the pronunciation of the names of ferries. All ferries in Washington State Ferry fleet with the exception of the OLYMPIC, the RHODODENDRON, and THE EVERGREEN STATE bear an honorable Native American title. This is a custom which was influenced by William O. Thorniley.

A number of the early day steamers bore familiar Indian names such as HYAK, WILLAPA or KITSAP but they were just as likely to be named for people: H.B. KENNEDY, ROSALIE, or LYDIA THOMPSON. Some names implied speed like FLYER, RAPID TRANSIT or TELEGRAPH, and many names reflected the region they served: PUGET, BELLINGHAM or CITY OF VICTORIA. Other names reflected former regions of service or Indian names from those regions: INDIANAPOLIS, IROQUOIS and SIOUX.

Among other scholarly pursuits, William O. Thorniley was a student of the Chinook jargon. He is credited as the organizer of the "name-calling" for the Black Ball Line. The KALAKALA was the first of a long train of Indian names for Puget Sound ferries. A few of these escaped Thorniley's wary attention like the SAN MATEO, SHASTA and the CITY OF SACRAMENTO but by 1945 the majority of the ferries in the fleet of Puget Sound Navigation Company bore Indian reference. Thorniley saw it as a way of preserving Northwest customs and recognizing native contributions on Puget Sound.

The State of Washington adopted a new policy for naming ferries after their purchase of the system. They were interested in tourists and promotion of tourism. Thus desiring to cater to these interests, the first two newly acquired vessels reflected a major mountain range (OLYMPIC) and the State flower (RHODODENDRON). The launching of the Evergreen Class of ferries touched off a furor of controversy when it came to names.

The first of this class of ferries, THE EVERGREEN STATE, launched in 1954, was the first ferry built by the Washington State Ferry System. Citizens calmly accepted her name. The vessels that followed in 1958 and 1959 were to be christened VACATION STATE and WASHINGTON STATE. Public officials stated that Indian names were difficult and captains attested that tourists were baffled with the tongue-twisters.

William O. Thorniley was not known for his idleness. He felt that these bureaucratic names were redundant and boring so he initiated an effort through the Seattle Chamber of Commerce to reinstate the tradition of Indian names. His remarks carried clout.

Practically every newspaper in Western Washington picked up the appeal to Governor Daniel J. Evans and the citizenry joined in with their pleas that old customs be honored. Thorniley kept the campaign humorous and the Governor, respecting public response, appointed a nine-member committee for name selection. Thorniley served as the Chinook jargon expert.

Thorniley's papers reveal his list of Chinook definitions and ferry names as follows. Pronunciations were not listed, for in Thorniley's words, "One must remember that the Chinook jargon never was a written language. It was strictly a spoken language until the early settlers put it down in writing as best they could.

"Many of these settlers weren't too literate. Consequently, when somebody tells you there's some other way to spell certain words in Chinook, he probably is just as right as the next person." These were Thorniley's definitions:

ORIGIN OF INDIAN NAMES OF PUGET SOUND VESSELS, PAST AND PRESENT

ALKI: Chinook Jargon "In the future; bye-and-bye."

CHINOOK: A large Indian tribe that was spread over the lower Columbia River area. Many of the words of the Chinook Jargon came from their language. There is no record of the meaning of the name.

CHACO: Chinook Jargon "Come."

CHETZEMOKA: A Clallam chieftain who enjoyed the friendship of the pioneers of the Port Townsend area who gave him the name, Duke of York. Chetzemoka Park in Port Townsend was named for him. His elder brother was called King George and his wife was Jenny Lind.

CLALLAM: The powerful Clallam tribe once covered much of the northern Olympic Peninsula. The name means "big brave nation."

CLATAWA: Chinook Jargon "Go."

COMANCHE: A Shoshonean Indian tribe of the western plains. There is no record of its meaning.

DUWAMISH: The Duwamish tribe, closely allied to the Suquamish tribe, lived at the mouth of and on the lower reaches of the Duwamish River. The name means "People who live on the river." Lake Washington was once called Duwamish Lake.

ELWHA: The Elwha River on the northern Olympic Peninsula takes its name from the word for elk in the Clallam tongue.

ENETAI: Chinook Jargon "Across; over on the other side or shore."

HIYU: Chinook Jargon "Plenty, much."

HYAK: Chinook Jargon "Fast, speedy."

ILLAHEE: Chinook Jargon "Land, place or location." Example: "Seattle Illahee."

IROQUOIS: A large and complex federation of Indian tribes widely scattered over the eastern United States and Canada. The name means "Heart people or people of God."

ISKUM: Chinook Jargon "To get hold of; to receive; to secure."

KELOKE: Chinook Jargon "Swan" or other aquatic bird. This is a variation of the word Kehloken.

KEHLOKEN: Chinook Jargon "Swan" or other aquatic bird.

KITSAP: Unfriendly chief and medicine man of the Suquamish Indian tribe which occupied a portion of Kitsap County. He was killed by his own people.

KLAHANIE: Chinook Jargon "Outside." The "Great Out-of-Doors."

KLICKITAT: An Indian tribe of south central Washington. Early explorers did not agree on the meaning of the name. Some claimed that it meant "Beyond," but the majority seemed to favor "Robbers" or "Dog Robbers."

KULSHAN: The Lummi Indian name for Mount Baker. It means "Great White Watcher."

LESCHI: Unfriendly chief of the Nisqually Indian tribe who was hanged at Nisqually for his part in the murder of white settlers.

MALAHAT: From Malahat Drive, Vancouver Island. Meaning of the name is unknown.

MOHAWK: A small tribe of Indians formerly occupying the Mohawk valley in northern New York State. There are two divergent opinions as to the meaning of the name. One is that it means "They eat what lives." The other is that it is an Indian word for "Muskrat."

MULTNOMAH: A sub tribe of the Chinook Indians. The name is believed to mean "Down the River."

NISQUALLY: An Indian tribe which headquartered at the mouth of the Nisqually River. Although there is some disagreement as to the meaning of the name, it is generally considered to be a corruption of a French-Canadian expression meaning "square nose."

NOOKSACK: An Indian tribe that lived on the river of that name. The name is said to mean "root eating people."

OSAGE: For the Osage Indians of south central United States, the name means "strong."

POTLATCH: Chinook Jargon "To give" or "a gift." When an Indian chief held a Potlatch, lavish gifts were presented to his friends in the expectation that they would return the favor when the occasion arose.

QUILCENE: Quilcene is a corruption of the name of a branch of the Twana tribe living on Quilcene Bay. The name, correctly spelled Quilceedobish, meant "salt water people." The other branch of the Twana tribe was the Skokomish or "fresh water people."

QUILLAYUTE: The Quillayute tribe has a small reservation at the mouth of the Quillayute River. The name is said to mean "gathering together." The Bogachiel, the Sol Duc and the Calawa gather together to form the Quillayute but a short distance from its mouth.

QUINAULT: An Indian tribe of the western Olympic Peninsula. There is no agreement as to the meaning of the name, but it has been claimed that Quinault means "the river with a lake in the middle of it."

SEHOME: The town of Sehome on Bellingham Bay was named for a Samish Indian Chief.

SHASTA: A northern California Indian tribe. Meaning unknown.

SIOUX: A large tribe of plains Indians. The name means "little snake."

SKAGIT BELLE: The Skagit Indian tribe lived at the mouth of the Skagit River and on parts of Whidbey Island. The meaning is unknown.

SKOOKUM CHIEF: Chinook Jargon. Skookum means "strong, powerful."

SNOQUALMIE: Snoqualmie Falls takes its name from the Indian tribe which lived in that vicinity. The name means "moon people." The upturned face on top of Mount Si nearby is supposed by the natives to have fallen from the moon.

SOL DUC: From the Clallam tongue "Sparkling mystical waters."

SUQUAMISH: A Salish Indian tribe which now occupies a reservation at Suquamish, north and west of Bainbridge Island. The meaning of the name is unknown. Chief Seattle was a member of this tribe and is buried on the reservation.

SWINOMISH: The Swinomish tribe was a branch of the Skagit tribe. The meaning of the name is not known.

TOLO: Chinook Jargon "To earn; to gain control; to win at a game."

TYEE: Chinook Jargon "Chief or leader."

WASCO: The Wasco tribe was a branch of the Chinooks living near The Dalles, Oregon. The name means "a cup or small bowl or horn."

WAKENA: Named for Wahkeena Falls (note difference in spelling) and the Columbia River Drive. The name is from the Yakima tongue and means "very beautiful."

WHATCOM: Whatcom, now a part of the city of Bellingham, is said to mean "noisy waters" and takes its name from the stream which connects Lake Whatcom with Bellingham Bay. Another source of information points out that Whatcom was the name of a chief of the Nooksack Indians who lived near by.

WILLAPA: An Indian tribe, long extinct, which lived in the Willapa Harbor area. There is nothing to indicate what the name meant.

YOSEMITE: The Yosemite Indians lived in, and around, the Yosemite Valley. The name is a corruption of their name for "grizzly bear."

ADDENDUM TO ORIGIN OF INDIAN NAMES OF PUGET SOUND VESSELS, PAST AND PRESENT

THE ORIGIN OF NAMES OF PUGET SOUND FERRY BOATS

CHETZEMOKA: Chetzemoka was a Clallam Indian Chief who befriended the early settlers at Port Townsend. A beautiful stretch of beach on the Strait of Juan de Fuca, in Port Townsend, has been set aside as Chetzemoka Park.

SKANSONIA: The SKANSONIA was named in honor of Mitchell Skansie, president and founder of the Washington Navigation Company, which built the vessel.

SAN MATEO: The SAN MATEO was a former San Francisco Bay Ferry. Her name, which is the Spanish equivalent of St. Matthew, was never changed.

KEHLOKEN: Kehloken is from the Chinook jargon and means "swan, or other aquatic bird."

KALAKALA: When she appeared in 1935, the KALAKALA was hailed as the world's first completely streamlined vessel.

ENETAI: is from the Chinook Jargon, and means "across—over on the other side."

WILLAPA: The WILLAPA carries the historic name of the first vessel of the Black Ball Line on the Puget Sound which, in turn, was named for an extinct Indian tribe which once lived on Willapa Harbor.

QUINAULT: The QUINAULT was named for Lake Quinault and the Quinault Indian tribe. The name is variously stated to mean "people of the big and little water . . . Lake Quinault and the Pacific Ocean, or the river with a lake in the middle of it."

CHIPPEWA: The CHIPPEWA was built in Toledo, Ohio, and was named for the celebrated Indian tribe.

ILLAHEE: Illahee is from the Chinook jargon, and means the "land or the place." (Siwash Illahee means an Indian reservation).

VASHON: The VASHON was built for the Vashon Island route. The island was named by Captain Vancouver for his friend Captain James Vashon who was later an Admiral of the British Navy.

KLAHANIE: Klahanie is from the Chinook jargon, and means "the great out-of-doors."

NISQUALLY: The Nisqually was named for the Nisqually River, which has its source in the Nisqually Glacier on Mt. Rainier. The river was named for an Indian tribe which lived at its mouth. The first settlement on Puget Sound was the Hudson Bay post near the river.

KLICKITAT: The KLICKITAT was named for the Eastern Washington Indian tribe. The name is said to mean "beyond."

ROSARIO: The ROSARIO was named in honor of

the home of Robert Moran on East Sound in the San Juan Islands. Robert Moran, celebrated Puget Sound shipbuilder, was Mayor of Seattle during the great fire of 1889. The name is from the Spanish and means rosary.

CROSLINE: The CROSLINE was built by the Crosby Direct Line Ferries, and is a contraction of that name.

LESCHI: The LESCHI was named for Leschi Park, which, in turn, was named for Chief Leschi, a troublesome Indian who was executed for his depredation against the whites.

KITSAP: The KITSAP was named for Kitsap County, which, in turn, was named for Chief Kitsap, sub-chief of the Suquamish Tribe under Chief Seattle.

SHASTA: The SHASTA was a former San Francisco ferry which was never renamed. She was named for Mt. Shasta which is a corruption of a name of an Indian tribe which lived in the vicinity of the mountain.

VESSEL NAMES ADDED AFTER ABOVE LISTS WERE PREPARED:

KLAHOWYA: greetings

TILLIKUM: friend

HYAK: swift

KALEETAN: arrow

ELWHA: elk

FERRIES NAMED FOR INDIAN TRIBES IN EASTERN WASHINGTON:

YAKIMA

SPOKANE

WALLA WALLA

REGIONS, LAKES, RIVERS AND A CITY'S NAMESAKE:

ISSAQUAH

KITTITAS

KITSAP

CATHLAMET

CHELAN

SEALTH

CODE OF FEDERAL REGULATIONS TITLE 46-SHIPPING
Excerptions

Chapter 15: Transportation of Passengers and Merchandise by Steam Vessels

Section 451: Number of Passengers Allowable.

The Coast Guard officials shall state in every certificate of inspection granted to vessels carrying passengers, other than ferryboats, the number of passengers of each class that any such vessel has accommodation for and can carry with prudence and safety. They shall report their action to the Commandant of the Coast Guard, who may at any time order the number of such passengers decreased, giving his reasons therefor in writing, and thereupon the Coast Guard officials shall change the certificate of inspection of such vessel to conform with the decision of the Commandant of the Coast Guard. Whenever the allowance of passengers shall be increased by any Coast Guard officials such increase shall be reported to the Commandant of the Coast Guard, together with the reasons therefor, and such increase shall not become effective until the same has been approved in writing by the Commandant of the Coast Guard.

The master or owner of the vessel, or either or any of them, who shall knowingly violate this provision shall be liable to a fine of not more than $100 or imprisonment of not more than thirty days, or both.

Section 452: Penalty for Carrying Too Many Passengers.

It shall not be lawful to take on board of any vessel a greater number of passengers than is stated in the certificate of inspection, and for every violation of this provision the master or owner shall be liable to any person suing for the same to forfeit the amount of passage money and $10 for each passenger beyond the number allowed.

Section 453: Special Permit for Excursions.

If any passenger vessel engages in excursions, the Coast Guard officials shall issue to such vessel a special permit, in writing, for the occasion, in which shall be stated the additional number of passengers that may be carried and the number and kind of lifesaving appliances that shall be provided for the safety of such additional passengers; and they shall also, in their dis-

cretion, limit the route and distance for such excursions: *Provided, however,* That the issuance of such special permit shall be reported by the Coast Guard officials to the Commandant of the Coast Guard, and such special permit shall not be effective until approved by the said Commandant of the Coast Guard.

Notes of Decisions:

1. Ferryboats: This section and sections 452 and 453 of this title, respecting the number of passengers that may lawfully be carried by a passenger steamer, have no application to a ferryboat, though temporarily employed as an excursion boat. Schwerin v. North Pac. C. R. Co., D.C. Cal. 1888, 36 F. 710.

A steamboat, having obtained a certificate as a general passenger boat, and not as a ferryboat, does not come within the exception in this section. The Hazel Kirke, D.C. and C.C.N.Y. 1885, 25 F. 601.

A ferryboat, when turned aside from its proper business to carry passengers on excursions, ceases quoad hoc to be a ferryboat, and as to that trip or voyage, it becomes, to all intents and purposes, a passenger boat. U.S. v. Burlington, etc., Ferry Co., D.C. Iowa 1884, 21 F. 331.

Where a boat is licensed to run as a ferryboat between a certain town and a point on the opposite bank of the river, the carrying of passengers and merchandise to towns above and below the ferry limits forbids the idea that she was exclusively engaged in ferrying. The Bright Star, C.C.Mo. 1868, Woolw. 266, 4 Fed. Cas. No. 1,880.

The ordinary character of a ferryboat, daily employed as such, and occasionally as a tug boat, is not changed by being employed in several trips in conveying visitors to a state fair, three miles distant, and penalties are not incurred for failing to have the boat inspected and licensed as a passenger boat, since the legislature evidently had in view the inspection of vessels constructed for voyages or trips of more than an hour's duration. U.S. v. The Steamboat Ottawa, D.C. Mich. 1857, Newb. Adm. 536, 27 Fed. Cas. No. 15,976.

2. Towing Vessels: A steamer usually employed as a tow boat, is liable to the penalties for having transported about one hundred passengers on a trip a distance of twelve or fifteen miles each way and receiving pay for the same when it was not inspected and licensed as a passenger boat, since the question is not whether the steamer has been usually employed in the towing business, but what was its employment and service at the time complained of. U.S. v. The Propeller Echo, C.C.N.Y. 1860, 4 Blatchf. 446, 25 Fed. Cas. No. 15,021.

A tugboat used for towing vessels to and fro which is accustomed to take on board the masters of the vessels thus towed and sometimes one or more of the crew and carry them from the shore to their vessels, or vice versa, is not a "passenger vessel" or a "vessel carrying passengers." 1883, 17 Op. Atty. Gen. 599.

3. Computation of Passengers: In estimating the number of passengers, no deduction is to be made for children or persons not paying, but the crew are excluded. U.S. v. The Louisa Barbara, D.C. Pa. 1833, Fed. Cas. No. 15,632.

4. Tonnage: In estimating the tonnage of a vessel bringing passengers from a foreign country, the custom house measurement of the port of arrival is to be taken. U.S. v. The Louisa Barbara, D.C. Pa. 1833, Fed. Cas. No. 15,632. See also, U.S. v. The Anna, D.C. Md. 1854, Fed. Cas. No. 14,457, affirmed Fed. Cas. No. 14,458.

SCRAPBOOK

Sequim, Wash.

A trip to Tacoma

Schedule subject to storms, break-
downs and conditions beyond
our control.

Deception Pass Ferry

Leave Mainland (Fidalgo) side,
7:30 a.m. and hourly to 7:30
p.m. Running time, 5 minutes
crossing.

Leave Whidby Island side, 7:45
a.m. and hourly to 7:45 p.m.

O. A. OLSON, Prop.
Special Night Trips Phone,
Anacortes 3452

Car and Driver 50c
Extra Passengers 10c
(Extra large car 75c)

Drive Carefully

JOHN PATRIC, WASHINGTON PRINTER

Charles E. Taylor

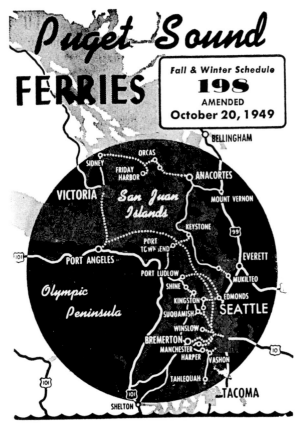

362

Automobile and Passenger Rates

The following rates on automobiles include driver's fare.

	One Way	Round Trip
Seattle and Vashon Heights		
Automobile under 2,500 lbs	$ .90	$1.75
Automobile over 2,500 lbs	1.00	1.75
Passenger	.35	...
Seattle and Harper		
Automobile under 2,500 lbs	1.20	...
Automobile over 2,500 lbs	1.30	...
Passenger	.35	...
Fauntleroy and Vashon Heights		
Automobile under 2,500 lbs	.75	1.50
Automobile over 2,500 lbs	.85	1.50
Passenger	.15	...
Fauntleroy and Harper		
Automobile under 2,500 lbs	1.00	...
Automobile over 2,500 lbs	1.00	...
Passenger	.20	...
Vashon Heights and and Harper		
Automobile under 2,500 lbs	.75	...
Automobile over 2,500 lbs	.85	...
Passenger	.15	...
Seattle and Port Blakely		
Automobile under 2,500 lbs	.90	...
Automobile over 2,500 lbs	1.00	...
Passenger	.35	...
Fletcher Bay and Brownsville		
Passenger Automobile	.50	...
Passenger	.10	...

Seattle and Brownsville via Port Blakely and Fletcher Bay

	Through Rate	
Automobile under 2,500 lbs	1.25	...
Automobile over 2,500 lbs	1.50	...

Ask the ticket agent for information regarding Commutation Rates.

Launching Party for the SOL DUC

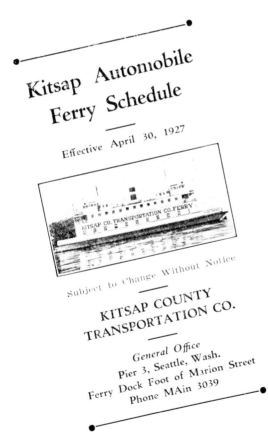

Kitsap Automobile
Ferry Schedule

Effective April 30, 1927

Subject to Change Without Notice

KITSAP COUNTY
TRANSPORTATION CO.

General Office
Pier 3, Seattle, Wash.
Ferry Dock Foot of Marion Street
Phone MAin 3039

BAINBRIDGE ISLAND—BREMERTON FERRY
OPENING CELEBRATION, OCTOBER 1, 1941

PUGET SOUND
SUMMER
RESORTS

A
GUIDE TO
THE
SUMMERING
PLACES
ON
PUGET SOUND
TOGETHER WITH
A LIST OF HOTELS AND
BOARDING-HOUSES
ISSUED BY THE
PUGET SOUND NAVIGATION Co.
COLMAN DOCK, SEATTLE, WASH.

INTERURBANS
AND
STAGES
SEATTLE + EVERETT
MT. VERNON + SEDRO-WOOLLEY
BELLINGHAM
AND OTHER POINTS

PUGET SOUND AND
BRITISH COLUMBIA
BY
INTERURBAN, STAGE AND FERRY

May, 1926

E.L. Franks

Capt. John A. "Dynamite" O'Brien

AFLOAT
in The
"Charmed Land"

Pug't S und Na igation Co.
S. . JONE . gt.
n.... 3 .5
MUNICIPAL DOCK   TACOMA

*'I will make a place
for you and me
Green days in forests
Blue days at sea'*

—STEVENSON

See **Puget Sound**
by Water

367

Christmas Chimes

Vol. III, No. 8   Seattle, Washington, Christmas Morning, December 25, 1962   Cultus Potlatch

CHRISTMAS QUIZ

1. Decorating a Christmas tree with candles is generally credited to: Franz Gruber......, Johann Eck......, Martin Luther.......
2. "Noel" means: gift......, birthday......, Christmas.......
3. "Hark! the Herald Angels Sing" was written on a Christmas morning by: Charles Wesley......, John Wesley...., Martin Luther.....
4. Frankincense and myrrh were obtained from: a quarry...., sap of a tree...., roots of plants.....

5. The wassail bowl is a custom in: Ireland......, Scotland......, England......
6. Christmas cards were started in the 1840's in: America......, England......, France......
7. Angels sang the first Christmas Carol over the: plains of Bethlehem...., hills of Galilee...., city of Nazareth.....

Answers on page four

Let no pleasure tempt thee, no profit allure thee, to do anything which thou knowest to be evil; so shalt thou always love jollity; for a good conscience is a continual Christmas.   —*Franklin*

CHRISTMAS SPIRIT REIGNS

If you doubt that there are angels, observe the little tots who believe Santa Claus won't come if they misbehave.

Christmas Is Here

Sing we all merrily
Christmas is here,
The day we love best
Of all of the year.
Bring forth the holly
And evergreens gay;
Deck out our cottage
For glad Christmas day.
Sing we all merrily,
Draw round the fire,
Brother and sister,
Grandson and sire.

Oldster Retaliates

As he finished his Christmas shopping at the New England village store an elderly gentleman unfolded, endorsed and handed to the clerk a rumpled government check on which was plainly printed: "Do not fold, spindle or mutilate."

The clerk looked at it, frowned and said, "You shouldn't do that, sir. The government doesn't like it."

The old man looked her straight in the eye and replied, "Young lady, the government does a lot of things I don't like either."

   —*Capper's Weekly*

Anybody who believes that old saw about "where there's smoke, there's fire" just has not tried to start a fire in the fireplace lately.

Christmas Comment In The Lighter Vein

Linda, who had been learning to sing Christmas carols in kindergarten, often sang herself to sleep. And one night, this is what her mother heard her sing: "While shepherds washed their socks by night."

At this festive season, you may be interested to know the derivation of the word "wassail." It comes from the old English expression, "Wassail the hollerin' about?"   —*Coronet*

An idea I'd like to propose is:
Give handkerchiefs rather than mitts.
No matter what size a guy's nose is,
A handkerchief always fits.
   —*Chicago Tribune*

Small boy to father playing with his Christmas train: "What this railroad really needs is a good retirement plan!"   —*Quote*

Each Christmastide I scatter wide Yule cards as a memento, but those to me are sure to be from folks I haven't sent to!   —*This Week*

The Christmas cigar a man really appreciates is the one that burns a hole in his Christmas tie.   —*Chatsworth Chatter*

A girl standing under the mistletoe isn't waiting for a gentleman to bring her a chair.   —*The Prism*

SINCEREST WISHES FOR YULETIDE AND THE COMING YEAR

May the wonderful Spirit of Christmas fulfill all your wishes for you. May the joys that you dream of and long for in some blessed moment come true.

May the faith that is part of the season hold promises perfect and dear and the wonderful Spirit of Christ-

mas bless your home through a wonderful year.

May the love of the grand old traditions, the friendship that rises anew make the way of life smoother and brighter in the true joys for yours and for you.

May the peal of the chimes and the carols, the peace and hope of the Star, make this a bright world of contentment and wonder, wherever you are.
   —*Mary and Bill Thorniley*

Another thing so simple a child can operate it is a grandparent.   —*Al Spong*

Most women don't mind Yule shopping — they charge right ahead! —*Arnold Glasow*

When we throw out the Christmas tree we should be especially careful not to throw out the Christmas spirit with it.
   —*The Scrap Book*

369

FOLLOW THE BIRDS TO VICTORIA, B. C.

The gateway to 1,000 miles of wonderland, evergreen forest glades, good roads, sandy beaches, wonderful climate and picturesque mountains.

Cross the International Boundary on the Ferries
NO RED TAPE

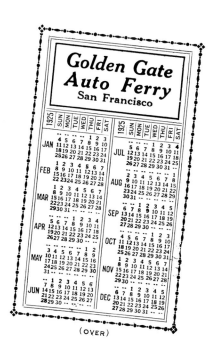

"The Ideal Summer Play Ground"

MOTOR TRIPS
DE LUXE
IN THE
Charmed Land

372

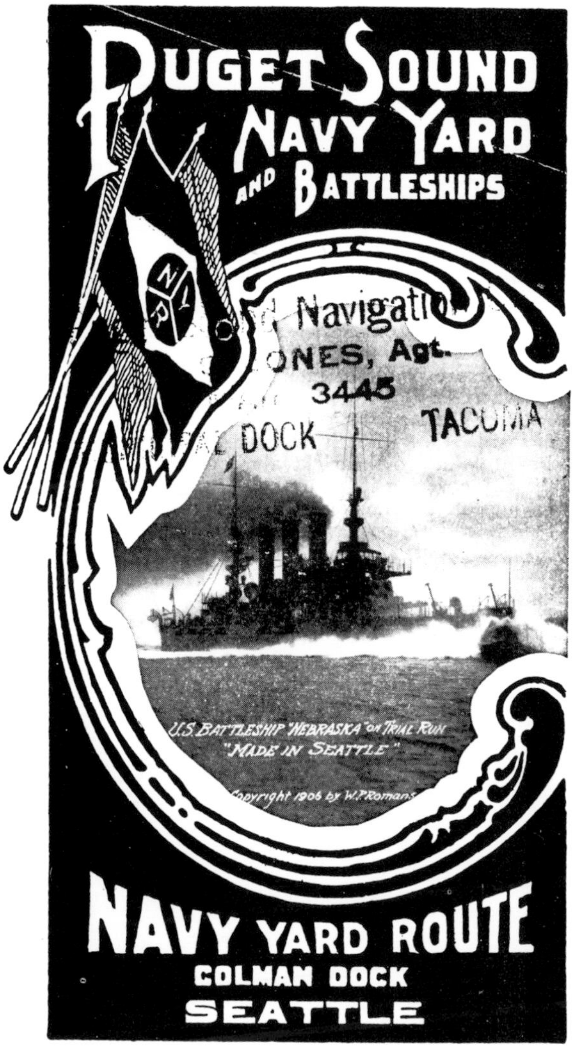

PUGET SOUND NAVY YARD AND BATTLESHIPS

Navigation
ONES, Agt.
3445
DOCK   TACOMA

U.S. BATTLESHIP NEBRASKA ON TRIAL RUN "MADE IN SEATTLE"

Copyright 1906 by W.P.Romans

NAVY YARD ROUTE
COLMAN DOCK
SEATTLE

8/13/1927

𝒯𝒽𝑒 MARINE DIGEST

DISTANCES ON SOUND, NAUTICAL MILES

Compiled by
CAPT. C. W. CALL
Puget Sound and Alaska Pilot

	Anacortes	Bellingham	Blaine	Bremerton	Cape Flattery	DuPont	Everett	Mukilteo	Olympia	Point Wells	Port Angeles	Port Gamble	Port Ludlow	Port Townsend	Seattle	Tacoma	Vancouver
Bellingham..	18																
Blaine	33	35															
Bremerton ..	72	85	100														
Cp. Flattery	92	107	108	130													
DuPont	96	112	124	40	155												
Everett	57	72	85	36	115	74											
Mukilteo	53	68	80	32	111	58	04										
Olympia	109	120	137	52	167	18	74	70									
Point Wells	51	66	80	21	109	46	15	11	59								
Pt. Angeles..	43	55	62	75	57	100	60	56	112	54							
Pt. Gamble..	45	60	72	41	103	66	27	23	78	22	48						
Pt. Ludlow ..	41	56	68	37	99	62	23	19	74	18	44	08					
Pt. T'nsend..	27	42	55	46	85	71	31	27	83	25	28	19	14				
Seattle	64	79	88	14	122	39	29	25	51	13	67	32	28	38			
Tacoma	83	98	103	26	142	20	48	44	37	32	86	52	48	58	25		
Vancouver ..	66	70	42	130	133	157	117	113	169	111	87	105	101	87	125	145	
Victoria	40	48	52	77	60	102	66	62	114	56	17	50	46	32	69	89	87

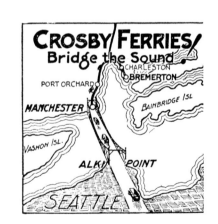

PUGET SOUND
AUTO FERRY
SCHEDULES
SUMMER 1935

FAST FERRIES OF THE BLACK BALL LINE FORM
THE SHORTEST CONNECTING LINKS BETWEEN
THE PACIFIC HIGHWAY, ITS BRANCHES,
THE OLYMPIC HIGHWAY AND THE ROADS
ON THE ISLANDS OF PUGET SOUND

PUGET SOUND NAVIGATION CO.
COLMAN DOCK   SEATTLE
MAin 2222

Uptown Travel Office   June 14, 1935   **65**
1306 Fourth Ave.   Schedule No.

PLEASE DESTROY ALL PREVIOUS ISSUES

Mrs. Charles Peabody with seven of her eight sons and their wives: (kneeling) Norman Penfield, (standing l to r) Alexander, Duane, Folger, Laurance, Charles, and Enoch W.

Larry Peabody

QUILCENE—Mrs. Charles Peabody and youngest son Duane in center

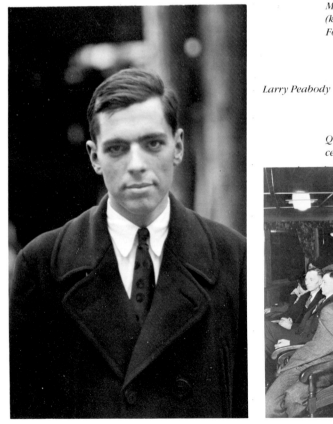

George, Woody, Larry and Mary at the Peabody Potlatch, 1983

Walter Green

Capt. Russ Taylor and author Mary Kline

Northwest Ferry Retirees 1983
(seated on floor) Larry Peabody, Clar Schleitweiler, Jan, George Mock (row 2, seated) Barbara Matson, Lloyd Atwood, Alice Bass, Louise Cook, Ann Levanavich, Capt. Tom Birkeland, Nina Birkeland, Ellen Van Nieuwenhuise, Eleanor Knudsen, Phyllis Eikum, Mary Fosse, Alice Nelson and Jerry Antovich (row 3, standing) Capt. Gunnar Joslyn, Woody Peabody, Eleanor Schleitweiler, Capt. Bill Anderson, Capt. George Kemp, Capt. Sig Sande, Joe Kasch, Capt. Earl Fowler, Capt. Cec Weyrich, Capt. Al Walker, Gary Van Nieuwenhuise, Capt. Dan Woods, Walter Green, Art Adamsen, Capt. Dick Cook, Mabel Maloney, Tony Overhouse, Marjorie Dean, Don Nelson (row 4, standing) Reg. Bass, Capt. Bob Matson, Maratha Anderson, Stan Osbeck, Capt. Ken Maloney, Capt. Ralph Petterson, Duane Davis, Capt. Norm Nelson, Mag Anderson.

SELECT BIBLIOGRAPHY

This is a listing only of the writings that have been used directly in the making of this book. This bibliography is by no means a complete record of all the works and sources that the authors consulted. It indicates the substance and range of reading upon which this history has been formed. It is intended to serve as a convenience to those who wish to pursue the study of Puget Sound's ferry fleet and maritime history.

Anges, H.L. ''Steamer ASBURY PARK in Service on the Pacific Coast.''*Marine Engineering.* (September, 1920):713.

''Annual Report Washington State Ferries, 1951-1952.'' Gov. Langlie's Papers, Washington State Archives.

Becker, Ethel Anderson. *Here Comes the Polly.* Seattle: Superior, 1971.

Benson, Richard. *Steamships and Motorships of the West Coast.* New York: Bonanza, 1968.

Birkeland, Captain Torger. *Echoes of Puget Sound.* Caldwell, Idaho: Caxton Press, 1961.

Brown, Richard E. ''Berkeley and Her Sisters: Their Architectual Style Changes.'' *Mains'l Haul,* (Maritime Museum Association of San Diego) Vol. XVIII, No. 2 (1982).

Brown, Richard E. ''San Francisco Bay Ferries.''*Sea Breezes.* (October, 1957):260-283.

Brown, Richard E. ''San Francisco Bay Ferries.''*Sea Breezes Magazine.* (October, 1957).

Brown, Richard E. ''Where Are They Now?—The Ferryboats of Yesteryear.'' *Mains'l Haul,* Vol. XVIII, No. 3 (1982).

Burke, Padriac. *A History of the Port of Seattle.* Seattle: Port of Seattle, 1976.

Calkins, R.H. (Skipper). *High Tide.* Seattle: Marine Digest, 1952.

Cammon, Betsey Johnson. *Island Memoir.* A Personal History of Anderson and McNeil Islands. Puyallup: The Valley Press, Inc. (no date).

Carey, Roland. *Isle of the Sea Breezers.* Seattle: Alderbrook Publishing Company, 1976.

Carey, Roland. *The Sound Steamers.* Seattle: Alderbrook Publishing Co., 1965.

Carey, Roland. *The Steamboat Landing on Elliott Bay.* Seattle: Alderbrook Publishing Company, 1962.

Clapp, Frank E. ''A Princess That Became a Queen.'' *Steamboat Bill.* (Spring, 1982).

Clarke, Norman H. *Mill Town.* Seattle and London: University of Washington Press, 1970.

Clausen, Walter P. *Peter Puget's Sound* Seattle: Ballard Printing and Publishing Co., 1979.

Cunningham, Ross. ''The State Had a Ferry Dream in 1951...but, Sadly, It Never Came True.'' *The Seattle Times.* (no date shown on clipping).

''Cupid's Work.'' *The Victorian Colonist* (May 27, 1891).

Demoro, Harre. *The Evergreen Fleet.* San Marino, California: Golden West Books, 1971.

Department of Transportation, State of Washington. ''Report of Investigation of the Earnings, Property, Operations, Rates, Services and Facilities of the Puget Sound Navigation Company, May, 1947.''

Diesel Engines in Ferryboats. *Pacific Motorboat Magazine.* (June, 1925).

Downs, Art. *Paddlewheels on the Frontier.* The Story of British Columbia and Yukon Sternwheel Steamers. Seattle: Superior, 1972.

Ely, Arline. *Our Foundering Fathers.* Kirkland: Kirkland Public Library, 1975.

Estep, A.C. interview. *The Sea Chest,* Vol. 11:91.

Evans, Elwood. *Puget Sound: Its Past, Present and Future.* 1869. Facsimile Reprint. Seattle: Shorey Book Store, 1964.

Faber, Jim. ''Ferry Guide.'' Washington State Ferries Brochure. (No specific date shown).

Ford, Robert S. *Red Trains Remembered.* Glendale: Interurban Books, 1980.

Fox, Captain John. ''A Glance Back and Looking Ahead with the Inlandboatmen of Puget Sound.'' pamphlet. Seattle: 1939.

''Get off This Run, Says Millionaire Greene.'' *Navy Yard American.* (Dec. 25, 1909).

''Golden Type Auto Ferries.'' *Pacific Marine Review.* (December, no year shown):564-559.

Gore, Willam J. and Evelyn Shipman. *Commuters vs. The Black Ball Line.* University of Alabama Press (Inter-University Case Program):1959.

Grant, Frederick James. History of Seattle, Washington. New York: American Publishing and Engraving Co., 1891.

Grun, Bernard. Timetables of History. New York: Simon & Schuster, 1979.

Hacking, Norman R. and W. Kaye Lamb. *The Princess Story.* Vancouver: Mitchell Press Limited, 1974.

Harlan, George H. "The Saga of the Ferries." *Sausalito News.* (February 27, 1941).

Harlan, George H. *San Francisco Bay Ferryboats.* Berkeley: Howell-North, 1967.

Harlan, George H. and Clement Fisher, Jr. *Of Walking Beams and Paddle Wheels.* San Francisco: Bay Books, 1951.

Harvey. "Ferry Skippers Were Artists at Warp, 2 Woofs." *The Seattle Sunday Times.* (no date).

Hershman, Marc J., Susan Heikkala and Caroline Tobin. *Seattle's Waterfront.* Seattle: Waterfront Awareness, 1981.

Hilton, G.W., R. Plummer, J. Jobe, and Carlo Demand. *The Illustrated History of Paddle Steamers.* New York: The Two Continents Publishing Company, 1976.

Hoffman, Fergus. Business Section. *The Seattle Post-Intelligencer.* (August 26, 1959).

"Island Ferry Problem Recalls Old Battles." *Bremerton Daily News Searchlight.* (December 30, 1935).

Johnson & Higgins, Average Adjustors. "Statement of General Average and Collision Claim Case of the Steamer IROQUOIS, New York to Seattle." (September 7, 1907). Thorniley files.

Johnson, Eads. "Ferryboats." *The Society of Naval Architects and Marine Engineers, Historical Transactions 1893-1943.* New York: The Society of Naval Architects and Marine Engineers, 1945.

Johnson, Eads. "Ferryboats." *The Society of Naval Architects and Marine Engineers, Historical Transactions 1893-1943.* New York: The Society of Naval Architects and Marine Engineers, 1945.

Joint Steering Committee of the Masters, Mates and Pilots, Local No. 6 and the Ferryboatmen's Union of the Pacific, Puget Sound Division. "Analysis of Award." (1935).

Jones, Robert D. *With the American Fleet From the Atlantic to the Pacific.* Seattle: The Harrison Publishing Company, 1908.

"KALAKALA Wins Battling Record." *Enetai* (February 18, 1983):8.

"Kasch Transportation Company." *The Sea Chest,* Vol. 16:12.

Kemble, John. "Chrysopolis." *American Neptune,* Vol. 2 (November 4, 1942).

Kemble, John Haskell. "Chrysopolis: The Queen of the Golden River." *American Neptune,* Vol. 2, Number 4 (1942).

Kemble, John Haskell. *San Francisco Bay* A Pictorial Maritime History. New York: Bonanza Books, 1957.

"Key System Ferries Building At Oakland Yard of Moore Dry Dock Company." *Pacific Marine Review.* (1926):250.

Kohl, J.G. "Geographic Memoir." *Reports of Explorations and Surveys,* Vol. 12, Book 1. Washington, D.C.: 1860.

Langley, Governor Arthur B. "T.B.A. and Ferries." Langley Papers. Washington State Archives, Olympia.

Leithead, Robert C. "Canadian Pacific Triangle Route." *The Sea Chest* (Sept., 1967).

Leithead, Robert C. "Captain Harry Crosby—Puget Sound's Energetic Ferry Operator." *The Sea Chest,* Vol. 12:27-34.

Leithead, Robert C. "The White Collar Line." *The Sea Chest.* Vol. :8.

Leithead, Robert C. and Louis Van Bogaert. "The Navy Yard Route." *The Sea Chest,* Vol. 2:96-117.

M'Donald, State Sen. Robert T. *Seattle Daily Times* (Sept.17, 1944).

MacMullen, Jerry. *Paddle Wheel Days in California.* Stanford: Stanford University Press, 1944.

Marine Digest. Jackson B. Corbet, Jr., editor. Vol. 1 - Vol. 21 (1922 - 1943).

Marine Engineers Beneficial Association. *Constitution of the National Marine Beneficial Association.* 1912. Pamphlet published by M.E.B.A.

Marine Engineers Beneficial Association. *Marine Engineers Annual 1901.* Seattle: M.E.B.A.

Marriott, Elsie Frankland. *Bainbridge Through Bifocals.* Seattle: Gateway Printing Company, 1941.

Matson, Captain Robert. "Leschi Park Shipyard." *The Sea Chest,"* Vol. 13:126.

McDonald, Lucile. The Lake Washington Story. Seattle: Superior, 1979.

McDonald, Lucile. Interview with Joshua Green. *The Seattle Times.* (January 17, 1965).

McDonald, Lucile and Austen Hemion. "Lake Washington Shipyard." *The Sea Chest,* Vol. 11:130.

McNairn, Jack and Jerry MacMullen. *Ships of the Redwood Coast.* Stanford: Stanford University Press, 1945.

Meany, Edmund. *Origin of Washington Geographic Names.* Seattle: University of Washington Press, 1923.

Meeker, Ezra. *Pioneer Reminiscences of Puget Sound.*

Seattle: Lowman & Hanford, 1905.

Men of the Pacific Coast, 1902-1903. San Francisco: The Pacific Art Company.

Newell, Gordon. *Ships of the Inland Sea.* The Story of Puget Sound Steamboats. Portland: Binfords & Mort, 1951.

Newell, Gordon. *The Green Years.* Seattle: Superior, 1969.

Newell, Gordon. *The H.W. McCurdy Marine History of the Pacific Northwest, 1895 - 1965.* Seattle: Superior, 1966.

Newell, Gordon. *The H.W. McCurdy Marine History of the Pacific Northwest, 1966 - 1976.* Seattle: Superior, 1976.

Newell, Gordon and Joe Williamson. *Pacific Steamboats.* New York: Bonanza, 1958.

"New Steamer ASBURY PARK, For the New York-Sandy Hook Route." *Marine Engineering,* Vol. VIII, No. 10 (October, 1903):495-502.

"New Steamer for the Pacific Coast." *Marine Engineering.* (April, 1903):188.

Pacific Northwest Goes to War. (State of Washington). Associated Editors. Seattle: Art Ritchie and William J. Davis, Publishers, 1944.

"Pacific Ports Department." *The Log.* Pacific Coast Association of Port Authorities. (no date shown):72.

"Pacific Workboat Builders." *Pacific Marine Review.* (December, no year shown):553-554.

Peabody, A.M. Collection. Archives, Museum of History and Industry, Seattle.

Peabody, Cornelia Marshall. Diary. (1855) Authors' copy, unpublished.

Perry, John. *American Ferryboats.* New York: Wilfred Funk, Inc., 1957.

Pratt. "The Active Washington Navigation Company." *Pacific Motorboat Magazine.* (January, 1938):26-7.

Puget Sound Navigation Company Corporate Papers. Archives of Puget Sound Maritime Historical Society. Seattle.

Rail and Water Edited by Ev Mills. North Highlands, California: History West, 1981.

Reh, Louise M. *Fifty Dollars An Acre.* A History of Puget Sound Naval Shipyard 1891 to 1916. Bremerton: Red Deer Press, 1983.

Root, Henry. *Personal History and Reminiscenses of Henry Root, 1845 - 1921.* Published privately. Bancroft Library Archives.

Report on Transportation Service to Golden Gate International Exposition 1939. (September, 1939):80. Bancroft Library.

Ruby, Robert H. and John A. Brown. *Ferryboats on the Columbia River.* Seattle: Superior, 1974.

Rushton, Gerald. *Echoes of the Whistle* Illustrated History of the Union Steamship Company. Vancouver: Douglas & McIntyre, 1980.

Rushton, Gerald A. *Whistle Up the Inlet.* The Union Steamship Story. Vancouver: Douglas & McIntyre, 1974.

Sachse, Richard. "Plan for Readjustment." Appraisal for the Key System Company. (July 20, 1929). Bancroft Library Archives.

Sayre, J. Willis. *The Early Waterfront of Seattle.* Reproduction. Seattle: The Shorey Book Store, 1971.

The Sea Chest, Vol. 3:15.

The Sea Chest, Vol. 8:87.

Seattle Daily Times. (August 6, 1939).

Seattle Daily Times. (August 2, 1939).

Seattle Daily Times. (May 23, 1934).

Seattle Post-Intelligencer. (January 10, 1904).

Seattle Post-Intelligencer. (May 2, 1903).

Seattle Post-Intelligencer. (Sept. 9, 1901).

Seattle Star. (May 17, 1912)

Shields, Captain Ed. "Puget Sound Freight Lines: A Dream That Came True." *The Sea Chest,* Vol. 12:85-98.

Shrader, Graham. *The Black Ball Line.* Edmonds: Edmonds Printing Co., 1980.

Smith, Virginia B. *A History of Labor Relations in the Puget Sound Ferry Boat Trade.* University of Washington Thesis (1950). Unpublished.

Southern Pacific Golden Gate Brochure. (April, 1929). Thorniley Collection.

Southern Pacific Railroad Brochure. "Treasure Island on San Francisco Bay." (1939) Bancroft Library.

Spaulding, Philip F. "Bridge of Bluewater—The Alaska Marine Highway." Presented to The Society of Naval Architects and Marine Engineers (May 22-25, 1974).

Spaulding, Philip F. "The History of Shipbuilding on Puget Sound." Presented to Waterfront Awareness Coastal Resource Program. (July 28, 1981).

Steamboats and Modern Steam Launches. Edited by Bill Durham. San Diego: Howell-North, 1981.

Stewart, Robert B. "Give the Ferries Back to Peabody." Letter to Editor, *The Bremerton Sun.* (no date shown).

Taylor, Russ. Letter to Walter Green, dated April 22, 1982. Copy in authors' possession.

Terkel, Studs. *Hard Times*. New York: Pantheon Books, 1970.

Thompson, Wilbur. "When It Was Fly on the FLYER." *The Sea Chest,* Vol. 13 (Dec. 1981).

Thompson, Wilbur and A. Beach. *Steamer to Tacoma*. Bainbridge Island: Driftwood, 1963.

Thorniley, William O. *The Seattle Sunday Times*. (March 9, 1958).

Thornton, Captain William. Tape Recorded Interview Conducted by Jervis Russell.

Timmen, Fritz. *Blow for the Landing*. A Hundred Years of Steam Navigation on the Waters of the West. Caldwell, Idaho: Caxton Press, 1973.

"To Get From Here to There a Pleasant Way, Take a Ferry." *Smithsonian,* Vol. 8, No. 4, (July, 1977):77-80.

Turner, Robert. *The Pacific Princesses*. Canada: Sono Nis Press, 1977.

Van Bogaert, Captain Louis. Scrapbooks of clippings. (1903 - 1960). Puget Sound Maritime Historical Society Archives.

Walker, Jim. *Key System Album*. Glendale: Interurbans, 1978.

Wallgren, Governor Mon C. "T.B.A. and Ferries." Wallgren Papers. Washington State Archives, Olympia.

Warner, Katy. "Katydids." *The Bainbridge Island Review.* (December 5, 1952).

Wells, Jay. *The Seattle Times,* (July 19, 1970):A21.

Western Writers of America. *Water Trails West.* New York: Doubleday & Company, 1978.

Wilkes, Charles. *Wilkes Survey, 1845*.

Williamson, Joe and Jim Gibbs. *Maritime Memories on Puget Sound*. Seattle: Superior, 1976.

"Worst Disaster in the Strait." *The Seattle Times*.

Wright, E.W. Lewis & Dryden's *Marine History of the Pacific Northwest.*(1895) Seattle: Superior, 1967.

Wright, Lawton. "Floating Bridges." *The Saturday Evening Post.* (April 5, 1941):40.

Wunder, John. *Pacific Northwest Sourcebook.*ASUW Lecture Notes. Seattle: Wunder, 1974.

Yakima Republic. (July 15, 1942).

A Special Thanks to C.W.(Bill) Somers for research materials and a grand tour of his fine maritime museum in the old winery at Grapeview, Washington. Mr. Somers and others like him have contributed significantly to the preservation of our maritime past through their private collections, many of which have been made available to the authors of this book.

INDEX

Acheson, Lois, 60, 63, 307-8
Acheson, Robert 60, 190, 307-8
ACME, 145-6
ACORN, 137-8, 140-1
ACTIVE, 260-1, 274
Admiral Line, 283
Agate Pass, 283
Agate Pass Bridge, 140, 301
AIRLINE, 126, 134-5, 249
AL-KI, 208
ALABAMA, 197
ALAMEDA, 249, 299
Alameda, CA., 27
Alaska-Yukon Pacific Exposition, 77, 148
Alaska Consolidated Canneries, 118, 120
Alaska Railroad, 100
Alaska State Ferry System, 13
Alaska Steamship Company, 13, 17, 19-20, 25, 34, 39, 41,
    45, 27, 67-9, 73, 182, 196, 208
  organization, 17, 19
  reorganization, 25
  officers, 34
  purchase of L.T.T., 39
ALBION, 102, 199, 241
Alexander & Baldwin, 155
Alexander, H.F., 197
ALF, 120
ALGOMAH, 50*
ALICE, 120
ALICE GERTRUDE, 21, 23, 32, 34
ALOHA, 180, 197, 213, 249
ALVARENE, 133
Ambrose, Vic, 59
American Express Co., 100
American Federation of Labor (AF of L) 208, 217
American Freezerships, 246
American Mail Line, 60
Ames, Capt. Charles "Big Ames", 27
Anacortes, WA., 101, 131-2
Anacortes-Sidney Ferry Lines, 132
Anderson, Capt. Henry "Harry" I., 59-60, 89, 94-5, 294,
    307, 309
Anderson, Capt. John L., 100, 118, 121, 130, 143-4, 146-50,
    152-7, 159-60, 162-6, 181, 196-7, 201, 212, 214, 218-9,
    225
  Anderson Shipbuilding Co., 148, 152
  Anderson Steamboat Co., 148

Anderson Water Tours, 154
  birth/early years, 143-4
  death of, 143, 157
  Ferry Dock Co., 181
  King County controversy, 155-7
  lake controversy, 146
  Lake Washington Shipyard, 147
  pallbearers, list of, 157
  purchase of K.C.T.C., 159
Anderson, Matt, 146
Anderson Shipbuilding Co., 148, 150, 152
Anderson Steamboat Co., 148, 150, 152
Anderson Water Tours, 154
ANNIE M. PENCE, 36, 38*
AQUILO, 8, 94, 148, 150, 153
Arey, Capt.Theodore, 208
ARGENTINA, 276
ARIEL, 126
Armit, William, 11
Arnold, F.K., 20
Arnold, George T., 50
Arnold, Mrs. George T., 50
Arnold Transportation Company, 50*
Arnold, T.T., Transportation, 50, 56
Arthur, President Chester A., 15
Artondale, WA., 124
ASBURY PARK, 278
Astoria, OR., 19, 191
ATALANTA, 12, 126, 166, 167, 169, 174, 178, 191
ATHLON, steamer, 39, 40, 41, 59-60, 84, 95, 104, 118, 167,
    199, 294, 307, 309
ATLANTA, 100, 142, 148, 153-4, 239
Atlantic Park, 148
Atlas Imperial engine, 191, 251
Atlas True diesel engine, 161
Aurora Bridge, 283
AVEN J. HANFORD, 250

B & T Transportation Co., 147
B.C.Steamship Service, 95
BABY MINE, 124
BAILEY GATZERT, sternwheeler, 47, 88-91, 197, 232, 241,
    309
"Bailey Gatzert Waltz", 89
BAINBRIDGE, ferry, 158, 164, 213, 261, 274, 310-1, 313
BAINBRIDGE, steamer, 133, 150, 160-1, 166, 178
Bainbridge Island, WA., 95, 111, 118, 160, 164, 244, 278
BALLARD, 111, 179, 202, 213, 214, 216, 276
Ballard, WA., 6, 38, 134, 200
Ballard-Ludlow Ferry Co., 212-3, 218
Ballard Line, 88
Ballard Marine Railway, 88, 133, 137, 184

Ballast Island, 12
Baltimore Steam Packet Co., 197
Banff National Park, 68
Barber Steamship Line, 164, 283-4
Barlow Brothers, 84
Barlow elevator, 11, 38, 93, 181, 183, 187, 191
Barlow, Capt. George W., 84
Barlow, Capt. Harry, 11, 31, 38, 85*
Barlow, Capt. Samuel, 21, 28, 31, 87-8, 244, 310
Barrell, George, 197
Barrington, Capt. Harry, 173-4
Bartsch, Capt. George, 147-148
Bath, ME., 102, 199
Baxter, Bill, 190
BAY CITY, 254
Bayless, Casey, 331
Beach, Edward, 45
Beach Comber, The, 100
BEAR, U.S.R.C., 83
BEAVER, S.S., 11, 12
Beckwith, Mayor of Victoria, 58
Beebe, Charles F., 20
Beecher, Capt. Herbert F., 20, 21
BEELINE, 135-6, 174, 249
BELANA, 186
Bella Bella, B.C., 21
Belle Rock, 39
Belleville, Ontario, Canada, 114
BELLINGHAM, barge, 23
BELLINGHAM, steamer (Ex-WILLAPA, EX-GENERAL
    MILES), 21, 23, 28, 74
Bellingham, WA., 3, 21, 28, 38-9, 101, 133, 160, 182, 191, 214
Bellingham Bay Transportation Company, 21
Bellingham Chamber of Commerce, 100
Bellingham Transportation Co., 146
Benson, George, 38
Berg, J.E., 23
Berg, Richard, 314
Bergeon, A.S., 310
Bethlehem Shipbuilding Co., 250, 276
BIANCA, 120
Bibbins & Wiman, 115
Bibbins, Frank B., 115, 126
Bills, Allen, 310
Birse, I.D. (Bud), 310, 314
Bishop, Charles F., 46-7, 50, 51
Bisset, Capt. A.R., 120
Black, Lloyd, 172
Black Ball Line, 15, 20-1, 23, 41, 51, 53, 121, 131, 164, 178,
    182-3, 189-91, 195, 203-4, 209, 211-3, 219-20, 222,
    225-6, 229, 231-2, 241-2, 244, 260-1, 274-6, 278-9,
    282, 284, 287, 293, 295-6, 298, 301-2, 305, 309, 311
Black Ball Ferries, Ltd., 311
Black Ball Freight Service, 183, 190, 278, 307

Black Ball Transport, Inc., 13, 31, 60, 63, 307, 309
Black Friday, 200
Black River, 146
Blaine, WA., 21
BLAKELY, tug, 208
Blakely Island, WA., 133
BLANCHE, 144
BLITHE SPIRIT, 310
Bloedel, J.H.196
Bloedel-Donovan Mills Co., 196
Blythe, Capt. C.C., 38*
Boeing Co., 229
Bogle, Lawrence, 196
Boldt, George H., 301-2
Boles, Joseph, 157
Bolton & Watt, 11
Borgholm Bada, Sweden, 41
Bothell Transportation Co., 146
Boxton, ND., 107
Boyd, Capt. George
Boyd, Capt. William, 208
Boyd, Fred, 243
Bremer, James, 83, 160
BREMERTON, 11, 113, 162
Bremerton, WA., 3, 83-4, 88, 92, 101, 104, 111, 115, 135, 160,
    183, 189, 209, 229, 242-3, 274-6, 279, 283, 286, 303
Bremerton Auto Freight, 182-3
Bremerton Car Ferry, 89
Bremerton Naval Shipyard, 166, 209-10, 216, 225, 260-1,
    274, 279, 309
Breyman, C.R., 89
Briscoe, Ray, 243-4
Brit, Walter, 38
British Columbia Marine Railway, 73
Bronson, Ira, 164, 196
Brooklyn, N.Y., 15
Brown, Joe, 241
Browner, Capt. George, 38
Brownfield, Capt. J.C., 78-9
Bryant, Walter C. & Co., 178
Buffalo, NY., 166
Bullene, Capt. George, 8
Burckhardt, Charles A., 118, 154, 157
Bureau of Navigation & Steamboat Inspections, 208
Burnham, Capt. A.B., 38
Burns, Frank E., 25, 45-6, 102, 200
Burnside, B.L., 155
Burrard's Inlet, 12
BURTON, 108, 126, 133
Burton, Vashon Island, WA., 115, 125, 161
Busch-Sulzer diesel engine, 52, 229, 232
''Business Man's Express'', 47
Byers, Alpheus, 121, 157, 163
Byers, Elizabeth, 163

Byers Brothers, 184
Byrdsen, Capt. Charles, 58

C.C. CALKINS, 143-4
Cable car, 147
Calhoun, Dr., 38
California Association of Port Authorities, 284
California Gold Rush, 9, 102, 199
California Marine Council, 204
CALISTA, 116-7, 184
CALISTOGA, 250, 259, 299
Calkins, Charles, 143
Calvert, William, 196
CAMANO, 184
Camano Island, WA.168
Campbell, Lynn, 157
Canadian Dept. of Marine and Fisheries, 182
Canadian Pacific Navigation Company, 74
Canadian Pacific Railway, 21, 46-7, 60, 67-8, 73-4, 77-9,
    95, 100-01, 131, 143, 188, 307, 311
Cannon Falls, MN., 107
Canora, Manitoba, Canada 16
Cape Blanco, 53
Cape Flattery, 6, 137, 274
CAPITOL, 186, 191
CAPITOL CITY, 102, 199
Carlander, Clarence, 155, 157, 184-5, 193, 211
Carroll, Dan, 59
Carroll, H.J., 176
Carson, D.B., 100
Carter, Capt. Henry, 28
Cary, George R., 155
Case, I.H., 162
Case, Margaret, 162
CATHLAMET, 318
Cedar River, 146
CENTENNIAL QUEEN, 276
CENTRAL, 94, 168, 171
CENTRAL II, 138-9, 168, 170, 249
CENTRAL IV, 174
Central Ferry Co., 168, 172-3, 175
Central Pacific Railway, 249
CHACO, 184-6
CHALCEDONY, 183
CHARLES H. MARSHALL, 15
Charleston, WA., 83-4, 92
CHELAN, 318
Chemainus, B.C., 17
CHETZEMOKA, 261, 264, 275, 314
Chicago, IL., 45
Chicago, Milwaukee & St. Paul Railway, 188
Chicago and South Haven Steamship Company, 58
CHICKAREE, 167

Chilkoot Trail, 25
CHIMICUM, 191
Chin Ling, 71
CHINOOK, 60, 287-90, 292, 298, 301, 310-1
CHINOOK II, 311
Chinook, WA., 84
CHIPPEWA, 45, 47, 50-6, 58, 74, 77-8, 83-4, 91, 95, 160,
    178, 226, 229, 232, 241-2, 249, 261, 275, 310, 314
CHIPPEWA II, 50
Chittendan Locks, Hiram, 6, 100, 154
CHRYSOPOLIS, 53, 249
Citizen's Dock, 182, 191
Citizen's Light & Power Co. (Ketchikan), 23
Citizens Utilities Co., 214
CITY OF ANACORTES, 133
CITY OF ANGELES, 80, 95-6, 100, 132-3, 197, 249
CITY OF BELLINGHAM, 249
CITY OF BOTHELL, 146, 152
CITY OF BREMERTON, 89, 91-2, 94, 197, 241, 249
CITY OF CLINTON, 174
CITY OF DENVER, 39-40, 102
CITY OF EDMONDS, 95, 98
CITY OF EVERETT, 116, 206
CITY OF KINGSTON, 18-9, 249
CITY OF MUKILTEO, 174, 249
CITY OF QUINCY, 41
CITY OF RENTON, 146
CITY OF SACRAMENTO, 250, 259, 271, 278-9, 310
CITY OF SEATTLE, 2-3, 5-8, 25-6, 78, 88
CITY OF STEILACOOM, 126, 129
CITY OF TACOMA, 94
CITY OF TACOMA (II), 123-4, 126
CITY OF TOPEKA, 208
CITY OF VICTORIA, 197-8
Clair, Donald, 53
CLALLAM, 45, 66, 68-71, 73, 303
Clallam Bay, 21
Clallam County, WA. , 71
CLARA BROWN, 114, 116, 124
CLATAWA, 138-9, 140, 166-7, 169, 249
Clay, Eula, 46
Clay Street Pier, San Francisco, 53
Clayton, New York, 146
Clifford, S.G., 197
Clinton, WA., 138, 168
Clough, William, 19
Coast Steamship Company, 20
Coffin, Capt. Everett B., 49-50
Coffman, Miles, 38
COHO, 307-9
Coleman, Jimmy M., 144
Collector of Customs, 100
Collinsville, CA., 53
Colman, James, 146, 182

Colman, Kenneth, 157
Colman Dock, 84, 135, 146, 160, 181-3, 196, 211, 231, 240-4, 279, 287, 303, 310
Colman Dock Co., 146, 182
Columbia & Puget Sound Railroad, 144
COLUMBIA, bark, 11
COLUMBIA QUEEN, 15
Columbia River, 11, 13, 19, 84, 89, 155
Columbia River and Puget Sound Navigation Company, Inc., 49
Columbia Steamship Co., 53
Colvin boiler (marine), 168
COMANCHE, 91, 213, 249
COMMANDER, 189-90, 213
Commercial Club of Tacoma, 58
COMMISSIONER, 261, 274
Commissioner of Navigation, Dept. of Commerce, Wash. D.C., 100
Congress of Industrial Organization (CIO), 217
Consolidated Builders, Inc., 299
CONSTITUTION, steamer, 67
CONSTITUTION, U.S.S., 53
Cookson, S.A., 231
Coolidge, L.H., 94, 134, 137, 168
Coombs, Judge Samuel F., 208
Coombs, William Mortimer, 206, 208
Coos Bay, Oregon, 20, 261
Copper River & Northwestern Railroad Co., 196
Corbet, Jackson B., 153-4, 157, 165, 216, 287
Cornell University, 283-4
Coronel, Chile, 46, 57
CORSAIR, yacht, 47
Coryell, George, 184
Coupeville, Whidbey Island, WA., 102, 199
Craig's Shipbuilding Co. (Shipyard), 46, 50, 56
Craig, George L., 50
Craig, John, 50
Craven, Donald, 53
CREOLE, 225
CREST, 124
Crosby, Capt. Harry W., 101, 131-5
Crosby, Roy W., 132-4
Crosby Direct Ferry Lines, 126, 134-5, 249
Crosby Marine Corporation, 133
CROSLINE, 122, 134, 136, 249, 274, 314
Crowley, Larry, 94
CROWN CITY, 317
Crown Zellerbach, 60, 63
Cunningham, Allan, 197
Cunningham, Ross, 302
Cushman, Judge E.E., 130
Cut Throat Bay, 124
CYRENE, 145-46

D.T. DENNY, 110
Daggett, H.L., 294
Dalles, Portland & Astoria Navigation Company, The, 88-9
Danforth, Manly, 8
Davis, James A., 130
Daw, Joe, 190
Day, W.P., 251
Deal, Clyde W., 211, 213, 217
DECEPTION PASS, 137-8
Deception Pass Bridge, 138
DEFIANCE, 110, 126-7, 129-31, 276
Delauney, Scott A., 69, 71
DENALI, 193
Denny, Capt. Sam, 36, 40
Denny, Henry, 36
Denver, CO.177
Deppman, C.F., 183
DES MOINES, 115
Detroit, MI., 45, 166
Detroit Trust Co., 60
Dieckhoff, E.W., 144
Dimond, C.L., 27
DIRIGO, 25, 27
Disappointment Slough, 53
Divine, Dr. Samuel L., 216
Dockton, WA., 95, 115
DODE, steamer, 21-2, 184
Dodge, Iowa, 196
Dodwell Line & Co., 94
Doheny, G.W., 69-70
DOLPHIN, 25-6, 73
Doney, Capt. William, 21
Dore, Mayor of Seattle, 219
Dority, Capt. Frank, 58
DOROTHY, 147
Doyle, Capt. Patrick, 114
Drakes Bay, 53
Driggs, Capt. Norman L., 133
Dudley, England, 166
Duncan, Capt., 18
Dungeness Spit, 70
Dunsmuir, Robert, 16-7
Durban, Gov. W.K., 46
Dutch Harbor, AK., 110
Duthie, J.F., 150
J.F. Duthie & Co., 162
Duthie Shipbuilding Yard, 150
DUWAMISH, fireboat, 23
Duwamish Head, 5-6, 243
Duwamish River, 134, 146, 162
Dyea, AK., 19

E.D. SMITH, 39
Eagle Harbor, Bainbridge Is., WA., 283
Eagle Harbor Transportation Co., 150, 166, 221
Easter, E.J., 147
EASTERN CLOUD, 164, 283-5
East River Pier, N.Y., 15
East Seattle Hotel, 144
East Waterway, 150
Echo pilotage, 31, 34
Eddy, John W., 118
EDITH, 21, 147, 241
Edmonds, WA., 197
Edmonds-Victoria Co., 197
Edmonds City Council, 178
EFFORT, 146
Eikum, Arnold F. (Spike), 306-7, 314
EL CAPITAN, 249
EL PASO, 250, 259
Electric Bond & Share Co., 196
Elevators
    Barlow marine, 11
    general discussion, 10
ELIZA ANDERSON, 166
ELK, ferry, 126, 128, 134
Ellicott, Maryland, 35
Elling, H., 17
Elliott Bay, 3, 12, 23, 51, 53, 100, 154
Elliott Bay Drydock Co., 184
Elliott Bay Towing Co., 83
Ellis, Capt. W.H., 83
Elwell, Capt. E.B., 124
Elwell-Parker lift trucks, 187, 191
ELWHA, 261, 264, 318
Embree, Jack, 307
EMILY KELLER, 147
Empire, OR., 260
Emmons, E.E., 38
Empress Hotel, Victoria, B.C., 68
EMPRESS ships, 68
ENETAI, 266, 274-5, 314-5
Esary, George W., 197
ESARY, JAMES, 184
Esquimalt, B.C., 73, 95
ESTELLA, 115
Estep, A.C., 163
EUREKA, 250
EVANGEL, 34
Evans, Daniel Jackson, 27
Everett, WA., 116-7, 184
Everett Tug & Barge Co., 60
Evergreen Floating Bridge, 155, 157
EVERGREEN STATE, 318, 320
Eyers, Walter, 190

F.E. LOVEJOY, 193
F.G. REEVE, 166-7
F.H. MARVIN, 186, 192
Fairbanks, Douglas, 78-9
Fairbanks-Morse engine, 23, 38, 60, 123, 126-7, 132-3
FAIRHAVEN, 37, 39, 169, 181, 183-4199, 241
FALCON, 108, 184
Falk, Peter, 36, 40-1
FANNY LAKE, 36, 38, 41
Farley, E.P. & Co., 284
FARRALON, 25
Fauntleroy, WA., 162
Fenner, E.B., 274
Ferry Building, San Francisco, CA., 250, 252
Ferryboat
    definition, 3
    double-ended, 10
    first on Puget Sound, 3
Ferryboat, def. (legal), 172
Ferryboatmen's Union, 157, 204, 208, 210-12, 217
Ferry Dock Co., 181, 188, 196, 200
Ferry Riders Association, 293
Ferry Users Committee, 221
First
    auto across Puget Sound, 83, 85
    cable car, 143
    diesel-powered autoferry, Puget Sound, 161
    drive-on, drive-off ferry, 95
    female ferry operator, 137
    female steamboat licenses, 115
    female wireless operator, 50
Fisherman's Wharf, San Francisco, CA., 250
Fitzgerald, William J., 42
Fitzpatrick, J.P., 197
Fleishhacker, Herbert, 197
FLORENCE K., 126, 167
FLYER, 21, 47-49, 241
Folger, Charles H., 15-16
Ford, W.T., 196
FOREST PRIDE, 104
FORTUNA, 91, 94, 147-8, 152
Foshay, Julianne, 197
Foshay, Wilbur Burton, 23, 195-7, 200-1, 251
Foshay, W.B., Co., 195-6, 200, 212
Foss, George, 193
Foss Launch & Tug Co., 53
Founders Syndicate, 196
Four Mile Island, 31
Four Winds Restaurant, Seattle, 276
Fowler, Capt. Lyle, 60, 306
FOX ISLAND, (EX-WOLLOCHET), 126, 129, 176
Fox Island, WA.131
Fox Island Clay Works, 124
Fox, Capt. John M., 157, 204-6, 208, 211, 214, 221, 296, 305

Francis, Capt. George, 19
Franklin, S.R., 157
Franks, E.L., 157
Fraser River, B.C., 110
Frese, Capt. Charles F., 275
FRESNO, 250, 257, 274
Friday Harbor, WA., 83
FULTON, 94
Furth, Jacob, 36, 147-8

GABRIOLA, schooner, 21
Gaines, William A., 204-5, 211
Gaines Board of Arbitration, 204-5, 211-13, 216
GALLOPING GERTIE, 130
Gard, Patrick, 8
GARDEN CITY, 5
GARLAND, 32, 34, 67, 83
Gatzert, Bailey, 35
GAZELLE, 147-8
Gazzam, Warren L., 108, 111, 121, 159-60
GENERAL CANBY, steamer, 19
GENERAL CUDAHY, 206
GENERAL FRISBIE, 189
GENERAL MILES, 19-20
General Motors engines, 287, 318, 324
General Strike, 91
GEORGE E. STARR, 21, 39, 41, 42
GEORGE W. ELDER, 143
Gibbs & Cox, 287
Gibbs, William Francis, 287
Gibson, Capt. J.S., 111
GIG HARBOR, 126, 128
Gig Harbor, WA., 124, 126, 128, 130
Gillespie, Capt. Harry, 19
Gilman, W.C., & Co., 300
Glacier National Park, 68
GLEANER, 132, 184
GLORIA, 135
Goff, John D., 28
GOLDEN AGE, 250, 260-1
GOLDEN BEAR, 250, 260-1
GOLDEN CITY, 250
GOLDEN COAST, 250
GOLDEN DAWN, 250
GOLDEN ERA, 250
GOLDEN GATE, 250
GOLDEN POPPY, 250, 260-1
GOLDEN SHORE, 250, 260-1
GOLDEN STATE, 250, 260-1, 265
GOLDEN WAY, 250
GOLDEN WEST, 250, 260
Golden Gate Bridge, 251
Golden Gate Ferry Co., 249-51, 260, 276

Golden Gate International Exposition, 251
GOLIAH, 23, 162, 276
Gordon, Bob, 161
Gottenberg, Sweden, 143
GOV. HARRY W. NICE, 317
GOV. HERBERT R. O'CONOR, 317
GOV. NEWELL, 115
GRACE, 166
Grady, A.C., 176
Graham, Harold, 60, 63, 150, 293
Grand Trunk Dock, 181, 188, 196, 200
Grande, Capt. Henry C., 60, 306
Gray, Capt. John Henry D., 19
Gray, Capt. Robert , 19
Grays Harbor, WA., 19-20, 186, 206
Great Lakes, 45, 50, 56, 58, 60
Great Northern Express Co., 110
Great Northern Railroad, 77, 160, 188
Great Western Iron & Steel Works, 35
Great White Fleet, 51, 77
Green, Hal, 35
Green, J.A., 174
Green, Joshua, 35-6, 38-9, 41-2, 45, 58, 73, 77-8, 84, 88,
    102, 104, 108, 121, 146-7, 157, 159-60, 164, 167, 182,
    184, 199-200, 225, 249
  birth/early years, 35-6
  investment in Puget Sound Day Line, 45-6
  organization of Inland Navigation Co., 41
  organization of L.T.T., 36
  resignation from P.S.N., 104
Green, W.H.H., 35
Green, Wagan, & Green, 11
Green, Walter, 31, 59-60, 92, 191, 229, 305, 307
Greenbaum, W.K., 46
Gregg, George, 59
GREYHOUND, 84, 102-3, 241
Gribble, Ernest, 302
Griffiths, Capt. James, 178
Griffiths, James & Sons, 305
Grounds, Henry, 38
GUARD, U.S.R.C., 83
GUEMES, 94
Guemes Channel, 39
Guerts, W.T., 221
Gunderson Brothers Engineering Corp., 318
Gunther, Earl, 211
Gustafson, John, 60
GYPSEY QUEEN, 124

H.B. KENNEDY, 84, 88-9, 102, 199, 241
H.B. LOVEJOY, 184-5
Hadley, Homer, 157
HALCYON, 170

Hall, Capt. L.J., 155
Hallanger, Capt. Don, 53
Hamilton, Capt. Frank E.45
Hanks, Mayor C.A., 134
Hannaford, J.M., 78
Hansen, Capt. J.J., 107
Hansen, Capt. A., 28
Hansen, Henry A., 107, 111, 159
Hansen, O.L., 107, 111, 159
Hansen Transportation Co., 107-8
Hanson, H.C., 286
Harbor Island, 3, 287
Harbor Tug & Barge Co., 226
Harkins Transportation Co., 191
Harnett, (artist), 88
Harrison, Pres. Benjamin, 108, 144
Harston, Millard T., 100
HARVESTER KING, 132
Haskell & Crawford Yard, 115
Hastings, Capt. L.B., 144
Hastings Steamboat Co., 20
Hatfield, Lloyd, 172
HATTIE HANSEN, 107
Hauan, Reuban, 197
Hawley, Dwight, 134
HAYWARD, 250-1, 298-9
Heath Shipyard, Tacoma, 25, 68
Heidelberg University, Germany, 15
HELEN, 83-4
Hemrich, Andrew, 148
HENRY BAILEY, 35-36, 41
Hibbs, McCauley & Smith, 231
Hile, Hoof, Shucklin Attys, 295
Hill, Capt. Minnie, 115
Hinckley, Lyman D., 94, 108, 110-1, 118, 120, 153, 159
Hinckley, T.D., 108, 110
Hinckley Block, 108
Hiram Chittendon Locks, Ballard, 6, 100
Historic Seattle Preservation & Development Authority,
    (H.S.P.D.A.), 276
HIYU, 118-120, 213, 318, 325
Hoboken, N.J., 51, 57
Hoffman, Fergus, 310
Hogan, J.P., 314
Holbrook, Capt. R.B., 89
Holland, John J., 88
Home, Capt. D., 11
Hood Canal, 101, 140, 283
Hoodsport, WA., 83
Hopkins, Hazel L., 118
Horluck Transportation Co., 175, 183, 315
Hostmark, Capt. A., 107, 111, 159
Houghton, (Kirkland) WA., 6, 95, 118, 144, 147, 152
Hubbard, Edward, 134

Hudson's Bay Co., 11, 13
Humboldt Bay, CA., 274
Hunes, Samuel J., 157
Hunt, A.M., 124, 126
Hunt, A.R., 124, 126
Hunt, Emmet E., 124
Hunt, F.M., 124
Hunt, James R., 67
Hunt, L.B., 124, 126
Hunt Bros. Boat Yard, 126
Hunter, Capt. J.C., 143
Hunziker, Stanley, 169
Hutchinson, Kansas, 196
HYAK, 106, 108, 110-1, 189
HYAK, (Super class ferries), 318, 324
HYAK's PUP, 111
Hyde St. Pier, San Francisco, CA., 250

ILLAHEE, 244, 270, 274-5, 314, 317
Illwaco Navigation Co., 19
Independent Ferry Co., 197, 200
Independent Ferry Lines, 155
INDIAN, 191, 193
INDIANAPOLIS, 44-9, 50-1, 57, 73-5, 84, 91, 177, 226, 249,
    309
Indiana Transportation Co., 46
Ingersoll-Rand engine, 261
Inland Boatmen's Union of the Pacific, 204, 217, 221, 293
INLAND FLYER, 39, 41, 84, 102, 145-6, 160, 167, 199
Inland Navigation Co., 21, 41, 49
Inter-American Navigation Co., 284, 286
Interlaken Steamboat Co., 148
International Longshoreman's Association, 210
International Steamship Co., 45
International Stevedoring Co., 111
International Workers of the World (I.W.W.), 116
IOLA, 241
IOWA, U.S.S., 84
Irondale, WA., 108
IROQUOIS, 45, 47, 50, 56-61, 63-4, 74, 83-4, 91, 105, 181,
    213, 232, 244, 249, 287-8, 309
Island County, WA., 172-3
Island Transportation Co., 116, 169, 184
ISLANDER, 162, 276
ISSAQUAH class, 318, 328-9
ISSAQUAH, steam ferry, 150-1
Isthmian Line, Inc., 53

J.B. LIBBY, 20
Jackson, D.B., 17, 25, 27-28
Jackson, Mississippi, 35
James, Capt. J.R., 155

James, Frank D., 157
JAMES MONROE, Black Ball packet, 15
JEFFERSON, 25-26, 73
Jenkins, V.S., 206
Jensen, Capt. "Chilkat," 19
Jensen, Capt. Ed, 8
Jitney ferry, 3
JOHN CUDAHY, 110
JOHN ENA, 204
Johnson & Higgins Average Adjustors, 57
Johnson, Capt. John J., 46, 57-58
Johnson, J.V., 146
Johnson, Mark, 146
Johnson, Capt. William, 167
Johnson Yard, Port Blakely, WA. 95
Johnston, Harry H., 130, 214
Jones Act, U.S. Government, 74
JOSEPHINE, 13, 124
Joyce, Alfred R., 168
Joyce, Arthur, 168
Joyce, Clarence J., 168
Joyce, Capt. O., 168, 200
Joyce, Percy, 168
Juneau, AK., 19, 143

KAHLOKE, 271, 278, 310-2
KALAKALA, 23, 60, 216, 218, 224, 229-47, 260, 275, 309,
    314
KALEETAN (Super class ferry), 318, 322
Kalispell, Montana, 110
Kalstrom, Capt. Charles E., 21
Kasch, Frank, 133
Kasch, William H., 133
Kasch Transportation Co., 133
Kayo, Felix, 38
KEEWEENAH, 208
KEHLOKEN, 261-2, 274-5, 278, 314
Kelsall, A.L., 38
Kennedy, H.B., 39, 84, 104, 199
Ketchikan, AK., 19, 23, 168, 195
Ketchikan Cold Storage, 23
Key Route System, 225-6, 231, 250-1
Keyport, WA., 260, 278
Keystone Landing, 176
King & Winge Shipbuilding Co., 23, 38, 118, 167
King & Winge Shipyard, 121, 138
King, James, 118
King, R.M., 188
King, T.J., 38
KING COUNTY, 147-8
King County, WA., 6-7, 94, 111, 114, 117, 149-50, 153-4,
    156-7, 160-2, 218-9
King County Board, 155

King County Ferry District, 314
King County Improvement Clubs, 300
King County Superintendent of Transportation, 153
King Island, Bering Sea 53
KINGSTON, 110, 166-7, 169
Kingston Transportation Co.
    organization, 110
Kirby, Frank E., 50
KIRKLAND, 144-5
Kirkland, WA., 149
Kirkland Fire Dept., 162
KITSAP of Seattle, ferry, 111, 117, 162-5, 225, 314
KITSAP (Issaquah class), 304, 318
KITSAP, steamer, 49, 108-9, 159, 160,
KITSAP II, 88-9, 108-9, 197
Kitsap County Transportation Co., 6, 8, 49, 94, 104, 108,
    111, 114, 117-8, 120-3, 135, 153, 155, 159-60, 162-3,
    165-6, 174, 181-2, 189-90, 195-7, 200-01, 203-4, 211-14,
    225
    change of officers/Anderson, (1924), 120
    controlling interests/reorganization (1905), 108, 111
    officers, (1905), 111
    organization of Ferry Dock Co., 181
    purchase of Poulsbo Transportation Co., 118
    sale to Foshay, 196
    sale to P.S.N., 214
KITTITAS, 318, 329
KLAHANIE, 256, 261, 263, 314
KLAHOWYA, 318, 321
KLAMATH, 250
KLICKITAT, 268, 270, 274-5, 314, 317, 331
Klondike, 10, 13, 19, 25, 39, 67-68, 110
KLONDYKE, 110
Knight, Leslie, 157
Kodiak, AK., 246
Kohl, J.G., 95
Kootenay, B.C., 166
Kraft, Capt., 107
KULSHAN (I), 60
KULSHAN, 249, 305, 317, 320
Kunkler, Capt. B.P., 157

L.P. HASFORD, 191
L.T. HAAS, 148-9, 184
Lacey V. Murrow Memorial Bridge (Mercer Island), 155, 157
LACONNER, sternwheeler, 36, 39
LaConner, WA., 36, 38, 114
LaConner Trading & Transportation Co., 36, 38-40, 73, 84,
    146, 183
    organization, 36
    stockholders, 39-40
    sale, 39
Ladd & Tilton, 17

LADY OF THE LAKE, 5, 146
LaFarge, Charles V., 19, 196, 277, 295
LAKE CONSTANCE, 140-1
Lake Louise, 68
Lake Ontario, 56
Lake Sammamish, 144
LAKE TAHOE, 248, 250-1, 274
Lake Union, Seattle, 6, 100, 108, 154, 283
Lake Union Dry Dock & Machine Works, 23
Lake Union Dry Dock Co., 94
Lake Washington, 6, 8, 78, 91, 94, 98, 100, 107, 118, 137,
     143, 146-7, 149-50, 153-7, 159, 161, 219
Lake Washington Cable Railway, 143
Lake Washington Ferries, 155-7, 212, 218
Lake Washington Land & Improvement Co., 143
Lake Washington Ship Canal, 6, 100, 134, 152, 154
Lake Washington Shipyard, 50, 60, 95, 115, 118, 120, 148,
     163-4, 191, 195, 197, 201, 229, 241, 261
Landes, Mayor Bertha K., 178
Landweer, Robert E., 53
Langlie, Gov. Arthur B., 300-2, 305, 317
Langley, WA., 169
Larsen, Joseph, 38-39
Lawrence, Capt. Tom, 71
Leach, George C., 174
Leary, John, 88
Lee & Brinton, 162
Lee, Edward, 147
Lee, Capt. Oscar, 176
Leighton, Capt. Bush, 176, 197
Lemolo, WA., 118
Lent, George, 17-18, 20, 45-46, 157
Leonard, Capt., 19
LESCHI, steamer, 146
LESCHI, ferry, 94, 142, 150-1, 157, 314-5
Leschi Park, 143, 147
Lewis & Clark Centennial (1905), 89
Lewis, Harry H., 294
Libby, Capt. Elmer E., 208
LIBERTY, autoferry, 94-5, 111-2, 118, 200
LIBERTY, steamer, 111
Liberty Bay, WA., 107
Liberty Bunch, WA., 107
Liberty Place, WA., 107
Lieseke, Mary, 175
Lift-truck operation, 187
LINCOLN, 94, 150-1, 153, 157, 314
Littleton, Rose, 178
Livingston, Capt. John, 47
Lloyd's Transfer, 190
Locomobile Co. of Seattle, 133
Lonergan, Charles R., 211, 305
Long Beach, CA., 162
Long Branch, WA., 138

Lorenz, Otto, 200
Los Angeles Harbor Dept., 161, 276
LOTTIE, 114
Lovejoy, Capt. Bart H., 168-9, 174, 183
Lovejoy, E.D., 183
Lovejoy, Capt. F.E. (Ed), 181, 183-4, 186, 191, 193, 196, 213,
     216
Lovejoy, Capt. Howard Bartlett, 116, 169, 183
Lovejoy, Capt. Howard Bentley, 183
Lovejoy, Howard, 191, 193
Lovejoy, L.B., 183
Lovejoy, Gretchen, 168
Lovejoy, Thomas E., 193
Ludlow-Kingston Transportation Co., 200
Luna Park, 5
Luna Park Natatorium, 5, 7
Lund, Ole, 184
LURA MAUD, 9
LYDIA THOMPSON, 21-22, 34, 83, 102, 160, 199
Lynch, Walter, 157
Lynn Canal, 27

M'Donald, State Sen. Robert T., 12
McAlpine, Captain A.N., 28, 47
McAteer, John, 162
McAteer Shipbuilding Co., 161-2
Macbride, Philip D., 94, 108, 111, 118, 157, 172, 181, 186,
     213-14
Macbride, Dr. Thomas, 111
McCaulay, Lilly, 16-17
McCaulay, William, 16-17
McClure, Capt. Charles C., 50
McCormick Co., Charles R., 178
McCormick Steamship Co., 184, 186
McDonald, D.J., 21
McDougall, Capt. Al, 38
McDowell, Floyd, 305-6, 314
MACKINAC, 50
Mackinac Island, MI. 50, 56
McMillan, Bloedel & Powell River Co., 17
McMillan, Capt. Bert, 8
McMillan, John S., 133
McNealy, A.L., 78-79
McNeil Island, WA., 131
Madison Park, 146-7, 149
Madison Street ferrydock, 11
MAGNOLIA, 126
Maine, State of, 45, 102
MAJESTIC, 34, 67-68, 73
MALAHAT, 272, 276, 310
Mangan, Capt. Gregory W., 242
Mangan, Capt. Jerry W. (I), 242
Mangan, Capt. Jerry W., 242

Mangan, Capt. Wallace H., 89, 91, 229, 232, 241-3, 309
MANHATTEN, 15
Manson, Harry E., 115, 214
Manson, John, 115
Manson, Peter, 115
Manson Construction Co., 115, 214
Manson, P. & Son, 115, 128, 176
MARIECHEN, 184
Marine Auto Freight Lines, Inc., 190
Marine Boiler Works, Toledo, OH., 58
Marine Construction Co., 134
Marine Engineer's Beneficial Association (M.E.B.A.), 204,
    206, 208, 293
Marine Power & Equipment, 318
Marion Street ferrydock, 4, 5, 111, 162, 181, 283, 321
Maritime Agencies Co., 283
Maritime Association, 155
Maritime Labor Board, 221
Markey Plant, 178
Marsh, Capt. Harry, 108
Marshall, Alexander C., 15
Marshall, Benjamin, 15
Marshall, Charles H., 15
Marshall, Edward C., 15
Martin, Gov. Clarence D., 216, 219
Martin, Hugh, 157
Martin, M.O., 307
Martinez & Benecia Ferry & Transportation Co., 8
Martinolich Yard, 95, 115, 167, 169
MARY F. PERLEY, 241
Mary Island, AK., 21
Mason, Capt. E.S., 38-39
Masters, Mates and Pilots Organization, 204, 208-10,
    212-13, 217, 293
Matson, Capt. Robert, 148, 150-1
MAUD, steamer, 71
MAUD FOSTER, 108
Maupin's University School, 35
Maxwell, Capt. Charles K., 133
MAY B. 2, 110
Medicine Hat, Alberta, 307
Meeker, Ezra, 41-42
Meinton Co., Inc., 299
MELROSE, 250
MENDOCINO, 251, 274-5
MERCER, ferryboat, 157, 161, 276
MERCER, sternwheeler, 147, 149
Mercer Island, WA., 143-4, 146, 155
Mercer Island Floating Bridge (Lacey V.Murrow), 155, 157
Merchant's Bank, 17
Merchant's Steamship Co., 19
Merchant's Transportation Co., 38, 186
MESSENGER, 114, 124
Metropolitan Electric Railway Co., 35

MEXICO, 208
Miller, David W., 206
Milton (West Seattle), 3
Milwaukee Dock, 188
Minneapolis, MN., 195-6
Mitchell, Emerson, 102, 199
Mitchell, Lewis Motors Co., 133
Mitchell, Capt. William E., 102, 197, 199, 200
Mitchell, W.J., 299
Mock, George, 310
Mock La Push, 146
Moe, Capt., 107
Moe Brothers, 107
MOHAWK, 188, 190-1
MOLLIE K., 133
MONONGAHELA, 283
Monroe, Capt. Joseph A., 8
MONTICELLO, 111, 118, 202, 209
Monticello Steamship Co., 250, 276
Montevideo, Uruguay, 57
Moore Shipbuilding Co., 231
Moore Dry Dock Co., 298-9, 317
Moran, Alice, 118
Moran, Robert, 33, 118, 206
Moran, Sherman, 118, 120
Moran Brothers, 110, 149
Morgan, J.P., 47
MORNING STAR, 31
Morre's Dock, 27
Morrice, William B., 307
Mosquito Fleet, 3-4, 12, 78, 123, 181, 191, 305
MOTOR PRINCESS, 95, 97, 100-1
MOUNTAINEER, 84, 166
MOUNT VERNON, 95-6, 100, 133, 176, 197, 249
Mount Vernon, WA., 133
Muckley, Joseph C., 303
Mukilteo, WA., 173, 182
MULTNOMAH, 84
MURIEL, 120
Murley, Bert S., 120-1, 157
Murphy, James E., 229-30, 232, 274

N.C. Price Construction Co., 152
Nafin & Levy, 168
Nanaimo, B.C., 131
NAPA VALLEY, 250, 271, 276
NARADA, 200
Natchess Pass, 108
National Labor Relations Board, 222
National Maritime Museum, 250
National Recovery Act, 210
National Steel & Shipbuilding Co., 318
National War Labor Board, 293

Naval Torpedo Station, 260, 278
Navy Yard Route, Inc., 84, 88, 95, 101-2, 104, 124, 183, 197, 199, 200, 211
Neah Bay, 21, 25, 180
Neah Bay Dock Co., 182
Nearhoff, Capt. Willis, 138, 168, 172-3, 175
Neider & Marcus, 21
Neifie & Levy, 47
NELLIE, steamer, 3
Nelseco engines, 287
Nelson, Charles E., 211
Nelson, Charles & Co., 283
Nelson Steamship Co., 307
Neptune's Barge, 23
NEPTUNE, 15, 261
Nevada, State of, 25
Newcastle, England, 73
New London, CT., 16
NEW ORLEANS, 250
New Westminster, B.C., 12, 110
New York Central Railroad, 196
NEWPORT, 250
Niagara & St. Lawrence Navigation Company, 56
Nibbe, Capt. John H., 84
Nicholaye, Rev. Father, 17
Nichols Bros., 175
Nichols, Capt. Melville, 17-9
Nickum, W.C., & Sons, 261, 299-300, 318
NISQUALLY, 269, 274-5, 314, 317
NORCO, (Ex-barge BELLINGHAM), 23, 200
Nord, Capt. J.G., 18-9
Nordstrom, Carl, 135
NORMANDIE, S.S., 240
Northern Pacific Railway Company, 19, 47, 49, 77, 78
NORTHLAND, 200, 206
Northland Transportation Co., 23, 195, 200
Northwest Rivers and Harbors Congress, 284
Northwest Seaport, 276
Northwestern Electric Co., 196
Northwestern Iron Works, 38
Northwestern Pacific Railroad, 250-1
Northwestern Steamship Co., 27
Northwestern Washington Community Council, 293-4, 296
NORWOOD, 115, 167
Nova Scotia, 110

O'Brien, Capt. John A. "Dynamite", 25, 177
O'Connor, Capt. J.C., 147
O'Neill, James, 8
Oak Harbor, Whidbey Island, WA., 137
Oakes, Walter, 17, 34, 41
OAKLAND, 249, 254

Oakland, CA., 226, 232
Oceanic Steamship Co., 208
OHIO, 133
Oland, Esther, 134
Oliver, Capt. J.L., 8
Olson, Agaton, 137-8
Olson, Berte H., 137-8, 140-1, 301
Olson Bros., 137
Olympia, WA., 12, 16, 27, 114, 138, 172, 188, 193, 286, 298
OLYMPIAN, 208
OLYMPIC, 101, 103, , 197, 249, 274
OLYMPIC (Ex-GOV.HARRY NICE), 317, 319
Olympic Ferries, Inc., 176
Olympic Navigation Co., 140
ONEYANA, tug, 53
Orcas Island, WA., 132
OREGON, U.S.S., 84
Osborn, E.A., 310
Pacific American Fisheries, 214
Pacific Coast Association of Port Authorities, 284
Pacific Coast Engineering Company, 144
Pacific Coast Steamship Co., 17, 19, 67-8
Pacific Marine Supply Co., 178
Pacific National Bank, 183, 260
Pacific Steamship Co., 188
Pacific Towboat Company, 78
Pacific Wharf Co., 27, 182
    organization, 17
    stockholders, 17
Panama Canal, 58, 60, 197
Parker, Capt. Frank, 208, 283
Parr-McCormick, 184
Pasco, WA., 155
Patterson, Capt.
Paul, Judge Timothy A., 216, 219
Paul Arbitration Board, 217
Paulin, Col. George, 310
Payne, Capt. J. Howard, 51, 155, 157, 176-8, 184, 197, 200, 213
Peabody, Capt. Alexander Marshall, 17, 20, 23, 138, 140, 157, 164, 181, 183, 195-6, 204, 210, 213-4, 219-22, 225-6, 229-30, 241, 245, 260, 274, 276, 279, 283-4, 286-7, 293-9, 301-3, 309-11
    birth, 17
    early years/education, 164, 283
    association with Inter American Navigation Corp., 284
    organization of Founders Syndicate, 196
    presidency, P.S.N., 195, 284
    purchase of K.C.T.C., 214
    cessation of P.S.N. ferries, 297-8
    sale of P.S.N., 302-3

Peabody, Charles, 15-19, 25, 33-4, 37, 41, 45-7, 58, 73-4, 78, 104, 126, 159, 164, 182, 232
    birth/education, 15
    death, 104
    early years/marriage, 16-17
    organization of Alaska Steamship Co., 17, 19
    organization of Pacific Wharf Co., 17
    reorganization of Alaska Steam, 25
    reorganization of P.S.N., 41
Peabody, Cornelia Marshall, 15
Peabody, Capt. E.W., 15, 104
Peabody, E.W. (Woody), 81, 104, 283, 286
Peabody, Folger, 17
Peabody, Lilly, (Mrs. Charles), 242
Peabody, Laurance (Larry), 81, 229, 245, 283
Peabody, Marie (Mrs. Alexander), 284, 287
Peabody, Norman Penfield, 47
Pebble, H.A., 299
Peel, William, 206
Penfield, Capt. Howard, 21, 47, 89, 177, 309
People's Saving & Trust Co., 104
People's Savings Bank, 35
People's Wharf Co., 182
PERALTA, 225-7, 229, 231, 240, 243, 250, 260
Percival, John Cushing, 188
Percival, Capt. Samuel W., 188
Percival Dock, 188
Percival Dock Co., 186
PERDITA, 102, 241
Peterson, Albin L., 294
Peterson, Capt. Lyle, 306
Peterson, W.C., 143
Phinney, Henry L., 157
Pierce County, WA., 6, 124, 128, 130, 134, 214
PIERRE VICTORY, 53
Pierson, Capt. R.H., 276
Pierson, R.R., 196
Pilot's Association, 60
PIONEER, 94, 138-9, 170, 184, 197, 249
Pioneer Square, Seattle, 33
Piver, Jack, 203
Plattsville, IL., 120
POINT ARENA, 20, 143
Point Roberts, 21
Point Turner, WA., 83
Polytechnic Institute, Brooklyn, 15
Pope & Talbot, 102, 199
Port Angeles, WA., 25, 101, 182-3
Port Blakely, Bainbridge Island, WA., 95, 118, 147
Port Blakely Mill Co., 118
Port Castries, St. Lucia, 57
Port Gardner Bay, 116
PORTLAND, 28, 30

Portland, OR., 3, 19-20, 39-40, 88, 108, 143, 146, 159, 196, 276, 299
Portland Rose Festival, 89
Port Ludlow, WA., 200
Port of Olympia, 302
Port Ludlow Mill, 178
Port of Seattle, 149, 162, 164
PORT ORCHARD, 102-3, 199, 241
Port Orchard, WA., 83-4, 91-2, 183
Port Townsend, WA. 3, 16-7, 20, 25, 46, 51, 56-7, 67, 69, 71, 73, 94, 111, 114, 182, 206
POTLATCH, 91
Poulsbo, WA., 107, 111, 120
Poulsbo Transportation Co., 118, 184
Prahl, Charles, 314
PREMIER, 208
Price, Capt. Frank, 8
PRINCESS BEATRICE, 46, 66, 72-3
PRINCESS ELAINE, 76
PRINCESS MARGUERITE, 74, 79
PRINCESS ROYAL, 74,
PRINCESS VICTORIA, 47, 72-4, 76-8
PRINCESS ships, 77, 197
PRINCETON, 120
Proctor, Gardner, 143
PROSPER, 34, 184
Public Service Commission, 172
Public Works Administration, 156
PUGET, 95-6, 197, 249
Puget Sound Bridge & Drydock Co., 309, 318
Puget Sound Day Line, 45-6, 56
Puget Sound Dry Dock Co., 115
Puget Sound Freight Lines, 114, 138, 155, 181, 186, 188-9, 193, 195-6, 200, 211, 213
Puget Sound Freight & Ferry Co., 186
Puget Sound Marina, 23
Puget Sound Maritime Historical Society, 23, 41, 244, 309
Puget Sound Mill Co., 102, 199
Puget Sound Motor Freight Co., 184
Puget Sound National Bank, 35-6
Puget Sound Naval Shipyard, 166, 209-10, 216, 225, 260-1, 274, 279, 309
Puget Sound Navigation Company, 8, 23, 25, 28, 31, 34, 39, 41, 43, 45-6, 49-51, 56-7, 60, 63, 67-9, 71, 73-4, 77-9, 81, 83-4, 88-9, 91, 94-5, 100-02, 104, 108, 121, 123, 126, 131-3, 135, 138, 140-1, 152, 159-60, 164-6, 173-4, 176-8, 181-4, 188-90, 195-6, 200, 204, 208-12, 214, 218-20, 225, 229, 232, 241, 244-5, 249, 260, 274-5, 278-9, 283-4, 286-7, 293, 296-9, 301-03, 307, 310, 311
    organization 1898, 25
    organization of Black Ball Ferries, Ltd., 310-1
    organization of Black Ball Freight Service, 183
    organization of Bremerton Auto Freight, 89
    organization of Navy Yard Route, 84

property holdings (1929), 182
purchase of K.C.T.C., 212, 214
purchase of Washington Route and W.I.T. Co., 212
reorganization (1903), 41, 43
reorganization (1951), 310
routes-1940, list of, 274
sale to Canadian govt., 311
sale to Washington State, 302-3
strikes against, 210-22, 293-8
Puget Sound Terminal Co., 186
Puget Sound Power & Light Co., 155
Puget Sound Tug & Barge, 155, 226, 260-1, 276
Puget Sound Tug Boat Co., 69, 184
PULASKI, U.S.C.G.C., 260
Puyallup River, 126
Puyallup Valley, 12

Quartermaster Harbor, WA., 116
QUEEN, 172
QUEEN OF THE PACIFIC, 19
QUICKSTEP, 12, 107, 146
QUILCENE, 213, 232
QUILLAYUTE, 213, 176, 178, 249, 310-2
Quillayute River, 178
QUINAULT, 269, 274-5, 314, 317
Quinn, Ray, 276

Race, Capt. H.M., 144
Racine, WN., 133
RAINBOW, 137
RAINIER, tug, 143
RAINIER, yacht, 148
Rainier Brewing Co., 148
Ralston, William, 249
RAMONA, 147
Ramwell, Capt. Harry, 173-4
Ransome, J.S. & Co., 178
RAPID TRANSIT, 168
Rat Portage, Manitoba, Canada, 16
Ready, Lester S., 251
Reconstruction Finance Corp., 284
RED JACKET, 283, 285
REDWOOD EMPIRE, 251, 274
Reeve, Capt., F.G., 115, 166, 168
Regatta Reef, 21
Reliable Welding Co., 193, 286
RELIANCE, 107-8, 162
RELIEF, 128
Renton, WA., 155
Revelle, Paul, 294, 296-8
RHODODENDRON, 317, 319
RICHARD HOLYOKE, tug, 69-71, 208

Riddel, Alexander, 38
Rindal, Capt. Ole, 244
RIVER QUEEN, 273
River Queen Restaurant, 276
ROBERT BRIDGES, 133, 162, 168
ROBERT DOLLAR, 133
"ROBERT E. LEE", 276
Roberts, Capt. George, 17-9, 25, 45, 69, 71, 196
Roberts water tube boilers, 58
Robin Steamship Line, 283
Robinson's Landing, 144
Roche Harbor, WA. 38, 114, 132
Rockefeller, Nelson A., 284
Rodgers, Capt. George H., 144
Roemer, Kathleen, 240
Rogers, W.G., 155
Roosevelt, Pres. Franklin D., 210, 217
Roosevelt, Pres. Theodore, 44
ROSALIE, 21, 24-5, 27-9, 31, 37, 42, 67, 74, 77, 83, 244
ROSARIO, 232, 314
ROSE, U.S.L.T., 150
Routes,
   see also Washington State Ferries
   Alki-Manchester, 134, 211
   Anacortes-Friday Harbor-Bellingham, 133
   Anacortes-Guemes, 94
   Anacortes-San Juan Islands, 274
   Anacortes-San Juan Islands-Sidney, B.C., 53
   Anacortes-Sidney, 100-1, 135, 274
   Ballard-Kingston, 110, 134
   Ballard-Ludlow, 200
   Bellingham-Pt.Roberts-Lummi Is.-Blaine, 146
   Bellingham-Sidney, 95, 101
   Berkeley-Richmond, 251
   Bremerton-Manette, 94, 152, 160
   Bremerton-Port Orchard, 152, 160
   Chicago and South Haven Line, 56
   Clinton-Everett, 168
   Des Moines-Portage, 161
   Dog Fish Bay Run, 107-8
   East Pass Mail , 84
   Edmonds-Kingston, 134, 274-5
   Edmonds-Port Ludlow, 169, 176, 178, 200
   Edmonds-Port Townsend, 50
   Edmonds-Olympic, 176
   Edmonds-Victoria, 197
   Everett-Langley-Clinton, 168
   Everett-Clinton, 94
   Everett-Whidbey Is., 173
   Fauntleroy-Vashon, 153
   Fauntleroy-Vashon-Harper, 274-5
   Fauntleroy-Vashon Hts.-Harper, 164, 219
   Fletcher Bay-Brownsville, 118, 213, 274-5

Gooseberry Point-Orcas Island, 138
Harper-Colby-West Bainbridge Is.-Brownsville, 108
Isle Royale, 56
Keystone-Port Townsend, 176
Kirkland-Madison Park, 157
Leschi-Bellevue, 148
Leschi-Mercer Is.-Newport, 150
Leschi Park-Mercer Slough-Newcastle, 144
Lofall-Southpoint, 141
Madison Park-Bothell, 146
Madison Park-Kirkland, 147, 149-50
Mare Is.-Vallejo, 8
Martinez-Benecia, 6, 8
Medina-Roanoke, 157
Michigan City to Chicago, 46
Mukilteo-Clinton, 94, 138, 173
Mukilteo-Columbia Beach, 174, 274-5
Mukilteo-Phinney Spit-Greenwood, 168
Mukilteo-Whidbey Is., 168
Navy Yard Route, 91-2, 100, 102, 135, 189, 199, 203, 218, 242
Olympia-Everett, 102
Olympia-Shelton-Tacoma, 146
Petoskey, Harbor Springs, Mackinac Is. & the Soo run, 56
Point Defiance-Gig Harbor, 6, 126
Point Defiance-Vashon, 126
Point Fosdick-Tacoma, 126
Point White-Bremerton, 275
Port Angeles-Clallam, 21
Port Angeles-Victoria, 101, 133, 274
Port Gamble-Port Ludlow, 140
Port Gamble-Shine, 138, 140, 168
Port Madison-Poulsbo, 107
Port Orchard Route, 19, 39, 84
Port Orchard-Bremerton, 175
Port Orchard-Bremerton-Manette, 175
Port Townsend Mill Run, 21
Port Townsend-Keystone, 274
Portage-Des Moines, 94
Portland-Astoria, 191
Portland-Willapa Harbor, 20
Renton-Leschi, 146
Rodeo-Vallejo Line, 250-1
San Francisco-East Bay Counties, 251
San Francisco-Marin County, 251
San Francisco-Oakland, 226
San Francisco-Sausalito, 250-1
San Francisco-Vallejo, 27
San Juan Is. run, 28, 31
San Pedro-Terminal Is., 161
Seabeck-Brinnon, 83, 140
Seattle-Anacortes, 39
Seattle-Anacortes-Bellingham, 60
Seattle-Bainbridge Is., 164

Seattle-Bellingham, 21, 199
Seattle-Bellingham-Vancouver, 58
Seattle-Bellingham-Anacortes-San Juan Is., 188
Seattle-Bremerton, 102, 189, 211, 213, 225-6, 232, 241-2, 274
Seattle-Bremerton-Port Orchard, 232
Seattle-Chico-Silverdale, 167
Seattle-Coupeville, 169
Seattle-Eagle Harbor, 261, 274-5
Seattle-Everett, 178, 199
Seattle-Everett-Whidby Is., 102, 166
Seattle-Fletcher Bay,
Seattle-Hood Canal, 102
Seattle-Indianola-Suquamish, 261, 274-5
Seattle-Irondale-Port Townsend, 108
Seattle-Kingston-Port Ludlow, 110, 200
Seattle-LaConner, 188, 199
Seattle-Liberty Bay, 107
Seattle-Manchester, 53, 274-5
Seattle-Milton (West Seattle), 3
Seattle-Port Angeles-Victoria, 178
Seattle-Port Blakely, 94, 111, 118, 164
Seattle-Port Madison-Manzanita-Brownsville, 111
Seattle-Port Orchard, 211
Seattle-Port Townsend-Victoria, 46, 51
Seattle-Port Townsend-Port Angeles-Victoria, 60, 244, 274
Seattle-Poulsbo, 111
Seattle-Roche Harbor, 133
Seattle-Rolling Bay, 111
Seattle-San Juan Island-Whatcom, 21
Seattle-Skagway, AK., 27
Seattle-Tacoma, 47, 165
Seattle-Tacoma-Olympia, 188
Seattle-Vashon-Harper, 94
Seattle-Vashon Heights, 6, 8
Seattle-Vashon Heights-Harper, 114, 117, 150, 153, 162
Seattle-Victoria, 25, 67-8, 73-4, 245
Seattle-Victoria-Vancouver, 188
Seattle-West Seattle, 94
Seattle-Winslow, 53
Shelton-Olympia-Tacoma, 114, 188
Steilacoom-Anderson Is.-McNeil Is.-Long Branch, 124, 126, 134
Tacoma-Fox Is.-East Cromwell, 126
Tacoma-Gig Harbor, 94, 115, 134
Tacoma-Quartermaster Harbor, 115
Tacoma-Quartermaster Harbor-Gig Harbor, 124, 131
Tacoma-Seattle, 124
Tacoma-Seattle-Victoria, 28
Tacoma-Sydney (Pt.Orchard), 11
Titlow Beach-Berg's Landing-Fox Is., 94
Titlow Beach-Point Fosdick, 130
Triangle Route, 73

Utsalady-Oak Harbor, 137
Vancouver-Nanaimo, 101
Vashon-Fauntleroy, 135
Vashon-Harper-Vashon Heights, 160
Vashon Heights-Harper, 135
Victoria-Port Angeles, 245
Victoria-Vancouver, B.C., 73

Russell, George, 110, 120
Rust, H. Arthur, 196

Sachse, Richard, 226
Sacramento Northern Railway, 250
Salmon Bay, 154
San De Fuca, Whidbey Island, WA., 184
San Diego & Coronado Ferry Co., 260, 317
San Francisco, CA., 5-6, 13, 27, 46, 133, 143, 183, 197, 226,
    249-53, 274, 276, 283
San Francisco Bay, 8, 12, 53, 204, 225-6, 249
San Juan Fishing & Packing Co., 196
SAN JUAN II, 133
San Juan Islands, 20, 25, 28, 31, 101, 111, 131, 133
San Juan Island Transportation Co., 133, 188
SAN LEANDRO, 250-1
SAN MATEO, 162, 250, 258, 276, 281, 314
San Pedro, CA., 162
SANTA CLARA, 299
SANTA ROSA, 251, 257, 274
Sausalito, CA., 8, 250
Sayre, J. Willis, 12
Schmitz, Helmuth W., 229, 232
Schuman, Capt. Charles, 38
Schutt, Mary, 134
Schwabacher's Bros. and Co., 35
Schwabacher's Wharf, 19
Scotch marine boiler, 20
SCOTIA, steamer, 71
Scott, Palmer, Co., 284
Scott, Capt. U.B., 47, 89
SCOUT, U.S.R.C., 83
Scranton, John Hart, 67
SEA BIRD, 84
Seaborn, Henry G., 197, 200
Seafair, 23
Seaforth Channel, 21
SEA LION, tug, 69-70
SEAL, 188, 191
SEALTH, 318
Sea Service Bureau, 178
SEATAC, 186, 192
SEATTLE, 83-4, 194, 197, 199, 241, 261, 294
Seattle, WA., 3-6, 9-13, 16, 21, 23, 25, 27-8, 31, 36, 39, 45,
    47, 49, 51, 57, 67, 69, 71, 74, 77, 83-4, 88, 91-2, 94-5,
    100-1, 110-1, 115-6, 118, 120, 131, 133, 155, 166, 168, 183,
    206, 209-10, 260, 274, 279, 283, 303
Seattle Chamber of Commerce, 35, 58, 154, 295
Seattle, Lake Shore & Eastern Railroad, 35
Seattle, Port of, 6
Seattle Drydock & Shipbuilding Co., 35
Seattle Industrial Traffic Managers Assn., 284
Seattle Iron & Steel Co., 71
Seattle Iron and Metals Corporation, 50
SEATTLE SPIRIT, 39
Seattle Steam Navigation & Transportation Co., 88
Seattle Yacht Club, 5-6
Seeley, Marvin, 243-4
SEHOME, 28, 241
Semar, William, 200
SENTINEL, 107-8, 124-5
Seward, Secretary William H., 13, 19
Seward Park, 155
Seymour, Mayor (Tacoma), 58
SHASTA, 250, 258, 273, 276, 296, 314
Shaver, Capt. H.T., 27
Shaw, Walter, 150
SHAWNEE, U.S.C.G.C., 274
SHEARWATER, 157
Shelton, WA., 187-8
Sheridan, Kitsap County, WA., 166
Shipowner's Association, 111
    also Washington Shipowner's Association
Shively, Otis, 23
Short, Ben, 169
Shrieber, Ontario, Canada, 143
Shuffleton Steam Plant, 155
Sidney, B.C., 101, 132
SIERRA, 208
SIGHTSEER, 147, 154-5
Singler, George, 56
Singleton, F.R., 157
SIOUX, 83, 101, 178, 181
SITKA, 249
Sitka, AK., 19, 143, 183
Six-Minute Ferry Co., 250, 276
SKAGIT CHIEF, 84-5
Skagit Railway & Navigation Co., 35
Skagit River, 36
Skagway, AK., 25, 27, 68
Skansie, Joe, 123
Skansie, Mitchell, 123, 127, 134
Skansie, William, 130
Skansie Shipbuilding Co., 124
SKANSONIA, 126, 130-1, 276, 314-5, 318
Skinner, D.E., 118, 197
Skinner, G.W., 200
SKOOKUM CHIEF, 186-8, 191
Slip Point, 21

Smith, Charles, 19
Smith, Capt. Jack, 38
Smith, Vice Adm. William W., 299
Smith Island, WA. 31, 70
SMOKWA, 311
Snake River, 172
Snohomish County, WA., 172
SNOQUALMIE, 208
Snyder, John A., 8
SOL DUC, xii, 60, 81, 83, 131, 178, 181-2, 213, 249
Solibakke, Al, 38, 191
SOPHIA, 115
Sorman, Capt. W.J., 260
Sound Ferry Lines, 134, 168-9, 176-8, 249
Sound Freight Lines, 184
Southern Pacific-Golden Gate Co., 249, 251, 274
Southern Pacific Railroad, 249-51
Southwark-Harris diesel engine, 162

Spaulding, Philip F., 135
Spaulding, Philip F., & Associates, 309, 318
Speas, Harry, 250
SPEEDER, 133, 166
Spieseke, Oswin, 19
SPIRIT OF 76, 175
SPOKANE, 318, 327
Sprague, W.P., 157
SQUAK, 147, 149
St. Lawrence River, 56, 146
St. Lucia, British West Indies, 57
St. Paul & Tacoma Mill Co., 115
St. Paul, MN., 78
Stahl, Charles, 174
Standard Oil Co., 3, 206
Stanley Steamer, 83
Stannard, E.T., 196
State Ex Rel Allen v Public Service Commission 111 Washington, 173
STATE OF WASHINGTON, 39, 83-5, 102, 199, 241
Steam schooner, def., 6, 172
Steamer, single-ender, def., 10
Steffen, John, 3
Stetson-Post Mill, 143
Stevens, Capt. Carl, 60, 310
Stewart, C.J., 155
Stewart, Gene, 167
Stimson Mill Co., 84, 206
STOCKTON, 250, 274-5
Stockton, CA., 53
Stoltenberg, C.H.J., 25, 28, 46
Strait of Juan de Fuca, 16, 101, 131, 197
Straits of Magellan, 46, 51, 57
Straits Steamship Co. of Oregon, 45
Strassburger, H.C., 303, 310
Strong, Fred, 20

Strong, H.C., 23
Stryker, Claude, 197
SUCCESS, 147
SUEJA III, 178
Suisan Bay, CA., 287
Sullivan, John E., 307
Sumner, Harry W., 135
Sumner, Capt. T.E., 310
Sunny Point Packing Co., 23
Supple, Joseph, 108, 146
SUQUAMISH, 111, 113, 115
Suquamish, WA.134
SUSIE, 124-5
SWAN, 152, 160
Swan & Hunter Yard, 73
Swaney, Homer M., 71
Sweet, J.B., 176
Swenson, Capt. O., 174

T.C. POWER, 110
T.W. LAKE, 38-39
TACOMA, 165, 241, 249
Tacoma, WA., 3, 5-6, 16, 25, 28, 35, 38, 47, 49, 67-9, 84, 88, 94, 107, 114, 115, 123-4, 133, 186
Tacoma Boat Building Co., 60, 274
Tacoma Chamber of Commerce, 115
Tacoma Machine Works, 115, 128
Tacoma Narrows Bridge, 130-1
Tacoma Oriental Lines, 60
Tacoma & Burton Navigation Co., 126
TAHOMA, 138
Talbot Coal Yard, 16
TAMALPAIS, 299
Tarrytown, N.Y., 196
Tatoosh Island, 71
Taylor's Mill, 23, 150
Taylor, Capt. Russel, 7-8, 34, 92, 94, 100, 174, 250
Taylor, Charles E., 115, 154, 188
Taylor, Courtland, 19
Taylor, Edward, 19
Teederman, W.A., 60
TELEPHONE, 89
Terminal Island, CA., 162
Thames River, 11
The Evergreen State College, 27
Thompson, Wilbur, 13
Thompson Steamboat Co., 34, 83
Thorniley, William O., ix, x, 100, 161, 173, 203, 229, 240, 245, 276-7, 309
  achievements, ix
  collections, ix-x
  employment with P.S.N., ix
Thornton, Capt. William P., 83-4

THOROUGHFARE, 249-50
Thurston County, WA., 172, 200, 298
Tibbetts, George W., 144
TILLICUM, 206, 318
Ting Hung, 71
Todd, A.E., 157
Todd Shipyard Corp., 53, 91-2, 197, 287, 318
Toledo, Ohio, 46
TOLO, 108
Tompkins, Capt. Harry E., 147-8, 152-3, 157, 160, 211, 212
Toner, Ward M., 294
TOURIST, 82, 84, 87-9, 191, 197, 213, 241, 249
Toy Look, 71
Tracy, Capt. Nicholas H., 306, 314
Tracytown, WA., 166
TRANSIT, 94, 124
Transportation Club of Seattle, 284
Treasure Island, San Francisco, CA., 251
Treiber, Capt. O.D., 161
TRITON, 148, 150
TROLD, 57
Troup, Capt. James W., 77-8, 95
Tucker, Mrs. R.H., 50
Turntables (marine), 10, 50, 92

UKIAH, 250
U.S. Army Transport Service, 276
U.S. Coast Guard, 3, 11
U.S. Coast Guard Academy, 16
U.S. Conciliation Service, 293
U.S. Customs Service, 16
U.S. Exploring Expedition (1841), 95
U.S. Marine Inspection Service, 115
U.S. Maritime Administration, 53
U.S. Maritime Commission, 298-9
U.S. Naval Academy, 241
U.S. Naval Reserve, 276
U.S. Naval Reserve Station, 110
U.S. Revenue Cutter Service, 16
U.S. Shipping Board, 51, 58, 95, 178, 184, 283
U.S. Steamboat Inspection Service, 71
U.S. Treasury Dept., 15, 16
Union Navigation Co., 114, 118
United Gas Improvement Co., 196
University of California, 249
University of Washington, 111, 184, 191
URANIA, 147, 150, 152, 160
U'Ren, R.R., 310
UTOPIA, 21-2, 28, 30, 39, 41

V.P. HANDY, 186, 191
Van Bogaert, Capt. Louis, 31, 45, 60, 62-3, 81, 132, 243-4, 260, 309

Vancouver, B.C., 101, 120, 160, 168, 283
Vancouver, Capt. George, 95
Vancouver Harbor, 12
Vancouver Hotel, Vancouver, B.C., 67-8
Vancouver Island, B.C., 16, 67, 69, 73, 101, 131-2, 261
Van Sant, A.R., 154
Van Tassel, William, 19
VASHON, ferry, 164-5, 201, 212, 221, 274, 314
VASHON, steamer, 115
VASHON II, 108-9, 111, 114-5
Vashon-Fauntleroy Ferry District, 150
VASHONA, 154
VASHONIA, 126, 128, 131, 275, 310
VASHON ISLAND (double-ended ferryboat), 94, 117, 161-2, 168
Vashon Island, WA., 111, 127, 164, 296
Vashon Island Navigation Co., 115, 117, 154
VERONA, 111, 114-7, 213-5, 215
VICTOR, 124
VICTORIA, 177
Victoria, B.C., 12-3, 16-7, 28, 45, 60, 65, 67-9, 71, 73-4, 78, 101, 131-2, 182, 244, 287, 291
Victoria, B.C. Board of Trade, 58, 67, 73
VICTORIA-ANACORTES FERRY, 132
Victoria-Anacortes Ferry Company, 100
Victoria Dock Co., Ltd., 182
Victoria Lumber & Manufacturing Co., 17
Viking semi-diesel, 178
VIRGINIA IV, 120
VIRGINIA V, 214-5, 218
VIXEN, 144
Voinot, Paul E., 154, 157, 241

W.B. FOSHAY, 195, 197, 200
W.P.A., Work Projects Administration, 138
Wabash River, 168
WAIALEALE, 21
Waitt, Capt. William J., 8
Wallace Equipment Co., 176
WALLA WALLA, 318, 325-6
Walla Walla Co., WA., 216
Wallgren, Gov. Mon C., 293-4, 296-301
WALLOWA, 88, 90
Wanamaker, Pearl D., 216
Warren, Capt. C.B., 155
WARRIOR, 191
WASCO, 102, 166, 199
Washington-Estep diesel engine, 163-4, 178
Washington Iron Works, 91, 197, 208
Washington Navigation Co., 123, 127-8, 130, 214, 218, 275
WASHINGTON of Kirkland, 8, 49, 94, 111, 117, 150, 152-3, 157, 162, 164, 167, 173, 219, 221, 249
Washington, D.C., 284

Washington Route, Inc., 104, 115, 166-7, 169, 173, 189, 212-3
Washington Shipowner's Association, 111, 210, 211, 213, 216-7
Washington, State of, 294, 305, 307, 309, 314
Washington State Dept. of Public Service, 183, 190, 203, 219-20, 275
Washington State Dept. of Public Works, 135, 172, 200, 216
Washington State Dept. of Transportation, 294, 297-8, 314
Washington State Federation of Labor, 209
Washington State Ferries, 8, 13, 181, 244, 246, 276, 309-10, 314-5
  ferries acquired, 314
  routes acquired, 315
  terminals acquired, 314
Washington State Highway Dept., 172
Washington State Mediation Service, 294
Washington State Parks Dept., 276
Washington State Supreme Court, 172, 189, 200, 301
Washington State Territorial Legislature, 172
Washington State Toll Bridge Authority, 157, 293, 296-301, 314
Washington Street, Seattle, 12-3, 69
Washington Tug & Barge Co., 78
Waterfront Employers Association, 208, 210
Watkinson, Capt. James, 15
Wayports Transportation Co., 188
Wenck, A.H., 157
West Pass Transportation Co., 184, 218
WEST SEATTLE, 5-8, 78, 88, 94, 114
West Seattle, WA. 3, 5-6, 8, 91
West Seattle Boathouse, 5-6
West Seattle Land & Improvement Co., 3, 5
West Waterway, Seattle, 31
Westberg, Alfred J., 157
Western Boat Building Co., 126
Western Mill, 110
Western Steel Corporation, 108
WESTERNER, 283
Westover, R.F., 38
WHATCOM, 73, 83, 91-2
Whidbey Island, WA., 199
  spelling, 95
WHIDBY, gas, 94, 168, 171, 177
WHIDBY, steam, 95, 98, 166-9, 172, 174, 249
Whidby Island Ferry Lines, 173-4, 182
Whidby Island Transportation Co., 95, 104, 138, 166-9, 172-4, 183, 212-3, 249
Whidby Stage, 174
Whitcomb, Harry, 38
Whitcomb, Capt. W.P., 19
White Collar Line, (K.C.T.C.), 121, 160, 214
WHITE FLYER (nickname for INDIANAPOLIS), 74
Whitehorse, Yukon Territory, 68

White Star Line, 56
WILDWOOD, 147
Wilkens, Mrs. M.A., 134
Wilkes, Charles, 95
WILLAPA, steamer, 19-21, 23, 25, 28, 208, 229
WILLAPA (Ex-FRESNO), 267, 274-5, 314-5
Willapa Harbor, 20
Willey, George T., 36, 39
Williams Line, 155
Williamson, Capt. William, 27
Wilson, Capt. Harry J., 100
Wilson, Judge, 172-3
WILSON G. HUNT, 13
Wiman, Capt. Chauncey, (Chance), 114-7, 167
Wiman, Gertrude, 115
Wiman, S.P., 114
Winchester, Capt. Frank, 38
WINNIFRED, 144, 146
WINSLOW, 213
Winslow, Bainbridge Is., WA., 283, 315
Winslow Marine Railway, 178, 261
WISCONSIN, U.S.S., 84
Wobblies, 116
WOLLOCHET, 130
Wollochet Bay, 124
Wolverton Auto Bus Co., 169
Women
  first ferry operator, 137
  steamboat licenses, 115
  wireless operator, 50
Wood, Capt. Alex, 8, 38
Woodruff, J. Knox, 188, 193
Woods, Charles, 8
World War I, 21, 58, 150, 152, 184, 283
World War II, 118, 154, 173, 191, 220, 222, 278-9, 287, 293
Wyatt, Capt. Cyprian T., 197-8

XANTHUS, 145-6

YAKIMA, 318, 322-3
Yamashita Shipping Co., 155
Yangste River, China, 34
YANKEE DOODLE, 133
Yarrows, Ltd., 95
Yellow Ferry Harbor, Sausalito, CA., 8
YERBA BUENA, 226, 228, 250-1, 257
Yesler Way, 143
Yesler Wharf, 143
YOSEMITE, 250, 255, 276
Yost Auto Co., 169
YUKON, 208
Yukon River, 68, 110

Zickmund, Frank, 36, 39-40
Zugehoer, Capt. Alexander J., 197

MARY STILES KLINE spent her childhood in Pasco, Washington. Her undergraduate and graduate work concentrated on maritime history and museology from The Evergreen State College and the University of Washington. She was curator and executive director of Northwest Seaport's fleet of five historic ships for over seven years.

Ms.Kline served as preservation consultant to Historic Seattle Preservation and Development Authority for the ferryboat SAN MATEO and research coordinator for the sternwheeler NENANA, Fairbanks, Alaska. She developed environmental living programs for the schooner WAWONA in Seattle and was museum and research consultant for the Coast Guard Museum, N.W. She serves as museum advisor to Archival Management, Inc.

Ms.Kline is a popular conference speaker in maritime circles. While writing this book, she continued her work as consultant to maritime organizations on the Pacific Coast. She and her family live in the Seattle area.

A native of Seattle, GEORGE A. BAYLESS's interest in maritime affairs dates back to his boyhood days. He was a persistent ship-watcher as he bicycled from his West Seattle home to the downtown waterfront.

A graduate of the University of Washington, he is a member of graphic arts and printing industry associations, Puget Sound Maritime Historical Society and the National Maritime Historical Society. He served on Northwest Seaport's Board of Trustees as restoration chairman for the tugboat ARTHUR FOSS.

He has been with Bayless Bindery of Seattle since 1949 and president since 1970. In 1972 he became the publisher of the *Marine Atlas,* Vol.I & II, a boater's piloting guide.

Mr. Bayless contributed his photographer's skills, his extensive collection of vintage maritime photographs and the results of his research to the making of this book.

Mr. Bayless' family divides their time between Bellevue, Washington and Whidbey Island homes.

WALTER GREEN, a native Texan, joined the ferry fleet of Puget Sound in 1927. He worked as deckhand aboard the SEATTLE and THE CITY OF BELLINGHAM for a year before his promotion to freight clerk at Bellingham for the Black Ball Line. In the 1930's Mr. Green assumed a public relations role for Puget Sound Navigation Company. When the company was sold to the state of Washington he helped organize Black Ball Transport, Inc., developing freight and ferry service between Port Angeles and Victoria, B.C.

Mr. Green has assisted in the research for this book with personal contacts, calling on former associates for insight into the history and current operation of Puget Sound's ferries. His charm and good humor have kept this book alive.

FERRYBOATS
A LEGEND ON PUGET SOUND

Designed by Herbert E. Carlson
Recorded and transmitted for type on a
Computek Word Processing Publisher's System
Composed by The Type Gallery in Garamond Book
Printed by Forward Press/Uniprint
on Simpson Shasta Suede
furnished by West Coast Paper Company
Bound by Bayless Bindery and Lincoln &
Allen in Holliston Roxite "C" Linen Cloth and
stamped in gold